How the New Deal Built Florida Tourism

UNIVERSITY PRESS OF FLORIDA

Florida A&M University, Tallahassee
Florida Atlantic University, Boca Raton
Florida Gulf Coast University, Ft. Myers
Florida International University, Miami
Florida State University, Tallahassee
New College of Florida, Sarasota
University of Central Florida, Orlando
University of Florida, Gainesville
University of North Florida, Jacksonville
University of South Florida, Tampa
University of West Florida, Pensacola

HOW THE NEW DEAL BUILT FLORIDA TOURISM

The Civilian Conservation Corps and State Parks

David J. Nelson

UNIVERSITY PRESS OF FLORIDA

Gainesville / Tallahassee / Tampa / Boca Raton
Pensacola / Orlando / Miami / Jacksonville / Ft. Myers / Sarasota

COPYRIGHT 2019 DAVID J. NELSON
All rights reserved
Published in the United States of America

First cloth printing, 2019
First paperback printing, 2023

28 27 26 25 24 23   6 5 4 3 2 1

Library of Congress Cataloging-in-Publication Data
Names: Nelson, David J., 1972– author.
Title: How the New Deal built Florida tourism : the Civilian Conservation Corps and state parks / David J. Nelson.
Description: Gainesville : University Press of Florida, [2019] | Includes bibliographical references and index.
Identifiers: LCCN 2018044932 | ISBN 9780813056319 (cloth) | ISBN 9780813080413 (pbk.)
Subjects: LCSH: Tourism—Florida—History. | Parks—Florida—History. | Florida Park Service—History. | Civilian Conservation Corps (U.S.) | New Deal, 1933-1939—Florida—History. | Florida—History—1865–
Classification: LCC G155.U6 N25 2019 | DDC 338.4/791759—dc23
LC record available at https://lccn.loc.gov/2018044932

The University Press of Florida is the scholarly publishing agency for the State University System of Florida, comprising Florida A&M University, Florida Atlantic University, Florida Gulf Coast University, Florida International University, Florida State University, New College of Florida, University of Central Florida, University of Florida, University of North Florida, University of South Florida, and University of West Florida.

UNIVERSITY PRESS OF FLORIDA
2046 NE Waldo Road
Suite 2100
Gainesville, FL 32609
http://upress.ufl.edu

This book is dedicated to

DAVID E. NELSON SR.
(February 6, 1923–January 14, 2008)
who inspired me to remember the past

CARTER COLE NELSON
(born April 17, 2006)
who inspires me to look toward the future

PATRICK ALAN SMITH
(January 11, 1967–April 22, 2018)
my late friend and colleague who reminded me
to focus on the present and to get "that damn book finished"
—thanks, friend

Contents

List of Figures ix
Acknowledgments xi
List of Abbreviations xv

Introduction 1
1. A Tropical Depression: A Tale of Two Floridas 7
2. A New Deal for Florida 18
3. Tourism, Conservation, and State Parks 33
4. The Mother Who Birthed the Florida Park Service 54
5. State-Sponsored Tourism and the Building of Florida's State Parks 69
6. Florida's Welfare State Parks: The CCC at Work and at Play 113
7. Improving Paradise: Nature as Commodity 137
8. The New Deal in Old Florida: Governor Fred Cone and Florida's Welfare System 153
9. Florida Crackers and Yankee Tourists: Class, Conflict, and Rejection in Paradise 164
10. The Sunshine State Emerges on the World Stage: Florida at the New York World's Fair 189
11. The End of the Beginning 198

Notes 211
Bibliography 263
Index 281

Figures

Figures follow page 96.

1. May Mann Jennings
2. Governor Dave Sholtz signing park legislation, 1935
3. Organizers of Florida National Exhibits
4. Florida Exhibition boat at the Century of Progress
5. CCC enrollees planting trees in Madison County
6. CCC reconstructing the Gregory House at Torreya State Park
7. CCC camp at Gold Head Branch State Park
8. Marjorie Kinnan Rawlings
9. Early depiction of a Florida cracker
10. Cow being dipped for ticks in Duval County
11. Turpentine worker with longleaf pine
12. Map of Florida state parks, 1939
13. Florida Exhibit at the 1939 New York World's Fair
14. Detail of diorama at the 1939 New York World's Fair

Acknowledgments

First and foremost, I want to express in writing how grateful I am to the historians over the years who guided, shaped, and improved this manuscript: Valerie Conner, Jim Jones, Frederick Davis, Albrecht Koschnik, Jennifer Koslow, and Jonathan Leib. And I especially want to express my immense gratitude to Elna Green, as no one could ask for a more supportive, protective, challenging, and nurturing mentor.

Several generous and supportive editors have also played a direct role in the shaping and molding of this work. Connie Lester of the *Florida Historical Quarterly* edited and published three articles of mine that later developed into portions of chapters 7, 9, and 10. Jack Davis not only published an essay of mine that would serve as the foundation for chapter 6 in his anthology *Paradise Lost? The Environmental History of Florida* but in doing so, he also gave me my first publication as an academic historian. For their encouragement, criticisms, and permission to use portions of these publications in this work, I remain forever grateful. And, of course, my sincere appreciation goes to editor Sian Hunter of the University Press of Florida, who carefully guided this book throughout the long process.

I am also grateful to the many scholars of history and other disciplines with whom I have consulted and from whom I have sought advice over the years: Keith Ashley, Gary Bilderback, Tina Bucuvalas, Robert Cassanello, Joan Denman, Jon Evans, Michael Francis, Craig Friend, Jacob Helt, Joe Knetsch, Barbara Mattick, Sean McMahon, Gary Mormino, Julian Pleasants, Tracy Revels, Joseph Sasser, Robin Sellers, Jon Sheppard, Robert Snyder, Claire Strom, Robert Thunen, Lu Vickers, Seth Weitz, Lee Willis, and Nick Wynne.

Several individuals with the Florida Park Service have greatly assisted with this study. George Apthorp, Sandy Cook, Ney Landrum, Triel Linstrom, Steve

Martin, Brian Polk, and Phil Werndli helped me with locating (and often archiving at the State Archives of Florida) records of the early park service. Renee Rau and Warren Poplin graciously granted me scholar-in-residence status at Gold Head Branch State Park during the research for this book. Several park managers opened their park files to me for research, including Pete Anderson (Highlands Hammock State Park), Steve Cutshaw (Torreya State Park), Robert Dye (Myakka River State Park), Bill Maphis (Florida Caverns State Park), Morgan Tyrone (Oleno State Park), Warren Poplin (Gold Head Branch State Park), and Robert Wilhelm (Hillsborough River State Park). And finally, to my close friend, former colleague, and current bureau chief with the FPS, Brian Fugate, who encouraged and challenged me during the entire process, I offer my sincere gratitude.

I am also grateful to the Florida Chapter of the CCC Alumni Association for assisting me with locating and interviewing several CCC veterans, especially two volunteers, Annemarie van Hemmen and Larry Levey, as well as being grateful to all the alumni who graciously agreed to be interviewed, on and off the record.

While my archival background may render me biased in this viewpoint, I nonetheless maintain that no researcher can survive without the tireless efforts of often nameless and forgotten archivists and librarians. I am no exception and would like to thank them by name: Burt Altman (Special Collections, Strozier Library, Florida State University), James Cusick (P. K. Yonge Library of Florida History, University of Florida), Gail Farr (National Archives–Philadelphia), Carole Goad (Sebring Historical Society), Gene Morris (National Archives–College Park), Salina Pavlovick (National Archives–Atlanta), the late Phil Werndli (Cultural Resources, Florida Park Service), and Debbie Wynne (Florida Historical Society).

Friends and colleagues who over the years have endured my endless ramblings about the project without complaint or (noticeable) eye rolling are Tony Attore, Matt Brackett, Julia Brock (thanks for the coffee), Melissa Euziere, Angie Fugate, Crista Hosmer, Lindsey Harrington, Matthew Harrington, Kimberly Luke (thanks for all the much-needed prayers, conversations, and support), Bob Pando, Karen Rubin, Holly Sinco, Bill Wilson, and Joshua Youngblood. I want to thank especially two of my closest friends and extraordinary scholars: archivist and historian Boyd Murphree and writer extraordinaire Patrick Smith. Both greatly assisted me throughout by personal example and with advice—plus by suffering through numerous long lunches, many of which were on their dime.

My former colleagues at the Florida State Archives have always offered selfless support and endless encouragement, including Jim Burke, Miriam Gan-Spalding, Beth Golding, Katrina Harkness, James Helms, Boyd Murphree, Candice Odom, Holly Sinco, and Adam Watson. And without the personal and professional support by my two supervisors (and close friends) Gerard Clark and Jody Norman, this project would never have been completed.

And finally, to my family: I can never repay what you have all done for me. To my parents, David and Mary Nelson: It's been a long road, but I hope I have made you proud. You two are my role models. And I am especially grateful for all those extra babysitting hours over the past years. To my other parents, Frank and Kathy Shuke, I thank you for the patience, assistance, and encouragement over the years. To my son, Carter, I apologize for all the times you wanted to play and I instead had to write. I will make it up, I promise. And to my wife, Heather—words cannot express my love and the gratitude I feel for you now and forever. All I can say is: We did it!

Abbreviations

CCC Civilian Conservation Corps
COP Century of Progress
CWA Civil Works Administration
FERA Federal Emergency Relief Administration
FFA Florida Forestry Association
FFS Florida Forestry Service
FFWC Florida Federation of Women's Clubs
FNE Florida National Exhibits
FPS Florida Park Service
FSA Florida State Archives
FSU Florida State University
FTU *Florida Times-Union*
FWP Federal Writers' Project
IIF Internal Improvement Fund
NARA National Archives and Records Administration
NPS National Park Service
NYT *New York Times*
OH Oral History
RFC Reconstruction Finance Corporation
RG Record Group
ROHP Reichelt Oral History Program
SPOHP Samuel Proctor Oral History Program
UF University of Florida
USFS United States Forest Service
WPA Works Progress Administration

Introduction

In 1999 the National Recreation and Park Association awarded the Florida Park Service (FPS) its coveted National Gold Medal for Parks and named the FPS the nation's best state park system. That honor has been repeated twice since, a feat not achieved by any other park system. Today residents and tourists alike consider the Florida Park Service one of the state's prized jewels. Numbering over 150 park units, the Florida State Parks are a major draw for visitors as well as a refuge for residents. The FPS has also given validity and visibility to the state government's environmental policies because one plank of the FPS mission has been the protection and restoration of Florida's fragile ecosystems. Yet despite the praiseworthy activities and excitement at today's state parks, the observant visitor may still notice at a few of the parks small metallic signs fastened to some of the older structures. The inscriptions on these signs read: "Built with the assistance of the Civilian Conservation Corps." Until quite recently these inconspicuous and seemingly insignificant signs were the only public recognition of the FPS's earliest days, a period when the agency was not quite so green-minded and when the CCC played a much larger role than is acknowledged today.

The following chapters examine the relationship between the Florida Park Service and the Civilian Conservation Corps between 1935 (when the FPS began) and 1945. It was clear early in my research that the CCC not only assisted the FPS in the early years; it funded, designed, built, and in large part ran the state park program. The FPS is financially, thematically, ideally, and literally a direct product of the New Deal. The New Dealers believed in conserving nature for society's use. This belief resulted not only in the CCC's highly publicized efforts in tree planting and fire prevention but also in the building of public parks and other nature-based recreational activities. The Florida Park

Service was one of the many manifestations of the New Deal programs and efforts to encourage a healthy society and put people to work.

From the perspective of Florida's civic elite, however, the New Deal meant other things—infrastructure, political patronage, and a steady supply of federal dollars needed to restore Florida's position as the nation's playground. The Florida Park Service was conceived as a way for Florida to take advantage of the New Deal's goals and ambitions in order to achieve its own agenda—namely, to help revive and expand Florida tourism by using the FPS. Florida leaders then took the New Dealers' desire to provide recreation, conserve resources, and offer work relief, and used it for their own ends. For them, state parks were not about restoring the state's ecosystems, changing society, or even bettering life for fellow citizens. For those leaders the state park system was, plain and simple, a tourism venture for which the federal government footed the bill.

There was also a third party who played an active role in the development of both the FPS and the CCC: enrollees who volunteered their time and efforts. The CCC was, after all, a voluntary organization, and people could leave at any time. Without their willing participation, the CCC and the FPS would not have been possible. There were other options available, though admittedly few as appealing as the CCC. They could have worked in other programs, migrated out of state, or even turned to crime. But the enrollees not only chose to sign up for the CCC; in so doing they also agreed to help their families, as most of their pay was sent home to dependents. Though they did not have access to the decision-making process, the enrollees nevertheless shaped how the FPS and the CCC were run in Florida. They sometimes rebelled and protested if their desires were not met. Some petitioned the government, others went AWOL, while still others took up the pen. Enrollees also offered insight and ideas for solving problems encountered in park construction and operation. Although their options were limited, enrollees exerted what agency they could within the CCC and the FPS.

In this book I argue that the desire of Florida's government and business leaders to create a Florida Park Service for tourism was often in conflict with the aims and goals of both the federal government and the CCC enrollees—as well as with those of some local citizens who resented the social, cultural, demographic, and political changes that tourism brought. The tensions that sprang from these conflicts required negotiation and compromise and resulted in a Florida Park Service that, in its final form, reflected the agendas of these parties.

As politicians, park employees, and citizens continue to debate the role and purpose of the FPS and argue over park planning and operations in the present—(the Florida Park Service has long been a favorite topic among both voters and elected leaders)—having a sense of the agency's origins may prove useful. Like most organizations, the FPS has been an evolving agency, reflecting the concerns and values of each generation since its inception. It turns out that many of today's debates over commercialization versus preservation, or balancing visitation and property protection, are nothing new. And all sides may be surprised to learn that today's thrice-awarded FPS bears little resemblance to its original incarnation. Readers can decide individually whether that is a positive or negative development.

But this is more than just the story of the CCC's creation of a few state parks. It also serves as a launch pad into understanding the larger story of Florida's current cultural and political climate. This story provides a window into the creation of modern Florida, a state where people debate whether it is southern or sunbelt. Who are "real" Floridians? Has Florida improved or declined over the past few decades? And are we paying too high an ecological and cultural price for commodifying the state's climate, history, and resources? In other words, the creation of the Florida Park Service is the story of modern Florida.

There is little scholarly doubt that tourism and other forms of commodification have played a crucial role in Florida's social, economical, and cultural past. Whether the topic is the environment, politics, race relations, or Florida's southern identity, at some point the discourse involves Florida's commercialized image as an inviting paradise. But few studies have dealt directly with that commercialization and its cultural and social effects upon the state. Fewer still have tried to locate the start of such commercialization. In this study I attempt to accomplish that by looking at Florida during the New Deal era. In its simplest form, the other major argument presented here is that Florida's commercialization in a modern sense began in the 1930s, although admittedly these efforts were a rebirth and intensification of earlier efforts. But what was unique to the 1930s was that these efforts were fueled in large part by federal relief programs as well as by an influential and largely non-native commercial-civic elite.

As English professor Anne Rowe explained it, "the ideal of Florida—the image of a tropical lush 'Good Place'—has been developed, explored, and interpreted by a series of American authors" from the earliest European explorers to the late twentieth century.[1] Yet for much of that time, most Floridians themselves did little to promote, expand, or duplicate that image. In fact, aside from a few entrepreneurs on the East Coast and at a few freshwater springs, most rejected such fanciful notions as "Yankee" ignorance of the South and of Florida. But by the 1930s a portion of the Florida populace took advantage of this centuries-old view of Florida to lift the quiet, agrarian southern state out of the Great Depression. In addition to the usual suspects (roadside attraction entrepreneurs, real estate agents, advertising firms, hoteliers), several groups embraced Florida's manufactured image, including citrus farmers, foresters, and conservationists, all of whom either serviced the influx of visitors and new residents or promoted their wares as components essential to the maintenance of that image. Many historians have discussed the earliest roots of this transformation in the early twentieth century as well as the cultural, environmental, and economic consequences in the later part of the century, but few have looked squarely upon the actual transformation itself.

While this book investigates that transformation primarily through the Civilian Conservation Corps' development of the Florida Park Service, it also branches out to explore how the federal and state governments, alongside the local civic-commercial elite, transformed Florida in order to make concrete Florida's long-standing literary and popular image. In addition, it also shows that such a transformation was not welcomed by all. In many ways, a cultural and political battle ensued over the future of Florida as economic and political priorities shifted from agriculture and extraction of the state's resources to a stance of promotion and attraction. For many residents, the consequences were not just economic and political but also personal.

While this cultural process and negotiation would not end in 1945, as this study does, nonetheless a conflict arose in the 1930s over regional and local identity. Long before Disney World opened for business and bold-faced the cultural divisions in the state, native white Floridians of the 1930s whose parents fought for and supported the "Lost Cause" were none too happy to find themselves residing in a state becoming more known for coconuts and flamingoes than for cotton and states' rights. A new white southern identity emerged to contest the prevailing tropical image. The Florida cracker, a long-used derogatory moniker, was repackaged and reformatted to provide the label for a diverse and often divisive group who were nonetheless united in their rejection of the state's catering to so-called foreigners. By the 1950s and 1960s when the image of the Florida cracker had solidified in the public mind, this conflict would combine with battles over segregation and even the Cold War to provide fertile ground for such phenomena as the Pork Chop Gang, the Johns Committee, the environmental movement, and such cultural products as the Florida Folk Festival and southern rock music. In other words, one cannot understand modern Florida history and its cultural and political milieu without a stronger foundation in the New Deal era. A similar claim can be made for the entire American South, as much of this region followed Florida's lead in commodifying its resources and image during the following decades.

Also of interest here is the effect these changes had, both upon the human relationship with Florida's environment as well as upon the physical environment itself. As so much of the image of Florida rested upon its climate, palm trees, sandy beaches, and tropical forests, much was undertaken to realize that image physically. Forest fires were extinguished, livestock fenced, ecosystems altered, and even local fauna such as panthers, bear, bobcats, and turtles slaughtered in order to provide a safe but exotic "natural" environment. Today thinking of state parks as tourist attractions is alien to most; we usually see such places as antidotes to the kitschy and overtly commercial theme parks and tourist attractions. Yet in the 1930s nearly all the state's tourist attractions utilized some natural aspect, including swamplands, beaches, natural springs, alligators, the climate, and limestone caverns.

This book is divided into eleven chapters. The first explores the social and economic conditions in Florida during the 1920s and early Depression. By providing a snapshot of Florida up to 1930, we can then gauge the social and cultural changes throughout the next decade. Chapter 2 explores both the nation's and Florida's reaction to the Great Depression, resulting in the New Deal and the creation of the CCC. The next two chapters examine the development of both conservation and tourism during the 1930s and how both led to the creation of the Florida Park Service. That is followed by a detailed look at the planning, construction, and advertising of Florida's state parks. Of particular interest here is how the FPS served as an example of state-sponsored tourism. The New Deal era was the only time when Florida's state government controlled the industry, using both local civic groups and federal relief programs to develop and sell its tourist resources. Chapter 6 looks at the CCC enlistees who built, staffed, and played in Florida's state parks.

Key to Florida's tourism was the commodification of the state's natural resources, tangible and otherwise. Florida developed a specific image of itself: tropical, exotic, safe, and natural. But reality did not always cooperate. In order to present the expected natural landscape to visitors, the CCC created state parks fitting the popular image of what Florida was supposed to look like: it began to remove native fauna and flora, alter water flow, introduce exotic species, and artificially landscape areas that were then presented as natural. Similar processes occurred in other areas of Florida. Although advertisements, publications, and other forms of popular culture celebrated Florida's Eden-like qualities, many in the state still believed that paradise needed improving. This is explored in chapter 7.

Conflicts over the resultant economic, environmental, and social changes in Florida make up the next two chapters. Chapter 8 follows Governor Fred Cone's failed attempt in 1937 to circumvent the federal restrictions over welfare funding in order to control state spending and patronage. This effort arose not only out of political motives but also as a way to challenge directly and reverse the efforts to commercialize Florida. And chapter 9 looks at those Floridians who rejected this manufactured version of a tropical paradise. Resentful of the changing political and economic priorities, these people (including ranchers, farmers, turpentiners, and North Florida politicians) saw "foreign" control over their livelihoods and culture. First, we look at the development of the Florida cracker as an idea and cultural construct. Although *cracker* was long used as a derogatory label, writers such as Marjorie Kinnan Rawlings converted that image into one of Jeffersonian frontier farmers whose lives illustrated an alternative and "authentic" Florida. The book concludes with two case studies, tick eradication among Florida's cattle and the anti-fire campaign, in which we see direct clashes between rural and agrarian people with those favoring the creation of a new image for Florida. While ultimately Florida tourism would survive these challenges to rise to astronomical heights by the 1970s and beyond, the cultural and social challenges to a commodified, commercialized Florida would remain as well.

1

A Tropical Depression

A TALE OF TWO FLORIDAS

On January 4, 1931, newspaper publisher and printer Thomas J. Appleyard died in a Thomasville hospital from a foot infection.[1] A native Virginian and a Civil War veteran who had served in the Confederate Navy as a young teen, Appleyard held the exclusive contract for printing for the State of Florida during his last decade of life. Upon news of his death, the state government brought his body to the Florida Capitol, where it lay in state.[2] Flags on state buildings were flown at half-mast, and a Confederate flag draped his casket. Pallbearers at his funeral included Governor Doyle Carlton, the speaker of the House, and several justices of the state's Supreme Court. A few months later the legislature passed a special resolution praising Appleyard for upholding the "ideals of the Old South."[3] It was a quaint and distinctly southern scene that took place in early 1931 and that is hard to imagine occurring in the state capital twenty, or even ten, years later. Culturally and economically, the Florida of 1930 resembled the Florida of 1910 more than that of 1950.

According to the 1930 census, half of its population still lived in rural areas and farmed.[4] The number one industry was agriculture, followed by manufacturing (which included sawmill workers, carpenters, and auto mechanics). Even in the field of transportation, the majority of the employees worked as tractor drivers. Most elected officials and local leaders kept the promotion of agriculture and extraction of natural resources their top priority. But by 1940 tourism and promotion had become the new goal for many. Even such "rural" pursuits such as citrus farming and seafood gathering were becoming directly linked to tourism and advertising. President Franklin Roosevelt was a regular visitor to the state, as were many of the nation's rich and famous. Florida was referenced often in Hollywood films and popular song. In the minds of many just the word "Florida" conjured up images of sandy beaches and swaying palm trees. And it was the tropical, exotic orange, not the cotton boll or the tobacco leaf, that became the international symbol for the state. Something had changed, and Florida hardly seemed the bastion for Old South ideals referenced in 1930 (although the seeds for this change can be seen as far back as the late nineteenth century). The brief, frantic Florida land boom of the 1920s was not a fluke nor an anomaly but rather a precursor. Yet behind the moss-draped sunny exterior and orange blossom–scented highways still lurked rural poverty and a conservative agrarian elite. Florida had transformed in many ways during the 1930s, and not everyone was thrilled about it.

Some people thought that the good fortunes of the stock market of the 1920s would last indefinitely. They were confident of it. It was that confidence that kept the Great Bull Market, which began in 1923, going. When the market slipped on September 3, 1929, few people worried or cared. Why should they? The "Great Bull" had already slipped twice before, in December 1928 and March 1929, and rebounded both times.[5] As writer Frederick Lewis Allen observed, September 3 was treated just as any other day. No headlines marked the occasion, and confidence on Wall Street remained high.[6]

Wall Street of the 1920s was where dreams were made. It was the proverbial street of gold—the fount from which the American Dream sprang. Rumors abounded of peddlers turning $4,000 into $250,000, and stock traders transforming $1 million into $30 million in mere months.[7] It seemed that the whole nation was trading in stocks. And yet no more than a million people out of a population of nearly 120 million actively participated in the market.[8] But for those one million participants, it was an incredible ride. In 1928 alone, the market earned $6.4 billion. By contrast, the U.S. government made only $3.9 billion that year.[9] As early as 1923 the market was exchanging 236 million shares annually. By 1928 that figure rose to 1,125 million.[10] As historian William Leuchtenburg put it, "the stock market was carrying the whole economy" in 1928.[11] But it was all a mirage, with no basis in any tangible reality, except for "an abiding faith in the permanent prosperity."[12]

As most historians agree, the real troubles began in March 1928. That was when the pure speculation period began. Traders bought and sold with margin buying—the use of loans to trade in stocks. This constant trading caused the market to rise to astronomical heights. A crash, in hindsight, seemed inevitable. Even President Herbert Hoover warned at the time against wild speculation and sold many of his stocks. No one took heed of his advice. Then in

1929, it happened. But contrary to popular belief, there never was a true crash. Instead, the end came in a long slide, from September 3 to November 13, 1929.[13]

By the last week of October, the end was in sight. Depression historian Robert McElvaine calls October 23 "the trigger."[14] On that afternoon the Dow Jones fell twenty-three points, wiping out all of July and August's gains. That was the signal for many to sell, and sell fast. The next day, October 24, soon became known as "Black Thursday" as thousands sold their shares. But even then, no one was ready to face the reality of the situation. The scene was set for October 29—"Black Tuesday." On that Tuesday, an all-out panic ensued. Over 16.4 million shares were sold.[15] No one will ever know for sure the exact figure. As has been widely reported over the years, sales were such that the stock ticker tape ran two and half hours late. The stock market boom was over.

By November 13 the market hit rock bottom for the year. Thirty billion dollars had been "blown into thin air."[16] Twice the amount of the national debt, and equal to the entire bill for United States involvement in the First World War. Over the next three years, it only got worse. From 1929 to 1930, the national suicide rate rose from 13.9 to 17.4 per 100,000 people.[17] There were 200,000 fewer marriages in 1932 than in 1929.[18] Companies began cutting budgets, and long lines began forming around unemployment offices and soup kitchens. America had entered the Great Depression.

But on that Black Tuesday, October 29, 1929, the state of Florida was already there.

As historian Robert McElvaine explained, the 1929 stock market crash did not cause the Depression. The crash only allowed it to occur, just as cold weather does not cause colds, but merely provides a suitable environment for the germs to prosper.[19] Overproduction, inequities in wealth, oligopolies, federal passivity, and international crisis were among the true causes. Likewise, many have written that Florida's land boom crash of 1926, and the two hurricanes that sandwiched it, were what brought Florida into the Depression three years earlier than the rest of the nation. But much of Florida was already deep in poverty, just as was most of the South. Widespread poverty was an established southern tradition by 1926.[20] The land boom's end was only the final blow to a state, and a region, that was already hurting economically and socially.

Few people realize the extent of Florida's poverty in the 1920s and 1930s because, as historian William Rogers pointed out, Florida's "playground" image coupled with its lack of factories and long lines of urban unemployed presented a false picture of prosperity.[21] Despite the success of the real estate and tourist trades (discussed later), Florida was no different than the rest of the South in its dependence on agriculture. And that dependence chained most of the state's citizens to the plow and the field. When the bottom fell out of southern agriculture in the early 1920s, most of Florida's citizens suffered right along with everyone else in the South.

Florida was as agricultural and rural a state as they came, with 54,005 farms in 1920.[22] Of those, fewer than 6,000 had tractors, while fewer than 8,000 even had running water. And most of the people who ran those farms were tenants and sharecroppers.[23] The tradition of tenancy has its origins in the antebellum plantation's slavery system. With the slaves' emancipation following the Civil War, cotton plantation owners lost their source of free labor. Unwilling to lose profits, they eventually devised a system within which they could continue to produce cotton for relatively little output—it became known as sharecropping.

Sharecropping was a system, reminiscent of antebellum plantations in structure and appearance, whereby a family agreed to live on and farm a section of an owner's land in return for a share of the crop. A few paid a simple rental fee for the opportunity to work the land. Because landowners knew they would lose a share of their profits each year to their tenants, many fixed the system to their advantage. They adopted a paternalistic attitude to excuse their behavior. Financial logs were often kept out of the croppers' reach. Educational opportunities were kept at a minimum. Most cropper schools met for only a few months out of the year, often in buildings with no windows or even desks, and classes were taught by teachers who were underpaid and often untrained.[24] Perhaps the cruelest, and from the planters' viewpoint the most effective, scheme was the notion of "furnishings." Since many croppers had no tools, and little furniture, clothing or food, the landowners would agree to furnish such necessities. These loans were made on a credit system, to be taken out of the family's share of the following season's crop. The interest rates ranged anywhere from 10 percent to well over 60 percent.[25] Usually tenants were unable to pay back the loans in a given year, so were forced to borrow again in order to survive yet another year. Like the infamous company store in the coal mines of Kentucky and West Virginia, this vicious cycle imprisoned the croppers on the farm year after year, guaranteeing continued labor and maximum profits for owners. From a production point of view, the scheme worked extremely well. By the 1920s croppers and tenants produced two out of every three cotton bales in the United States.[26]

Yet despite the prevalence and "success" of the system, it was a harsh and brutal life for the sharecropping families. New Dealer and journalist Lorena Hickok labeled it a form of slavery.[27] Bound indefinitely to the land and the hope of the next year's crop, they were the sector of the population most vulnerable to financial hardships. They lived in one- to three-room wooden cabins, often with no window glass and no running water, screens, or electricity. Their diet consisted almost entirely of salt pork, dried beans, flour, molasses, and corn meal. In the 1930s the Federal Emergency Relief Administration under President Franklin Roosevelt discovered that 20 percent of tenant farmers had no pillows until the federal government provided them.[28]

Though cotton was a major crop in Florida, especially in the northern part of the state, it was not the only crop. Compared to the rest of the Southeast, Florida had a diversified agriculture that included tobacco, citrus, strawberries, peanuts, celery, and corn. But workers in these areas were treated in much the same manner as the cotton-farming sharecroppers.[29]

Then in the 1920s the unimaginable happened—conditions grew worse for the average agricultural worker and his family. After an agricultural boom during World War I, resultant overproduction caused agricultural prices to tumble in the early 1920s, and they continued their downward spiral across the South through the 1930s. From 35 cents a pound in 1919, cotton prices fell to 28 cents in 1923, and by 1933 cotton was selling for a paltry 6 cents a pound.[30] In Florida corn and cotton values fell from $27 million to $10.2 million.[31] Similar results were seen across Florida's agricultural spectrum. But low prices and overproduction were not the only causes for the worsening conditions in Dixie. Southern agriculture also suffered from soil depletion, the boll weevil, and unfavorable weather conditions, especially in hurricane-prone Florida.[32]

"I mean things were tough," remembered Tarpon Springs resident George LeCouris. "We were running around with patches on our pants and holes in our shoes."[33] Sneads resident Fred Williams had "to wear my mother's shoes to school. And the kids laughed at me."[34] Many nights, all they had to eat were "milk and bread, which was like corn flakes, it was corn bread. . . . That kept us from starving."[35] Mulberry resident Ansley Hall recalled: "Well things were pretty tight back at that time. My Dad used to grow a garden and he'd take the greens and stuff like that, he'd take them down to the market and trade the greens in for some bacon. That, they give us, back there when things were really tight, they'd give us products instead of money in order to get something different to eat from what you got in your garden."[36] "If you were making six or eight dollars a week, you were making good money," declared one resident.[37] "Farming was hard," explained Buck Heath, a son of a farmer in Wewahitchka in the 1920s. "Cotton was bringing four cents a pound . . . peanuts, six cents a pound . . . Hogs—you couldn't even sell them on the market . . . and beef, you couldn't sell that."[38] Farmer Gilbert Tucker remembers the primitive conditions his best friend's family endured near Christmas, Florida. "They had no outhouse, only a 'relief spot' for a toilet. The area was designated by a big peeled cypress pole fastened between two trees in a palmetto clump near a swamp. There was a trail going from the house to this outdoor relief spot. The signal if the toilet was in use was a palmetto fan put on the trail . . . When it began to smell too bad, they just changed palmetto patches."[39]

As a result of these economic woes, the health of Florida's agricultural families worsened. Hookworm, pellagra, and typhoid were rampant. Malaria was six times worse in Florida than the rest of the nation.[40] A 1934 federal survey found that 80 percent of the children in rural Jackson County suffered from hookworm.[41] A WWI veteran's description of a bus ride through North Florida in 1939 provides a picture of rural Florida poverty that could just as easily have been written in 1925. As he wrote, the bus was full of "cullud folks and yaller folks—malaria, hookworm, pellagra and korn likker—babies with redbugs and bedbugs."[42] One passenger was nursing ("country style") her child who obviously had "the barber's itch. Poor babe—chiggers, itch, skeeters and the whole parade of bugs, no doubt."[43] All the passengers described were obviously poor and hungry, and many were demonstrably bitter.[44] But perhaps the most telling feature of the piece was that it was not written as an exposé, but rather as a humorous article for a CCC camp newsletter. The descriptions of poverty were mentioned only incidentally and in a matter-of-fact manner.

Also on that bus could easily have been representatives from some of the other trades prevalent in Florida: cowhands from the central and southern flatlands, cigar rollers on the west coast, citrus pickers from the state's remnant dune system, which runs like a backbone through the peninsula's center, loggers of the pine forests of the north and panhandle, and the shrimpers and fishers who encircle them all on the Atlantic and Gulf coasts. These were people perpetually stationed near the bottom of the economic ladder. Perhaps the group who came closest to the croppers' brutal lives were the turpentiners of the north and the panhandle regions. Kept as close to slave labor as legally possible by their bosses, the turpentiners lived in rough camps of sixty to ninety men each, situated in the scrubby sand hills where the longleaf pines grew, scores of rattlesnakes and deer ticks resided, and an understory of thick, lacerating palmettos flourished.[45] Florida folklorist Stetson Kennedy gave a hint of the brutality of their lives when he wrote for the Works Progress Administration that the typical camp owner "carr[ies] a revolver, sleeps with two double-barrel shotguns by his head, and keeps another shotgun and automatic rifle near the front door."[46] But unlike for the sharecroppers, few details of the lives of all of these workers have been recorded or are known. Nevertheless, one fact is unmistakably clear for this era—most of Florida was poor, and no improvement was anywhere in sight.

While a major portion of the state's population was struggling to put food on the table, Florida, Janus-like, had another face to show. This face was one of sunny beaches, fulfilled dreams, and incredible riches. This face was shown to the world and, more often than not, the history books. Everyone referred to this face as the Florida land boom.

Called by some the "dress rehearsal" for the 1928–29 national stock boom and eventual crash described at the beginning of the chapter, the Florida land boom likewise was built upon a foundation of speculation and confidence in perpetual good fortune.[47] After the Great War investors began moving to Florida. Land was cheap and plentiful. Several entrepreneurs had already paved the way, including Carl Fisher, who arrived in Florida in 1910 to the young town of Miami. Within a decade Fisher had built an adult playground of posh resorts, designed neighborhoods, and restaurants and horse tracks.[48] He followed in the footsteps of the two Henrys, Flagler and Plant, whose railroads opened up the southern peninsula for travel and trade in the late nineteenth century and whose grand resorts gave hints of the luxuries to come. Right behind Fisher were Addison Mizner, the mastermind behind Boca Raton and Palm Beach, George Merrick of Coral Gables, and the designer of Hollywood, Joseph M. Young. Though these men had wealth and power to start with, they grew still richer and demonstrated to an ambitious nation the riches waiting in the Sunshine State. The people who came to these resorts and fabricated cities soon realized that they, too, wanted to own a piece of the dream. Carl Fisher's Miami became the focus of the resultant land boom. And as with all dreams, someone is always willing to make a profit fulfilling it. Thus the Florida realtor was created.

In 1920 the number of realtors was relatively low. But Florida leaders decided to help matters along. Already Florida was the land of few taxes, with no sales, land, or property taxes. So when the Florida government banned all state income and inheritance tax in 1924, the floodgates were flung open. Florida quickly gained a reputation as a place where one could make tons of money and keep nearly all of it. By 1925 there were 12,000 realtors in Miami alone.[49] In 1920 some 22,000 land transactions were recorded. By 1924 there were 61,000.[50] In 1925 that figure skyrocketed to a whopping 174,530 transactions.[51]

The 1920s were the era of real estate fraud and sleight of hand, where out-of-state buyers could own a piece of paradise, located somewhere in the middle of the Everglades. Buses of prospective land buyers were shown beautiful parcels of land—visible only at low tide. But during the boom, there was actually little need for much conning. Speculation took care of that.

Perhaps no group symbolized the Florida land boom and its speculation craze so much as the "binder boys." As one eyewitness described them, binder boys were "some of the lowest and least scrupulous gentry probably to be found in the whole of the United States."[52] Binders were salesmen who dealt not in land but in paper options on real estate. The system worked like this: one could buy an option on a piece of land by paying 10 percent down, with the understanding that the other 90 percent would be paid within thirty days. Meanwhile, within those four weeks, there was no limit on how many times that option could be resold. So, for example, a binder could buy an option priced at $500 by paying $50 down, then turn around on the same day—even within the hour—and resell it for $1,000. By the end of thirty days, it was not unheard of for an option to go for more than $20,000 from an initial investment of less than a $100. By one estimate, there were as many as 25,000 binder boys working in South Florida at the height of the boom.[53] Binders, though impossible to quantify because most of their transactions went unrecorded, no doubt contributed to the meteoric rise in land prices. Land that sold in 1920 for $8 was selling in 1925 for $150,000.[54] This was pure speculation at its worst. The publicity over the land frauds and the binder boys grew so bad that Florida's Governor John Martin—worried over the effect this might have on the boom—traveled to the Waldorf in New York City to speak in an effort at damage control.[55]

The speech worked, for Florida's land boom continued unabated. It was helped along by prominent people such as the "Great Orator" himself, William Jennings Bryan—who was paid $100,000 a year by Coral Gables founder Merrick to hawk real estate.[56] Baseball great Ty Cobb's brother was a Florida realtor who convinced the Boston Red Sox to conduct spring training in Sarasota.[57] Even God was pulled into the act when Bible quotes were used to lure buyers (e.g., "Arise and go toward the south" from Acts 8:26).[58] Miami's newspaper, the *Miami Herald,* printed the nation's largest single issue at 504 pages with twenty-two sections—most of it real estate ads.[59] In 1925 there were 425 permits issued for hotel construction between January and May. In October of that year alone, seventy-six hotels were built, nearly all of them in South Florida.[60] Beautification projects abounded, and roads were improved. Along with the land boom, an accompanying population boom developed in South Florida. Between 1923 and 1925, 300,000 residents moved to the Sunshine State, with the majority settling in South Florida (though most would not stay).[61]

At the core of the land boom was tourism. It was tourists who first saw the potential in Florida. And it was overwhelmingly tourists who bought the land. Most of the significant population growth was either winter residents (i.e., long-term tourists) or those hoping to make a mint off other tourists. Simply put, without tourism, there was no land boom. In hindsight, it is obvious that the land was not the best investment for the future of the state; the people that the land boom brought in were. But no one had yet made that connection in 1926, which was unfortunate for them, because the land boom was about to come to an end.

John Kenneth Galbraith once described Florida's land boom as a "classic speculation bubble." As all bubbles must eventually pop, the Florida land boom's demise was inevitable. And that demise came to South Florida with little warning in late summer 1926.

In the early days of meteorology and mass communications, hurricanes could hit coastal areas with all the stealth and surprise of an enemy attack. Between September 18 and 20, 1926, such an attack hit South Florida in the form of the strongest hurricane ever recorded by the weather bureau up to that time.[62] Miami was pummeled for twelve hours, with winds that reached as high as 160 mph, while the hurricane moved its way slowly west across the peninsula. No building in downtown Miami was spared damage. Its streets were under three to four feet of water.[63] The town of Moore Haven, on the shores of Lake Okeechobee, was completely destroyed by tornados and flooding that killed 120. Finally, the storm exited into the Gulf of Mexico at Bonita Springs, from where it moved north toward the panhandle. Though it missed Pensacola by only a few miles, it spared the colonial city none of its fury. In the end the storm caused $10 million in crop damage. Florida's string bean and pepper crops were lost, as was a third of the state's cotton.[64] The newly begun avocado trade was halted in its tracks. The state lost 27 percent of its overall citrus for that season, though some counties, such as Lee and Dade, lost over 90 percent.[65]

Though the destruction left behind in the hurricane's wake was significant, the lasting damage came with the aftermath. Potential investors and speculators suddenly and collectively realized that Florida was not a calm paradise, and that hurricanes were not just a once-in-a-lifetime event. If a hurricane could do this much damage in just two days, many investors thought, what else lay in store for them? It was that potential for more disasters that planted the seed of doubt in investors' minds and dispelled the confidence in Florida realty. In a matter of days the Florida boom was over.

Almost to the day, two years later, potential became reality. On September 18, 1928, another hurricane hit South Florida, killing 1,800 people, leaving 35,000 homeless, and ending once and for all any hope of a renewed land boom.[66] By this time many of the investors had headed north, just in time for Wall Street's speculation frenzy. What these speculators left behind was South Florida's entrance into the depression already gripping the South.

The boom's end hit Florida hard. The exodus of cash that accompanied the northbound investors perhaps had a devastating effect on Florida's banking system. By 1926 the banks were beginning to close. Yet it was not sudden withdrawals that caused many of the closings. Instead, as Raymond Vickers demonstrated in his pioneering work *Panic in Paradise*, the problem was rooted in Florida's banking system, which allowed bankers to operate shrouded in secrecy, behind a complex and secretive regulatory system.[67] As Vickers discovered, many bankers invested huge sums of their banks' funds into land speculation. When the boom ended, the land deals fell through, and all the money the banks invested vanished. Between 1926 and 1929, 125 out of 335 banks failed, with a combined loss in assets of $375 million.[68]

When the boom ended and the banks collapsed, people all across Florida felt the effects. Fred White, whose father was a sharecropper in the 1920s, explained, "When the banks started closing, we did not have any money, so we didn't lose any, but it hurt us indirectly because we were working for people who had money."[69] Compounding this was the further lowering of agricultural prices. Lumber demand fell as construction ceased, hurting loggers and mills in North Florida.[70] By 1929 three-fourths of Florida's city governments had defaulted to some degree.[71] In Marianna several businessmen committed suicide in the late 1920s.[72] In Miami a resort hotel—unfinished after the 1926 hurricane—was converted into a chicken farm, with incubators and coops housed in the elegant bedrooms.[73] In 1931 the East Coast Railroad and the Florida Panhandle Hotel Corporation were in receivership.[74] And in Sun City, located just west of Tampa, a resident trying to protect his $50,000 mortgage investment purchased the entire town "lock, stock, and barrel," including "its water tower, its electric plant, a sizable motion picture studio, and numerous smaller buildings . . . all for $100 cash."[75]

Florida had the highest unemployment rate in the Southeast.[76] Florida farmers and sharecroppers were reeling from the low agricultural prices, bad weather and environmental conditions, and a low money supply. Turpentining, logging, and other traditional jobs were also declining. Direct relief appeared to be the only remedy for them. Granted, not everyone was a starving sharecropper living in a wooden shack. Along with the rural poor was a small but steady professional class that included merchants, lawyers, and landowners. But even in the urban areas, most worked in the low-paying and slowly declining service trades, such as being maids and cleaners. But regardless of economic standing, people were not as well off in 1929 as they were in 1925. The average annual income in 1929 was $521, $200 below the national average. By 1932 that average in Florida fell to $314 a year.[77] With banks closing and a low tax base, localities had no infrastructure to provide either relief or change. But there was hope for the state, first noticed in Miami. Even in the depths of the Great Depression, people still came to Florida for recreation. Although Florida shared with the rest of the South a distinctive dependence on agriculture and an aptitude for poverty, Florida also had something all its own. It had tourism.

But first, Florida had to solve its immediate problems. The state needed relief, and a way to funnel that relief to where it was most needed. Florida had neither funds nor any effective relief programs, while its constitution prevented direct relief and deficit spending. It was not until 1933 that two men from New York would succeed in changing Florida's economic and social landscape.

2

A New Deal for Florida

On the night of February 15, 1933, President-Elect Franklin Roosevelt capped off a weeklong cruise aboard Vincent Astor's yacht sailing along Florida's coast by parading down Bayfront Park in Miami.[1] Thousands were in attendance for a chance to see the nation's new leader. Florida had voted overwhelmingly Democratic, contributing to the restoration of the South's solidity after a brief Republican flirtation to avoid electing the Catholic Al Smith president in 1928. As Roosevelt greeted people, and Chicago's Mayor Anton J. Cermak approached the motorcade, five shots rang out. A "stubby, curly-haired man" named Joseph Zangara, bent on killing the president, missed his intended target but mortally wounded Cermak and struck three others.[2] Once hit, Cermak was rumored to have said to the president, "I'm glad it was me instead of you."[3] Roosevelt amazed onlookers by refusing to leave the scene and personally rode with Cermak to the hospital. Zangara (also known as Giuseppe Zangara) was quickly apprehended, convicted within days, and given three consecutive twenty-year sentences for the three citizens shot. Three weeks later he was given the death penalty for Cermak's murder when the mayor died.[4]

Meanwhile, Florida Governor David Sholtz rode the train with Roosevelt to accompany the mortally wounded Cermak back to Chicago. They spoke at length during the trip of future relief efforts, politics, and Florida's recovery.[5] A couple of weeks later, on March 4, Sholtz attended the presidential inauguration in Washington, D.C.[6] Thanks to Zangara's failed attempt to kill the president, a relationship developed—one that Sholtz would always henceforth refer to as a friendship—that had profound consequences for Florida in the 1930s.

As one historian put it, "Few figures have more significantly shaped the South's destiny than FDR."[7] Though Roosevelt spent most of his early career in the North, it was another tragedy that first brought Roosevelt to the South.

In 1921 Roosevelt contracted polio, which rendered his legs useless.[8] In 1924, on the advice of a friend, Roosevelt traveled to Warm Springs, Georgia, to seek a cure for his disability in the town's warm mineral waters.[9] During his many visits to the rural community (forty-two altogether), he developed an affinity and understanding for the South and its people. Already a firm believer in the "country life," he befriended many of the region's farmers and local leaders. He even set down roots when he purchased over a thousand acres on Pine Mountain, just outside Warm Springs.[10] Roosevelt knew the South and its problems with poverty, ecological disasters, and sharecropping when he took office and began his relief programs.

As New York's governor since 1929, Roosevelt had already garnered a reputation for progressive relief programs when he chose to run for president in 1932. One of his New York relief programs in particular would have profound influence once Roosevelt was in the Oval Office. For that program, Roosevelt used state funds to hire more than 10,000 out-of-work young men to reforest New York's depleted forests.[11] His progressive reputation served him well in the election, for the United States was slipping ever further into the depths of the economic depression. Unemployment figures were between 12 million and 14.6 million in 1932, for a nation of 125 million.[12] By February 1933, 15 percent of the nation was on some form of relief.[13] People wanted action, and as he promised in his inaugural address, Roosevelt was a man of action.

When Roosevelt took office, he wasted little time in demonstrating the differences between his activist administration and Herbert Hoover's overly cautious and locally oriented relief methods. Roosevelt immediately called a special session of Congress to deal with the banking emergency. Congress passed his banking bill sight unseen.[14] All told, the Hundred Days, the busiest three-month period in congressional history, saw fifteen major relief bills passed, which served as the foundation of what became known as the "New Deal."[15] The New Deal created profound changes for the South, which Roosevelt later said was "the nation's number one economic problem."[16]

As the Roosevelt-inspired legislation piled up over the next twelve weeks (and over the next nine years), federal relief fell into four categories.[17] These were direct relief for the unemployable; work relief for those able to perform labor; public assistance for the aged, blind, and young; and insurance for the unemployed, injured, and retired.[18] Eventually the New Deal framers (known collectively as the "Brains Trust") aimed at curbing the causes of poverty. But in this early stage their goals were only to curb the immediate effects of the Depression. One after another, the many "alphabet" programs emerged: the Federal Emergency Relief Administration (FERA), the Tennessee Valley Authority (TVA), the Agricultural Adjustment Administration (AAA), the Public Works Administration (PWA), and National Recovery Administration (NRA). In the winter of 1933–34 social worker and fellow New Dealer Harry Hopkins urged the creation of the Civil Works Administration (CWA) to aid the unemployed through a predicted brutal winter. In 1935 the New Deal expanded further, aiming at reform as well as relief. Urged by Dr. Francis Townsend, among many others, the federal government created the Social Security system to assist the elderly. That year also saw the emergence of the National Youth Administration (NYA) and the gargantuan Works Progress Administration (WPA).

For the South, one of the first New Deal programs to have any major effects was the Agricultural Adjustment Administration, an attempt to bring parity to farmers by restoring crop prices to 1917 levels by decreasing supply. In essence, the federal government would pay farmers not to grow a certain percentage of their crops. Because of the bill's relatively late passage—May 12, 1933—most of that year's crop was already planted. Therefore the government paid many farmers to plow up their fields. In 1933 some 10.4 million acres were plowed up, and the government shelled out over $161 million.[19] While southerners benefited from other New Deal programs, the South's rural nature, along with the South's powerful presence in the Congress, limited the New Deal's impact, especially concerning labor. But one program did have a noticeable southern presence: the Civilian Conservation Corps.

The CCC was without a doubt a pet project of FDR's. Over the years scholars have debated the degree of FDR's centrality to the New Deal. But no one denies that Roosevelt was the driving force behind the creation of the Civilian Conservation Corps. As former labor secretary Frances Perkins wrote in 1946, the CCC "was really his own."[20] It could be argued that because Franklin Roosevelt felt so strongly about reforestation, he would have pushed for the creation of a conservation corps even without an economic depression. By most accounts, Roosevelt was a devout conservationist. At Hyde Park he cultivated one of the nation's healthiest private forests, planting ten to fifteen thousand trees a year.[21] He hated seeing trees cut and not replaced.[22] As early as 1910 Roosevelt fought for reforestation programs for New York

State's Fish and Game Commission.[23] Even the oft-critical New Deal scholar Paul Conkin admitted that on conservation, Roosevelt never wavered.[24] For Roosevelt, forest management was more than good stewardship—it was a societal necessity. Roosevelt believed many of civilization's ills could be cured by a return to the country. This Jeffersonian belief in the powers of an agrarian or rural lifestyle fueled many of Roosevelt's New Deal efforts. Never was this more obvious than with the CCC.

Many have tried to decipher the influences upon Roosevelt's CCC program. The obvious suspect is Harvard scholar William James and his 1912 essay "The Moral Equivalent of War." In that essay James argued for transforming the destructive tendencies inherent in all young men to public service through a conscripted work force.[25] Though Roosevelt always denied reading James, he could not deny the many similar conservation armies prospering in the early 1930s. Germany, Austria, Bulgaria, Denmark, and Norway all had reforestation work relief for young men.[26] (In fact, after the Nazi takeover in Germany in 1933, the reforestation program became a Nazi propaganda organ. The few CCC critics tried to make a connection between the Nazis' "tree army" and the CCC.[27]) In the United States many states turned to arboreal work relief as an answer to combating unemployment. Washington, Pennsylvania, Michigan, Virginia, and Wisconsin all had some form of forestry work relief, usually involving tree planting.[28] California, the most organized of them all, had twenty-five camps under an agreement with the U.S. Forest Service to plant trees and fight forest fires.[29] And finally, in August 1932, the Society of American Foresters advocated a reforestation relief program.[30] But while the originality of his idea may be questioned, Roosevelt's desire and personal involvement in the creation of the Civilian Conservation Corps cannot be.

Concerns over the natural environment led to the creation of the CCC, but so did widespread worries for the social environment. When the Roosevelt Administration assumed power in spring 1933, there was much concern within educational, social, and political circles about the effects the economic depression was having upon the nation's youth. Throughout Europe, youth dissent aided the rise of communism and fascism. For many, fear of such revolutionary activities closer to home led to the conviction that youth relief was needed in the United States. As President Franklin Roosevelt's Brains Trust began developing a series of regulatory laws and relief programs, many simultaneously pushed for action for the country's youth, which at the time referred to those between sixteen and twenty-five years of age.[31] As many have noted, one-third of the nation's unemployed fell within that age group.[32] Each year 2.25 million students dropped out of school in search of work.[33] Charles Taussig, American Molasses Company president and Brains Trust member, warned of the possibility of America's youth fostering undemocratic opinions, as the German and Italian youth were doing.[34] Senator David Walsh of Massachusetts stressed the need for a youth relief program so that the young would not "become demoralized and disheartened, and thus constitute a dangerous addition to discontented and radical minded elements."[35] In 1934 one social worker wrote to Roosevelt's chief relief administrator Harry Hopkins: "The young are rotting without jobs and there are no jobs."[36] Even the president's wife, Eleanor Roosevelt, used her newspaper column "My Day" to champion youth relief, arguing that "an embittered, unfulfilled and disappointed youth will be more dangerous to our future happiness than any loss in material possessions."[37]

Roosevelt needed little convincing, since his concerns for youth welfare dated back to his gubernatorial reign, and to his visits to Warm Springs for polio therapy during the 1920s. He always felt that the nation's youth were "special charges" of the federal government. However, Roosevelt often differed with members of his administration on how to help youth. It was clear that FDR already believed young adults' energies and emotions should be channeled into socially positive good-works projects, such as planting trees and large-scale public works.[38] FDR was also influenced by psychologist Stanley Hall's work on adolescence, likewise arguing for physical outlets for healthy citizen development, and for not allowing young adults to mature too quickly.[39] His ideas led to several youth-oriented programs in the 1900s, such as the YMCA and the Boy Scouts. By the 1930s Roosevelt felt that students' choice to drop out of school was often a rational reaction to an education system that remained uncommitted to students' needs in the real world.[40] Roosevelt would later argue that his CCC program offered an alternative to traditional schools. In addition to completing conservation projects, the enrollees took classes in the evenings, and participated in hands-on job training.

Meanwhile others around FDR, such as his wife, relief administrator Hopkins, and Aubrey Williams, wanted to attack the problem driving so many youth to leave school in the first place. They felt that educators had failed at their job. Too many youth were dropping out and entering the adult job market, competing with older workers struggling to support families. They wanted to democratize education by serving "a wider spectrum of the nation's youth."[41] Not only should students still in school be encouraged to remain there, but youth who quit for employment—either to help out their family, or merely out of frustration—should also be coaxed back. One way was through job training, which would offer immediate real-world benefits to those students not on a college track.[42] The idea would be to "shock an American education system" into changes, with the federal government leading the way by example. Such a program would also transform the government pedagogical role from a mere "financier of the schools to a schoolhouse in and of itself."[43] But the first steps were more conservative, focusing on maintaining those students currently enrolled in school.

The resultant program, based on plans drawn up by Secretary of Labor Frances Perkins and Aubrey Williams, was the National Youth Administration (NYA), created by executive order on June 26, 1935.[44] But two years earlier, these concerns and searches for a solution to the youth problem had also lent "Roosevelt's tree army" a strong educational element that stressed citizenship and patriotism to keep youth away from radical ideas.

Within eight days of taking office Roosevelt drew up plans for a national conservation army. As he would soon explain in a "fireside chat" (the "informal" and very effective radio speeches he made sporadically throughout his presidency), Roosevelt proposed a civilian corps "to be used in simple work" that would "confine itself to forestry, the prevention of soil erosion, flood control and similar projects."[45] Roosevelt explained that the work would benefit more than just forests: "We can eliminate to some extent at least the threat that enforced idleness brings to spiritual and moral stability."[46] For Roosevelt, the restoration to America's youth of a connection with the outdoors was as important as the actual forestry work. This idea would influence many New Deal projects.

To make the corps a reality, Roosevelt first had to organize it and get it passed through Congress. He personally drew up an organizational chart. At the head would be the director, overseeing all operations. Representatives from the departments of Labor, War, Interior, and Agriculture would oversee various logistics of the program. Labor would be in charge of selection. The transportation, conditioning, policing, and housing of the enrollees (as the corps volunteers were called) would be handled by the U.S. Army. As for the choosing and handling of the various work projects, Roosevelt chose two government service organizations. The Forest Service would oversee all forestry projects—whether on federal, state, or private property—which constituted the majority of CCC work projects. The Interior Department's National Park Service would supervise any park projects, including those in state parks. To handle the various agencies, an advisory council was set up, with representatives from all participating agencies as members. The same executive order (#6101) that set up the council also named a director—former labor leader Robert Fechner, former president of the International Association of Machinists, and one-time vice-president of the American Federation of Labor (AFL).[47]

Fechner was chosen in order to silence the only major critics of the CCC plan—organized labor. Fearing job competition from the relatively high salary proposed for enrollees—$30 a month—they began calling the plan militaristic and decried the army's role.[48] Some labor leaders went so far as to call the CCC forced labor.[49] AFL's president William Green worried that the corps would undercut private jobs.[50] In effort to please these critics, Roosevelt chose the Tennessean Fechner.[51] Though chosen by FDR, Fechner was no New Dealer. Unlike New Dealers Harry Hopkins, Frances Perkins, Henry Morgenthau, and Aubrey Williams, Fechner was not steeped in the Social Gospel tradition.[52] Withdrawn, homely, and a self-labeled non-intellectual, Fechner once described himself as a "potato bug among dragonflies."[53] But he was easy to get along with and very devoted to the CCC. Once when Postmaster General James Farley pointed out the patronage opportunities of the corps, Fechner was outraged, and said such activity would be "harmful to the project."[54] As his assistant, Fechner chose James McEntee, a fellow machinist who was equally devoted to the CCC. Thus, with labor appropriately appeased, the CCC was ready for Congress and implementation.

On March 21, 1933, Roosevelt sent a message to Congress asking for an Emergency Civilian Works (ECW), the official name for the CCC until 1937.[55] Ten days later the bill passed. As set up, the corps would accept all single, unemployed men between the ages 18 and 25 (later expanded to 17–28 years). On April 14, Native Americans were allowed into the corps. Because of the Bonus Marches of 1932 and 1933, provision was also made to include WWI veterans.[56] Enrollees would be paid $30 a month, with $25 sent home to their dependents.

They would be organized into camps of 200 men, for six-month terms with the option of renewing their stints for up to two years. Roosevelt wanted the men recruited quickly, with a goal of 250,000 enrollees by July 1, 1933.[57] The first camp was in Luray, Virginia, set up on April 17, 1933.[58] When the July deadline rolled around, director Fechner reported there were 274,375 enrollees, with camps located in every state.[59] The Association of American Forestry reported that also by July 1933, 16,000 civilians were employed as auxiliary help.[60] The CCC was under way.

Quickly, the Civilian Conservation Corps proved to be the New Deal's most popular program. For reasons of both personal pride and political gain, Roosevelt always made known his connection with the CCC. Almost from the start, the CCC was known as "Roosevelt's tree army." On May 7, 1933, FDR spoke at length on the CCC during one of his fireside chats. "We are conserving not only our natural resources," he pointed out, "but also our human resources."[61] In August that year Roosevelt personally visited five CCC camps in Virginia's Shenandoah Valley. Along with a full press corps, Roosevelt brought with him Secretary of the Interior Harold Ickes, Secretary of Agriculture Henry Wallace, and AFL President William Green.[62] The press stemming from the trip, along with the speeches and the program's success, forever linked Roosevelt intimately with the CCC. Few if any of Roosevelt's political opponents would attack either the program or the president's role in it.

Although it has had its share of critics in the post–New Deal years, the Civilian Conservation Corps remains popular. This fact is more remarkable considering the relatively small number of people who were directly affected by the CCC. Its peak year was 1935, when 500,000 enrollees were reported.[63] The average yearly enrollment was 250,000, though by the last years, the figures were much lower.[64] Overall the total nine-year enrollment was 2.5 million.[65] Although from a relief viewpoint the CCC was in T. H. Watkins's assessment "insignificant," it was effective in accomplishing its goals.[66] CCC enrollees planted more than half of all the trees ever planted in the United States.[67] The CCC was also nearly scandal-free. The only incidents of consequence were the National Park Service "phony camp"—where an employee of the NPS set up a faux camp and collected the phantom enrollees' paychecks—and the "toilet-kit incident," involving the purchase by the CCC's administrative staff of overpriced mess kits.[68] Neither story received much attention. Yet the main reason for the popularity of the corps was that it was a simple idea offering easy-to-comprehend and tangible results, which tapped into America's agrarian myth.[69] The image of young men trotting off into the woods, improving the land the nation's forefathers had settled, carried a powerful resonance. Unlike the WPA and other work-relief program recipients, the CCC's enrollees were seen as earning their pay through sweat and hard work restoring the country's resources. It was an image that would not go unnoticed by state and local leaders.

Despite the popularity of some of its programs, the New Deal did not end the Depression. Nothing would until World War II brought pump-priming defense industries and a dramatic rise in factory and military jobs. Although 36 percent of the population received some form of relief, it was not enough.[70] In fact, it can be argued that for some sectors of the citizenry, the New Deal made matters worse. An example was the AAA. Aimed at increasing farmers' purchasing power, the program entrusted farm owners with the responsibility of dividing the money paid for the destroyed crops among their tenants and sharecroppers. Instead, most simply "fired" their tenants and croppers and pocketed the cash. While the AAA effectively ended the harsh sharecropper system, it also offered few options for the cropping families now out of work. As historian James Patterson wrote in his study on American poverty, no group was better treated by the federal government of the 1930s than the large landowners of the South.[71]

Though not perfect, the New Deal was nevertheless relief on a scale never imagined at any previous time in the nation's history. And relief was what Florida desperately needed. Florida's economic and social conditions from the 1920s only grew worse by the early 1930s. It seemed that Mother Nature was not yet finished with Florida. First came the citrus industries' infestation by the Mediterranean fruit fly in 1929–30. Discovered in Orlando, the fly soon infested nearly an entire year's crops, affecting 40 percent of Florida's total rural population.[72] Over 70 percent of that year's citrus fruit was destroyed to control the fast-reproducing insect. Then it was the cattle ranchers' turn. In the early 1930s the cattle tick fever broke, causing ranchers to agree to state-sponsored bimonthly cattle dippings in arsenic solution. Expensive and time-consuming, the frequent dippings forced the small to mid-size ranchers out of the cattle business. Such disruptions only added to the misery. In 1934 there were 250,000 cases of hookworm and between 80,000 and 90,000 malaria cases in Florida.[73] Average per capita income in 1932 was $289.[74] By 1933, 36 percent of African Americans and 22 percent of whites were on some form of relief.[75] According to a 1935 state government report, 110,000 families were on relief, among whom 140,000 people were under sixteen years of age.[76] Florida was one of only four states in which more than 20 percent of citizens were on relief.[77] And those figures would have been much higher had more relief been available. Less than twenty Florida counties had any public relief.[78] One reason for this was that many cities and towns were bankrupt. Several municipalities had floated large bonds in the 1920s to accommodate growth that defaulted with the land boom and stock market crashes.[79] Aggravating matters was the nearly non-existent tax base in Florida. As shown in the previous chapter, only two taxes were available to governments in Florida: a gas tax and the ad valorem tax. Florida's first gas tax was in 1921, at one cent per gallon. In 1923 Florida raised the tax to three cents, but the revenue could still be used only for road building.[80] The State of Florida would not collect a sales tax until 1949.[81] But the relief problem went beyond mere cash availability and was firmly rooted within Florida's government and its politics.

Florida had a long tradition of laissez-faire relief policies. In fact, Florida's expectations of its government were limited in most matters. The office of governor was weak, with an elected cabinet and a law against running for successive terms. The governor's only power came from the bully pulpit and his appointee powers. The Florida Legislature was hardly stronger—it met for only sixty days every two years. Florida residents liked state government weak, distant, and uninvolved in their lives. Florida's early relief efforts reflected this relationship.

Florida's first welfare law, which allowed judges to help "pauper" children through apprenticeships, was passed in 1828. At the age of twenty-one they received a blanket, one hundred dollars, and a horse.[82] That law was altered in 1866 to require that orphans be taught a trade during their apprenticeships. Ten years later the state government started the Florida Asylum for Indigent Lunatics, and nine years after that the state-run School for the Deaf and Blind opened in St. Augustine.[83] That same year, 1885, Florida rewrote its constitution. Its only welfare provision was its requirement that counties provide for "inhabitants who by reason of age, infirmity or misfortune may have claims upon the aid and sympathy of society."[84] This was the start of Florida's poor farms. And aside from the monthly Confederate pensions for the widows of Confederate veterans—who were not eligible for federal pensions—the Florida

Constitution forbade any direct relief by the state. There would be no other state-sponsored relief until the 1920s.

Florida politics also inhibited much progressive action. State politics had traditionally been fractious with an "every man for himself" atmosphere tainting the issues.[85] Several factors contributed to this divisiveness: the state's large size; the lack of adequate transportation and communication; diverse trade and agriculture; and the aggregation of political power in rural North Florida coupled with the growth of South Florida's population.[86] Gubernatorial elections often saw ten Democratic candidates to represent the many factions of the party. (Republican campaigns were inconsequential.) Unlike other states, Florida had no statewide political machines to unify factions.[87] This divisiveness meant that each law, proposal, act, or idea was fought tooth and nail by the other factions (political, geographical, and social) within the Democratic Party. It stifled all innovation. The economic crisis of the late 1920s only heightened the divisions.

When the real estate market crashed, Florida was still operating under the 1885 constitution (and would continue to do so until 1968). Despite this, the State Board of Public Welfare was created in 1927 to oversee city, county, and private relief agencies. Relief efforts involved mostly child welfare programs such as schools, orphanages, and adoptions agencies.[88] The new board offered no relief of its own. It was to inspect all public and private relief agencies, oversee all state parolees, license maternity houses and child-boarding homes, request reports from such agencies, and encourage county-level welfare.[89] It was under-funded and under-staffed even in "normal" times, and was inadequate for the Depression.[90] The board's first biannual budget was a meager $20,000.[91] Except for a few county relief efforts, it was all Florida had to offer.

Few governors across the nation had clear economic plans for battling the depression. Budget slashing was the usual tactic, and Florida's Doyle Carlton was no different.[92] A Tampa citrus farmer and lawyer, Carlton was elected governor in 1928 and soon cut both state employee salaries and the government's budget.[93] He feared new taxes, and opposed attempts to create them. Inheritance, income, and gambling taxes were all offered by the legislature and vetoed.[94] Carlton believed that the Depression was cyclical and would soon blow over. He targeted the banks. In 1931 he sponsored the Florida Banking Act, which limited deposit withdrawals.[95] The only other economic measure Carlton supported was President Hoover's Reconstruction

Finance Corporation (RFC). The RFC was trickle-down economics that gave loans to banks and businesses to spread "confidence" throughout the nation's economy. Hoover's supply-side answer to widespread suffering gave to many the false, if long-lasting, impression that he cared more for banks than for people. Carlton, like all governors, requested RFC loans. In September 1932 Florida received its first of four payments—$500,000.[96] By May 1933 Florida had already received $3 million from the federal government.[97] But it was not enough. And it went to the wrong people. By the 1932 elections many Floridians were angry and looking for a change.

David Sholtz represented that change for many. Riding the same wave of discontent that swept Roosevelt into office, Sholtz used his outsider image to win the gubernatorial race. He was born in Brooklyn to Russian—and perhaps Jewish—immigrant parents.[98] (His staff would often claim his parents were German.)[99] Sholtz followed degrees from Yale and Stetson with a law career in Daytona Beach.[100] After gaining political clout from his presidency of Florida's State Chamber of Commerce, Sholtz entered the 1932 gubernatorial race, which was already crowded with seven other candidates.[101] Called Florida's first modern campaigner by Jacksonville's *Florida Times-Union*, Sholtz used loudspeakers, radio speeches, and a chartered plane to campaign on a platform of free textbooks and tax reduction.[102] Sensing the electorate's mood, Sholtz emphasized his outsider reputation. He called his opponents "politeers."[103] Ex-governor and fellow candidate John Martin unintentionally added to the image with his comment that Sholtz was "unknown, untried and untested."[104] Sholtz surprised all when he won the election by a 71,000-vote margin.[105]

Sholtz, once described by *Time* magazine as "plump-jowled and energetic," did not start out as a New Deal governor.[106] He pledged once inaugurated to shrink the state's government and not to add new agencies and programs.[107] His free textbooks plan was honorable but hardly the answer to Florida's poverty. And his tax reduction ideas were just a continuation of the same policies Florida government had practiced for generations. He even told FDR when they first met that he wanted Florida free of all federal money.[108] But he was a skilled politician—Secretary of State R. A. Gray described him as "clever"— and when he saw Roosevelt's growing popularity, he began to change his approach.[109] He was helped along in this apparent transformation by Senator Duncan Upshaw Fletcher. The long-time Florida senator, who supported Sholtz during the election, was close to FDR (he often visited Roosevelt in

Warm Springs), and his support of FDR's New Deal was "near perfect."[110] Sholtz and Fletcher worked closely together, and the newly elected governor soon saw the advantages of siding with President Roosevelt. Besides, thanks to would-be assassin Joseph Zangara, Sholtz was a "friend" of Roosevelt's. By the time the Florida Legislature met in 1933, the New Deal had begun, and Sholtz was—at least outwardly—a Roosevelt man.

In his first message to Florida's legislature, Sholtz said, "President Roosevelt has boldly shown the way to the nation," and he asked for the same legislative cooperation that had been afforded the president.[111] But his Roosevelt connection was little more than image, for what he asked for from the legislature was only a slightly expanded version of what he had campaigned upon: free textbooks, the creation of a state board of conservation, and reduction in vehicle license tag fees.[112] But he did reverse himself on accepting federal funds, and the legislature and Florida public followed his lead. The FERA, WPA, and CWA were soon active in Florida, with the funds dispersed through the Board of Public Welfare. This was a major change for a southern state because the South had traditionally shunned any federal involvement in its affairs.[113] But by 1933 Florida, along with the rest of the South, was ready for a change. For a politician like Sholtz, taking advantage of such a change was very lucrative: he kept the constituents satisfied while supplying local leaders and fellow colleagues with plenty of federal funds. Best of all was that Florida spent very little of its own money. And with the CCC, Sholtz scored one of his biggest political successes.

As many governors across the nation learned, the CCC offered them many advantages. It enjoyed huge popularity, employed thousands, and brought in federal dollars to the state and local businesses. Towns, communities, and other localities fought for CCC camps. Camps meant locally bought supplies, publicity, and two hundred or more new customers for food, recreation, and beer. It was political patronage without the negative stigma. Plus the CCC would improve the state's natural resources as the enrollees planted thousands of trees, fought fires, built roads, and developed state forests. To be associated with the CCC meant political gold for politicians. And in Florida, it was Governor Dave Sholtz who reaped the credit.

The CCC in Florida was up and running in less than six months. The first camp opened in the Olustee National Forest in August 1933.[114] By October there were 3,500 Florida enrollees in twenty-two camps.[115] By the second period (the CCC enrollments were divided into six-month periods), there were twenty-six camps; and by the third, twenty-five.[116] The State Board of Public Welfare chose the enrollees, and the Board of Forestry was the local agency that chose and supervised the projects (in consultation with and under the overall jurisdiction of the U.S. Forest Service and National Park Service).[117] The Florida Forestry Board was, by any measure, the major driving force behind the Florida CCC program. By 1933 State Forester Harry Lee Baker was the de facto head of Florida's CCC work projects. Throughout the nine years the CCC was in Florida, the only projects not under Baker's supervision were the Seminole camps, run by the United States Department of the Interior. Though Baker predated Sholtz by five years, the two enjoyed a good working relationship. While the state's initial contribution was minimal, the CCC was nevertheless an early success for Sholtz.

The governor wasted little time in exploiting the CCC's success. In his correspondence Sholtz made clear that he was a firm supporter of Roosevelt's CCC. His letter to the American Tree Association in 1934 was typical of this period: "I am more than ever convinced that the CCC is one of the greatest achievements of our great leader, Franklin D. Roosevelt. Seldom has the world experienced a movement that has so completely benefited the present by rendering a service to the future."[118] Around the same time Sholtz personally wrote to two newsreel production companies, Pathé and Movietone, to ensure news footage of his inspection tour of CCC camps.[119] Also in 1934 Sholtz organized the Forest Fire Prevention week as a way to celebrate the CCC's achievements in Florida. Held in December, it involved over twenty Florida cities and more than three thousand CCC enrollees and included parades, posters, radio programs, and movie trailers that were displayed before every movie in Florida theatres during that week.[120]

Yet it is still unclear just how devoted Dave Sholtz was to the larger New Deal. Historians have alternately described the governor as a dedicated New Dealer and as a conservative who was motivated only by political gain.[121] One fact is clear. Before 1933 Sholtz had never shown any inclination toward social welfare in any form. Moreover, before entering office, he displayed decidedly pro-business leanings, and once in office, Sholtz was not above using the CCC for political gain. Before the state hired anyone for CCC work, it ran a political background check to ensure loyalty to Sholtz, usually performed by Sholtz's executive secretary James "Jim" P. Newell.[122] Forester Harry Lee Baker typically wrote Newell asking whether he could hire candidates for CCC positions.[123] An example of such a background check was one for potential employee, Glen Tyler. In a confidential letter, lawyer William Fills informed Newell that "you may safely assume that Mr. Tyler was no friend of the Governor, and did not support him when he was running for office."[124] Senator Sam Lundy of Milton, Florida, had a similar assessment for another potential employee, who also "was not in sympathy with the administration."[125] Neither candidate was hired.

For this reason Harry Hopkins, head of the FERA, CWA, and later the WPA, was skeptical of Sholtz. To restrict Sholtz's meddling in New Deal affairs, Hopkins moved the major New Deal state facilities—including the WPA, CWA, Florida ERA, State Welfare Board, and the CCC—from Tallahassee to Jacksonville. Hopkins's suspicions are attributable to one person—Lorena Hickok. A journalist who was a close friend to the Roosevelt administration (she was especially close to Eleanor Roosevelt), Hickok was one of the New Deal's most avid supporters. In 1934 Hopkins asked Hickok to be his eyes and ears in gauging how the New Deal was working around the nation. For several months Hickok traveled in her car and sent Hopkins word about what she saw and learned. In late January and early February of that year Hickok spent time in Florida. She was not impressed. "I have seen more greed in this state than anywhere else I've been," she wrote at one point.[126] Hickok was especially harsh on Dave Sholtz. "The Governor [Sholtz] has a bad reputation around the state, and it's getting worse. . . . It's generally assumed on the part of the public apparently that he is playing politics with the CWA."[127] E. R. Bentley, a county administrator for the CWA in Lakeland, told Hickok that he "voted for that blankety-blank, but I'm ashamed of it now."[128]

For two years Sholtz fostered an image in Florida of total cooperation with the Roosevelt Administration on the New Deal. But by 1935 it was time for the state to ante up its fair share of the relief burden; the federal government was demanding change. Some leaders in Florida, including Dave Sholtz and Harry Baker, saw more opportunity for the state. If Florida now had to foot some of the bill for the CCC, then they would ensure that the CCC worked for the state as well. Therefore, among the many changes that 1935 brought was a new state government organization—the Florida Park Service.

3

Tourism, Conservation, and State Parks

To a large degree, the modern image and commodification of Florida sprang from the initial reaction of visitors to the Sunshine State. The warm climate, the exotic looking vegetation and animal life, and the relative lack of human development offered new arrivals what seemed an inviting tabula rasa. But as they acclimated and familiarized themselves with the area, many attempted to re-create that initial reaction through tropical plantings, "exotic" architecture, and importation of tropical animals. As in earlier eras but more widespread and intensified, we see this with roadside attractions in the 1930s and 1940s. As non-Floridians grew increasingly familiar with the state, many developers increased their dependence upon genuinely exotic elements—eventually bypassing Florida elements altogether, leading to the Disney era and beyond. But at the start of the decade, the native flora and fauna of Florida were often enough for those initial visitors.

In January 1930 a family of initial visitors to Florida experienced that first reaction from a bird's-eye view when Ronald Roebling flew his parents in his private plane over his hometown of Sebring, Florida, in the southern Central Florida Highlands—the southern end of an ancient dune system dating back over 300,000 years. They were building an estate in nearby Lake Placid, and he wanted to familiarize them with the area. On that flight they saw the miles of citrus groves that carpeted these rolling dune hills. Snaking through the orange groves was U.S. 27, the new highway that linked the small towns of the area: Lake Placid, Avon Park, Lake Wales, and Sebring. Rising above this landscape was Bok Tower, a 205-foot-high marble and coquina carillon situated atop Florida's highest point, 285 feet above sea level, on the outskirts of Lake Wales. Barely a year old (it was built by *Ladies Home Journal* editor Edward Bok on land originally designated as a bird sanctuary), the tower and adjoining gardens designed by Frederick Law Olmsted Jr. and constructed by William Lyman Phillips were already one of Florida's top tourist draws.[1] Then Ronald's mother, Margaret Roebling, noticed an area that stood out (and up) from the orange and green landscape—a lush hammock known locally as Hooker's Hammock.

Located just outside Sebring, Hooker's Hammock was South Florida's last remaining virgin forest.[2] A vestige of an ecosystem that once extended across Florida from Orlando south to the Everglades, this surviving 500-acre tract was home to native trees that stood well over 100 feet tall, as well as lush ferns, rare flowers, and a thriving bird population. The hammock was unlike any other surviving Florida ecosystem in the 1930s. The contrast between the dry sand hills of the Lake Wales Ridge and this tropical forest was startling. In an account written much later, Margaret Roebling reputedly said as she saw the hammock, "People have taken most of the state of Florida for their playground. I want to save a bit of it."[3] She soon wanted to buy the hammock and turn it into a public park.[4]

The Roeblings, a well-known New Jersey family—John Roebling's father built New York City's Brooklyn Bridge as well as the railroad bridge over Niagara Falls—paid $25,000 for the land. The sale created a buzz locally. Margaret soon discovered that others in the area also wanted to turn the hammock into a park, with the hopes of attracting to Sebring the crowds visiting Bok Tower just up U.S. 41. A year earlier several local leaders—including Avon Park Mayor C. S. Donaldson, Harder Hall hotel owner Ray Green, realtors B. L. Laird and William A. Davison, and novelist Rex Beach—formed the Tropical Florida Parks Association, with the goal of turning Hooker's Hammock into a national park. They invited NPS officials to Sebring, offered them free board, and gave them a tour of the proposed park. Although impressed, the NPS visitors decided the area was much too small to warrant national park status. Therefore when Margaret Roebling entered the picture, the association—which was still eager to attract tourists to the area—paid a visit to her Lake Placid home. In April 1930 they changed their name to Highlands Hammock, Inc., and made Mrs. Roebling (later replaced by W. A. Davison) its president.[5] By summer, with an initial financial grant by Mrs. Roebling, park construction was under way.[6]

The original plan was to sell subscriptions and solicit donations from local residents and prominent individuals across the state. But when the response proved lackluster, the Roeblings decided to foot the bill themselves. The sole assistance they received was when the association asked for, and received, funds from the Highlands County Board of Commissioners for a county road to the newly renamed Highlands Hammock.[7] The Roeblings put their estate's engineer, Alexander Blair, in charge of the project, and hired over forty out-of-work Sebring locals for labor. Registered state engineer Joe Hawkins handled the day-to-day park operations. With Margaret Roebling's untimely death in October 1930, the project went into high gear as John Roebling labored to complete the park in her memory. Expenses included building roads, staff residences, property fences, bridges, fire lanes, and a ranger station; restocking the hammock with deer and turkeys; conducting surveys; and maintaining a large labor crew. Tree surgery on three massive oaks that Margaret was particularly fond of, which involved filling the trunks with steel rods and concrete, cost John Roebling over $10,000.[8] Some additional funds were raised through the selling of fruit produced by the hammock's citrus grove. Oranges and grapefruit had been cultivated on the site for decades, although by the time the Roeblings purchased the hammock, "the groves were in a very run down condition."[9] While there was little market for grapefruit, the oranges brought in some profits. For instance, in 1934 the organization sold over "one hundred and fifty boxes of Valencia late oranges," and 1,424 field boxes of sweet oranges.[10] They expected twice as much the following year.[11] By 1933 when the park was opened to the public, Roebling had spent well over $300,000 of his own money.[12]

That same year Governor Dave Sholtz began receiving reports on the park's progress. For instance, in 1934, Fred Gadsby, regional supervisor for the National Park Service, sent along a note from District Inspector Orin Bullock that remarked, "This area should surely be acquired by the State of Florida and made into a State Park. The vocabulary of an Architect is staggered in an attempt to describe the wonders nature has wrot [sic] in this location."[13] Many, including Rex Beach and Alexander Blair, wrote that they believed John Roebling would donate the completed park to the state.[14] Sholtz resisted, citing the Florida government's poor financial situation.[15] When State Forester Harry Lee Baker reported that Roebling was willing to contribute funds covering half the maintenance costs for the next five years, the offer became more enticing.[16] Sholtz advised Baker to consider the deal "if you think this can be handled without any obligation financially upon the state."[17] He would visit the park himself the following February.[18]

As Sholtz realized, throughout 1933 and 1934 the CCC proved itself a successful avenue for building infrastructure and offering political rewards to local leaders at little cost to the state. So when the Federated Garden Clubs of Florida began expressing interest in building a Florida State Garden and Arboretum at Highlands Hammock, it seemed to be a good project for a new CCC camp.[19] In 1934 the private park printed and sold thousands of copies of its *Guide to Highlands Hammock State Park,* and the park was already attracting a fair number of visitors and might bring a profit to the state.[20]

In 1934 the state accepted Roebling's offer and assumed ownership of Highlands Hammock, though specifics of the park's management were left undecided.[21] The Roeblings' share of the funds would be handled through a board of trustees set up under Highlands Hammock, Inc. and would match state funds for the next six years.[22] In the meantime a CCC camp was set up to begin construction of the State Garden and Arboretum. This was fortuitous timing. The following spring when the federal government demanded more commitment from Florida in its relief programs, Sholtz already had an ace in the hole. He introduced legislation that created the Florida Park Service, and without a penny spent by the state, Highlands Hammock became Florida's first state park and one of its earliest roadside attractions.

In May 1933 Governor Sholtz was still finding his way, awkwardly transforming himself from the champion of no taxes and smaller state government to a full-fledged New Dealer. But that month a simple informational request would set him—and Florida—on a path toward national, even international, aspirations. On May 3, 1933, first-time legislator Ben Wand of Duval County wrote to Sholtz asking him "to secure and transmit to me figures concerning certain expenditures of the Dept. of Agriculture . . . for the payment of advertising, the printing of booklets or pamphlets, and a breakdown of amounts advanced for the account of the Committee on the Century of Progress Exposition."[23] Both the advertising funds and Florida's involvement in the upcoming Chicago world's fair were news to the governor. He immediately responded to Wand that he would do so, then wrote both to Agricultural Commissioner Nathan Mayo for the desired information and to State Auditor Bryan Willis for his own informational purposes.[24] Mayo responded the following day with a copy of his department's biennial report for 1930 to 1932.[25] Again, with speed rare for governors, Sholtz responded that "this report . . . does not show the information requested [and] I have no record of any other report covering the full operation of your office."[26] Finally, after more requests by Wand and Sholtz, Mayo relented. He revealed to Sholtz his rather substantial, and rarely publicized, advertising fund and the large plans for it for that summer.

Historically, the Florida Department of Agriculture had been the government's largest agency and its commissioner among the state's most powerful politicians. Elected independently of the governor, commissioners faced no term limits. In fact Nathan Mayo, agricultural commissioner since 1923 (he was first appointed by Governor Cary Hardee when W. A. McRae died and then was elected the following year) would serve in that office until his death in April 1960, the state's longest-serving public officer.[27] (His successor, Doyle Conner, would serve another thirty years, from 1960 to 1990.) Born in Whitaker, North Carolina, in 1876, Mayo and his family moved to Marion County, Florida, in 1887.[28] By 1923 Mayo was an ambitious civic and economic leader and counted among his many interests a general store, two sawmills, a cotton gin, a citrus nursery, and a turpentine still.[29] Once appointed commissioner, with agriculture still dominating the state's economy, Mayo not only enjoyed extensive patronage power but also found some of the state's most powerful individuals—from citrus growers to cattle ranchers to tobacco and cotton planters—attempting to curry favor. And in 1925 Mayo sought to expand his office's power even further.

Within the department's vast bureaucracy was the small Bureau of Immigration. A relic of the nineteenth century when sparsely populated Florida desperately needed residents to develop and cultivate its untamed forests, sand hills, prairies, and wetlands, the commissioner's office was charged with attracting potential farmers to the state. But in 1925, during the peak of the Florida land boom, such cultivation was no longer a priority. Yet Mayo used this to seek out legislation in order to create an advertising fund for the nearly forgotten bureau. On May 29, 1925, the legislature created an advertising fund for "the varied resources and possibilities of our entire State."[30] The legislation included a $25,000 budget. But in a surprising move, Mayo successfully sought approval at the next legislative session in 1927 to cancel this appropriation and instead to remove the department's excess inspection fees from the General Revenue Fund and transfer them to funding advertising. As the inspection fees (making up the General Inspection Fund) collected by department officials "for inspection services on gasoline, kerosene, signal oil, fertilizer, stock feed, citrus fruit, and fees collected from milk dealers" as well as on poultry, packaged food, and drug stores was extensively above and beyond the necessary operating expenses of the Inspection Bureau, this removed the advertising from gubernatorial and legislative regulation.[31] In 1934 alone these inspection fees ran to more than $300,000.[32] In essence Mayo enjoyed a private fund to use however he saw fit. And as Sholtz (and Ben Wand) discovered in 1933, this fund was not even reported in the department's biennial report (although it would be in later years).

But despite whatever nefarious, secret, or private affairs toward which Mayo may have utilized this fund, by 1933 the Bureau of Immigration published well over a hundred publications, including brochures, pamphlets, booklets, and posters, as well as fair exhibits and programs, discussing everything from Florida's agriculture and natural resources to its weather and real estate. As Mayo once stated, "tourist patronage is vital to our welfare."[33] But in the summer, the advertising fund was involved in the state's largest outreach project to date, a project that would awaken many, including Dave Sholtz, to the state's economic potential: Chicago's Century of Progress Exposition.

Two days after Christmas in 1930, then Florida governor Doyle Carlton received an invitation from Rufus Dawes (whose brother was vice president under Calvin Coolidge) to participate in an event to "celebrate the 100th anniversary of [Chicago's] organization into a municipality. The subject of the exposition is the progress which has been achieved by mankind within the century by the use of science."[34] And he was offering "a cordial invitation [for] Florida to participate."[35] This was to be the first American-sponsored world's fair since the cessation of the Great War. Before then, world fairs were a semi-regular occurrence in Europe and the United States. The phenomenon had started in earnest in 1851 with England's Crystal Palace Exposition in London's Hyde Park. Over the next fifty years France and the United States (with their industrial fairs) along with England, Italy, Germany, and Spain (focusing primarily on their colonial wealth and possessions) sponsored numerous fairs and expositions. Present-day icons such as the Eiffel Tower (1889), the Statue of Liberty (1876)—both designed by Gustave Eiffel—and the Ferris Wheel (1893) began as world's fair exhibits. The 1889 Industrial Exposition in Paris had attracted 28 million visitors, while the 1904 St. Louis world's fair's visitation topped 50 million. One of the most famous and influential in the United States was the 1893 Columbian Exposition, with its White City and symbolic closing of the frontier, held in Chicago. Forty years later, planners designed an even larger fair on the same site.[36]

Carlton's initial reaction to Dawes's invitation was lukewarm: "Our state shall look forward with interest to this exposition."[37] But as Chicago began to publicize the extent of its fair—over 640 acres with exhibits by the nation's top corporations, a world showcase, plus a Midway area, and an expected attendance of 70 million—many in Florida became excited about the possible repercussions of Florida's participation. That spring, the legislature created a Century of Progress (COP) Commission.[38] State senator William C. Hodges, who would often support the efforts to promote Florida throughout the 1930s and personally led the initial efforts to create the COP Commission, wrote to Carlton that "this is important because this is Florida's opportunity to again put itself in the eyes of the Nation in those months just immediately preceding Florida's winter season."[39] When the commission met at Hodge's Goodwood Plantation, those in attendance included the State Forester Harry Lee Baker who would later put this experience to use in the coming years.[40]

The initial plans stressed advertising agriculture, history, government, and manufacturing. Aside from Hodges, the tourism potential had hardly registered except for a brief mention of an exhibit on "amusements."[41] But by late fall, led in part by William Hodges and Nathan Mayo, attitudes changed. This was further fueled as other states revealed their plans, especially California. Long considered a rival of Florida, California was seen by many as possessing similar attributes to Florida (e.g., a productive citrus industry, a dependably sunny climate, extensive sandy beaches, and a romanticized Spanish colonial past), but it proved more effective in advertising its wares than the other Sunshine State. In fact, many in the state argued that Florida—home to the oldest permanent European settlement in the nation, site of the famous Suwannee River, the nation's only subtropical region with its native orchids, mangroves, palm trees, and Everglades, the largest producer of oranges and other citrus fruit in the nation, and the site of hundreds of natural springs—actually surpassed California in many respects. As one of the first press releases by the Century of Progress Commission stated, "Our greatest competitor is California. . . . Already it has recognized the magnitude and importance of the World's Fair [and] will tend to draw people to enjoy 'our unequalled climate.'"[42] Another release stated more plainly, "We must do something finer than [the 35 other states with fair exhibits], especially to fabricate and maintain a more alluring exhibit than our only competitor, California, which is expending $1 million."[43]

The COP continued to issue weekly, even at times daily, press releases, which in large part were designed to sell both the exposition and a full-fledged return to the promotion of Florida to a skeptical public. After the crash of the land boom, many Floridians believed the combination of greed and a loss of the state's agrarian focus had led to financial disaster. For some, the natural disasters that followed the crash—hurricanes, a drought, and the Mediterranean fruit fly infestation—were perhaps divine retribution for the state's rampant capitalistic pursuits. Therefore many viewed a return to those heady days with concern and wariness. Hodges addressed this in a letter to a critic while maintaining the competitive theme, arguing that the COP "will show that the State will no longer take criticism or undervaluation lying down but having shown its inherent strength by recovery from the harmful features of the boom, has come back and is ready to invite residents, investors and visitors to participate in its further development."[44]

One must also remember that in the early 1930s, Florida was still very much an agricultural state. The extraction and cultivation of natural resources dominated the economy. Therefore the COP had to assuage potential critics through press releases and correspondence. One release utilized agricultural imagery: "Roger Babson [famed entrepreneur and founder of Webber College in Babson Park, Florida] states that the tourist crop is worth six times [the value] of the citrus crop."[45] Hodges, in a letter to another critic, wrote: "The idea is not new to you and yet it bears repeating—the more men and women living in Florida the better for every profession, every seller and every grower or producer. . . . We are an empty state. Please regard the Century of Progress Commission as therefore directly aimed at bringing a larger dependable population into the State."[46]

But in the meantime, Nathan Mayo and banker–railroad magnate Edward Ball teamed up to form the not-for-profit, quasi-governmental Florida National Exhibits (FNE). Based out of Deland, Florida, and funded through private donations, a legislative appropriation, and Mayo's aforementioned advertising fund, the FNE was created to plan and construct the state's ever-growing exhibit. Earl W. Brown, Deland's current mayor and former resident of Milford, Pennsylvania, was hired to oversee daily operations.[47] Exhibit plans became increasingly elaborate as the FNE attempted to re-create for fair visitors the impression newcomers had of the state on their first visit. As environmental historian Jack Davis has stated, "Florida is an imagined place. It has long been so, with outsiders historically acting as the creators of its image."[48] And few places offer better places to create an image than a world's fair, which as one scholar describes it, is "like a good sci-fi movie, is a plausible fantasy."[49] For the fair FNE spared few expenses, with a total cost of more than $250,000, and that does not factor in the services FNE did not have to fund, such as free rail shipping, donated supplies, and volunteered services.[50] More than $100,000 came from public funds, including state gasoline tax, tobacco tax, and taxes on bottled drinks as well as direct legislative appropriations.[51] As Earl Brown argued, "We must give the visitor beauty, color, the strange, the exotic, light, water, music, a veritable Arabian Night fairyland that will draw them again and never cease to charm and fire the imagination of the dullest. It must be the talk of the hotel lounges, vast spaces of the Fair. . . . It must be made an outstanding attraction of the tens of thousands of attractions."[52] And the COP promised that "Florida is not going to Chicago with a mediocre exhibit of fruits and flowers and fish, cabbages and cauliflower—that is only incidental. It will dramatize Florida to the world—Florida in all its glamour of romance, in its dignity and majesty."[53]

Completed in May 1933, the exhibit was above and beyond what any other state presented. It was housed in the Court of States, which was an "immense building, shaped like an inverted U with a the Federal building in the center. . . . The approach to the Court of States is by a main entrance . . . and leads directly to the Florida exhibit, the first of the states' exhibits."[54] The theme of the exposition was the scientific and technological progress of the past century. Awkwardly, Florida claimed it pioneered the "science of showmanship" with its innovative exhibits. According to Brown, "the diorama is the latest science of showmanship. The whole technique of exhibiting has been revolutionized by it. Dull and monotonous displays are, as if by magic, made highly dramatic and fascinating . . . [giving] depth and color and animation to backgrounds, akin to looking through an old fashioned stereoscope."[55] Charles Plastow of Rollins College in Winter Park made sixteen dioramas, starting with Bok Tower. "Each hour, a reproduction of the chimes will be heard," explained another press release. "Lighting effects will further attract the people and the fidelity of details will be truly marvelous."[56] Continuing with the scientific pretense, a release explained that a "diorama is a pictorial representation in three dimensions: width, height, and depth. You have a feeling of looking into the far distance.... People are beginning to realize what a tremendous psychological effect color and form have upon the well-being of the individual and how it is possible to obtain certain reactions thru [sic] the medium of the eye.... All these points have a direct bearing on the making and showing of the diorama—the new science of showmanship."[57] Each diorama was five feet by nine feet, two feet in depth. "After the Chicago fair, they will be placed on exhibition in some building in Tallahassee" and used "for future exhibits."[58] One popular diorama was a dramatization of Stephen Foster's "Old Folks at Home" (Way Down Upon the Suwannee River).[59] "The diorama has been animated or humanized to the extent that by the use of mechanical devices instrumental and vocal renditions of the song [are featured] and the figures of the negroes gathered around the old cabin home."[60] Other dioramas included a turpentine camp, a citrus grove, an Ybor City cigar-making factory, Silver Springs, St. Augustine, beach fishing (labeled "Playground of the Nation"), seafood gathering, and hunting (titled "Year 'Round Sports.")[61]

Once the concept of a science of showmanship was established, the FNE proceeded to create a huge advertisement for Florida tourism. FNE divided the two-level exhibit into six sections. Each section illustrated the new focus of Florida's tourist industry—attracting middle-class tourists to Florida for summer and winter vacations. The first section was the Land of Romance, which featured Spanish discovery and colonization, including sculptor George E. Ganiere's *Ponce De Leon*, welcoming the exhibit's visitors. In a shift from earlier images (aside from in the Foster diorama), Florida's southern past was nowhere in sight, replaced by the more exotic and popular Spanish past. The next section was the Land of Sport, which began with the following text: "Florida has been termed the 'winter playground of the nation.' The term should be changed by elimination of the word 'winter.' Florida is the all-year playground." This was followed by the Land of Homes, which mentioned that "an erroneous idea prevails . . . that Florida is only for those possessed of great wealth." Then followed by Land of Health, Land of Agriculture, and Industry. The focus of the last two sections included citrus, strawberries, seafood, and sponge fisheries—all of interest to tourists. Also featured in the exhibit was a live citrus grove re-created on the fairgrounds, actual Everglades muck brought in for an exhibit of the River of Grass, an aquarium of Florida fish and animals, mural paintings, five statues, relics, an exotic lily pool, and an orange juice bar.[62]

Will Rogers wrote on Florida's exhibit: "If you only have one day at the COP, there are two things you must be sure to see—one is the General Motors building... and the other is the Florida Hall." And in the ongoing rivalry with California, Rogers awarded this round to Florida: "If you want real oranges, get them at the Florida exhibit, if you want wax oranges get them in the California hall."[63] In 1933, with the possible exception of President Roosevelt, Florida could not have asked for a better recommendation.

Because the Florida exhibit was in the Court of States, it had to talk about specific Florida features, a shift from the neutral advertising of the 1920s when Florida tried to associate itself more with the Mediterranean or the French Riviera. This specificity worked with the general public and led to a more uniquely Florida focus throughout the 1930s. More than anything else, the experience of creating the exhibit at the world's fair focused and fueled the tropical and exotic image of Florida. Alligators, hammocks, springs, citrus, Seminoles, and Spanish conquistadors were no longer background decorations for ostentatious resorts and themed nightclubs but rather were now the main attractions for the state. Florida itself was an attraction, not the architecture or hotels. This realization fueled the rise in roadside attractions, including springs, alligator wrestling shows, marine aquariums, citrus fruit stands, and Spanish mission sites.

The full extent of the effect of Florida's Chicago exhibit upon the state's economy and socio-political culture would not become apparent until the end of the 1934–35 winter season (and even then not completely.) Conservative estimates were that 23 million people visited the fair that first summer, with at least 9 million of those visiting the Florida exhibit.[64] The 1934 version of the fair attracted even more, with 13 million visiting Florida Hall.[65] But as early as January 1934 many observers could already detect a tangible increase in the state's visitation, the highest since 1925.[66] *Business Week* reported on February 17, 1934, that "for the first time in years, hotels were overbooked and not accepting any reservations, railroad traffic neared the peak years of 1926 and 1927 and bus lines showed a 50% increase in business."[67] The following year, the same journal reported that tourists spent $500 million in the state.[68] The State Road Department estimated that motor tourists in 1934 exceeded 1.4 million, spending well over $90 million (averaging $2.50 a person per day).[69] Inquiries to both state chambers of commerce and the Florida Department of Agriculture's Bureau of Immigration were the highest to date. The *New Republic* reported in March 1934 that "Florida was the first state to witness the full effect of the return of a 'feeling of optimism.'"[70] And most tellingly as far as the fair was concerned, the sale of citrus fruit to Chicago alone rose 26 percent, while sales to the surrounding Midwest were skyrocketing.[71]

More than any other moment, the Century of Progress exhibit marked the start of modern tourism in Florida; a rebirth after the tourism-ending land bust that made earlier, pre–land boom marketing efforts near obsolete. From this point on, Florida would continue, until the end of the twentieth century and beyond, to promote and depend upon tourism more than any other industry. More significantly, this was also the start of the brief period when the state government and its public officials controlled the message of state advertising while also actively creating Florida's image. This was the moment when Florida, for many at least, ceased to be viewed as distinctly *southern* in the popular mind and began to assume the image of a more racially and regionally neutral land of sunshine, fun, and endless opportunity, although segregation and other racial considerations of course still played a strong role in the state's tourist trade. Slavery, cotton, the Civil War, and other decidedly "southern" elements were downplayed by many. For most outside the state, Florida became genuinely exotic and tropical. And as presented at the fair (and elsewhere), this was a playground devoid of class, race, unemployment lines, labor disputes, or foreign immigration. It was a revolution from above, a civic-elite revolution; quiet and subtle but revolutionary nonetheless, with far-reaching consequences for the state's economic, political, and social future.

By the end of the decade, the private sector would take precedence in how the state was marketed and sold, both through commercial outlets (e.g., the local media, roadside attractions, hotels, and private corporations) and by private citizens contesting this newly created state image. But in 1933 the state government, partnering with the state's chambers of commerce, controlled Florida's image and advertising. Yet many of those in control at the time knew that good advertising and clever fair exhibits were not enough to maintain the momentum. A state needed unique attractions to promote and sell, especially if it wanted visitors, like farm crops, to return year after year. And in 1933 and 1934 there were still few bona fide tourist attractions or other selling points. Over the next several years, many people involved with the Century of Progress, both directly and peripherally, worked toward that goal of increasing Florida's tourist attractions and selling Florida to the world.

Yet the tourist trade was nothing new to Florida. As early as Reconstruction, northern visitors were trekking to Florida for health, hunting, and adventure. Many of these early visitors were Civil War vets who had served in or near Florida and were now bringing their families.[72] Communities on Florida's east coast coped with the economic hardships of the post–Civil War era through exploitation of the leisure and health markets. Although, as historian W. Fitzhugh Brundage has pointed out, the South was seen as unhealthy before the Civil War, by the 1880s several sites—a large number of which were located in Florida—became health resorts and sanitariums, often located next to natural freshwater springs.[73] (Thanks to yellow fever, malaria, mosquitos, and the South's extreme summer heat in an era before air conditioning and DDT, many continued to view the South as unhealthy up through the 1920s.) Soon reporters were writing guides and articles about "exotic" Florida, many of which were authored by people who had never set foot in the Sunshine State.[74] Several communities wasted little time joining in on Florida's promotion, fueling the mythical aspects of the state's advertising. Stories about "old Indian legends," romantic Spanish explorers, fountains of youth, and the medicinal qualities of natural springs began to crop up in Florida newspapers and brochures. Stereoview cards of tropical Florida were purchased by armchair travelers along with those depicting such exotic locales as Europe and Egypt. By the 1870s and 1880s cheap land, warm weather, and the lure of effective promotions brought hundreds of northern residents to Florida. In his popular guide *Florida for Tourists, Invalids and Settlers*, George Barbour wrote in 1882, "Florida is rapidly becoming a northern colony."[75] By the winter of 1874–1875, over 33,000 tourists came to Florida annually.[76]

Also by the 1870s and 1880s, new transportation systems were developing in Florida. Steamboats made their first appearance in the 1870s, sailing up and down the St. Johns and Ocklawaha rivers.[77] Not long after leaving office, even President Ulysses Grant enjoyed a steamboat voyage along Florida's waterways. But it was the railroads that had the most impact upon Florida tourism. In 1878 Standard Oil cofounder Henry Flagler took his first trip to Florida and immediately saw the potential for exploitation.[78] Soon he and others, including railroad owners Henry Plant and William D. Chipley, were constructing rail lines and developing support communities. These new rails became prime movers for the citrus and timber industries. Flagler's East Coast railroad also emerged as the dominant player in the tourist trade. Almost single-handedly, Flagler transformed sleepy, vacant East Florida into a resort mecca. First St. Augustine, then West Palm Beach, Miami, and Key West were given the Flagler treatment, complete with extravagant resort hotels, new roads, and trains full of curious onlookers. As early as 1888, Ward G. Foster, originally of Albion, New York, and the executive in charge of Flagler's construction in St. Augustine, could profitably open the Ask Mr. Foster Travel Service.[79] On the west coast of the Florida peninsula, Plant was likewise developing Tampa and St. Petersburg—albeit on a much smaller scale. As trains began using these rails at the turn of the century, Floridians saw a major influx of retirees, millionaires, invalids, writers, and realtors into their state. And these tourists were hungry for things to see and do. Fortunately for them, many Floridians were happy to oblige.

The first tourist attractions were modest affairs. The target audiences were primarily from the upper classes, as few others were able to enjoy the luxury of leisure trips. These first attractions included alligator and ostrich farms, fountains of youth (which were usually simple artesian wells), horse and car races, freshwater spring sanitariums, and military forts. In addition, coastal areas developed grand resorts and hotels that catered to the elite visitors. Surprisingly, the beach itself was rarely used other than for scenic value. As the beach and sun craze would not take off until the late 1920s, vacations to Florida were usually long-term excursions, often lasting the entire winter.[80] And unlike other southern states, where "the struggle to cultivate and perpetuate historical memory in the South was incorporated into the commerce of tourism" so that "the tourist South became a stage on which southerners presented the South both as they wanted to see it and as they imagined tourists wanted," Florida boosters and promoters offered a new, regionally neutral tropical image, closer in spirit and advertisements to the French Riviera or the Mediterranean than the romanticized Old South of Charleston or Richmond.[81]

But by the 1920s the makeup and activities of Florida tourists began to change. While the upper crust still ventured south to Florida, now so did upper middle-class families, taking advantage of the nation's newfound prosperity and its affordable assembly-line-manufactured cars. The natives called the new visitors "tin can tourists" for the canned food they brought with them.[82] These mobile vacationers changed forever Florida's physical and economic landscape and, in doing so, altered the nature of Florida tourism.[83]

Commenting in the 1930s on modern tourists, one Tennessee Valley Authority planner said, "A generation ago, vacationists still sat on their front porches of resort hotels all summer long and enjoyed a static holiday. Today, they move, they investigate, they mingle."[84] This new breed of active, impatient tourist required new facilities. Unable to afford the large resorts and hotels that marked the Flagler era, tin can tourists demanded cheaper lodgings. One of the first features to spring up was "tent cities," large campgrounds that offered running water and sanitation facilities for tin canners. St. Petersburg, in Hillsborough County on Florida's west coast, was one of the first areas to develop tent cities.[85] Before long though, motels and motor lodges replaced most of these tourist campgrounds. Miami also began catering to this new addition to the leisure class. Often the children of immigrants, these travelers exhibited tastes strikingly different from those of their Gilded Age counterparts. In Miami many of these hotels—today hailed as icons of the Art Deco movement—were located between 5th Street and 23rd Street, painted in such "exotic" hues as sea foam green, flamingo pink, and sunshine yellow.[86] In a trend that would come to full fruition in the 1930s, these hotels were uniquely Florida in style, color, and effect. (By 1939 there would be more than three hundred Art Deco hotels in Miami alone.) But the most profound changes in Florida were the new federal highways upon which the tin canners drove.

Many visitors to Florida complained of cattle and other animals roaming the poorly kept and primarily dirt roads.[87] (Florida did not enact its first fence law until 1949.)[88] Shrimper Albert Gufford claimed that in the 1910s it took his family seventeen days to travel from Brunswick (just north of the Florida border in southeast Georgia) to Maitland, Florida. "The only paved road that was in this area at all was part of Main Street in Jacksonville. . . . [Driving] down the coast, you'd come to a little town, and maybe you'd have about two blocks of pavement. And the rest of it was rutted roads."[89] Even as late as 1929, Edward Ball reported to his boss, Alfred DuPont, on a fact-finding mission in North Florida: "Leaving Live Oak . . . the next paved highway was nine miles outside of Pensacola, 320 miles distant . . . the Old Spanish Trail (US 90) was about as the Spanish had left it."[90] Until Florida developed a State Road Department in 1915, counties had the sole responsibility for maintaining roads. Even then, the legislation only authorized the department to advise counties. Then in 1917, to meet the requirements of the Federal Road Act, Florida began building state highways.[91] By the 1920s roads had become big politics, for each town wanted to boast that it had the best roads in the state. For instance, Marion County billed itself as the "Good Road County of Florida."[92] An ad for Deland invited visitors to "Come, ride around our streets and learn why competent authorities have stated that this is the best-paved city per capita in the U.S."[93] Getting a road built in one's area was a major coup for Florida politicians. But it was the federal government that provided Florida with its best roads.

In 1923 U.S. 90 opened between Jacksonville and Lake City and became Florida's first paved highway.[94] Next came U.S. 1, the "Dixie Highway," instigated by Florida realtors and eventually running over two thousand miles, it connected Florida's east coast to New York State and later all the way to Maine.[95] This was followed in quick succession by U.S. 27 ("The Orange Blossom Trail"), which ran through central Florida, U.S. 441 ("Uncle Remus Route"), U.S. 41, and U.S. 17, the St. Johns River Trail, which ran south from Jacksonville to Miami.[96] Although it took nearly thirteen years to complete, due to a lack of funding (finally provided by millionaire Baron Collier in exchange for the creation of Collier County) and environmental constraints, the Tamiami Trail finally opened in 1928 to much fanfare, connecting for the first time the east and west coasts in South Florida by crossing the Florida Everglades.[97] By the end of the 1920s the majority of Florida tourists came by car along one of these highways. Land boom observer T. H. Weigell described traffic on the Dixie Highway in 1926 as an "incredible assortment of humanity that in Ford and Rolls-Royces, on bicycle and on foot was pouring towards Miami. . . . Most of these equipages had the family goods roped on to the rear; camp beds, washing stands . . ."[98] By 1925 over 500,000 cars drove these roads south each year.[99]

The sudden end of the Florida land boom and the subsequent stock market crash of 1929 placed a damper upon Florida's tourism trade—but did not end it. In fact, the golden age of Florida attractions is considered by some scholars to have begun in 1929, with the opening of Bok Tower Gardens.[100] Sarasota, which throughout the 1920s was one of three key destinations for winter visitors (along with Miami and St. Petersburg), successfully shifted its advertising by appealing to the financial concerns of potential visitors: "Cancel your coal bills—and cold bills—by substituting the glorious climate of Sunny Sarasota for those bleak winter months," suggested the Sarasota Chamber of Commerce's visitor guide in 1931.[101] Miami was considered by many at the time the barometer for tourism in the state, and several observers reported on Miami's apparent success amid economic depression. As editor Oswald Garrison Villard observed in the *Nation* in the 1930s, "If one were to judge Florida by the appearance of Miami, one would have to say that the depression is over in this state. The streets are thronged with tourists."[102] Journalist and confidant of the Roosevelts Lorena Hickok echoed this same sentiment in one of her letters from Florida to New Dealer Harry Hopkins.[103] Miami was eased through the depression by middle-class—"tin can"—tourism.[104] A few entrepreneurs noticed this trend and acted accordingly.

By the early 1930s several in Florida refused to give up on tourism's promise, including owners of gas stations, fruit stands, and souvenir shops.[105] As Stuckey's founder William Stuckey only half-jokingly said in the 1930s, "Thank God the North won the war. It would have been awful if there hadn't been any Yankees to sell to."[106] But most believed that while it was not awful, Florida tourism was not realizing its full potential. Florida had nearly two million tourists in 1925.[107] By 1932 that figure was down to less than 500,000.[108] The success of the Century of Progress was most encouraging, but its full impact would not be realized until after the 1934–35 season. And as many would state throughout the decade, "Florida is within 48 hours of 90 percent of the people of the United States."[109] Therefore, although the trade was not disappearing, it appeared to need additional help to attract those 90 percent of Americans. And some officials in the Florida government—including several of those behind the Florida exhibit at the Chicago world's fair—were prepared to deliver some help.

One additional boost to the tourism industry would originate in 1934 from a relatively obscure agency. The Florida Forestry Service was created, more than for any other reason, to fight forest fires, both naturally occurring and human-caused fires. But not everyone welcomed such an agency. Contrary to popular beliefs, fire suppression was not a widely practiced policy in Florida until well into the 1920s. Up to that time, many Floridians practiced a primitive form of controlled or prescribed burning for land clearing, pest and disease control, fire fuel reduction, and the replenishment of native grasses. By the twenties, as Florida began to urbanize and its population grew, several groups, including foresters and the timber industry, pushed for state control over Florida's woodlands. Using scientific research on fire from the emerging forestry field—most of which was conducted in the less incendiary northern regions—foresters and the timber interests argued successfully for the creation of the Florida Forestry Service in 1927. For this anti-fire faction, such a service was essential to ending wasteful fire practices and ensuring future wood supplies. They also believed that unless controlled, nature would not only become unproductive but would also prove dangerous to humans. Timber interests realized that such an agency transformed Florida's government into a virtual forester and a de facto business partner with a vested interest in the welfare of forests.

"Fire destroys!" So began a small publication printed by the four-year-old Florida Forestry Association (FFA), which in 1927 created an uproar within Florida's political and industrial circles. Entitled *Forest Fires in Florida*, and written by Harry Lee Baker when he was still a district forester with the U.S. Forest Service (USFS), the pamphlet blamed many native Floridians for thousands of destructive forest fires across the state.[110] Using words and arguments as incendiary as the destructive wildfires he described, Baker lamented the annual loss of $8 million in timber sales that stemmed from over 15,000 yearly fires—97 percent of which Baker said were "man-caused."[111] Only the remaining 3 percent were started by natural means—namely lightning. "Enough young growth is destroyed every year in Florida to build 100,000 six-room homes," at 16,000 board feet each.[112] As for mature trees, Baker claimed that "fire scars develop into 'cat-faces' on merchantable timber and are fertile spots for damaging fungi and insects," a statement accompanied by photos of longleaf pine rotting from the inside out.[113] Baker further claimed that fire impoverished forest soils—resulting in native grasses dying out, killed native game animals ("fox, squirrel, and opossum are frequently killed outright by forest fires"), and robbed birds such as quail of their nesting areas. As Baker concluded, "everybody loses when timber burns."[114]

By 1927 the leading agency in the nation for fire suppression was the U.S. Forest Service. Although foresters early on had conducted research on the causes and effects of woods fires—and many recognized multiple sources for the fires—by 1908, they adopted a singular explanation. For the sake of securing long-term congressional funding as well as for clarity of its public message, the USFS adopted a "simple, tough message" that all fires are bad and must be prevented at all costs.[115] That unilateral stance emerged out of the "light burning" controversy in California, sometimes called "Indian burning." Land managers in California were split on whether to use small-scale controlled burns to reduce fuel and fire hazards, just as the Native Americans of the area had done for centuries. Debates swirled around the issue for years, confusing the lay public, and threatening the young USFS's status and its congressional backing.[116] By 1910 most—although not all—foresters adopted a similar no-fire tolerance stance.[117] In Florida support of the development of similar policies within the state government pitted the powerful timber interests, enthusiastic backers of the anti-fire campaign, along with the emerging forestry profession, against turpentiners, ranchers, and small farmers, all of whom at some point used fires to clear land, replenish grasses, and kill ticks.

In Jacksonville in 1923 the stage was set for a showdown with these "fire bugs" when timber leaders created the Florida Forestry Association (FFA) and immediately began publishing articles and pamphlets on forestry and fire.[118] Political activist May Mann Jennings joined future legislator Ben Wand, who at this time was the publisher of the *Southern Lumber Journal*, to co-head the new organization.[119] The bylaws stressed that the volunteer organization was "to represent the interests of all people, the sportsmen, and the wood-using naval stores, agricultural, and horticultural industries."[120] But the creation of a state forestry department was their ultimate goal. Wand and his associates sought governmental protection of their financial interests, while Jennings was more concerned with conserving natural resources for future use. Demand for such an agency had grown since the passing in 1911 of the Weeks Act, a federal law that allowed states to accept federal funds in order to create forestry services as well as to enter into cooperative agreements with the U.S. government.[121] In 1924 the Clarke-McNary Act strengthened the Weeks Act, expanding the lands on which such funds could be expended.[122] In addition widespread apathy toward fire further fueled their efforts. As forester Inman Eldredge remembered: "Nobody cared. The people in the city didn't care; the people in the small towns didn't care. They were accustomed to having the air full of smoke at certain times of the year. The politicians didn't even care."[123] In 1925 the FFA ventured to Tallahassee to lobby the state legislature, with little luck. For the next legislative session—at the time the legislature met only once every two years—the FFA raised its public relations profile.

In 1927 the FFA hired Baker to author the aforementioned *Forest Fires in Florida*. Born in Pueblo, Colorado, in 1888, Baker grew up in Michigan.[124] Upon receiving his B.S. in forestry at Michigan State Agricultural College in 1910, he went to work for the USFS in several districts across the nation, including the Virginia Forest Service.[125] By 1927 he was the assistant forest inspector for the southern region. To Baker, trained in the fire-vulnerable northern forests, the indigenous fire practices in Florida were truly abhorrent.

In language that reflected the mindset of many foresters of the time, Baker wrote passionately against what he saw as foolish, even pre-modern, attitudes toward fire and natural resources. Words such as *scars, menace, destroyed*, and *killed* are found throughout the text. As with later writings on fire, Baker described burned forests as both destroyed and irretrievably lost. He placed the fault for such losses at feet of cattlemen and small-time farmers.

Baker's fiery booklet, coupled with the rise in forestry across the nation thanks to the Clarke-McNary Act, made the creation of a state forestry board inevitable. In May 1927 the state legislature created a governor-appointed forestry board. This board, to be made up of timber industrialists and forest enthusiasts, would set state forestry policy and hire a state forester to enforce that policy. On August 1, 1927, Governor John Martin appointed the board, who then held their first meeting on December 13, 1927.[126] As set up, the agency—which adopted the name Florida Forestry Service in April 1928—consisted of a board, a state forester, and four branches: Information and Education, Applied Forestry, Administration, and Fire Control.[127] At their second meeting, held February 23, 1928, the Board chose Harry Lee Baker to be Florida's first state forester.[128] The newly christened FFS maintained that "practically all woods fires are caused by man, and therefore are preventable."[129] With Baker personally assuming the fire control branch, the FFS made fire suppression in Florida its main mission.

To accomplish this, the FFS embarked on an extensive public education program—a considerable undertaking when one considers their meager $12,000 annual budget—called the Southern Forest Education program, a cooperative effort with FFA and the American Forestry Association (AFA). Two "motion picture trucks" were sent out across the state, showing films such as *Burnin' Bill* and *Pardners*.[130] The program originated with AFA president Ovid Butler, who brought together the "Dixie Crusaders," a group of foresters who traveled the South—focusing primarily on Mississippi, Alabama, and Florida—and lectured, set up fair exhibits, and showed educational films.[131] The Florida version of the program, which consisted of the movie trucks emblazoned with the slogan "Stop Woods Fires—Growing Children Need Growing Trees," reached over 250,000 Floridians by 1930.[132] While their reach was impressive, they still faced growing resentment from many in the rural areas angry at this governmental intrusion into their long-held autonomy in all matters natural. But the desire to spread and enforce their no-tolerance fire policy would lead to the

FFS enthusiastically latching onto the New Deal's vastly popular CCC program. The state's chief forester offered additional reasons for partnering with the CCC as well.

In 1934 Florida state forester Harry Lee Baker began making the argument that the government could develop state parks as a way "to develop the largest industry in the state—recreation."[133] Adding parks meant extending vacation trips by providing visitors with more choices. The longer people stayed in Florida, the more money they spent. As Baker observed, "They [tourists] soon tire of the races, night clubs and man-made recreation. They sit in the lobbies of our hotels wondering what to do with themselves. If a park system were shown on the highway maps and their wonders described in the literature of a state department, the tourists would flock to parks by the thousands."[134] In a letter to the Florida State Planning Board, Baker argued that Florida had features to attract visitors in addition to the roadside attractions. "The tourists come to our state to see Florida the Beautiful, the land of moss-covered oaks, our waterways, and lakes to fish, ride and hunt and live in outdoor Florida."[135] A year earlier, in an attempt to wrangle more state forests out of the short-lived Florida Agricultural and Industrial Relief (FAIR) Commission, Baker had argued that forests could not be concerned only with timber. "We should not overlook the fact that public support will depend largely upon the recreational advantages of such areas."[136] In what can be seen as a proto-version of the Florida Park Service in 1934, Baker argued that these proposed state forests must "appeal to the people in the cities. Tourists will enjoy hunting, fishing, and camping in these public forests and will appreciate the fact that there are no landowners to drive them away. Sportsmen and recreationists . . . will be the strongest boosters for state forests."[137] And with the New Deal in full swing by 1934, Baker—who had assisted with the Century of Progress planning, and could see the proverbial handwriting on the wall for Florida's future—knew this was the best time to start. But Baker was not the first to suggest a state park system that year. His suggestion, in large part, was lifted from the ideas of former first lady of Florida, long-time conservationist and park enthusiast May Mann Jennings.

4

The Mother Who Birthed the Florida Park Service

May Mann Jennings's ideas for a park system in Florida had their roots during the state's Progressive era. In Florida, as in much of the nation, many people by the early 1900s began to formulate and follow the ideals of conservation. Unlike preservation, which involved removing untouched natural areas from human development, conservation embraced the concept of "wise use"—in forester Gifford Pinchot's much-used phrase.[1] For conservationists, nature was valuable only when humans were able to use it. And anything that was considered unusable—such as a wetland—was seen as wasteful. Wetlands, Florida conservationists believed, should be transformed into a useful resource, such as farmland. The greatest good for the greatest number of people was the driving motto of Florida progressives.[2] These were not supporters of John Muir's deferential view of natural preservation. Nature required action, not passivity. Ecosystems, wildlife, and natural resources represented potential, which humans needed to realize. But conservationists also believed that natural resources, such as water, woods, minerals, and soil, were vulnerable to careless choices, including overproduction, uncontrolled fires, and poor planning. Therefore, "wise" planning and use were needed to ensure resource availability for future generations.

No one in Florida better represented this ideal than Jennings herself, often referred to as the "Mother of Florida Forestry." The wife of Governor William S. Jennings (1901–5), May Mann Jennings was a powerful political activist in her own right.[3] Raised in Crystal River, Florida, during the 1880s, Jennings was educated in St. Augustine.[4] But she learned about politics and government from her father, Austin Mann, a state representative from Hardee County from 1883 to 1891 and a Populist who in December 1890 organized the national convention for the Farmers' Alliance—one of the precursors to the Populist

Party—in Ocala, Florida.[5] These skills May learned in her youth were put to use aiding her husband (whom she married in Brooksville in 1891) when he was elected Florida's governor in 1900. She was commonly referred to as his "right hand man."[6] But it was when the Jenningses moved to Jacksonville after William's term was finished (at that time Florida governors were constitutionally forbidden to run for a second term immediately), that May Jennings emerged as a stand-alone political figure.

Soon after she arrived in Jacksonville, May Jennings joined the Florida Federation of Women's Clubs (FFWC), an umbrella group that orchestrated activities and causes of women's clubs across the state. Organized in February 1895 in Green Cove Springs, the FFWC took on many causes, which included promoting the passage of state health laws, establishing county libraries, bettering public education, and undertaking several beautification projects.[7] Two major overriding themes guided FFWC's work: women's rights and social morality.[8] For instance, they were integral in raising the age of consent in Florida from ten to twenty-one years.[9] But for Jennings, who would become the FFWC's director (1914–17) and eventually its longest-serving member, conservation was the most important issue. When her husband was still governor, Jennings pushed for drainage of the Everglades, which she and others felt was a "moral imperative."[10] They felt that under this "river of grass" lay Florida's richest soils, a resource that would benefit thousands of people. Though the project ultimately failed, and in the process wreaked environmental havoc upon the fragile ecosystem, it vividly demonstrated how Jennings and many of her fellow progressives looked toward natural conservation as an answer to solving society's ills; and not just material ills. Beyond sustenance and utilization of natural resources, quality of life also depended upon beauty, relaxation, and recreation. For Jennings, through wise planning and management, nature could provide these needed qualities as well.

In the early 1900s several South Florida women's clubs began to rally around the preservation of the nation's largest stand of royal palms on Paradise Key. Located on the edges of the Everglades, Paradise Key was a twelve-mile-long islet southwest of Homestead in Dade County.[11] Unlike at other islands in the Everglades, a wide slough protected Paradise Key from nearby fires, thereby allowing a mature hammock to develop.[12] Yet other threats loomed. Development was taking off in South Florida at the turn of the century, and the clubs wanted to ensure that the Key and its palms remained intact. Around this same time May Jennings bought a house in Homestead, not far from Paradise Key. She soon learned of the campaign for the royal palms, and before long, saving Paradise Key became her pet project. Given a chance to express her views of nature's role in society, Jennings stressed that Paradise Key must become a public park for all to enjoy. With the zeal of a missionary, she spent the next decade gathering support for her park plan. Few in power cared for the idea. There was no profit in it, and with women unable to vote, there was also little political pay-off for supporting it. But Jennings was adamant. When elected FFWC's president in 1914, she wasted little time placing Paradise Key's preservation at the top of the agenda. Her tenacity paid off. Using a network of fellow wives and daughters of Florida's political and business leaders, along with the contacts she gathered through her many activities for her gubernatorial spouse, May Jennings managed to provoke growing interest in the state's capitol for creating a Paradise Key "state park." Armed with draft legislation authored by herself and husband William—as well as a donation of 960 acres on Paradise Key by Mrs. Kirk Monroe—May Jennings met with Governor Park Trammell and several legislators in 1915 to discuss plans for what she now called "Royal Palm State Park."[13] Her lobbying proved fruitful, because that legislative session recognized the key as a state park and gave it a one-time appropriation of one thousand dollars. The Congress also donated to the FFWC the state's portion of the island.[14] Florida now had its first state-funded public park.[15]

In November 1916 Royal Palm State Park was formally dedicated with a 168-car cavalcade and over a thousand people in attendance.[16] Before long it began attracting a steady flow of tourists. Yet its paying visitors never provided enough to make ends meet. Despite its name and initial state appropriation, Royal Palm State Park remained a private park and was usually in need of additional funds. For the next thirty years Jennings spent a majority of her time scrimping, saving, and begging various organizations, politicians, and friends for donations to keep the park afloat. Eventually several facilities were built, including a lodge. Then in 1933, through her connections (especially her son S. Bryan Jennings, then president of the Board of Forestry), Jennings secured for Royal Palm State Park Florida's first state park CCC camp: SP-1. The park survived for another fourteen years, after which she donated it to Everglades National Park.

Journalist, author, and Everglades activist Marjory Stoneman Douglas offered a less than flattering portrayal of Jennings's work with Royal Palm State Park in her as-told-to memoir, *Voice of the River*, in 1987. "This little park got its start due to the pushing and prodding of Mrs. Mary [sic] Mann Jennings, wife of the ex-governor. The state built the road and so forth and the Jenningses owned a lot of land nearby. I cast no aspersions, but there is something inevitable in thinking the Jenningses wanted to develop the land and that having the road built with public funds didn't hurt."[17] Jennings and Douglas originally knew each other from their activist work during the suffrage movement, though their respective work on behalf of the "river of grass" never coincided.[18]

Buoyed by her success with developing Royal Palm State Park, Jennings continued her work in recreation and conservation throughout the 1920s. First, she organized the Tropical Everglades National Park Association to promote the conversion of the Everglades into a national park.[19] Then in 1925 Jennings wrote legislation that enabled the state to accept lands for use as state parks. Its passage was an early attempt at the creation of a state park system.[20] As no money was set aside for such a program, however, the park system suffered stillbirth. Ironically, Jennings's greatest contribution to Florida parks was through the indirect result of another piece of legislation passed in the 1920s. Beginning in 1921, the FFWC—under Jennings's urging—began lobbying for the creation of a forestry board composed of a forester and a board of governor-appointed citizens to regulate and manage the state's growing timber industry. True to her Progressive roots, Jennings was calling for "wiser" planning for Florida's timber resources. Her idea involved more than mere fire prevention and included the promotion of tree planting, an educated selection in tree cuttings, and the preservation of beautiful, health-restoring forests. Assisted by her son S. Bryan Jennings, she drafted a bill outlining such a board and passed it along to her contacts in the state capitol. After years of lobbying, the bill passed virtually intact in 1927—aided in large part by Baker's aforementioned publicity efforts—and the Florida Board of Forestry was born. Governor John Martin appointed S. Bryan Jennings as the board's first president, who in turn guided the hiring of Baker as Florida's first state forester.

The joining of Jennings's progressive ideals on conservation, beauty, and recreation with Baker's and Sholtz's more commercial ambitions occurred in early 1934. At a February 1934 meeting of the Trustees of the Internal

Improvement Fund, a committee that included S. Bryan Jennings and May's friend Senator W. C. Hodges of Tallahassee submitted a proposal for acquiring over five thousand acres of land for state parks in Duval and Nassau counties and along the Suwannee River.[21] Earlier in 1933 May Jennings wrote a pamphlet for the Florida Women's Clubs called "Parks and Natural Scenery," which chided Florida for wasting the opportunity to build parks back in 1925, with the first state park law. As she bitterly wrote, "the first steps had yet to be taken."[22] Eager to jump-start a state park program, Jennings took her case to the Trustees of the Internal Improvement Fund, a governmental board that controlled all federal and state lands not under the control of other state agencies.[23] Created in 1855 and composed of the governor, attorney general, comptroller, state treasurer, and commissioner of agriculture, the Trustees had the authority to sell and lease lands and then use the resultant revenues to fund improvements throughout the state.[24] Therefore, until a state park system was created, the IIF was the only agency that could accept lands donated to the state for park purposes.

At that IIF meeting Baker agreed with Jennings's assertion that CCC camps were available to Florida for state park development, and added that his Board of Forestry would cooperate in any way it could.[25] Jennings pointed out that her Royal Palm State Park already had an established CCC camp, SP-1, in operation since October 1933. Also in Dade County was Matheson Hammock Park, a county recreation area that was currently being built by SP-2, another CCC camp.[26] That spring, in preparation for a park service, Baker commissioned forester Winton Reinsmith to search for the elusive Torreya tree along the Apalachicola River on land that the Forestry Service could easily acquire.[27] Local lore held that the tree (and its close relative the Florida yew) could only be found in a twenty-mile stretch along the historic river, where bluffs soared nearly a hundred feet. Baker knew that such a tree, coupled with the dramatic scenery, would make for a fine state park. His report confirmed the local beliefs.[28] States across the nation were expanding their state park programs through the use of CCC labor and funds. It was time for Florida to take advantage of this labor pool and start a park system for its citizens.

Baker and Jennings were correct in their belief that the U.S. government would aid Florida in state park development. On April 29, 1933, less than a month after the CCC's creation, its director Robert Fechner—at Secretary of the Interior Harold Ickes's urging—approved state park work for CCC camps.[29] For the CCC's first enrollment period, there were CCC state park camps in twenty-six states, for a total of 105 camps.[30] By October 1934 state park camps increased to 265 in thirty-two states.[31] Several states, such as Virginia and Louisiana, began state park systems as a direct result of the CCC.[32] But New Deal involvement in recreation went beyond the Civilian Conservation Corps. With the exception of roads and public housing, the majority of funds spent for New Deal work-relief projects were for recreational development, including parks, ball fields, public pools, trails, and historic monuments.[33] Just about every New Deal program worked on at least one recreation project. The Works Progress Administration's Federal Writers' Project wrote guides to cities and states, directing people to recreation areas. Beginning in 1936 the WPA conducted the Park, Parkways, and Recreational Areas Study as a way to coordinate the development of recreational projects throughout the nation.[34] As stated in a federal brochure on the CCC in 1941, recreation "contributes to the conservation of human wealth of the U.S."[35]

As with conservation, this devotion to recreation was rooted in the progressive origins of many New Dealers. "Play" was for many progressives a didactic, morally uplifting activity that served as a primary component for any healthful society. As First Lady Eleanor Roosevelt pointed out in 1936 in an essay in *Scribner's* magazine, Americans now enjoyed an increased amount of leisure time and needed opportunities for quality recreation.[36] Her husband was likewise a believer in recreation, and under his governorship New York had acquired the most state park acreage in the nation.[37] Just as Progressives believed conservation was needed to give Americans equality of access to public lands, they also believed Americans needed access to recreational areas. As *Conservation* magazine put it, recreation should provide "the maximum happiness to the greatest number of people."[38] The journal warned Florida that "it is not hard to envision a future when thousands of our citizens in modest circumstances, who cannot afford to pay for the privilege of using private facilities, will be unable to find a place along our highways or in our recreation centers where they may legally enjoy the scenic beaches and recreation opportunities of their native state."[39] The most obvious evidence of Progressives' commitment to recreation was the development of the National Park Service under progressive president Woodrow Wilson.

Though its beginning can be traced back to the 1870s, the National Park Service was not organized as a government agency until 1916. The first national parks were little more than fenced off wilderness areas with army rangers patrolling on horseback. The first park was Yellowstone in 1872, established for public use by President Grant.[40] This was followed by Sequoia National Park in 1890, Mount Rainier National Park in 1899, and Crater Lake National Park in 1902.[41] From 1872 until 1916 the secretary of the interior was in charge of maintaining the national parks.[42] Then in 1915 an ex-Borax manufacturer named Stephen Mather mentioned to his friend Franklin Lane, President Woodrow Wilson's secretary of the interior, that he believed the national parks were being poorly handled.[43] In response Lane made Mather an assistant to run the parks. Mather began to publicize the idea of a National Park Service by writing essays in magazines such as the *Saturday Evening Post* and *National Geographic*.[44] Finally on August 25, 1916, Woodrow Wilson signed legislation creating the National Park Service. The U.S. Army stepped down, and park rangers took over the park duties.

Soon after its creation, Mather used the NPS as a vehicle for promoting state park development. In 1921 Mather and his assistant Horace Albright started the National Conference of State Parks.[45] By the 1920s the interest in state parks had developed into a national movement. The first state park was Niagara Falls in New York, in 1885.[46] By 1900 Ohio and Minnesota began setting aside areas for state parks, followed by Idaho (1909), Illinois (1911), and North Carolina (1915).[47] But these early parks were small affairs with little or no funding. After 1921 state parks development increased, with Arkansas, Missouri, Iowa, Maine, Texas, Utah, Oregon, Kansas, Washington, and Nebraska all starting full-blown state park systems.[48] In 1927 California hired landscape architect Frederick Law Olmsted Jr. to choose and design park sites.[49] When the NPS was chosen to be one of the agencies to aid with CCC work by overseeing park projects, it wasted little time promoting state park development. Director Horace Albright wrote to all existing state park agencies and informed them that money was available.[50] Conrad Wirth, Albright's chief planner, was placed in charge of CCC state park work.[51] On average, the NPS supervised over four hundred camps.[52] The NPS also aided with the Park, Parkway and Recreational Areas Study.

Therefore Harry Baker's suggestion that Florida develop its own state park system using federal labor and dollars was nothing radical. However, his suggestion to link these potential state parks with tourism was indeed new. Baker realized that Florida's economic future rested upon an expanded and fully supported tourist industry. In July 1934 Baker wrote to Ed Ball, a member of the State Planning Board (Baker was an affiliate member), making his case for a Florida Park Service to expand Florida tourism.[53] This letter was the catalyst for moving the Florida Park Service beyond a mere idea. Ball, who ran his brother-in-law Alfred DuPont's interests in Florida, agreed with Baker's notion: "The time has come for Florida to have a state system of parks. It is my belief that if Florida would make an effort to attract the tourists, instead of only being interested in milking the tourists, that we could greatly increase the natural influx of pleasure seekers."[54] As Ball explained in 1936, "after visiting Florida's initial exhibit at the Century of Progress . . . I was convinced of the real results being obtained for this state by . . . advertising" itself.[55] Referring to the federal government's willingness to provide funds, Ball argued that it would be "criminal" if Florida did not create a state park system while such a program was "on the bargain counter!"[56]

A product of the New Deal, the State Planning Boards were an emulation of the National Resources Board and were found in most states.[57] Essentially, the concept behind the boards was similar to conservation's "wise use," only now applied to governmental policies. The federal government believed that before a state could spend federal dollars wisely, it had to assess its needs and develop a long-range, comprehensive plan for spending. Again, as with conservation and recreation, the idea was "to insure equitable participation in our national gains to those who make the nation what it is."[58] In the beginning Florida's board lacked any teeth. Florida's State Planning Board was created on March 7, 1934, by executive appointment—an earlier version was created in 1933 at the request of the PWA's Harold Ickes, but the legislature failed to fund it—with former CWA and State Road Department chairman (and citrus grower) C. B. Treadway as chair.[59] This would soon change; it became official in June 1935 by a legislative act.[60] But in 1934 it was little more than a self-described advisory board composed of prominent citizens, including Ed Ball (along with fellow Century of Progress planners Lorenzo Wilson and Nathan Mayo).[61]

No friend to the New Deal, Ball was only interested in securing for DuPont favorable conditions, such as good roads in Florida's panhandle and CCC camps for DuPont's forests, as well as mustering business for the Florida

East Coast Railway.⁶² After Jennings's presentation in February, Ball agreed to set up a committee to investigate possible park sites for counties and cities, prompting Baker to seek him out.⁶³ Baker wrote that he was "confronted with the problem of recommending park areas to the NPS where CCC camps could be located."⁶⁴ He asked the Planning Board to seek out FERA funds to conduct a state park survey because he "needed advice and assistance," and there were "no funds available to the Florida Forest Service to make examinations and reports."⁶⁵ Ball agreed, and in the fall of 1934 two State Planning Board–sponsored and FERA-funded surveys for state park sites were conducted under the guidance of the board's newly created Park and Playgrounds subcommittee, chaired by Ball.⁶⁶ Landscape architect Walter Coldwell, assisted by fellow architect Felix Benton, conducted the first state park survey, and Walter Coachman handled the second. Both reported their findings to Florida Forest Board member Mrs. Linwood Jeffreys, and the Leon County WPA typed up the final results.⁶⁷

The surveys identified more than fifty possible parks areas. Not only did they recommend the sites that eventually comprised the original seven Florida State Parks, but they also identified sites that would become state parks as late as the 1990s. Using guidelines set out by Baker and the National Park Service—which afterward graded each recommended site for its possible park value—the two surveys investigated sites for their scenic grandeur, boating, fishing and swimming possibilities, population centers in vicinity, possible camping facilities, and historical values.⁶⁸ The Planning Board hoped for a total of thirteen state parks so that one would be located within reach of most residents.⁶⁹ But a recommendation for a site did not automatically produce a state park, for as Coldwell explained to May Mann Jennings, many sites were unavailable because of their "prohibitive purchase price."⁷⁰ The intense and comprehensive surveys also recommended many sites that became popular tourist attractions later in the decade, including Rainbow Springs, Homosassa Springs, and Wakulla Springs.⁷¹ That latter spring was purchased in 1935 and transformed into a successful tourist attraction by none other than Edward Ball, who had resigned from the State Planning Board just after the surveys were completed.⁷²

Baker's idea was just the catalyst that Florida governor Dave Sholtz wanted as the 1935 legislative session approached. As early as 1933 Sholtz had received hints that the federal government wanted more financial commitment from

Florida in its participation in the New Deal. In May 1933 CCC director Robert Fechner urged Sholtz to demand from the Florida Legislature, "if now in session or if not, in the next succeeding session," legislation to maintain and take responsibility for projects started by the CCC.[73] For the moment Fechner was assuaged by Board of Forestry member William L. Wilson's letter suggesting that Florida would soon, among other things, enact legislation "to set up state forests as well as parks."[74] In October 1934 Fechner urged Florida to base its law for a park service on New York's system.[75] Then in January 1935 Sholtz received a telegram from President Franklin Roosevelt. "It seems to me that the time has come for each state to make proper provisions for taking over this part of the work," Roosevelt wrote.[76] Only those states that enacted such measures "will be entitled to receive first consideration."[77] The implication was clear. If Florida did not take on a more fiscally active role in the New Deal, federal funding would cease.

Sholtz, anticipating such a demand, appointed in December 1934 a six-member panel to study new social welfare legislation.[78] Their recommendation was a new State Welfare Board that would handle all welfare disbursements and coordinate Florida's New Deal efforts. Harvard alumnus Conrad Van Hyning was brought in to study Florida's current welfare situation and offer suggestions. His report on Florida welfare legislation recommended a State Welfare Board that consisted of representatives from eleven regions.[79] The board would oversee the regions, one region each for Duval, Dade, and Hillsborough counties, with the other eight regions representing the remaining sixty-four counties. Aware of the risk of losing federal funds if Florida did not create a new agency, officials brooked little opposition to the plan.[80] The bill was entitled the Ward-Banks bill.[81] It passed the House with one amendment: a Florida residency requirement for the board's director.[82] Hoping to keep control of federal funds in "friendly hands," the measure was meant to bar welfare-minded Van Hyning from assuming control of the board. But Roosevelt's relief administrator Harry Hopkins wanted the bill passed with Van Hyning's proposal intact. So on May 27, 1935, the Ward-Banks bill passed the Senate with no residency requirement and a $100,000 budget.[83] There would be seven members appointed by the governor and a local welfare board located in each of the eleven districts.[84] Along with welfare disbursements, the State Welfare Board would handle CCC enrollment for Florida. The State Planning Board was also given a budget of $25,000 by the 1935 legislature.[85] Other boards created that year included the State Liquor Board, Everglades Park Commission, Board of Workman's Compensation, State Tuberculosis Board, and Florida Citrus Commission.[86] As Florida historian Charlton Tebeau wrote, this was the true start of the New Deal in Florida.[87]

As these bills were being debated in the spring of 1935, Fechner continued to press Sholtz to accept more responsibility for CCC work. In February 1935 Fechner again asked Sholtz "what provisions have been made" to assist the CCC.[88] Specifically, he was looking for a larger Florida Forest Service budget and a Florida Park Service. Five days later, Fechner wrote yet another letter to Sholtz. "I do know that the President is quite sincere in his view that the states should accept a proper proportion of the financial cost of the work."[89] Finally Sholtz instructed the Board of Forestry to create the Florida Park Service.[90]

The board, with May Mann Jennings's son Bryan as its president, was quick to oblige.[91] It soon drafted a bill (in consultations with Mrs. Jennings) and sent it to the legislature, where it became Senate bill 558. The bill established the Florida Park Service, which would operate in cooperation with the IIF and the NPS.[92] The Florida Forestry Board would have sole supervision over the FPS and would employ a director "whose qualifications for such service are certified to by the National Park Service and to employ such other assistants as may be necessary."[93] It also enabled counties to accept land for state parks and then to donate those lands to the IIF. Finally, it made all earlier state park laws null and void. The bill moved through the state legislature with little fanfare, passing the Senate on May 16 and the House on May 27, 1935.[94] But before Sholtz signed the law, he asked Baker for reassurance that it was what Fechner desired. Baker wrote that "the bill is designed to meet the point of view of President Roosevelt. . . . We do not have and cannot get Florida's full quota of CCC camps unless the state takes steps to provide work projects."[95] This law would do just that. It would also give the Florida Park Service a $25,000 annual budget.[96] For good measure, Baker also pointed out that for $50,000 (the total budget of the Florida Forest Service, including the FPS), Florida would receive in return $500,000 in land purchases and $1,500,000 a year for CCC camps.[97] Satisfied with Baker's answer, Sholtz signed the bill on June 4, 1935.[98] Florida now had its own Florida Park Service.

With legislation and funding in place, the FPS needed a director. Although Harry Lee Baker had fought for the park service and seemed an obvious choice, as chief forester he wielded supervisory powers over both the Forest and Park services and therefore had little incentive to step down to FPS director. That left May Mann Jennings as the next logical choice, but that was not how things turned out.

Jennings was Florida's most knowledgeable park authority, not only having authored legislation and lobbied for state parks in Florida but also having been in charge of a park, Royal Palm State Park, for nearly twenty years. She handled all matters ranging from advertising to managing employees to development of the park's features. Unlike any other likely candidate, Jennings alone had successfully applied for, received, and overseen a CCC camp of two hundred, in this case for her Royal Palm State Park (designated as CCC project SP-1). CCC Company #262 (first created on April 17, 1933, for a CCC camp in Missoula, Montana) arrived on October 20, 1933, with landscape architect William Phillips handpicked by Jennings as its project superintendent; he had been the landscape architect for McKee Jungle Gardens and Bok Tower Gardens and was the current CCC project superintendent for Miami's Greynolds Park.[99] With work commencing on November 5, 1933, the company completed over five miles of roads, created a five-acre deer park, cleared 1.5 miles of trails, provided general clean-up on sixty acres, built a six-acre campground, planted several royal palms (using dynamite to excavate holes in the limestone), dug fire breaks, and constructed a 20 × 40 foot garage and a concrete-lined lily pool.[100] Jennings had then not only lobbied the IIF to accept John Roebling's donation of Highlands Hammock, but also sanctioned the removal of her Royal Palm State Park CCC camp to Highlands Hammock to begin work on the Florida Garden and Arboretum.[101] (The NPS was anxious to leave Royal Palm State Park before summer because of worries of a malaria outbreak. The original plan was for the company to return in the fall, setting an alternating seasonal pattern between the two parks.[102]) In May 1934 and 1935, Governor Sholtz chose Jennings to represent Florida at the annual National Conference on State Parks.[103] Unfortunately, despite NPS requests that she attend, he did not provide any expenses for travel, and she had to decline both years.[104] In spring 1934 Jennings approached the Putnam Lumber Company in Dixie County for a donation of several hundred acres of Suwannee River property to supplement a friend's proposed donation in order to provide one thousand acres on river with suitable land for campsites.[105] Just as with the donations for Duval and Nassau counties, the proposed Suwannee River State Park could not attract enough donors or state commitment.[106] But Jennings proved she was aggressive and, with proper backing, could produce results.

When the Florida Board of Forestry began showing interest in creating a state park service with its application for the FERA park surveys in the summer of 1934, Jennings began a year-long lobbying campaign to be appointed director of the future FPS. Knowing that the NPS would be intimately involved in any proposed FPS, Jennings first wrote to Herbert Evison, the CCC supervisor for the southeastern region. "I would very much like to ask that state parks in this state not be approved by the NPS without also giving me an opportunity to pass on their desirability," she wrote, and proceeded to list her park credentials.[107] She also began lining up support for herself as FPS director. Throughout that summer and the following year Sholtz received several letters recommending Jennings as FPS director.[108] Jennings probably felt confident when she received two letters from Sholtz in May 1934. In them he wrote that Jennings would receive his endorsement as "supervisor" for state parks.[109] He further wrote that he would "like to appoint those who have been doing the major portion of the work, and who are really interested."[110] He went on to describe Jennings as just such a person.

However, once the FERA survey was under way, and it was obvious that she was not being consulted on the park selections, Jennings must have become worried that she was being left out of the loop. She first wrote to Florida Senator William C. Hodges—a longtime friend as well as a supporter of both parks and tourism—to offer her opinions on the survey. Jennings disapproved of using Baker and his men for the survey, explaining that she "believed a very definite and decided line should be drawn between forestry work, which is commercial, and the park work, which is recreational." She also began writing letters to head surveyor William Coldwell and Harry Lee Baker, offering suggestions in an attempt to play a role in the now developing park service.[111] She formatted her letters to match the style of the survey entries for each site. But her letters were never answered.

Unsuccessful with the survey, she returned to Sholtz in a series of letters. In them, she argued that "if given a free hand in the matter of state parks, I can accomplish a great deal. . . . I would like very much the opportunity to dedicate my services to the building of a Park System for Florida under your administration."[112] Two months later she wrote more emphatically, "I beg that you do not forget that I am your best, possibly your only, applicant for State Director, Commissioner, or whatever you choose to call it."[113]

As the park service legislation was moving through the Florida Legislature, Jennings became increasingly concerned over her chances for being chosen FPS director. Section three of the proposed law stipulated that any director appointed must be approved by the National Park Service. This was stronger wording than her son S. Bryan Jennings's original wording in his draft of the bill.[114] As Jennings pointed out, "this would preclude my being appointed Park Director."[115] She and the legislature knew that the NPS would require someone who was a university-trained landscape architect or park professional. It appeared that someone did not want her as FPS director. In a letter to Senator W. T. Edwards, she argued that she would be more successful than an NPS-appointed landscape architect and begged that he get the bill amended.[116] But the bill passed with the stipulation left intact.

Jennings tried a last-ditch effort in June 1935 in a final letter to Sholtz. Playing upon his sympathy and pride, she wrote that she was facing financial hardships. "I am really very much in need of some rather good paying job. I am relying on your friendship over a matter of years, as Governor to another Governor's widow, to see that I have something with an adequate compensation."[117] The letter did not work and that summer, Baker's assistant C. H. Schaeffer was chosen as the director for the newly created Florida Park Service.

In retrospect, Jennings's bid for directorship was doomed from the start. While her initial idea to create the FPS might have given Sholtz a way to ensure further CCC camps, it was in actuality a dead issue until Baker infused it with commercial possibilities. It seems likely that Baker and Sholtz did not want Jennings as FPS director. Her Progressive ideals would have clashed with their vision for a tourist-based, commercial Florida Park Service.

(Jennings was not down for long. Later in 1935 she was hired as the secretary for the Everglades Commission, a state agency designed to secure an Everglades National Park in South Florida. The new national park was finally dedicated in 1947 after thirty-two years of concerted efforts, with Royal Palm State Park one of the key components in its fruition—although the park's lodge was not used as the visitor center, as originally hoped, and was eventually removed to unspecified private property somewhere in Homestead, its whereabouts unknown.[118] At the dedication President Harry Truman singled out Jennings for her unwavering efforts in seeing the park to completion.)

By the end of 1935 the FPS had acquired all seven of its original state parks: Gold Head Branch, Hillsborough River, Myakka River, Florida Caverns, Fort Clinch, Torreya, and Highlands Hammock.[119] It had funding, statutory authority, a director, and federal backing. The only component still missing for a completed tourism-boosting Florida Park Service was labor to build the parks. And that would come in the form of CCC enrollees.

5

State-Sponsored Tourism
and the Building of Florida's State Parks

The Florida state parks were built almost exclusively by CCC labor, following the ideals, plans, and standards created by their supervisors, the National Park Service. In fact, the first park employee was Mr. Pantzer, a CCC enrollee at Highlands Hammock State Park, who in May 1935 began offering guide services to visitors between 1:00 p.m. and 5:00 p.m. on weekdays and from 9:00 a.m. to 4:00 p.m. on Sundays.[1] The Florida Park Service, with its small staff and budget, was more of an advisory group. It offered ideas and, more often, critiques while reluctantly assuming financial responsibilities in the latter years as the projects were completed. The bitterness that FPS director Lewis Scoggin and others would display toward the CCC in the postwar years (Scoggin once called the CCC "a haphazard program of keeping men at work on virtual leaf-raking jobs in the parks") more than likely stemmed from the near-constant conflicts between the FPS and NPS over park plans and implementation.[2] At the root of these conflicts were the often incompatible goals of the two agencies. The National Park Service wanted to build state parks in the mold of its own parks, using such ideals as master planning, compatible designs, and resource protection. The Florida Park Service, on the other hand—created to maintain as well as further fuel the momentum in tourist visitation gained by the Century of Progress Exposition exhibit and other advertising ventures in 1933 and 1934—was less concerned with recreation and conservation than with creating parks that were simultaneously marketable as tourist attractions, and that could also be built fast using as little state funding as possible. The result was a system of state parks, built between 1935 and 1942 by CCC workers, that was a compromise between these commercial and recreational interests.

While the National Park Service was busy using the CCC enrollees (the common term used to refer to the relief workers who were enrolled in the corps) to plan and construct the parks, others in the state government, including the Florida Park Service, were busy promoting Florida to tourists. Chief among these was the staff of the Office of the Governor, fresh from their success with a second year at the Century of Progress Exposition in Chicago (extended due to unexpectedly high profits in 1933). This was followed up with the same exhibit—with only minor changes—displayed at the Rockefeller Center in New York City in winter 1935 and at the Great Lakes Exposition in Cleveland in summer 1936. The *New York Times* extensively covered both events, and even President Franklin Roosevelt commented on Florida's exhibit in Cleveland, noting "that people all over the East are visiting this exposition in Cleveland [and] that the State of Florida has put up a fine building here."[3] Sensing he was onto something that could possibly lead to national office (a U.S. Senate run was already in the works), Governor Dave Sholtz decided to up the ante for tourism.

On July 11, 1935, in Jacksonville, Florida, Sholtz arranged a statewide conference of two hundred of Florida's civic and business leaders at which he called for the organization of the "All-Florida Advertising Campaign."[4] And again Sholtz played upon the ongoing rivalry with the other land of sunshine, California.[5] As he pointed out, California was spending nearly $900,000 a year in tourist advertising.[6] In his letters inviting people to the conference, Sholtz said one of the reasons he dreamed up the idea was because "of the renewed activity on the part of California and its business interests" in promoting itself to the nation.[7] At the meeting Sholtz stated that his goal was for Florida to raise at least $500,000.[8] He urged that "all sectional, inter-community and personal jealousies and prejudices be laid aside in the common effort . . . to advertise Florida nationally."[9] Of course those who harbored reservations and hostilities toward such a campaign—for example, farmers, ranchers, and turpentiners—were not a part of this campaign. Those present, however, were thrilled with the plan, and it was agreed at a smaller second meeting in Tallahassee on July 22, 1935, that "all money raised shall be spent in recognized national advertising media outside of the State of Florida, and that all monies raised shall be spent for this purpose and for no other."[10] They would target hotel chains, rail, ship and bus lines, realtors, banks, and the national media. Sholtz became chairman of the advertising committee, Charles Overman of the Association of County Commissioners of Florida was chosen as vice-chair, and Robert Grassfield of the Florida State Chamber of Commerce was secretary.

Taking a page from Commissioner of Agriculture Nathan Mayo's playbook, Sholtz funded this new campaign with the "breaks" from the State Racing Commission. Created by the legislature in 1931—the same year that parimutuel betting was made legal—the Racing Commission regulated the state's popular horse and dog tracks, most of which were located in South Florida.[11] As a way to sell the gambling idea to all the counties, the law required tracks to pay the state 10 percent of the track winnings, with the race tracks allowed to keep only 7 percent.[12] The state then distributed these funds equally to all of the sixty-seven counties. By 1939 this amounted to roughly $29,000 per county, most of which the counties used to fund public education.[13] But these funds were derived by rounding down—and never up—a winning to the closest dime. The left over odd cents were called "breaks" and were also given to the State. It was these breaks that Sholtz used to fund his advertising campaign, along with contributions by the county boards of commissioners. And as with the Agriculture Department's inspection fees, the race breaks were neither regulated nor subject to biennial legislative approval. Such a fund could not come at a better time, as Mayo discovered his own advertising stash depleted: "For the past two years, the major part of this fund has gone toward keeping the Florida Exhibit at the Century of Progress and we still owe several thousand dollars."[14] His department was also "depleted of booklets, bulletins, etc."[15]

By fall 1935 the All Florida Advertising Committee was already showing signs of progress. In its first step the committee hired a New York advertising firm, Eastman, Scott and Company.[16] Vying for such lucrative business during the midst of a national depression, letters from media outlets poured into Sholtz's office, including from the *New York Law Journal, New Yorker, Brooklyn Daily Eagle, New York Daily News, Dynamic Pictures, Christian Science Monitor, New York Times*, General Outdoor Advertising Company, National Sportsmens Inc., and numerous hotels and rail lines.[17] Many newspapers, in hopes of securing future advertising, published complimentary stories about Florida and its promotion campaign. One such story appeared in *Town & Country* in December 1935 and another in the *Christian Science Monitor* in February 1936.[18] Just the idea of promoting Florida appeared to be news in 1935. For many it was a sign of impending economic recovery.

With $67,000 "actually on hand" by October 1935, the committee began purchasing ad space.[19] A half-page Florida ad was purchased that fall for the January issue of *Time* magazine, at the height of Florida's winter season.[20] Another ad was purchased in *Fortune* magazine for October.[21] By December Florida advertisements could be found in all the major newspapers on the East Coast. Even the popular daily comic *Dick Tracy* mentioned Florida. In a cartoon on March 1, 1936, a hospitalized Tracy is given three tickets to Florida by a young boy, who exclaims, "Dick! Think of it! Bright sunshine, bathing in the ocean, deep sea fishing." An adult in the next panel adds, "Look at these pamphlets, Tracy. Palm trees, a southern moonsoft sea breeze—," interrupted in the next panel by the hero: "Stop! I'm licked! I surrender! I give in!"[22] Therefore by early 1936 even the nation's top crime fighter was choosing sunny Florida over sunny California. The committee also placed full-page ads in both the *New York Times* and *New York Herald Tribune* throughout the month of February. Their plan was to try to convince travelers in New York and New Jersey—by far the two largest sources of Florida tourists—to extend their vacations into March and April. Until then Florida's tourist season traditionally had run from November to a peak in January and February and tapered off by early March. As late as March 15, 1936, a full-page ad was placed in both the *New York Times* and the *Chicago Tribune*. Committee advertising executive R. H. Scott was pleased that articles on President Roosevelt's upcoming Florida fishing trip were found in the same issues. "The President is actually doing what we are urging thousands to do in the full-page ad, and probably because he realizes just the facts we are trying to get across."[23] Florida's "inside man" at the *New York Times*, Harris Sims, a Stetson University graduate and avid promoter of Florida, made sure many of the committee's achievements and goals made their way into the paper. One article, "Florida's Season Lengthens," quoted Sholtz arguing that "Florida is lovelier in March than at any other time and because of the fact that mortality rates from pneumonia are higher in March in the cold Northern areas, practical-minded vacationists will . . . escape into sunshine."[24]

Such season lengthening was one of the committee's goals. Another included convincing people to vacation in Florida during the summer months (a tough sell in the years before widespread air conditioning and the invention of DDT), expanding the number of visitors, and increasing agricultural sales—although aside from citrus, always a strong selling point that was innately linked to Florida's sunny climate, this last goal was not actively pursued.[25] By late 1936, through an internal document the committee announced that it achieved most of its goals (ignoring the lack of increased sales of agricultural products), even stating that "Florida is having the best summer in its entire history" with thousands, instead of hundreds, traveling to the State of Florida.[26] One of their measuring tools was a cut-out coupon that appeared in most of the ads and could be redeemed for promotional literature from the Florida State Chamber of Commerce.[27] Over 13,000 had been received by summer 1936.[28] To handle these, as well as the more than 21,000 inquiries, the committee received federal assistance through the Professional Service Project of the Florida WPA, with William Wilson providing supervision.[29] These relief workers created a synopsis of each inquiry, including name, address, and nature of question or concern (much as a commercial sales firm does in order to create a databank of potential future customers). Each person sending either a coupon or letter inquiry received the brochure *Florida—The March of Progress* and a signed facsimile letter from Governor Sholtz welcoming them to Florida.[30] The winter campaign cost approximately $30,000, while the summer campaign cost considerably less, at around $5,000.[31]

With three years of national fairs under their belts and millions of tourists responding, Sholtz and his staff decided to go international. In the fall of 1936, with the assistance of the W. H. Rankin advertising firm in New York City, they began a second advertising campaign, this time focusing on potential European tourists. One plan was to arrange a major passenger ship, preferably the *Queen Mary*, to dock at Port Everglades near Fort Lauderdale, Florida. The idea was that passengers would disembark in South Florida—perhaps with cars in tow—and enjoy ten or more days motoring around the state. "This year the *Queen Mary* brought 32 British motor cars with their owners to New York," Rankin wrote to Sholtz.[32] Even better would be to suggest to these passengers that they bring bicycles and "ride from Ft. Lauderdale, Miami, Tampa, Lakeland, Orlando, Tallahassee and thence over to Jacksonville, from there take the Clyde Line Steamer to New York and return to London via the regular Cunard White Star Liners."[33] This new advertising campaign presented Florida as the "New World's Riviera."[34] It was a calculated shift from the middle-class, family-oriented advertising Florida had advanced since 1933, and for Rankin, one of the promotional architects of the Florida land boom, it was an attempt to "recapture the glory days of the 1920s."[35] Apparently oblivious to world events erupting in the mid-1930s, Rankin convinced Sholtz that "we could not only bring tourists by the shipload from Great Britain, France, Italy, Germany, Holland, Sweden and Denmark to Florida"—they could also get them to visit in the summer when Europeans usually traveled.[36] Sholtz immediately began writing letters to European travel agencies and major newspapers in London, Paris, Rome, and New York, along with the large steam ship companies. Recipients of his letters included the *Washington Post, New York Sun, Boston Herald, London Times, London Daily Telegraph,* London's Advertising World, the London Press Exchange, the Victoria Hotel, and the *Christian Science Monitor.*[37] As Sholtz explained to one travel authority, "as soon as the Europeans know what we have to offer . . . they are sure to come in thousands."[38] It might even promote "world Peace," he wishfully suggested.[39]

In both visitation and world peace, the plan failed miserably. The first snag came with the discovery by Rankin that "on account of the laws, there is no chance to have foreign ships go direct to Port Everglades. I also learned that Port Everglades could not harbor ships of the size we intended . . . a large ship cannot turn around in the harbor but must back out."[40] In many cases Sholtz was fishing for free articles in his letters to media announcing the plan, which had worked with the All Florida campaign. As Rankin suggested, "Send out a press release . . . then watch the newspapers give the idea publicity!"[41] But by this point the major publications were tiring of offering free publicity with empty stories of Florida's travel plans. Florida's initial novelty was wearing off. Instead, most of the papers suggested Florida buy advertising. Although Cunard White Star Line placed ads in English and Scottish newspapers using the line "Come to the New World's Riviera," it produced only about a "half dozen" people "to call the Cunard office."[42] One steamship agent offered Sholtz and company a reality check on their plans: "To sell Florida to the European will require a little more than the cooperation of steamship lines, newspapers, etc. Today the German stays in Germany because he is not allowed to take any money out of Germany. The Italians have none. The French have but they are not spenders and they do not travel to any extent. The Russians are too busy with their 5-year plans."[43] The only people left were the English, but Florida would have to compete with established places such as "Las Palmas, Madeira, and Teneriffe, also . . . South Africa." Furthermore, as one London journalist explained to the governor, the purpose of cruises "is to get people to pass as much time as possible on the boat and to spend their money there. You want to get the people ashore and spending their money in the State of Florida. . . . Attractions in Florida are only known here amongst a very small circle of rather wealthy people."[44] The solution was to offer more than merely climate and beaches. Although advertising and fair exhibits had proven successful, tourist attractions—created by local entrepreneurs jumping on the promotional bandwagon—were only just starting to appear by 1935 and 1936. There was the risk that even Americans might start going elsewhere, perhaps to California. And this European fiasco further illustrated the need for the State of Florida to build and promote its own attractions, in particular its seven new state parks.

As the Florida State Planning Board reminded people in 1940: "The tourist industry is Florida's greatest source of revenue . . . greater than the total net income from agriculture and industry combined."[45] But the FPS needed little reminding. Forestry staff were usually present at all the All Florida Advertising Committee meetings. And in September 1935 forester C. H. Coulter sent out to park and forestry staff a circular ordering employees to give the campaign "as much publicity as possible. . . . The more money to advertise the attractions and resources of Florida outside the State, the more visitors we will have . . . thus resulting in the increased interest in state parks and forests and forestry in general. This means you are fully justified in giving as much of your time as you can" to the campaign.[46] In a 1936 radio broadcast on the Florida Park Service on WTAL in Tallahassee, Harold Foley of the Board of Forestry explained: "Florida, a Mecca for tourists for a large part of the year[,] has often been referred to as Nature's Wonder Garden. . . . We have needed parks in the true sense of the word . . . for our tourists [and] for our citizens."[47] One U.S. Forest Service CCC inspector, in a confidential memorandum, criticized State Forester Baker for "not [being] familiar with the conditions and problems which exist in the State camps nor is he making any efforts to familiarize himself with these problems," presumably spending his time on advertising and the development of state park camps.[48] Even the way the FPS chose park locations reflected its goal of promoting Florida tourism across the state. Three of the state parks—Hillsborough, Myakka, and Highlands Hammock—were located in tourist-friendly South Florida. Fort Clinch was also well situated in northeast Florida to capture many of the travelers along U.S. 1 en route to St. Augustine, Daytona, and beaches farther south. The other three, Florida Caverns, Gold Head, and Torreya, all in North Florida, were not in prime tourist areas. Their development was an attempt by the FPS to expand tourism across the state. The idea was either to attract tourists from more popular areas or, as in Marianna's case with the

Florida Caverns, to catch visitors as they passed through the town en route to well-known sites in Central and South Florida. As an article in the *Jackson County Floridian* pointed out, of the 1,395,650 tourists who visited Florida in 1935, more than 500,000 came through Marianna.[49] But with the caverns developed as a state park, the article argued, visitors now had a reason to pull off the highway.[50] Harry Baker called Marianna the "gateway to Florida for tourist travel."[51] On another occasion, speaking on the merits of all state parks, Baker explained, "There are thousands of tourists coming to Florida each year in search of naturalistic features."[52] These visitors "are willing to spend their money in order to see things for which Florida is famous."[53] And the FPS could provide those things.

An example of the strategic location of the parks is illustrated in a 1941 letter from FPS director Lewis Scoggin to State Senator Dewey Dye, in preparation for Dye's address at Myakka's grand opening on February 28, 1941. The event included speeches by C. R. Vinten of the National Park Service and Project Superintendent A. B. Edwards and featured a picnic lunch in the CCC camp. Scoggin wrote:[54]

> A tourist might begin a tour of the state at Fernandina where he may inspect Fort Clinch State Park. Proceeding down the coast, he would stop at Fort Marion National Monument, St. Augustine, and Fort Matanzas National Monument. He might then cross the state to Tampa and visit Hillsborough River State Park, to Sarasota where he could linger a while at Myakka, then across the state to Sebring to see Highlands Hammock State Park, which has been described as the third most important park of its kind in the United States. From there the visitor might go south through the muck lands around Okeechobee to the very heart of the proposed Everglades National Park lying between Myakka and the lower east coast, and complete his tour by proceeding up the west coast to Tallahassee then to Torreya State Park on the Apalachicola River, Florida Caverns State Park at Marianna, and end his tour in Santa Rosa Island National Monument near Pensacola. So it is seen that Myakka River State Park is a pleasant stop-off place on a tour of the state and national park areas within the state.[55]

One way to promote the parks was to highlight one feature at each site. Torreya State Park became known for its "rugged topography" and for the Torreya tree (*Tumion taxifolium*)—"one of the rarest trees on earth," exclaimed one FPS brochure.[56] One early park brochure featured an "Indian Relics" hill just south of the Gregory House, "evidence of a forgotten Indian village" where visitors were encouraged to gather Native American artifacts, such as "Indian pottery."[57] (A 1938 Torreya State Park location map showing land ownership boundaries also shows one topographic feature labeled "Indian Relics Ridge."[58]) In the 1937 edition of her guide to Florida (written under the supervision of and funded by the Florida Department of Agriculture), Marjory Stoneman Douglas wrote that the bluffs landscape of Torreya "reminds one of the mountains of Virginia, North Carolina or Tennessee."[59] Highlands Hammock State Park became a "tropical wonderland," while Myakka's prairie was like the "African veldt."[60] Fort Clinch State Park highlighted its historic namesake, and Hillsborough River State Park was advertised as "Florida's jungle."[61] In an attempt to add some drama to the park's promotion, Douglas wrote of its river that "on the bottom can be seen turtles and fish. Poised in the stream can be seen hundreds of ferocious garfish, and if one tarries to watch, occasionally he can witness a kill."[62] Gold Head Branch State Park came the closest to a traditional park image, billing itself as a sportsman's paradise with fishing, boating, diving, hiking, and camping. Yet Douglas managed to add a bit of allure regarding its tropical ravine, which she wrote was full of "beautiful palms, a great variety of flowers and shrubs and trees of a subtropical nature," all of which had been added by the CCC.[63] Florida Caverns State Park, however, received the most publicity and, with its cavern tours, emerged as the closest of the parks to bona fide roadside attractions. Comparisons to Luray Caverns in Virginia and Mammoth Caverns in Kentucky were common in its promotional literature. Baker once claimed, with enthusiasm if not much factual evidence, that the Florida Caverns were "equal to some of the most widely publicized wonder-spots in the entire nation."[64] Meanwhile, some officials in the NPS believed otherwise. As one NPS geologist wrote in 1936: "It is doubtful if the visitor from the North—most of whom have seen at least one of the larger caverns in Kentucky or Appalachian valley will be much impressed."[65]

Yet even with the hyperbole of some of the FPS publicity, the finished park system was a much scaled-down version of the original plans. At the time of acquisition, the FPS was going to develop Torreya into an "Old South" plantation, complete with cotton fields and a working cotton gin. The FPS also planned to rent out the restored and relocated the antebellum Gregory

House as a bed and breakfast. At Gold Head, a water mill that once operated on park grounds at the turn of the century was to be rebuilt. And plans for another state park property, Suwannee River State Park—purchased in 1936 and 1937 but not developed until after World War II—called for the revival "of old Negro plantation life."[66] Located on U.S. Highway 90 between Lake City and Madison in North Florida, this was not the same Suwannee property that May Mann Jennings had attempted to develop in 1934, which would eventually become an FPS property in 1993 as Fanning Springs State Park. The park's entry in a 1940 brochure, *Florida State Parks Invite You*, runs alongside an Uncle Remus image.[67] Gold Head Branch State Park, which had the least ambitious of all the park plans, was going to build a large community house and reconstructed water wheel to be located at an old mill site along the park's titular stream.[68] But again Florida Caverns trumped the other parks for the elaborateness of its original plans. In what would be called "Sholtz Park," the CCC was to develop bridle paths, a museum, a post office, an "Indian pottery stand," an Olympic-sized pool, docks, a small zoo, picnic area, gas station, twenty cottages, a sandwich stand, souvenir stand, restaurant, photo studio, and if time and budget permitted, a small airport.[69] Such plans reflected how the state parks might have developed if Florida had possessed the funds to eschew NPS/CCC labor. As completed, the state parks reflected the guidance of the NPS more than the grandiose plans of the FPS.

From 1936 until the outbreak of the Second World War, the FPS consistently promoted its parks. Brochures such as *Florida State Parks Invite You*, a sixteen-page glossy publication from 1940, were regularly produced. Each park had its own handout as well as publications on topics common to state parks. Highlands Hammock had several handouts on flowers, birds, and trees. Hillsborough River superintendent and biologist Oscar Baynard helped produce many of the handouts and brochures. His *Birds of Highlands Hammock*, produced in 1940, was still being used as late as 2002. He also created bird lists for Oleno State Park (when it was still a Forestry Training Camp) in 1937, and for Hillsborough River State Park.[70] Baynard was instrumental in the creation of the many signs, labels, and other interpretive materials present at the parks. FPS director Scoggin credited Baynard's signs and brochures with the 74 percent increase in visitation at Hillsborough River.[71] Beginning in January 1936 the FPS also had a fifteen-minute weekly radio broadcast on WTAL, broadcast on Fridays at 6:00 p.m.[72] Unfortunately no recordings of this radio show survive and we have only one script, from the premier broadcast.[73] Gold Head developed an exhibit showcasing the park's features with electrically lit panels consisting of large photographic slides situated on light boards, which traveled to several hotels along the East Coast.[74] Probably influenced by the success of Florida's exhibits at the various world fairs in the 1930s, the Florida Caverns superintendent Clarence Simpson created a diorama of the caverns out of cypress knees that went on permanent display at Jacksonville's bustling Union Station.[75] Highlands Hammock's staff borrowed an idea from its roadside attraction neighbors and began placing park bumper stickers on the cars of park visitors.[76] Soon thereafter, Fort Clinch employed the same tactic. Even before most parks were officially open, park officials were soliciting visitors through radio shows, newspaper stories, and press releases.

The Florida Park Service was a small organization when it began in 1935. At the time, it was only one of five branches of the Florida Board of Forestry, the other four were the Applied Forestry, Publicity, Fire Control, and Fiscal branches.[77] The young park agency consisted of a director, procurement officer, stenographer, landscape architect, and construction architect. The first FPS director, Charles H. Schaeffer, served from 1935 till 1937, at which time he resigned to become assistant state forester in South Carolina (although he would return in the 1950s as chief of education and information.)[78] Before his selection as director, Schaeffer had been in charge of the Forest Service's state nursery in Olustee.[79] Former procurement officer Henry J. Malsberger replaced Schaeffer as director until 1940, when he replaced Harry Lee Baker as state forester.[80] Lewis Scoggin, who earlier replaced Malsberger as procurement officer, became the FPS director that year, and remained so until 1952, when he was fired over a dispute with the Board of Parks and Historical Memorials. The rest of the FPS staff included Vera Glisson as stenographer, Walter Coldwell as the landscape architect, and Felix Benton, followed by D. A. Finlayson, as the FPS architect throughout the majority of the pre-WWII years.[81]

As the parks grew, employees were added to the FPS payroll. Park guards and superintendents were hired to protect and manage park facilities as well as offer visitor services. A special coup for the FPS was the hiring in 1936 of Oscar Baynard as park superintendent of Hillsborough River State Park. A well-known ornithologist, Baynard began his career in the early 1900s as a naturalist working for the Audubon Society to protect egrets from hunters in the Florida Everglades.[82] Landscape architect Hayden Williams began at Highlands Hammock in 1941 as superintendent, while Donald K. Plank was simultaneously brought on as park naturalist.[83] For Florida Caverns, the FPS hired an eleven-year veteran with the Florida Geological Survey named Clarence Simpson as that park's superintendent in 1941.[84] Biologist Leonard Giovanoli, first hired at Highlands Hammock as a naturalist, was transferred in 1942 to aid Simpson at the caverns.[85] Former CCC employees M. B. Greene and Clayton Perreault were hired as superintendents for Fort Clinch and Gold Head Branch state parks respectively, also in 1941.[86] Last hired was Allen Crowley at Myakka River State Park in 1942.

But most of the time the CCC project superintendents and the camp enrollees ran the camps and provided visitor services. CCC superintendents solved design and construction problems, developed public programs, and maintained the park facilities. The enrollees—in addition to park construction—cleaned, repaired, and interpreted the parks to the public. Enrollees at Highlands Hammock, Florida Caverns, and Fort Clinch state parks gave regular tours to visitors, often before the parks were officially opened. At all the state parks, enrollees and superintendents participated in park promotions—through word of mouth in local towns, supplying information to local media, and staging events such as CCC anniversaries and local dances. These public events made the parks household names across the state and familiarized the public with the parks' features.

Although they worked on CCC projects, these project superintendents were National Park Service employees. Despite a large national bureaucracy and federal funding, the NPS in Florida was a rather small affair. Besides the project superintendents, the state inspector for the NPS, C. R. Vinten, was the human face of the NPS in Florida. Vinten relayed instructions and criticism from the NPS regional office in Richmond, Virginia, to the FPS administrators. As the NPS's sole authority in the state, Vinten also had the power to decide how federal funds were spent, approved plans, and controlled the project superintendents.[87] Vinten hired most of the project foremen and superintendents.[88] He also made sure that NPS standards were followed in the state parks. Any problems the FPS had with the NPS were dealt with through, and often originated with, Vinten. As with all NPS-hired project superintendents, the state inspector was a landscape architect—a designer of outdoor spaces. The NPS insisted upon hiring college-educated workers familiar with outdoor engineering and design.[89] Project superintendents included Claude Ragan (SP-4, Myakka), Arthur B. Weissinger, and later Tracy Baker (SP-5, Gold Head), A. D. Lawson (SP-12, Florida Caverns and Torreya), A. C. Altvater (SP-10/SP-3 Highlands Hammock), H. B. Andrews (P-71, Hillsborough River), and M. B. Green (Fort Clinch).[90]

As all landscape architects know, a state park must possess several basic elements. Features such as trails, contact stations, fencing, park roads, picnic areas, and restroom facilities were common to most state parks. And by the late 1930s, park designers could consult several standard works. Park buildings were designed in the "rustic style," defined as "the use of native materials in proper scale, and through the avoidance of rigid straight lines and oversophistication, giving the feeling of having been executed by pioneer craftsmen."[91] These buildings were usually patterned after the work of NPS architect Albert Good, whose book *Park Structures and Facilities*, published in 1935, was the "bible" for the nation's park designers.[92] Most structures built in Florida's state parks by the CCC, including cabins, shelters, contact stations, picnic benches, drinking fountains, fences, and even latrines, were derived from Good's book. Even the layout of campgrounds had set standards. The "Meineche Plan," developed by E. P. Meineche in 1932, guided park planners in campground design, including the use of circle drives and spurred sites, each equipped with a fire ring and a table.[93] A botanist who demonstrated that campgrounds coexisted best with nature when specific soil types and plant communities were chosen, Meineche wrote his study when he noticed the number of trees and other plant life that died in several early National Park campgrounds. The study became the monograph *Campground Policy*.[94] CCC project superintendents and NPS inspector Vinten strove to include these elements and standards in their work in Florida's state parks. But beyond the common elements such as roads, fences, shelters, sewage and water systems, power lines, picnic areas, and restrooms, CCC camps also added features unique to specific parks, differentiating one Florida state park from another, a practice that lent itself to easy marketability.

The first state park to receive a CCC camp was Highlands Hammock in 1934, although the Florida Board of Forestry did not officially approve the transfer of the private park to the state until February 23, 1935.[95] As the park was finished when acquired, the camp—designated FL SP-3 (later SP-10)—was originally intended "to prepare the physical structure and background for a botanical garden and arboretum, as a complement for Highlands Hammock State Park."[96] However, after a couple of years, NPS inspector Vinten allowed the CCC to improve the park's infrastructure, including building a park office and records house, a contact station, improved roads, a refreshment house, and fencing.[97] This was partly because of the state's delinquency in its financial commitment to the park, even though the park had been charging admission since the creation of the FPS in June 1935. Visitors 18 years and up were charged 25 cents, those aged 12 to 18 were charged 10 cents, and children under 12 were admitted free.[98] Only the Sunday Vespers Services were completely free of charge.[99] Yet as early as fall 1935, FPS director C. H. Schaeffer asked the Trustees of Highlands Hammock, Inc.—the private nonprofit body that John Roebling set up to oversee the park's development—to turn over all of Roebling's $25,000 set aside as matching funds for the park's upkeep for six years.[100] The Board of Forestry's minutes reflect that in addition to having "full authority for the administration of the park" they expected full access to the trust fund "to supplement any funds appropriated by the legislature."[101] His stern suggestion was unanimously voted down, as the conditions of Roebling's trust fund limited the options available to the trustees.[102] A compromise was finally reached whereby one member of the Board of Forestry was to become a trust fund trustee to ensure that the needs of the Forestry Board were financially met by the trustees.

In addition to sustaining the majority of park funding, Highlands Hammock, Inc. continued to provide much of the publicity for the park. One example was from early 1935 when the organization hired the Tampa-based Burgert Brothers to produce a fifteen-minute color film of the park for viewing at movie theatres across the state.[103] They also placed bumper stickers on cars that visited the park, and they passed out illustrated folders and other promotional materials.[104] The organization sent frequent press releases to major publications and courted any reporter, writer, or promoter who would listen to them. In the early years the park also allowed visitors to pick their own oranges in the hammock's groves. As one publication explained, "you can secure permits to pick oranges from the park guides and they will even furnish ladders. Many visitors . . . make up small souvenir packages [while] others just pick for immediate consumption after learning from the accommodating guide the trick of peeling an orange 'cracker style.'"[105] Park staff even made arrangements with local groves to direct visitors "if all the oranges and grapefruit have been picked in the park."[106] The park emerged as one of the most popular attractions in southwest Florida in the 1930s.

Less than an hour's drive from Highlands Hammock was the CCC SP-4 project at Myakka River State Park. Much of the property was acquired in 1934 (originally to be either a game preserve or state forest) from Phoenix Insurance Company executive A. B. Edwards, but state officials and locals had always hoped for at least a portion of the land to be dedicated as a state park.[107] The first CCC company actually arrived on November 10, 1935, although they would not conduct park work for a few months.[108] Under project superintendent Claude Ragan's supervision, the CCC there built shelters, the park drive, fences, contact station, latrines, and an amphitheatre.[109] But the most striking park feature was the set of five rental cabins made of sabal palm logs.[110] Rental cabins were also built at Hillsborough River (P-71) and Gold Head (SP-5) state parks to the north of Myakka, near Tampa and Keystone Heights respectively.[111] Hillsborough's five cabins were equipped with rustic furniture, electricity, water, and hand-hewn tables.[112] But the most popular feature at Hillsborough River State Park was the swinging bridge that enrollees built across the eponymous river. CCC crews there also built several picnic tables, twenty tables with benches, two miles of park roads, three drinking fountains, a recreation shelter, and a latrine and landscaped more than one hundred acres.[113] Gold Head Branch State Park consisted primarily of land donated by Mike Roess, secretary for the Virginia-based Columbia Forest and Farms, Inc., along with parcels from Roswell Penny (of Penny Farms) and R. L. Dowling and Sons.[114] Gold Head's veteran CCC company (#2444) built four overnight cabins, though fifteen were originally planned.[115] In addition to building cabins, Gold Head's camp made furniture for the cabins at other state parks.[116] They also constructed a boat house (complete with CCC-built rowboats for rent), a garage, caretaker's house, gatehouse, trailer camp, recreation hall, lake bathhouse, and a stairway down into a ravine where the park river ran—a freshwater, spring-fed stream flowing into Lake Johnson, around which the majority of the park's facilities were located.[117]

Historic restoration and rehabilitation projects dominated at Torreya (SP-6) and Fort Clinch (SP-8) state parks. Enrollees at Torreya in Liberty County dismantled, moved down river, and rebuilt the Gregory House, an antebellum cotton plantation, on park grounds. The house was reassembled on a high bluff overlooking the Apalachicola River, next to several gun works dating from the Civil War. Fort Clinch also dated from the Civil War. It was built in the 1850s on the northern end of Amelia Island in northeast Florida and named for Seminole War General Duncan Clinch.[118] The fort was a Union-occupied site by 1862 and was abandoned soon after the war. Except for a brief reoccupation during the Spanish-American War, Fort Clinch sat empty until the CCC arrived in 1936. The CCC cleaned, landscaped, restored, and re-created the military fort, and they added a series of groins to prevent further erosion.[119] Enrollees built a lodge on the park's beachfront as well as two campgrounds.[120] Plans for five cabins at Fort Clinch were never completed.[121]

Perhaps the biggest accomplishment of Florida's CCC state park camps was Florida Caverns, SP-12, originally a side camp from Torreya (SP-6). Occupied by three separate companies, a junior African American company, a white veteran company, and finally a junior white company, SP-12 not only built an entire park but also excavated and developed a system of caves for public tours. Originally the enrollees worked on a locally well-known and widely used cave called the "Natural Bridge Cave." Its walls were covered in graffiti, and more of its formation sat in Marianna living rooms than in the cave. Then in 1937, while on an inspection of the state, NPS geologist Oliver Challifeux discovered two new caves, designated as caves #2 and #3.[122] Suddenly cavern development switched to the two caves, where enrollees excavated dirt and rock, built walkways, added a lighting system, and wrote a tour script.[123] Nearby, the NPS, along with FPS architect D. A. Finlayson, designed a two-story combination museum-office building that the enrollees constructed out of local limestone and which overlooked the nearby ravine and Chipola River.[124] At the other end of the park, enrollees developed a swimming and picnic area at a natural spring called Blue Hole.[125]

While excavating the two new caves, CCC workers began to pull out items among the debris that appeared to be human-created, including pottery sherds and flint flakes, contradicting park engineer John Lowrie, who remarked to NPS staff that "no Indian artifacts or any other cultural material have been found in any of the caves now under development."[126] The reason, according to Lowrie, was that "early Indian tradition existed that no Indian came near the caverns due to the constant smoke and steam arising from the various outlets."[127] He explained that "the vapor is caused by the various changes of temperature outside the caves coming into contact with the moist air from the interior. The average temperature within the cave is 63 degrees."[128] But the steady stream of artifacts seemed to belie such local lore.

NPS policy forbade the "the demolition of present historic structures and remains without proper examination" and instead promoted the "salvaging of valuable scientific collections."[129] In addition to the two caves, CCC enrollees also found artifacts in the parking lot area. The NPS called for a proper archaeological excavation of the three areas, and the FPS obliged, sensing the exhibition possibilities in the park's museum then under construction.[130] After going through several candidates, including future Florida archaeological luminary John Goggin (then a graduate student at the University of New Mexico), William Kary with the CCC company (#1445) in Vilas working for the Apalachicola National Forest, and W. J. Winter with the St. Augustine Historical Program, the two park agencies finally settled on park superintendent J. Clarence Simpson, who also worked for the Florida Geological Survey.[131] Simpson's subsequent excavation (referred to as Job 147), for which he was paid ten dollars a day through PWA funds between February 26 and March 7, 1941, resulted in sherds from three vessels in one cave and several ceramic pieces from the other.[132] The parking lot produced the most material. Simpson and men from the park's CCC camp swept clean the floor of the two caverns and dug several test pits and trenches.[133] The artifacts were bagged and stored onsite.

Later that summer Simpson with Julian Granberry of the National Park Service discovered a new cavern, "a small opening in the ground about 300 yards south west of the combination building" that "developed into a large cave."[134] Of interest were the bear tracks and "other prints that have every appearance of moccasin tracks" and "two shallow pits in the clay floor where clay had been dug with some pointed tool."[135] The NPS's Southeastern Archaeological Center (SEAC) located at Ocmulgee National Monument in Macon, Georgia, sent a young archeologist, Charles Fairbanks, to investigate. Later to reach academic prominence with his groundbreaking plantation excavations and his authoritative 1980 book, *Florida Archaeology,* Fairbanks in 1941 was just starting his career.[136] In October 1941 he dated the materials (which he took back with him to Ocmulgee) from Simpson's excavations to the Mississippian and Weeden Island periods (1000–1500 A.D.).[137] As for the new cave, Fairbanks confirmed the presence of human footprints. "The tracks are of bare feet and there is no possibility of determining the cultural affiliation . . . it is probably safe to assume they are Indians."[138] But in the end the park was disappointed with the Fairbanks report, which concluded that "the evidence points to more or less casual visitations to caves," mostly during the proto-historical periods.[139] Visions by park administrators of Indian cave tours and aboriginal souvenirs and trinkets vanished in the face of the empirical evidence.

The FPS would be further disappointed when the materials Fairbanks took away were not returned. In 1944 Simpson unsuccessfully attempted to recover the restored vessels form Ocmulgee.[140] At the time, Fairbanks was in the U.S. Army, and the promised restoration work had not been completed.[141] Two years later the materials were finally returned to the park, where in 1948 they were found simply "stored in the woodwork shop" at the park by then FPS archaeologist John Goggin.[142] Florida archaeologist Ripley Bullen at last wrote up a final report in 1949 on the 1941 excavations and reached the same conclusions as Fairbanks. Considering that the southeastern archaeologist Gordon Willey visited the park in October 1940, every major archaeologist working in Florida in the 1940s researched the park's artifacts, although the proposed park exhibit never materialized.

Former CCC enrollee Buck Heath, who was briefly stationed at Florida Caverns, described an interesting discovery in the caves. "We found a skeleton and it was on display down there for years. We found a rifle . . . but it didn't have no stock on it. It's all gone now." According to Heath, the discovery was made while enrollees dug out the cave in 1939. "We dug out all kinds of stuff . . . Indian arrowheads and dug that gun and that skeleton." Heath speculated that "somebody went in there and hid and died in there or something."[143] Yet none of the surviving reports from the park's excavation mention such a finding.

However those reports do mention the discovery of another skeleton at the caverns, though one that was decidedly not human. In fall 1941 Simpson "located the skeleton of an extinct whale or Zeuglodon. The specimen was from the genus Basilosaurus, and in recent years it has been suggested by some cryptozoologists to be the basis for the Loch Ness Monster myth. At the time, only one other complete fossil was known to exist. There are at least seven vertebrae visible on the surface of a limestone ridge."[144] As with the Native American artifacts, this raised hopes for the developing park museum. State Geologist Herman Gunter found the discovery to be of "inestimable value."[145] Scoggin immediately asked Vinten to set up a CCC excavation job, referring to the discovery as "the best fossil in the State."[146] But on second thought Scoggin began to "fear that we will not be to able count too much on CCC labor" as well the possibility of "the loss of the fossil to our Service" once the NPS saw the potential of the find.[147] "There will be slack times probably during the summers when some of the personnel and myself may be able to work it out bit by bit. The cost would be high if we were to hire men."[148] But it was not to be. As late as 1946, it was still in the ground.[149]

Throughout the 1930s and early 1940s tensions between the two park agencies grew increasingly acute as their differing goals became clearer. The NPS personnel wanted to build state parks in its own mold. They were concerned with maintaining high park standards, regardless of how long it took to achieve those standards, and relied on a large staff of biologists, geologists, landscape and construction architects, and inspectors to guide them. The FPS on the other hand, concerned with shrinking budgets and an acute need to justify its existence to an obstinate administration, wanted parks built fast, cheaply, and wanted them easily marketable. Park standards were desirable only if they did not get in the way of the park's completion and promotion. An example of this concerned Fort Clinch. Although all involved wanted the fort restored, similar to those in both St. Simon's Island and St. Augustine, the FPS changed its stance when work took too long. While awaiting the park's first full camp (up to that time, park work was completed by a side camp from Gold Head) FPS director Malsberger decided the fort was a "ruin" and that only minimal work should be done, since "to go farther would spoil the effect we are trying to achieve."[150] As many in the NPS believed, such rash and irrational decisions were the result of poor park training and planning on Florida's part. According to Park Board member Mrs. Linwood Jeffreys, the NPS officials felt the FPS director and staff should be landscape architects, not foresters.[151] Dependent upon the NPS's leadership and expertise, as well as the CCC labor it controlled, the FPS steered clear of any actions that would jeopardize NPS support. However, administrators on both sides became increasingly vocal about their frustrations.

Several of the interagency conflicts arose out of NPS insistence upon following proper park standards, which was in sharp contrast to the pattern in Florida, where attractions overemphasized an area's "exotic" qualities in both advertising and construction, including the planting of exotics and the removal of unwanted fauna and flora. The NPS believed parks should blend with their surroundings and not detract from the visitor's enjoyment of natural and cultural features. That was why so many parks, including Florida's state parks, used natural, local materials for constructing buildings and other facilities. Use of lime rock, pine, and cypress dominated park structures in Florida. Details as small as which colors park buildings should be painted were a major concern for the NPS. In 1939 Vinten and FPS director H. J. Malsberger had a running argument over whether to paint Gold Head's structures with a uniform stain, as Vinten proposed, or rather with a variety of colors, as Malsberger desired.[152] As was usually the case, Vinten won out. Another time, Malsberger had finished touring Gold Head Branch State Park and promised the veteran enrollees there a baseball park built on park grounds. He then wrote to NPS inspector Vinten to authorize the building of one.[153] Scoggin argued that the enrollees wanted to join a local league, which was always good for park publicity. Vinten refused to allow it, stating that such a ball field would require bleachers, dugouts, and fencing, and it would distract from the park's natural features.[154] Malsberger was so angry at what he considered micromanaging that when he wrote to park workers to tell them the bad news, he could muster little more than: "I do not care to enter into any further correspondence with Mr. Vinten."[155]

For the NPS, planning was the key. The NPS required its parks, and the state park projects with which it was involved, to develop master park plans long before any physical work was undertaken. These master plans were studied, discussed, and altered before the NPS regional offices approved each project. Before the plans passed, the NPS biologists, wildlife technicians, geologists, architects, and landscape architects pored over them, checking for any flaws in design. As Vinten wrote to Malsberger in reference to painting Gold Head's buildings, "evident lack of planning" was unacceptable in the NPS.

The in-depth planning and quality control resulted in lengthy timetables for projects. Local leaders, eager to reap the benefits from an operational state park, wrote often to the FPS director's office demanding results. The FPS was also eager for parks to open for business, out of fear of their becoming obsolete if construction took too long. As Malsberger wrote to Vinten about one project at Florida Caverns State Park, "It does not seem logical that after two years work, the only concrete evidence of progress is about two-thirds completion of the combination building."[156] Highlands Hammock project superintendent A. C. Altvater remembered having to rebuild a wall in one park structure four times before Vinten was satisfied. "The stress was always put on quality."[157] Much of the FPS's frustration began to center upon the project superintendent at Florida Caverns State Park.

Not far from Tallahassee and deep in the heart of politically powerful North Florida, Marianna was a hotbed of political activity. Because of its close proximity to Tallahassee, Florida Caverns State Park, located just outside the Marianna city limits, received more attention from the FPS's central office than any of the other state parks. Tours for prominent groups were a regular feature of the project. Several enrollees spent more time giving tours than they did building the park. The Junior Chamber of Commerce, State Welfare Board, Governor Spessard Holland, the state legislature, and most out-of-state visitors to the capital were given tours of the caverns. With such scrutiny, it was perhaps inevitable that SP-12, and its project superintendent A. D. Lawson (formerly of SP-4 Myakka), would become the target of criticism for directors Malsberger and Scoggin.

The frustration was usually over how long it took for the enrollees to develop the park. At the Torreya side camp, for which Lawson was also superintendent, the FPS lost its first naturalist because the custodian's house was not finished. "We should experience the same difficulties with anyone else we hire until living quarters are provided."[158] Vinten countered that the state had done much too little to meet its park responsibilities.[159] This was a common complaint of the NPS, and one the FPS could not refute. Operating on a minuscule budget and with a small staff, the FPS was dependent upon the NPS and the CCC for nearly everything. Therefore it rarely did more than complain. But when scheduled tours of the caverns for the Junior State Chamber of Commerce and the State Welfare Board were botched, tensions boiled over. As Scoggin complained to Vinten, the State Welfare Board arrived to find the caverns' lighting system malfunctioning and superintendent Lawson nowhere to be found. The tour was rescheduled for the following day, but according to Scoggin the tour guide "was on the toilet. . . . After a most unnecessary delay, the Welfare Board returned to Marianna, and did not get to see the caverns."[160] Scoggin and Malsberger demanded that Lawson be pulled from the project. He was "anything but satisfactory."[161] Vinten reminded them that Lawson was an NPS employee, and threatened that if they did not want him working on the project, then perhaps the NPS would pull out altogether.[162] The FPS backed down, but the bitterness remained.

By 1940 several of Florida's state parks were opened to the public, even as the CCC continued their work on the facilities. Also by 1940, three state parks were already charging admission: Highlands Hammock State Park charged 35 cents a driver and 15 cents for each additional passenger; Gold Head Branch State Park's admission price was a flat 10 cents per visitor; and Hillsborough River State Park charged 25 cents per car. They were open daily from 6:00 a.m. to 7:00 p.m.[163] Vinten, not surprisingly, felt that the fees at Highlands Hammock were financially restrictive, limiting the park's visitation. He recommended that the park install a flat fee of 25 cents per car.[164] Torreya and Fort Clinch opened their gates to the public later that year, with Myakka following in 1941.[165] Gold Head's grand opening on April 15, 1939, attracted well over 3,000 people to the 1,240-acre park for an "all-day dedicatory program."[166] Planned to coincide with the sixth anniversary of the CCC's creation, the grand opening featured over 1,222 pounds of free barbecue, group singing of Stephen Foster songs, a dance sponsored by the Starke American Legion, boat and swimming races, and speeches by state forester Baker, NPS supervisor Vinten, FPS director Malsberger, and camp superintendent Weissinger.[167]

By 1939 Florida was attracting nearly three million visitors annually—the highest number since the end of the land boom.[168] In 1940 Highlands Hammock saw visitors from Indiana, Chicago, Cleveland, Virginia, Alabama, Maine, Minnesota, Boston, and Norway.[169] Gold Head counted more than 6,000 visitors in less than two months.[170] In a 1940 letter attempting to get that park's abandoned CCC camp reoccupied, Vinten wrote enthusiastically that Gold Head was "receiving very encouraging public support. [The cabins] have been very well filled even during the week days [by] a very high class of people."[171] Park staff were especially pleased with such success as a rumor had began circulating in Starke and Jacksonville in 1939 that the park's lakes were contaminated, which briefly but severely hurt attendance.[172] Only after the FPS released an official statement assuring people that the water quality was good did the rumor finally die down. Most surprising was Fort Clinch, which boasted the highest visitation of all the parks, averaging nearly 3,000 visitors per month.[173] Florida tourism had returned, and the FPS, its goal reached, now for the first time had to deal with visitor service issues.

One of the first steps the FPS took was to create a set of rules for visitors.[174] Hunting, vending, advertising, gambling, speeding, and drinking were forbidden within state parks. Also forbidden were "possession of dynamite, dynamite caps, or blasting fuses" as well as "fishing with nets, traps, drugs, or dynamite."[175] Camping was allowed with the park superintendent's approval. Once approval was gained, prospective campers simply looked for any open spot they desired and set up camp. Campers could use dead and fallen trees as firewood. All combustible waste was to be burned, and the rest buried. For their camp fires, campers were to "scrape all vegetative matter down to mineral earth for a distance of five feet from the fire."[176] As FPS brochures reminded visitors: "Fire is the greatest threat to our parks."[177]

Another threat to the parks was the lack of staff. The FPS was still dependent upon CCC labor to handle most of the visitation. Enrollees conducted tours at Fort Clinch, Florida Caverns, and Highlands Hammock. Douglas mentions this fact twice in her 1937 edition of *Parks and Playgrounds of Florida*—first for Gold Head, where "the [CCC] custodian of the property will gladly show you the park or take you to a good picnic area."[178] Then she noted it for Myakka, where "the project superintendent at the CCC camp acts in the capacity of park custodian and he and his staff will gladly show you through the park and will courteously see that you secure whatever accommodations you desire."[179] Superintendent Lawson urged Scoggin to hire more staff to handle the surge in visitation at Torreya and Florida Caverns. "These people in some cases come from a long distance and express keen disappointment and anger," he observed, when the park was closed or tours were canceled because of lack of help.[180] Whoever they hired needed to be "willing to work, and work hard."[181] The situation grew worse in 1941, when another state park was added to the FPS: Oleno State Park, located near Lake City.[182] Built jointly by the local WPA office located in High Springs, Florida, and a Forestry CCC camp out of Olustee, Oleno was designed as a boys' summer camp and a forestry training facility.[183] But with the success of the FPS, Malsberger and the FFS decided to open Oleno up to the public. Its sole employee, Carlos Maxwell, became the park's superintendent.[184] The FPS was on the verge of over-extending itself.

Besides using CCC labor to handle many daily park tasks, Scoggin had to stretch the budget in other ways as well. Park caretakers were originally expected to create subsistence farms so that the parks could "be practically self-sustaining."[185] Concession agreements were another option for funds and labor. At Fort Clinch, Scoggin struck a deal with former traveling showman William Decker. Despite concerns over his German accent, the FPS agreed in 1940 to allow Decker free room and board in exchange for the development of a museum as well as routine park maintenance.[186] The two-year contract allowed Decker to charge ten cents per visitor to the museum and keep all profits made, up to $2,400 a year. Also in 1940, Hillsborough River State Park superintendent Oscar Baynard hired his brother to run a concession and perform routine park duties on a deal similar to Decker's.[187]

In June 1942, however, Scoggin managed to scrape together enough funds to hire the Florida Park Service's first (and for years, only) female field employee.[188] Botanist Carol Beck, later to became the FPS's first chief naturalist, was originally hired to work alongside superintendent Oscar Baynard at Hillsborough River State Park. Her duties were to provide natural education, to design and create exhibits and labels, to write interpretive materials such as program scripts, brochures, and signs, and to make animal and plant surveys and check-lists for all the parks.[189] Yet despite the hiring of Beck, park interpretation and programming remained small in scale. Jim Stevenson, the chief naturalist from 1969 to 1985, described the situation when he started in the FPS in 1965, which apparently closely resembled the 1940s. "There was no park interpretation, no resource management, no law enforcement. All there was [was] maintenance and administration. . . . The only interaction was when the visitor paid the fee at the entrance and if they happened to track a ranger down if they wanted to ask a question. But there was no visitor services. The typical ranger's day was doing maintenance—cleaning restrooms, hauling garbage, mowing grass, repairing buildings, that kind of thing."[190] Stevenson, who knew Beck well and often spoke to her about those early years, described the trouble she faced: "A lot of resistance. It [park interpretation] was new. The old-timers didn't believe in it. So it was a struggle."[191] Unfortunately records of her office no longer exist, but Beck remained in the naturalist position until 1969, when Stevenson replaced her.

Stevenson also provided insight into the nature of park rangering in the FPS's early years. Many of the original rangers were still active when he came along in 1965. As he explained in a 1999 oral history: "There was no training. You hired on, you rode around for a day or part of the day with another ranger or with the assistant superintendent and learned what to do. You learned how to clean a restroom from somebody that's cleaning restrooms."[192] And in the early 1940s cleaning restrooms was about all the park service could handle.[193]

When the idea for a state park system was first seriously considered, Florida had few roadside attractions. Bok Tower, Silver Springs, and McKee's Monkey Jungle were open for business, though not as developed, landscaped, or marketed as they would be in the years to come. But with the success of the fairs and the advertising campaigns, many entrepreneurs realized there was a ready market waiting for exploitation. And when the state began to use the CCC to build parks—coupled with the CCC's efforts constructing several county and city parks—they inspired enough confidence and motivation for many local promoters to leap in.

In 1935 Florida welcomed Monkey Jungle, at Goulds; Ravine Gardens, Palatka; Eagle's Nest Gardens, Bellaire; and Sunken Gardens, St. Petersburg. The following year brought Floating Islands, at Orange Lake; Lewis Plantation and Weeki Wachee, Brooksville; Parrot Jungle, Miami; and Cypress Gardens, Winter Haven. The peak year for new attractions was 1937, with Everglades Wonder Gardens, Famous Trees Botanical Gardens, and Rare Bird Farm, Miami; Florida Wild Animal Ranch, St. Petersburg; Jungle Gardens, Brooksville; Moon Lake Gardens, Dunedin; Oriental Gardens, Jacksonville; Rainbow Springs, Dunellon; and Wakulla Springs, near Tallahassee. Rounding out the decade were Orchid Gardens at Fort Myers; Homosassa Springs; Rattlesnake Headquarters, Kendall; Tropical Hobbyland, Miami; and Marineland Studios, south of St. Augustine. Considering the publicity and visitation Highlands Hammock received—including for its new CCC-constructed Florida Gardens and Arboretum—along with the garden-like aspect of other CCC-built state and county parks, it was no accident that Florida saw a rash of new tourist gardens and "jungles" in the mid- to late 1930s.

Yet despite the financial hardships, the FPS attempted to expand its holdings, no doubt hopeful that CCC labor would last indefinitely. The first effort was Suwannee River State Park near Madison, Florida, in what was then Ellaville. From the start, as board member Harold Foley once explained, "the Florida Board of Forestry has felt . . . that it is highly desirable that a state park be established along the Suwannee River."[194] Local residents in Live Oak created a Suwannee River State Park Association to further those plans.[195] The state purchased the first parcel of 300 acres on June 27, 1936, for $10 from Minnie and S. A. Hinely.[196] Over the next year several other parcels were purchased, the most expensive costing $800 for 80 acres.[197] Tomoka State Park near Ormond Beach on the East Coast came next, with initial land purchases in 1939. While mentioned in several early publications and reports including the 1940 brochure *Florida Parks Invite You* (in which it was called Volusia State Park), the park's current unit management plan asserts that the official acquisition did not begin until 1946.[198] Also acquired in 1939 was the undeveloped 240-acre Pan-American State Park, given to the State of Florida by Robert Hayes Gore, former governor of Puerto Rico.[199] The donated area was strewn with native wild orchids, not surprising as Gore was an avid orchid collector.[200] Bordering on the Everglades and the New River west of Fort Lauderdale in Broward County, it was described by the Florida State Planning Board as "the only sub-tropical area completely unspoiled on the American mainland accessible by water," with "cypress and low-lying lush swamp land" and "several natural streams and rivulets" as well as a "Lost Lake" of "some ten acres which is almost inaccessible on foot" and which was initially "discovered from the air."[201] The park property was never developed by the state—as late as 1951 a bill was introduced to initiate state park development—and it was eventually rolled into the Everglades National Park in the late 1950s.[202]

A fourth park property came as a gift out of the blue. Wealthy Chicago attorney Hugh Taylor Birch decided at the age of ninety-three to donate his land in Fort Lauderdale to the State of Florida for use as a public recreation area. Acquired by the Board of Forestry and Parks on December 31, 1941 (although they would not physically assume ownership until his death in 1943), the gift came after Birch became concerned at the rapid rate of development in South Florida, ironically an indirect result of some of the FPS's attempts to boost tourism. Born in 1848, Birch was a longtime winter resident of South Florida. He first came to the Fort Lauderdale area in 1893 and ten years later began buying shoreline property. Situated between Highway A1A and East Sunrise Boulevard, for some time this would be the second beachfront property the FPS owned. The Florida State Planning Board had been calling for such acquisitions since at least 1937, when it called for a public beach within fifty miles of any community.[203]

The FPS almost succeeded in acquiring more beach property in 1943, however. Repeatedly voted decades later by several recreational organizations as one of the nation's most beautiful and pristine beaches, Little Talbot Island at the time was owned by Florida's State Road Department. The agency offered the property to the then struggling park service. As board member A. B. Edwards argued to Governor Spessard Holland, "It has excellent potential park and recreation advantages.... In view of the large population in the northeast corner of the state, particularly in Duval County, ... the people were entitled to a recreation center, especially on the ocean front. When we are in position to develop it, it should be a valuable adjunct to the park system of the state."[204] It could also have led to more visitors to Fort Clinch on Amelia Island, located just to the north of Talbot Island. At the time, Amelia Island was only accessible to vehicular traffic from the west on A1A by way of Yulee. Edwards argued that this might "lead to the extension of Heckscher Drive, especially through the island to the ultimate construction of a public highway on up the coast to connect with the present coastal highway."[205] Holland concurred, arguing that he believed "a highly desirable state park [could] be developed at the spot which will be utilized by many people from the heavily settled Duval County area."[206] But it was not to be, as Scoggin among others nixed it over concerns of cost and labor.

The most intriguing near miss for the FPS was the historic Fort Caroline on St. Johns Bluff near the mouth of the St. Johns River in Jacksonville. Built by French Huguenots in 1564, the fort site represented the first successful European settlement in North America, pre-dating St. Augustine by over a year and the more celebrated English colony of Jamestown in Virginia by over seventy years. Destroyed by the Spanish in 1565, the fort was never rebuilt. Today historians and archaeologists contend that the site of the original fort is unknown and was likely washed away by the St. Johns River in the late 1800s when the U.S. Army Corps of Engineer built jetties and dug channels that altered the river's course. But in 1943, many believed the site remained intact. The property's biggest booster was a young Jacksonville lawyer and local historian named Charles E. Bennett. For years Bennett worked to convince the state to purchase the site. Governor Holland, who in the 1930s always voted with Senator W. C. Hodges and others to promote Florida tourism, agreed with young Bennett and tried to get the Florida Park Service to buy the property, which was then for sale.[207] While the property had appeared on the two FERA surveys back in 1934 as a highly desirable park property, Scoggin shot down the proposal, again over financial concerns. He suggested that Bennett convince Duval County to buy the property and then donate it to the Florida Park Service.[208] (Instead Bennett waited until he became a representative to the U.S. House of Representatives and orchestrated the creation of a national monument at the historic site nearly twenty years later. And forty years later in 1989, U.S. Representative Bennett created the Timucuan Preserve, a federal umbrella organization that united Little Talbot Island and Fort Clinch state parks with Fort Caroline National Monument, Kingsley Plantation National Historic Site—formerly a state park from the 1950s until 1989—and Huguenot City Park.)

Despite these expansion attempts, the Florida Park Service would have to wait for the postwar economic and tourism boom to expand, a growth that was further fueled by the merging of the Board of Historical Memorials with the newly independent park service in 1949. Tomoka State Park would begin development in 1946, as would Hugh Taylor Birch State Park (as it came to be known). Suwannee River State Park opened to the public in 1951. And even Little Talbot Island eventually emerged as a state park in 1952, complete with two beaches and two entrances: North Beach for white visitors, and South Beach for African Americans. But in the early 1940s, the FPS would remain an organization of only the eight parks funded almost entirely through federal relief dollars.

For the immediate future Scoggin managed to avert financial disaster, but his dependence on CCC labor would soon prove problematic. For the nation was on the brink of world war, even as the NPS and enrollees continued to build Florida's state parks and superintendents dealt with ever-increasing visitation, and the Civilian Conservation Corps and Florida tourism would become two of its earliest casualties.

Figure 1. May Mann Jennings became a leader in the Florida Forestry Association, founded in the 1920s. State Archives of Florida, Florida Memory, https://www.floridamemory.com/items/show/136897.

Figure 2. Governor Dave Sholtz signing the Florida Park Service into existence, 1935. State forester Harry Lee Baker is on the left. State Archives of Florida, Florida Memory, https://www.florida memory.com/items/show/136951.

Figure 3. Organizers of Florida National Exhibits (*left to right*): Lorenzo Wilson, Nathan Mayo, Ed Ball, Earl Brown, and William C. Hodges, Tallahassee, 1930s. State Archives of Florida, Florida Memory, https://www.floridamemory.com/items/show/10275.

Figure 4. Florida Exhibition boat (with John Roebling's Sky Ride in rear) at the Century of Progress Exhibition in Chicago, 1933. State Archives of Florida, Florida Memory, https://www.floridamemory.com/items/show/157423.

Figure 5. CCC enrollees planting trees in Madison County, 1935. State Archives of Florida, Florida Memory, https://www.floridamemory.com/items/show/62638.

Figure 6. CCC reconstructing the Gregory House at Torreya State Park, 1937. State Archives of Florida, Florida Memory, https://www.floridamemory.com/items/show/150122.

Figure 7. CCC camp at Gold Head Branch State Park, 1930s. State Archives of Florida, Florida Memory, https://www.floridamemory.com/items/show/116189.

Figure 8. Marjorie Kinnan Rawlings at her home in Cross Creek, 1940s. Today her home is a state park. State Archives of Florida, Florida Memory, https://www.floridamemory.com/items/show/28042.

Figure 9. An early depiction of a Florida cracker, from *Harper's New Monthly Magazine*, 1871. State Archives of Florida, Florida Memory, https://www.floridamemory.com/items/show/154288.

Figure 10. A cow being dipped in arsenic solution to eradicate ticks, Duval County. State Archives of Florida, Florida Memory, https://www.floridamemory.com/items/show/1349.

Figure 11. A turpentine worker with longleaf pine, 1910s. Note the cleared understory—evidence of regular controlled burning. State Archives of Florida, Florida Memory, https://www.floridamemory.com/items/show/151994.

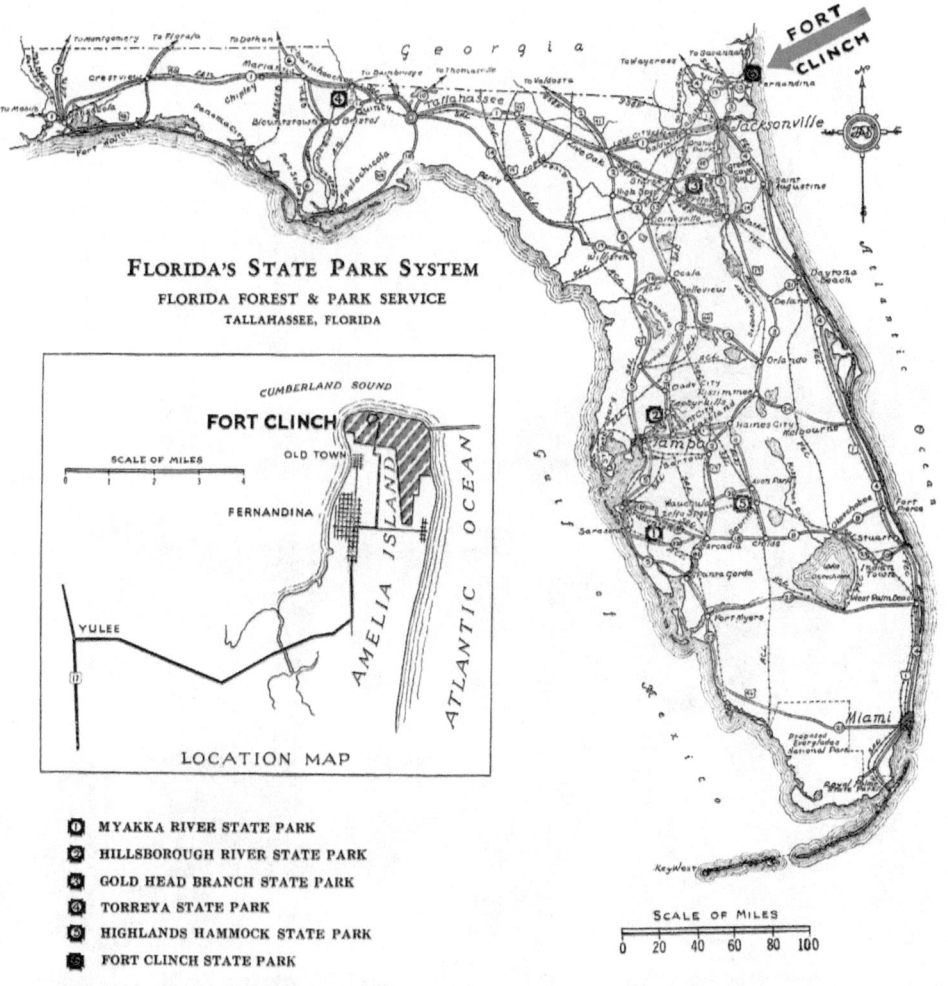

Figure 12. A map of Florida state parks from a Fort Clinch State Park brochure, 1939. From author's collection.

Figure 13. View of the Florida Exhibit at the New York World's Fair, 1939. State Archives of Florida, Florida Memory, https://www.floridamemory.com/items/show/12086.

Figure 14. Detail of one of the original dioramas from the 1939 New York World's Fair for Stephen Foster's "Old Folks at Home," now housed at the Foster Memorial in White Springs, Florida. Photo taken by Francis Johnson, 1953. State Archives of Florida, Florida Memory, https://www.floridamemory.com/items/show/71744.

6

Florida's Welfare State Parks

THE CCC AT WORK AND AT PLAY

It usually began by word of mouth—often from a brother or a friend who joined first. In some cases it was a neighbor. As one veteran said of a nearby family with an enrollee, "You could tell that the $25 pushed that family up. They ate good."[1] Another veteran said he hoped to join because he "was looking for groceries on the table."[2] As he went on to explain, in the CCC "you had a place to stay, you had groceries to eat and you had exercise . . . just about everything you needed."[3] Many were also eager to leave home. "I just wanted to get off the farm," remembered another CCC enrollee.[4] Uncritical newspaper and newsreel stories also extolled the program's virtues and added to the lure. But regardless of the reasons, the Civilian Conservation Corps enjoyed a good reputation in Florida and had no problem meeting the state's quota of CCC enlistees each year. The need and desire was so great that the CCC had little need to advertise.

The few brochures that did appear in the program's later years left little doubt of the CCC's benefits. With titles such as *Builder of Men* and *Work Experience That Counts*, the propaganda used simple repetitive language (words over two syllables were rarely used) aimed at addressing the twin worries of most young men in the 1930s: work and food.[5] Calling the CCC "a school of work and experience," one brochure featured a photo of a shirtless enrollee lifting a heavy log as his friends watch in amazement—masculinity obtained through steady work.[6] And for the other concern for young men in the 1930s, the advertisements were likewise persuasive. As another brochure declared, "three times a day, CCC enrollees get ravenously hungry, and three times a day, they eat their fill of good food."[7]

Once interested, young men were directed to visit their local recruiting office, where CCC selecting agents were waiting. Under the jurisdiction of the state's selection director—Jack Horne of the State Welfare Board—the agents followed a list of guidelines to determine a candidate's eligibility. A CCC enrollee had to be between seventeen and twenty-five, unmarried, unemployed, not currently in school, a U.S. citizen, and "of good character."[8] Anyone who had been convicted of a felony, previously dishonorably discharged from the CCC, or unable to perform hard labor was ineligible.[9] Coercion, pressure, and discrimination "of any kind" were to be avoided at all costs by the selection agents.[10] Agents were also to stress that despite the U.S. Army's involvement, the CCC was a non-military, voluntary agency. In overall procedure, nevertheless, CCC offices "were more or less like an army recruiting station . . . there was an officer sitting up there in a central place, and you go in and you sign up."[11]

Once it was decided they were qualified for work relief, candidates were asked to fill out applications, listing their physical attributes, health history (especially of communicable diseases—a consistent concern for the CCC), and family's financial situation. Then came the physical exams.[12] Enlistments were for six-month periods, and candidates were told to be at the departure point on a specified date.[13] Instructed to bring only one suitcase with toiletries, one suit, and a musical instrument if they possessed one, the enrollees—as they were known from this point on—were then sent to conditioning camps.[14]

Run by the U.S. Army, conditioning camps were designed to acquaint the enrollees with army-style life. On a WJAX radio show, Florida State Supervisor of Selection Jack Horne, when asked if he "had to deal with a lot of softies," answered that this was not a problem thanks to the conditioning camps.[15] By 1939, 31,491 Floridians had been through the CCC's conditioning camps.[16] On the first day, enrollees were given haircuts, issued two sets of clothes (dress khakis and work denims), given a trunk, and assigned to a company.[17] Along with the daily exercise regime and educational lectures, enrollees received shots for typhoid fever, smallpox, and parathyroid.[18] This was most enrollees' first experience with a regimented, structured lifestyle. "You talk about hollering and swearing and jumping. We were just on pins and needles all the time because you did not know what you were doing."[19] Many "caught hell because they did not know what was expected of them."[20] Over time most came to realize that life as a CCC enrollee was less strenuous than that of a soldier. "It was not like military. We had a little freedom, not like the military. We had to follow the rules, though. We had rules that we had to maintain," explained one former enrollee. "You can't go out. You have to work in the daytime, you can't just take off whenever you want to, or anything like that. [It was as] simple as that. We had to go to work. And take care of ourselves. And keep clean. You can't be going around like a bum."[21]

Most enrollees from Florida were stationed at Fort Benning in western Georgia, though a few were sent to Fort Barracas in West Florida.[22] As CCC veteran George LeCouris remembered of Fort Benning: "We got our inoculation, and we lived in tents. They had these tents up there, and everything.... We slept in tents and cots, but we had to go down to the horse barn, and get straw to put in our mattress."[23] Once the two-week stint was up, the companies were sent on to their assignments. "We got our bedding, our canteens, and our mess plates," explained LeCouris. "And things that you would need in camp. So when we left out of there, we left as a convoy . . . [and] we came down into Florida."[24]

Beginning in 1934 several CCC companies were sent to Florida for state park projects operated under the jurisdiction of the National Park Service.[25] Florida now had the free labor it needed to build its new Florida Park Service and restart Florida tourism.

The CCC enrollees were the Florida Park Service's labor force. At the time the FPS consisted of little more than a director, an assistant, and a procurement officer. The first park superintendent was not hired until the late 1930s, and the first rangers date from the early 1940s. Until World War II the CCC's staff and enrollees were the de facto park rangers. They were the public face of the FPS. But park construction and management were not on the enrollees' main agenda. They enlisted for money, food, social activities, training, and education. The state parks were merely the means to an end.

Most of the enrollees who worked on state park projects were young Floridians. Many, such as enrollee Fred White, who helped develop Fort Clinch State Park, were from sharecropping families. White dropped out of school in the third grade and was plowing fields by the age of nine.[26] Talmadge Holmes was also from a sharecropping family—for strawberry farmers in Hillsborough County.[27] He was educated in the strawberry schools for migrant families. Enrollee James Keene came from a family of "citrus pickers," while Fort Clinch and Gold Head Branch state parks enrollee Hillary

Cowart's father worked as a minister and a fish hatchery operator.[28] Over 50 percent of the enrollees were from rural areas, and most had not finished high school.[29] Many signed up to help ease their families' financial burdens. "Back then, you could live pretty well off $25 a month," explained one former enrollee.[30] Paul DeGirolamo, who would work at Highlands Hammock State Park while in the CCC, described the effect that his older brother's check from the CCC had on his family: "At that time, that money, you know, you could buy a lot of stuff with twenty-five dollars. I remember when I used to go to the grocery store with mother. Heck, with twenty-five dollars a four-wheeled wagon would just be loaded up with goodies."[31] When his brother left, DeGirolamo decided to go in. "With ten children, we needed the help. . . . And I only stayed six months. Got a little homesick."[32] Beyond work relief, there was little else available to them. CCC veteran Talmadge Holmes best summed up the enrollees' Depression experience as "pretty rough."[33]

But junior enrollees—as those enrollees under twenty-five were called—were not the only CCC companies to serve on Florida state park projects. Because of the large number of permanent structures required by the state park plans, World War I veteran companies—with their more advanced skills and experience—served at all the state park camps except Hillsborough River and Oleno state parks.[34] Called "the career men of the CCC" by historian John Salmond, WWI veteran companies were normally used during the final stages of a park's development and provided the polish of a finished park.[35]

Finally, in addition to the enrollees there were the LEMs—the "local experienced men"—who were hired by the CCC to offer guidance and knowledge to projects. Salmond stresses that LEMs were "vital to the initial success of the whole CCC venture."[36] Soon after the CCC's creation, Fechner and others realized that unskilled young workers—even under the supervision of the army, the USFS, and the NPS—needed direction and guidance. On April 22, 1933, it was decided to hire unemployed local talent to supplement the enrollees' efforts and to serve as their mentors. In the Florida state park projects that extra guidance was crucial. While there were usually eight LEMs per CCC camp, the FPS camps had an average of fourteen.[37]

Because the first state parks were nothing more than undeveloped wilderness—they were not even fenced off—early state park camps in Florida were primitive affairs. Enrollees lived in army tents as they built their camps, used crudely constructed "straddle pit" latrines, and drank from hand-dug wells. Often roads had to be cleared just to reach the campsites. An enrollee who was stationed at a forestry camp in Olustee, near Lake City in northern Central Florida, described life in an early CCC camp: "We had to build a camp . . . no toilets, no facilities. We had to have tents, and they provided cots. We got moss from the trees and made a mattress for the cots."[38] Even the sanitary improvements after a couple of weeks offered little relief. "Later, they built a big kiln where they had these toilets that were made of iron. They set up on a platform, and underneath was a furnace. They'd get wood from the woods, and build a fire there, and just incinerate the waste. . . . when they'd have a burn, the wind would blow it right through the mess hall where we ate."[39] In 1936 CCC director Robert Fechner required that all camps consist only of pre-fabricated buildings.[40]

Most campsites were located on high, dry ground that required little clearing. At Torreya the camp was on a bluff a hundred feet above the Apalachicola River. Gold Head Branch State Park's camp was also on high, sandy ground. The camp for Hillsborough River State Park was twenty miles away in Sulphur Springs, on the banks of the freshwater spring, a few miles north of Tampa. At Fort Clinch the CCC stayed just outside Fernandina city limits on northern Amelia Island, approximately a mile from the park boundaries, in barracks with no screens or windows.[41] Bedbugs and mosquitoes were a major problem for the Fort Clinch–stationed enrollees. The Florida Caverns State Park company camped on the grounds of the West Florida Industrial School before they converted the dorms into barracks.

The most inhospitable location was Myakka River State Park's campsite, situated on the bank of the slow, meandering Myakka River, which was prone to yearly flooding. Because the park consisted of 20,000 acres of prairie, the river's bank was the only shaded area for miles around. While the army, which had final say on CCC campsite locations, expressed concerns over mosquitoes and water supplies, they were assured by District Forester Carl Bohleber and Myakka's Project Superintendent A. B. Edwards that the river's flow meant "the mosquitoes would not breed out there like they do along the coast" and that for "ten months in the year the Myakka River valleys are practically free from mosquitoes."[42] In addition, the site, located "right on the bank of the Myakka River on the left hand side of the road, just before you cross the bridge on the Sugar Bowl Road to Arcadia," featured a four-inch artesian well that had a "very strong flow of water."[43] But the well proved too sulphuric to be potable, and the mosquitoes were often unbearable. The lack of adequate facilities for the first months meant bathing was usually done in the alligator-infested river.[44] Malaria was common among the enrollees.[45] Flooding was also common. Along with the soggy conditions, Myakka State Park was also prime snake habitat. In the first two months of the camp's existence, enrollees killed well over thirty rattlesnakes. A survey crew killed one rattlesnake that measured over seven feet long.[46] Hunting and hiding rattlesnakes became a hobby for many of the junior enrollees. Staged snake fights between rattlers and King snakes were common leisure activities.[47] Newsletters often reported on the numbers of snakes killed per month.[48] In 1939 the camp relocated approximately a mile from its original site. The river's yearly flooding had taken its toll on the patience of the army and the project superintendent.[49]

The CCC workers stationed at Highlands Hammock State Park lived a wholly different life. Because of the Roeblings' $300,000 contribution, the park itself was a finished product by 1934 when the first enrollees arrived. Their job was to build the Florida Gardens and State Arboretum, not to develop the state park (although the various CCC companies stationed at the park continued to add to the park facilities). The first company to arrive was the New York–based Company 453, fresh from work at May Mann Jennings's Royal Palm State Park. They were housed three miles southwest of the park on the grounds of the lodge on Rex Beach Lake.[50] DeGirolamo remembers: "We had cabins all along the lake, and there were six people in the cabin. . . . We had a nice big mess hall." About the only complaint camp residents had involved insects. "We used to have these mosquito bars [fine-mesh mosquito-netting] at night—the mosquitoes were bad at the time," explained DeGirolamo.[51] Ticks were also a problem, explained another former resident. "Most ticks I ever seen in my life in one place. Just a whole handful."[52]

Generally the first building constructed at a CCC camp was the garage, followed in succession by the supply house, mess hall, barracks, officers' quarters, project supervisor's office, and infirmary.[53] At Myakka, for example, it was a month before the barracks were constructed. As time and labor permitted, other buildings were added to the camps, including flush-toilet latrines, recreational halls, libraries, workshops, and storage sheds. Along with a parade ground, flagpole, and playing field, these features were the basic elements of most CCC camps in Florida. Specialized structures were often added as projects developed. For instance, the Highlands Hammock company built a nursery because they were constructing a garden and arboretum. Gold Head Branch State Park had a sawmill to supply lumber for the vacation cabins being built.[54]

Most CCC camps were set up in the same manner. The U.S. Army was in charge of all in-camp activities. They provided cooking, supplies, medical care, religious outlets, transportation, and leadership.[55] "The Army is their provider and tailor, doctor and teacher, spiritual advisor and paymaster," wrote CCC promoter Ray Hoyt in *We Can Take It*.[56] The U.S. Army divided the nation into nine corps areas, each headed by a major general.[57] Florida was located within the army's Fourth Corps area, headed by General George Van Horn Mosely, who wanted military discipline for the enrollees.[58] In charge of the entire operation at the camp level was the camp commander, the camp's highest-ranking army officer. He had full authority over the camp. The camp commander, also known as the commanding officer (CO), set the rules and regulations for the camp and settled any disputes between enrollees and between camp staff.[59] Second in command was the subaltern, followed by the camp doctor.[60] While most in the army looked upon the CCC camps as more of a nuisance than an opportunity, they were determined to maintain military discipline at all times. Perhaps due to the army's lackluster opinion of the CCC, most camps had several COs over time.

While the army ran the camps, the National Park Service oversaw all matters concerning park development.[61] The project superintendent, an NPS employee, was in charge of the park construction. He made the work orders, chose the LEMs, consulted with the NPS and the FPS to develop park plans, divided up the work duties, gathered supplies, wrote progress reports, and appointed camp leaders. Generally project superintendents divided enrollees into anywhere between five and eight work crews, each with a specific task. For instance, at Highlands Hammock, work crews included picnic bench making, furniture making, nursery management, building construction, road clearing, and trail development.[62] Each work crew had its own leader, sometimes an LEM, other times an enrollee from the ranks.

The day usually began with a 5:45 a.m. reveille, followed by exercise, barracks cleaning, and breakfast.[63] By 7:00 a.m. the enrollees received their job assignments and were transported to the work sites. Enrollees worked eight-hour days, forty hours a week. They usually ate lunch in the field out of mess kits and returned to camp between 4:00 and 5:00 in the evening.⁶⁴ After dinner the rest of the day was spent either in classes or as free time. Weekends were also considered free time for the enrollees, provided the camp was clean and passed the CO's inspection. Often enrollees were required to watch for forest fires or perform KP (kitchen patrol) duties, usually on rotation.⁶⁵ At Hillsborough River State park, because their campsite was located over twenty miles away, enrollees took turns patrolling the park on weekends. Once, when Leonard Hendry and another enrollee were patrolling the park, a major storm broke, flooding the park. "We had to stay out there a whole week."⁶⁶ Hendry and companion had nothing to eat by the third day but bread and onions, and they spent most of their time beating back snakes off their cabin's porch.⁶⁷ Sometimes enrollees were issued leave time, which allowed them to visit family and friends. Other times, the army provided transportation for recreational field trips to surrounding areas. The earliest such trip was made by Highlands Hammock enrollees to Bok Tower in August 1934.⁶⁸

The CCC offered two types of jobs: those that were required at all CCC camps, including truck drivers, clerks, cooks, leaders, mechanic helpers, and night guards; and those that were camp and project specific.⁶⁹ These latter jobs included dam building, tree planting, building construction, landscaping, drafting, carpentry, wildlife management, and survey work.⁷⁰ In Florida state parks the jobs included fence building, landscape design, road construction, trail clearing, forest fire prevention, building construction, dynamiting tree stumps, building culverts and mosquito ditches, historic restoration, and sign painting.⁷¹ While these project jobs were done without the aid of power tools and with little work experience, there were few problems getting them accomplished. The lack of administrative and office skills of the enrollees and the locals, however, often made such duties hard to complete. Highlands Hammock Project Superintendent A. C. Altvater complained to his superiors: "Every effort has been made to obtain a competent clerk from the ranks of the enrolled men, or by inducting a LEM, but these efforts have all failed."⁷² As an antidote to the often grueling manual labor of park development, some enrollees turned to KP duty for relief. "We had to dig up stumps and palmettos," explained one enrollee. "I did that for two or three weeks before I decided that I wasn't much of a person for something like that, so I got a job in the kitchen."⁷³

Staff in the kitchen were usually the most popular people in the camp. That was because of the near universal opinion that the CCC served excellent food. Almost every article, interview, or brochure on the CCC mentioned the quality of food found in CCC camps. "It wasn't how your mother cooked. But it was good," remembered one enrollee.[74] According to Florida State Welfare Commissioner C. C. Codrington, the CCC spent forty-six cents a day per person on food. "Every man gets five pounds of food per day."[75] An oft-stated bit of trivia of the CCC is the average weight gain for enrollees within the first six weeks—twelve pounds. Former enrollee Malcolm Oliver remembers, "When I went into the CCC, I weighed 127 pounds and I had a 27-inch waist. From August the 9th till December the 18th or somewhere along there, I went back home and I weighed 156 pounds. I still had a 27-inch waist, and I was as hard as that wall there, just like a brick."[76] Then again, Oliver's experience was above the norm due to his role at Highlands Hammock as his camp's cook. He explained that after suffering a work-related illness, "I stayed in the kitchen. . . . I finally wound up as mess hall director. In other words I was responsible for setting the tables, lining them up, you know you had to do it army style. The knives and forks had to be in a straight line. Every cup had to be in line and I just had to see that it was taken care of. The first and second cook would pass down an order [and] you go make the biscuit or you make the cornbread or you make the pot roast. I was cooking for 250 men. I'd make cornbread, biscuits, rolls, cooked beans, greens or whatever was to be cooked. Meat, eggs."[77] Not everyone was as happy in the kitchen, though. "If you wasn't careful they'd put you in the kitchen peeling spuds," remembered fellow Highlands Hammock enrollee Ansley Hall. "That's the part I didn't care much about. I got to where I could go wash dishes for over 200 men. If all the stuff was brought to me to the sink and I could wash it and someone would take it away I could wash dishes for 200 men in 45 minutes."[78]

Meals were abundant in meats, starches, and vegetables and usually ended with a dessert. A menu found in the Highlands Hammock State Park camp inspection report from 1935 is typical for CCC meals.[79] On Monday breakfast included eggs, cornflakes, milk, grapefruit, coffee, bread, oats, and juice. Lunch consisted of baked beans and pork, boiled potatoes, buttered beets, dill pickles, salad, grape drink, bread, and butter. That evening's dinner was fried beef liver, fried onions, sweet potatoes, fried peppers, tea, bread and butter, cocoa, and bananas. The menu for the rest of the week was in the same vein. For the enrollees in the middle of the Great Depression, these meals must have been a daily feast. It was a long way from corn meal, dried beans, and salt pork. As a former enrollee pointed out, "Nobody ever turned down food."[80] "Yeah, we had good food," remembered another.[81]

To ensure that the food and other conditions at the camps were satisfactory, the Office of the Director of the CCC conducted annual inspections of their camps. These inspections graded camps on their sanitation, recreational activities, budgets, dietary provisions, safety program, educational efforts, morale, equipment, and the camp's facilities. For Florida camps Neill Coney Jr. conducted all the inspections for the full nine years of the CCC program. The resultant inspection reports serve as a window into the camps' operations, as they listed menus, numbers of enrollees, size of park, nature of work accomplished, types of buildings in camp, classes offered, sports played, and even the types of toilets used.[82] Venereal diseases were a prime concern for inspectors, who noted how often the enrollees were inspected medically—which was usually once a month. Those on the kitchen staff were checked more often, normally once a week. At Gold Head Branch State Park, veteran company 2444 set up a "prophylactic facility" to combat VD.[83] Typical citations for camp commanders included rotten wood found in buildings, lack of proper lighting in latrines, sandy walkways, unsafe vehicles, and poor paint jobs.[84] At the Hillsborough River State Park CCC camp, which was located several miles away in Sulphur Springs, the administration was criticized in a 1937 report for "inadequate" bathing facilities, and the barracks were deemed "too crowded for good sanitation."[85] The camp with the most consistently favorable inspections was Gold Head Branch State Park, while Fort Clinch State Park was the most often criticized—usually for its dilapidated buildings and camp grounds. To counteract any possible complaints of socialism, the CCC director's office had inspectors check for any communistic influences in the camps. According to the camp inspection reports, the Florida state park CCC camps were free of radicals.

The main concern of all the inspections was the safety and welfare of the enrollees. An inspection in 1935 of Highlands Hammock (SP-3) shows just how concerned the CCC was about its enrollees and about offsetting any complaints about their treatment. In February 1936 Neill Coney wrote to Assistant Director James McEntee that SP-3 project superintendent A. C. Altvater was working the camp's enrollees in two crews for twelve-hour days alternately, giving them every other day off.[86] The practice "does not seem to be within the spirit of the regulations on this subject."[87] Further, because the alternating workdays included Saturdays, the practice meant that Sundays were the only days when equipment was cleaned and repaired, "robbing some people of a day off."[88] But as Altvater reported in December 1935, the camp suffered from a "lack of adequate transportation," and there were "times when two hours elapsed between the arrival of first and last man on the job."[89] It often took more than two weeks for the camp to receive parts for repairs on the few trucks the camp possessed, Altvater complained.[90] McEntee responded to Coney's letter by contacting NPS Assistant Director Conrad Wirth to look into the "direct violation of the regulation."[91] Finally, in April 1936, Herbert Evison, NPS deputy assistant director, wrote to McEntee that after a special inspection by Florida's NPS inspector C. R. Vinten, the practice had stopped, although the practice "was the enrollees' idea."[92]

Another concern for the CCC was the hazing of rookies—as new enrollees were called—by their fellow enrollees. Often the army took part in this, such as by sending rookie enrollees on searches for left-handed wrenches or latrine oil.[93] But a letter from an enrollee's mother to Florida Governor Fred Cone revealed that the practice often took a more malicious turn. She described how "rough necks" would get drunk, physically abuse the new rookies, and once "even threw a knife at one of the boys."[94] In response the CCC's director of selection W. Frank Persons wrote to Jack Horne that "excessive hazing" was becoming a problem.[95] Although hazing was never reported for any of Florida's state park camps, it did occur. Fort Clinch enrollee Hillary Cowart described how one of the leaders roamed the barracks intoxicated and beat the rookies in the camp: "He would start on one side and he would go down the thing, whipping somebody."[96] Myakka River State Park's camp newsletter explained how its hazing ritual worked. Called the belt line, it involved rookies running the gauntlet between "two lines of boys armed with belts."[97] "The Monday night recruits were given the works Tuesday afternoon," the account noted. The Myakka enrollees also ran a kangaroo court that found all rookies guilty. They either had to pay the others in cash or suffered a paddling. "Quite a few bought out as the pants they wore were thin, and the paddles hot."[98] Buck Heath described an incident at Florida Caverns:

We had this boy in the company. He was a bully; he'd haze the new people.... So he told this boy one night, "Go up there to the captain's office and get some striped paint—we got to paint the flagpole." So the old dumb country boy . . . the captain was in his office and he went over there . . . and he said, "I come up here to get some striped paint." [The captain] said, "Okay. Can you show me who told you to do that?" The next four or five nights that old boy didn't come in until ten o'clock—the captain had him out there in the woods hunting some striped paint. I bet he never hazed nobody else.[99]

Despite the inspections and other precautions, life in a CCC camp was not worry-free. Accidents were common, especially among the junior enrollees. There were often mishaps with trucks, tools, and each other. At Highlands Hammock, the Highlands County forester cited the young enrollees for several fires that originated in the camp, which led to the firing of the camp's commander.[100] Also at Highlands Hammock, Company 262 member Albert Oliva drowned while swimming in Rex Beach Lake.[101] The most serious accident within a state park CCC camp occurred at Torreya State Park in Liberty County. One of the major projects at the park was the dismantling and floating down the Apalachicola River to the park grounds of an antebellum mansion, the aforementioned Gregory House. On one trip the overloaded barge tipped, dumping into the turbulent river the enrollees operating it. Two enrollees could not swim and drowned.[102]

But the work projects were only eight hours a day, five days a week. Therefore once the work was finished for the day, enrollees had many hours in which to find ways to occupy themselves. Sports, girls, beer, movies, and evening classes were the major leisure activities, usually in that order of priority. There were also games, radio, music, fishing, and staged shows. Life in a CCC camp was more akin to a summer camp than to the army or a steady job.

Sports constituted the prime off-hour activities. Every kind of organized sport could be found in camp. These games were encouraged by both the army and the CCC to promote team building, social skills, and athletic prowess. Sports played at Florida's state park camps included baseball, basketball, volleyball, horseshoes, boxing, swimming, track, football, and softball.[103] Baseball teams were organized at all the camps, and most were members of city and regional leagues. This was also true in the winter for the basketball teams. Camp newspapers were full of stories and box scores for CCC baseball and basketball games. But the sport that received the most attention from the U.S. Army was boxing.

Just as they did while training soldiers during the First World War, the army used boxing to settle disputes within the CCC camps.[104] And CCC boxing bouts were also popular public events. At Myakka enrollees fought weekly at the Sarasota American Legion Arena.[105] As the popularity of the fights grew, the enrollees built a regulation-sized boxing ring in the camp's recreation hall. The only state park camp in Florida that did not have boxing at all was Gold Head Branch State Park, home to a veterans' company. Its youngest member was thirty-four years old, and its oldest was sixty-three.[106] While this was never directly stated, it is probable that the army used boxing as a subtle method of training potential recruits for warfare. It also served as a way to relieve much of the aggression and tension (sexual and otherwise) inherent in groups of young single men.

And boxing was indeed popular among the enrollees. "If you want to get in the ring with somebody," explained one enrollee, "all you had to do was tell him—he'd crawl in there. He wasn't afraid of you. They [the U.S. Army] had rings and somebody would referee it. They'd say, 'Hey, come over here and referee these. . . . ' Nobody in particular but just anybody. But when you said, 'Stop,' they stopped, too."[107] Another from Highlands Hammock explained, "It was just more or less for fun. No [one] was mad at each other. You know, just get in there and box. I took a crack at it."[108] But not all was fun and games, remembered Malcolm Oliver, also of Highlands Hammock:

> But the bad part about [boxing] . . . was you'd go into a new camp and of course you're the rookie. And some of the fellows that I went to this camp with told them that [I] used to fight a little in the ring in Florida. . . . And they matched me up with a fellow who was a professional. And of course you know being in the ring and doing a little fighting I could tell. . . . It was a frame up . . . Well I got in the ring with him and I kept him off of me for that first round. But it made me angry to think that they would want to have some fun out of me. They wanted to see him knock me out, you know. So when the first round was over I told them to take these gloves off of me. . . . I got angry and I wouldn't fight with him anymore.[109]

Dances and other social events with the local girls also served to relieve frustration and sexual tension among the enrollees. Often the army volunteered to transport local girls to Friday night dances in the camps. At Highlands Hammock, girls from the Lake Bird Lodge, a vocational school for girls, visited the park several times for dances.[110] At one dance enrollees were given initialed handkerchiefs and each had to locate the girl with initials matching those on the handkerchief.[111] That dance, like most, consisted of music, dancing, ice cream, cake, tea, and a show put on by the enrollees.[112] At one Myakka dance the army hired a local orchestra to provide the music.[113] Enrollees from the local areas were also encouraged to bring their girlfriends. Aside from the dances, enrollees found other chances to meet girls during trips to the local towns, such as at the movie theatres, local restaurants, and ice cream shops. Quick to recognize this new breed of consumer, such businesses placed ads in CCC camp newsletters, offering special discounts to entice the enrollees. Although enrollees were allowed to keep only five of their monthly thirty dollars, that was enough to fund several romantic evenings, which trumped the wallets of other would-be Romeos. "We had $5 to spend that they did not have," explained former enrollee Willie O'Neal.[114]

In addition to romantic endeavors, the U.S. Army also transported CCC enrollees to local towns on weekends. This influx of federal funds into the local economy—via the enrollees' monthly five dollars (which was in addition to the camp's purchasing of food and supplies)—was one of the attractions of having a CCC camp. "We went in Army trucks, yeah," remembered one enrollee. "We'd leave town about eleven o'clock [p.m.] to go back to camp. Then on Sunday, you could go back."[115] Ansley Hall of Highlands Hammock explained, "The only trouble about going to town if you couldn't catch a ride [was] you'd have to walk to town."[116] Beyond the excitement of escaping from camp, entertainment opportunities were limited in small-town Florida in the 1930s. The food offered at camp generally surpassed the local cuisine. The U.S. Army provided church services on Sunday mornings—at least for Christian enrollees. And as one enrollee described it, the problem with shopping was "the limitation of where to put some of that stuff. You had a footlocker and you cram it down in there. There was no other place."[117] Enrollee Thomas Hutchison spent his first wages going to the movies. "It cost twenty-five cents and I said, 'No, that costs too much. I don't want to be going back there,' which I didn't."[118] But despite Hutchison's experience, watching

Hollywood films was by far the most popular off-campus activity. Enrollee George LeCouris echoed a sentiment many shared: "When we went to town, most of the times [it was] to the picture show. That was the main thing. Why go sit around in the park? Unless you had a girlfriend. But most of the time, you went to the movie show."[119]

Yet most enrollees spent their money in camp at the local canteen, which was usually located in the recreation hall. The canteen sold candy, cigarettes, matchbooks, toiletries, writing paper, and other necessities. Some camps used canteen booklets, small pieces of paper stapled together inside a cover, as cash, which was purchased at the beginning of the month by the enrollee. This reduced opportunities for losing cash while providing enrollees with small discounts for using canteen coupons. A cover on an issue of the *Myakka Rattler* demonstrated the importance of the canteen to enrollees. It read: "The saddest words in tongue or pen—My canteen book is gone again."[120]

Also located in the recreation hall were the camp's games and its radio. The 1930s were a golden age for table games, including bridge, Parcheesi, Monopoly, checkers, and poker. Games were cheap, usually required little skill, and could be played anywhere at any time. Puzzles were also prevalent in the 1930s.[121] Most enrollees grew up listening to the radio. Some of the most popular radio shows of the time included *Amos and Andy*, *Little Orphan Annie*, *Jungle Jim*, and *The Shadow*.[122] Crooners Rudy Vallee and Bing Crosby, swing pop artists such as Benny Goodman, and western and hillbilly music were also available on the camp's radio.[123] Disputes over the radio were common in CCC camps.

But another activity that attracted many enrollees in the evenings was attending night classes. Although not talked about as much today, education was the most publicized feature of the CCC during the 1930s and 1940s. For many supporters, the educational aspects of the CCC were what legitimized the quasi-military relief agency. In a 1940 publication sociologist Marian Wright wrote that the CCC could "easily justify its existence" on its education alone.[124] Promotional articles and brochures always made it a point to emphasize that the CCC was about "the conservation of natural as well as human resources."[125] The educational goals of the program were designed to make enrollees "more employable and better citizens" through a program of academic and vocational training.[126] Many, including the U.S. Army and CCC director Robert Fechner, wanted a more vocational-centered "learn by doing" program.[127] As one army officer expressed it, "We have in our charge poor boys who should be taught how to earn a living, not how to make a rug."[128] But New Dealers strove to instill an academic slant to the education, focusing especially upon eradicating illiteracy.[129] They also wanted to emphasize developing healthy social skills, such as proper personal hygiene, cooperation with others, worthy use of one's leisure time, and good work habits like adhering to "factory time."[130] As the nation mobilized for World War II in the early 1940s, some promotional brochures began to link education with creating patriotic citizens who were valuable members of the "American democracy."[131] The CCC educational program remained popular with the public throughout its run.

Yet education, which was not originally included in the organization of the CCC, was often the most controversial aspect for the agency's leaders. W. Frank Persons, who was in charge of the CCC selection division, was directly responsible for its inclusion with his idea in May 1933 of having an educational advisor at each camp. This notion soon caught on with Ickes, Roosevelt, and most important, Commissioner of Education George Zook.[132] Soon thereafter, Harold Oxley was chosen as director of CCC education and oversaw the selection and management of the camps' educational advisors. But not everyone in the federal government supported expanded education for the enrollees. CCC director Fechner wanted to emphasize vocational training and believed that too much academic training took time away from learning job skills.[133] As a result Oxley often encountered difficulty in prying money from the director's office for educational supplies and programs.[134] The army, especially General Douglas MacArthur, was also against it and never enthusiastically backed education for enrollees. The army, moreover, was able to influence the content of the classes and steered classes toward such traditional values as self-reliance and individualism and away from New Deal ideals such as collectivism and active government.[135] The army was particularly sensitive to classes that dealt with current issues and politics. Its goal was to keep conflict and tensions to a minimum. Not surprisingly, the camp commanders were often at odds with the camp educational advisors.

The camp educational advisor was in charge of all educational activities in the camp. Usually a college graduate, the advisor decided on the curriculum, taught classes, trained staff, offered personal guidance to enrollees, and coordinated many of the enrollees' leisure activities, such as field trips and personal projects.[136] Some of the classes that educational advisors offered at Florida's state park camps included typing, current events, wood shop, poultry, nursery, civics, reading, arithmetic, rabbit raising, beekeeping, cooking, first aid, forestry, basketry, drama, music, auto repair, sign painting, and photography.[137] In 1940 Highlands Hammock offered over forty-one classes for its Company 453.[138] To supplement the classroom, educational advisors maintained a camp library filled with classic and popular books, current magazines, daily newspapers, and government booklets and brochures. The State Library of Florida in Tallahassee assisted in this by lending over a thousand books a year to Florida's CCC camps.[139]

Between 1934 and 1936 the University of Florida provided staff and aid to camp advisors, including those in state park camps. Using its General Extension Office, the university appointed a state educational officer—P. G. Reynolds—to oversee dispensing information to advisors, loaning the camps equipment such as projectors and other visual aids, and organizing and assigning student teachers. Reynolds's newsletter, the *Florida Advisor*, served as the clearinghouse for these activities.[140] Probably the most helpful to the camp educational advisors were the FERA-paid student teachers Reynolds supervised, who were available during the summers.[141] These teachers were college students who lived in the camp for six-week periods, during which time they aided in teaching, maintaining the library, and creating reports.[142] Myakka River and Highlands Hammock state parks received student teachers in 1934 and 1935.[143] After 1936, as the CCC's education program matured, the university backed off in its direct involvement with the CCC.

For the enrollees in the state parks, however, education was not their main priority. While some companies, such as Myakka River State Park, whose African American company 5480 reported 100 percent enrollment, others such as Gold Head Branch State Park once reported that only three out of the 194-man strong Veteran Company 2444 were enrolled in classes.[144] The average enrollment for Florida state park camp enrollees in night classes usually hovered around 50 percent. Vocational training usually proved to be the most popular with the young men. As one former enrollee described it, "If I had to choose between education and common sense I'd take the common sense. I knew one fellow. He'd give you a legal pad and you could start writing down figures on it . . . just as fast as you could write them down. You get down to the bottom, and he'd write the answer to it. But he couldn't put a light bulb in a fixture."[145] That enrollee became a mason in later years, a trade he learned in the CCC. When asked about his educational experiences in the CCC, former enrollee Ansley Hall only remembered making "a radio-magazine combination table and it took every power tool that they had in the woodwork shop to build that table. The reason for that was to familiarize you with all the tools."[146] Former enrollee Buck Heath also favored technical training. "They offered . . . going on a survey crew or working surveying. Now that was educational. Anybody could handle a shovel to dig dirt, but not everybody could [work] a surveyor instrument."[147]

But for some, the CCC still offered valuable classroom time. "They had what was called the education building and had a man in there that we could go in," former enrollee Thomas Hutchison explained. "We could study and read books and if we needed help, he helped us." The problem for many like Hutchison was the lack of educational opportunities in their home environment. "I had a part-time education—about sixth grade. Back in them days, they had three months out of the year of schooling, and if there was work to be done, it come ahead of the schooling. But we could go in the [CCC] educational building and lot of us got a lot more education than what we got out of school, that's for sure."[148] Buck Heath had a similar experience. "I went to fourth grade in school. . . . Before I went in the CC [sic] camp, it was just an old one-room schoolhouse we went to. We'd start going to school about October on to January. Then Daddy would pull us out to the field for the plowing."[149] Yet overall, for most enrollees, usable job skills were the educational priority.

Advisors also fought a losing battle in trying to persuade enrollees to read books of substance from the camp libraries. Comics, westerns, and adventure novels were the perennial favorites with enrollees at both junior and veteran camps. And according to the annual camp inspection reports, book circulation per year in the libraries rarely reached over a third of the library's holdings (anywhere between 200 and 600 books) and was generally considerably less. Company 2444 at Gold Head Branch State Park checked out only fifty-seven books out of a thousand volumes for the entire year of 1940.[150] In the Florida Caverns camp newspaper, enrollees complained that the library contained no "all-fiction magazines," and the scholarly journals it stocked were "practically never touched by our members."[151] Camp newspapers, however, did announce the arrival of pulp novels such as *The Face of the Men from Saturn, Shudders and Thrills,* and *Daredevils of Mars.*[152]

The one educational publication enrollees did read voraciously was the camp newspaper. Camp newspapers were the domain of the camp educational advisor and usually were integrated within a journalism class.[153] But more often than not it was the enrollees who wrote the articles, supplied the artwork, and served as its audience. Camp newspapers varied wildly from camp to camp. Some newspapers were crude, mimeographed affairs (e.g., Myakka's *Myakka Rattler* and Torreya's *Torreya Park Chronicle*), while others, such as Highlands Hammock's *Roger's Post* and Fort Clinch's *Barrack's Bag*, were professionally printed.[154] The newspapers provided the enrollees a chance to vent their frustrations and opine upon camp events. Veteran enrollees at the Florida Caverns maintained the most critical camp newspaper out of all the Florida state park camps—the *Veterans Viewpoint*. They wrote critically on intolerance in the country, "goldbrickers"[155] in the government, and the rise of dictatorships.[156] In an investigation of the camp by the CCC Director's Office for several regulation violations, the newspaper was labeled "subversive," and its content was used as partial justification for the sacking of the camp's CO.[157] (Gold Head's *Pick and Spade*, another veteran' camp newspaper, featured similar if less vitriolic articles.) For the most part, however, camp newspapers were benign, filled with gossip, attempts at humor, and announcements of upcoming social events.

Camp newspapers in Florida state parks offer a unique snapshot of camp life. Throughout the papers are ads for local businesses, such as movie theatres, beer joints, laundries, and drugstores. Sports recaps, reviews of camp events, and sketches of camp life were regular features. Most articles rated as little more than high school fodder, in columns such as "Camp Chatter," the "Key Holer," and "Overheard in Camp." "Why are all the boys giving up smoking? Christmas must be coming along," observed one newspaper in a typical fashion.[158] "We wondered if the girls in Quincy like to see the boys come to town every Saturday night. I should say they do," boasted another.[159] Yet one can decipher the enrollees' priorities and self-images through the simple writings. Also decipherable are the enrollees' habits and vices, best seen in the cautionary articles written by the camps' doctors and advisors. Topics included profanity ("The Most Useless Habit"), feigning sickness, drinking ("A Father's Advice to a Son"), and venereal diseases ("stay away from prostitutes").[160] Although limited by army supervision and CCC regulations, the camp newspaper was one of the few voices of enrollees in the

CCC, and with every Florida state park camp possessing its own newspaper, the enrollees used that voice often.

For enrollees in the "colored" companies, having any voice in the Deep South was an accomplishment in itself. Representative Oscar De Priest's amendment to the CCC bill prohibited discrimination of any kind in the selection of enrollees.[161] African Americans were therefore allowed into the CCC.[162] But despite the legislation, de facto practices meant that many African Americans were rejected for service. Once a "colored company" was formed, the CCC then had a difficult time finding a community willing to house them. Pennsylvania lost two CCC camps because the state refused to allow two African American companies within its borders.[163] New York was also a problem, of which Fechner once wrote, "No other state . . . has so many communities that have vigorously, and at times, bitterly opposed placing a Negro company anywhere in their vicinity."[164] But Fechner, a native Tennessean and a devout segregationist, was no freedom fighter, and rarely fought the racism that black camps encountered, especially in the most segregated of all regions, the Jim Crow South.[165]

The CCC's record on race relations in the South, where four out five of the nation's African Americans resided, represented for historian John Salmond "one of its few areas of failure."[166] Four southern states—Georgia, Arkansas, Alabama, and Florida—refused to enroll blacks until 1935, when the federal government threatened to cut off federal funds.[167] In Mississippi whites made up 98.3 percent of the enrollment, despite a black majority population.[168] Even though many of the barriers to African American enrollment were removed by 1935, black enrollees continued to face racism and resistance throughout the South, including Florida.[169]

Jim Crow was alive and well in Florida in the 1930s. Unlike in other southern states, the Ku Klux Klan remained a powerful force in the Sunshine State throughout the decade.[170] As late as 1939 the KKK paraded through downtown Orlando.[171] Lynching was still a common practice in Florida as well. The year before a black CCC camp arrived at Florida Caverns State Park in Marianna, an African American named Claude Neal was brutally lynched—with his toes, fingers, and testicles severed—by a crowd of Marianna men, women, and children. The body was then hung in front of the Jackson County Courthouse in the town's square.[172] Though Claude Neal's case was extreme even for the times, most blacks throughout the state were disfranchised, poorly educated, and lived in fear and poverty. CCC enrollee George LeCouris, a son of Greek immigrants, remembers seeing a lynching in Quincy while on weekend leave from his CCC camp in the Apalachicola National Forest. He was dropped off by a U.S. Army truck in the downtown square. Because the town square was full of people, food and other make-shift vendors, George presumed he had lucked onto a local carnival. But he quickly realized the festivities were of a much darker nature. "There was a colored [male] that had raped a white girl in Quincy, Florida. And when they caught him and found him, they drug him with a car all around the streets and everything." Off tape, LeCouris said the man had also been castrated. "And then they hung him in the courthouse lawn under one of them oak trees. And when we got there that afternoon, it had all happened. But he was still hanging there when we got there."[173] Into this violent racial climate in 1935 arrived several African American CCC camps, including three stationed at Florida state parks.

In 1935 Myakka River State Park near Sarasota and Torreya State Park in Liberty County received African American CCC companies. The following year a side camp from Torreya was established at Florida Caverns State Park in Marianna.[174] The racism enrollees encountered at these camps can be seen in how the camps operated. All officers and supervisory staff were white and had their own private restrooms and bathing facilities—unlike at other CCC camps, where facilities were shared. Any white visitors, including student teachers and other enrollees, slept in the officers' quarters and never with the black enrollees. Even the camp newspapers differed. Newspapers at Myakka and Torreya contained less gossip and humor and featured more articles on religion and patriotism, most likely the product of the white educational advisor's interventions.[175] Not until an African American educational advisor was hired in the late 1930s did Torreya's newspaper ever mention that the camp had black enrollees. Previously, in all the drawings and sketches the enrollees were shown as white. Recreation at the camps also differed from that in other state park camps. Baseball teams played only other black camps, and boxing was mysteriously missing from most inspection reports (although boxing was sporadically practiced).[176] Willie O'Neal, an African American former enrollee, whose experiences paralleled those in state parks camps, described life in a forestry CCC camp as a mix of racism and opportunity.[177] The training, money, food, and education he received in the CCC was a blessing for O'Neal, but the racism he faced reinforced the limitations on African Americans in Florida.

While O'Neal's camp would play informal games with the white CCC camp located just across the lake, there was friction between the enrollees once in town on weekends.[178] One of O'Neal's jobs was to drive the white camp doctor to the other two camps he supervised. "I would take him in his truck and we would go to Marietta [a black CCC camp], stop there, and check in, and I would then carry him on to Fernandina [Fort Clinch State Park, a white CCC camp]. See, I could not stay at Fernandina. I would come back to Marietta. Then the next day the white people would bring him back to Marietta, and I would bring him to Olustee."[179] Yet for O'Neal and other African Americans, the CCC offered an opportunity for education and job training not found anywhere else.

African American enrollees faced their largest challenges from outside the camps as communities throughout Florida refused to allow black camps in the area. Communities such as Sumatra, Foley, Hilliard, and Santa Rosa County fought successfully to keep out black camps.[180] One of the largest fights occurred in Sarasota, when the federal government replaced a junior white camp with a black camp in 1935 to continue work on Myakka River State Park.

In August 1935 Governor Dave Sholtz received letters and telegrams from angry and politically influential citizens in Sarasota, upset over the switch in camps at Myakka River State Park. A letter from George Randall was typical: "The replacement of whites by blacks in any walk of life is deplorable enough without the shame of turning our beautiful Miakka [sic] into a varitable n[———] heaven. What can you do to remove these negroes, and prevent the complete ruin of the Miakka region as a tourist attraction so soon after its inauguration?"[181] Congressmen Park Trammell, Duncan Fletcher, and J. Hardin received similar telegrams.[182] Senator Trammell urged Sholtz to intervene, claiming that this "condition ruins state park for sportsmen and visiting tourists."[183] But as Sholtz sent his executive secretary Jim Newell down to investigate, it became clear that not all in town were against the move. Despite the fact there was a "mass meeting" of citizens, one newspaper editor noticed that the meeting's leaders were from the anti-Sholtz camp and were using race baiting as way to gather support among the "young Florida Crackers" who attended—and who voted against the switch in camps "strictly from a racial standpoint."[184] Most of the town's leadership was absent, and no mention of the meeting was posted in the newspapers.[185]

Although it soon became obvious to leaders in Tallahassee and Washington, D.C., that the protest was begun merely as a political ploy, the issue of race, once raised, could not be ignored. The public was outraged, while businesses feared that tourism would plummet if people discovered that African Americans built the park. Therefore the Sarasota Chamber of Commerce voted to oppose the camp officially.[186] Baker reminded Sarasotans that the loss of the park would result in the loss of "about $100,000 a year that is being spent locally to maintain the camp."[187] And Schaeffer argued through the local paper that the park "under the CCC program in cooperation with [the] National Park Service could be successfully completed, but under any other form of relief development completion would be questionable and local and state governments would have to contribute funds to project."[188] The FPS director C. H. Schaeffer, desperate to keep the camp for fear of losing it altogether, devised a plan to allow the original opponents to save face and yet still appear the winners. With the support of *Sarasota Herald* editor J. B. Riley, Schaeffer asked the National Park Service if the camp could be moved "three to four miles from its present site."[189] The argument he devised was that the opponents simply did not want Negroes bathing in the river. The NPS agreed.[190] But Fourth Corps Army Area General Van Horn Mosely refused and pulled the black company out of the camp. The army was already unhappy with the environmental conditions, and the addition of an unfavorable social climate was the final straw. Faced with a choice between a black camp and no camp at all, the citizens of Sarasota backed down. The lure of a finished state park proved irresistible to locals, despite their racial concerns. As *Sarasota Herald* editor Riley described it, "even some of those who have switched were originally bitterly opposed to the presence of the negro CCC."[191] An example was "E. J. Bacon, former mayor of the city, [who] was one of those opposed to the negroes at the park, but since the civilian forces was transferred and he lost four tenants, he is in favor of their return."[192] The local Kiwanis Club also agreed that "the possible colored manning of the camp" was acceptable since the FPS was capable of "intelligently and agreeably" handling the situation.[193] In late September 1935 Governor Sholtz asked for reoccupation of the camp at the park, and after assurances that he had full support of the local community, Mosely complied—with one condition: that the camp be moved to higher ground of the army's choosing.[194] The FPS agreed, and the CCC company returned on September 24.[195] A similar series of events also accompanied the occupation of Torreya State Park.[196] When NPS authorities began considering a new CCC camp to reoccupy Gold

Head Branch State Park near Keystone Heights, NPS inspector C. R. Vinten warned his authorities that "owing to the fact that the park is already in use by the public, together with the fact that there will be a heavy work load of structural jobs, we do not consider that the assignment of a colored company at this area would be necessary."[197] In both cases the economic promise of tourism trumped racism.

Despite the CCC's failings in Florida with race and other issues, former enrollees, black and white, continued to view their time in the CCC as a valuable experience.[198] As one enrollee put it: "It was the finest thing to ever come to this country."[199] The opinion appears to have been unanimous among the former enrollees. With a summer camp–like atmosphere, the large amount of relief paid to Florida families (which by 1937 was a whopping $5,537,770), and the public's high opinion of the CCC, it is little wonder that enrollees had high regard for the program.[200] For them, it was the job training, social experiences, and developed friendships that remained most important. They were oblivious to the idea of conserving Florida's natural areas and indifferent to the development of the state's tourist trade; neither was a motivation for them. Putting food on their family's table was their prime motivator. And in turn, the governors and FPS administration never mentioned the enrollees or their welfare. Yet the enrollees played an integral role the development and operation of state parks and in the development of modern Florida tourism. Without the enrollees providing the labor, there would not have been a Florida Park Service in the 1930s.

7

Improving Paradise

NATURE AS COMMODITY

In 1941 Highlands Hammock State Park's Civilian Conservation Corps camp published a brochure that directed visitors to "see the beauty of Florida's unspoiled nature." But in the state parks, as well as the other recreation areas and forests that the CCC created, the result was anything but unspoiled. Vistas were created, trees planted, native species removed, natural processes such as fires and water flow were halted, and exotics were introduced. Unlike on the issues covered in earlier chapters, the one area for which there was little conflict between the NPS, the CCC, and the FPS was in the altering of Florida's natural environment to achieve their goals, and in so doing they brought about long-lasting environmental change to Florida. All three agencies believed that parks were built environments—not preserved wildernesses simply made accessible to the public. As the CCC superintendent for Myakka River State Park, A. D. Lawson, wrote in a narrative report from 1935: "It seems to have always been the rule for men to pick up where nature left off, and complete a beautification project."[1] One enrollee at Gold Head Branch State Park wrote in his camp newspaper that the park was "carved out of the wilderness," as though the natural features were unfinished and required human intervention.[2] In another report, this time at Highlands Hammock State Park, the superintendent described their efforts as the "work of a creative artisan."[3] The root concept informing these statements was the idea that nature was a wild entity that needed to be tamed, beautified, sanitized, and improved upon. This was park creation in its most literal sense. And it was a viewpoint shared by creators of other types of parks, roadside attractions, and highways, and was even to a degree applied to Florida's human environment.

The CCC and FPS were not operating in a vacuum. From the start of the decade, 1930s writers and promoters saw the state as a natural playground, wherein all its native features were to be beautiful, safe, and useful to tourists. In 1932 Marjory Stoneman Douglas published the first edition of her popular visitor's guide to Florida, which began: "In a very large sense the entire State of Florida is a park and playground. [All of Florida] constitutes an area being devoted in a large measure to the pleasure of a whole nation of people. Fishing, sailing, swimming are freely possible to everybody everywhere. . . . And to those who love to study raw nature, this land is indeed a glorious haven."[4] But throughout the 1930s Florida's "raw nature" would in fact become manicured, altered, beautified, and in some cases wholly created.

More than anything else, to attract visitors to the state, Florida's natural world had to be visually attractive. Arthur Hale of the State Road Department said: "All highways are scenic highways."[5] As John Taylor, president of the Florida State Horticultural Society, argued in April 1933: "Occupying the position geographically that we do makes us the natural playground of our nation. This being true, it behooves us all the more to make Florida beautiful."[6] The following year he continued his argument. "Permit me to call to your attention the importance of making Florida a beautiful state. . . . I do not believe we could spend money in any form of advertisements that would bring a greater return than put into the development of parks, playgrounds, and beautification . . . which would attract thousands and more thousands of people every year from the frozen regions of the North."[7] He compared the need for beautification with citrus. Growers spend much effort and time to make their crops "pleasing to the eye, not that it adds much if anything to the quality of the juice . . . thereby creating consumer demand."[8] A couple of years later the Florida State Planning Board made the same claim: "There is no better way to conserve and expand the tourist industry than by increasing the State's facilities for the entertainment of winter visitors. Well-kept forests and the beautiful clear streams and lakes of the State have scenic value as well as a recreation value."[9]

Not surprisingly, considering her work with parks and forestry, one of the prime movers of Florida beautification was May Mann Jennings. As early as 1932 she pushed for a state beautification program, focusing primarily upon the state highways, which she said "emphasizes advertising value."[10] At that time Governor Doyle Carlton and his successor Dave Sholtz faced public criticism over the state's use of convict labor. Much of that scrutiny stemmed from the controversial but popular Paul Muni film *I Was a Fugitive from a Chain Gang* then playing in Florida theatres, which was based upon the bestselling expose of Georgia's chain gangs by former prisoner Robert Burns. Jennings therefore became worried that highway beautification would cease over such public concerns. Since like most state agencies at the time the State Road Department had to cut its funds, and convict labor was cheaper than prison maintenance, Jennings argued, "I think the general idea that the convicts were being used for Beautification work throughout the state would to some extent take the sting from the idea that they [the convicts] were being terribly driven and overworked. . . . There seems no good reason to me that Florida with its climatic conditions and marvelous growth should not have only the best roads, but the most beautiful as well."[11] Her efforts even found their way into the *Christian Science Monitor*, which quoted her saying, "The business man is awakening to the fact that beautification and . . . conservation . . . together constitute an indispensable factor when reckoning the dollars that will circulate in his home town markets. . . . The careless indifference of [past times] has given place to city planning, county and state beautification associations, organized effort on the part of business men and women working together for beauty."[12]

The terms *beautification, beauty, attractiveness*, and other synonyms were floated with much regularity by many civic groups, elected leaders, and local journalists. And as the preceding Jennings quote illustrates, the idea of "improving" and beautifying paradise tied together conservation, tourism, and advertising. Even citrus growing was affected by the aesthetic movement. Throughout the 1930s citrus growers and buyers in the nation debated the use of food color to make oranges more attractive. And at the heart of this beautifying impulse was the argument that all of Florida was an attraction and therefore all of it must be attractive.

It was inevitable that the issue would move toward improving Florida society. As the Florida Federation of Women's Clubs declared, "The community must be beautiful. Woman with her housecleaning bent had to clean and make beautiful the streets of the town as well. . . . They have run the pigs and cows off the street . . . next is cows off the highway!"[13] John Taylor argued that beautifying highways made "a better citizenship so that future generations may be content to spend all their time in their native state adding millions to its wealth and beauty."[14]

And to keep those highways attractive meant allowing only the "beautiful people" to use them. In 1935 Governor Dave Sholtz decided to set up a "border blockade" on all the road arteries in order to keep out migrant and itinerant workers. He argued that the policy was a crime prevention measure. The first year, more than 50,000 transients were turned away from the state.[15] But as the *New York Times* stated, the prime motive behind the policy was that Sholtz "does not want Florida's 2,500,000 visitors annoyed by hoodlums."[16] Florida stopped the restrictive program in 1937 over constitutional concerns.[17] Governor Fred Cone, no fan of Florida's advertising and beautification efforts, pointed out, "Why some of the worst people that come to Florida in the Winter time are racketeers in fine limousines and Pullman cars. There are plenty of crooks in fine automobiles."[18]

Even the CCC partook in the beautifying efforts. Florida's CCC educational advisor wrote *A Suggested Outline for a Course in Camp Beautification* in 1935.[19] The idea was twofold. "As the CCC camps are the semi-permanent home of over 5 million young men, all that is possible should be done to instill in them a consciousness of, and a desire for attractive surroundings."[20] As with so much else in Florida, the state's CCC administrators were concerned with how the camps appeared to visitors. "Beautiful grounds will do much to give the camp the right kind of publicity."[21] But the young enrollees, the supervising forester and park planners, and the U.S. Army officers all cared little for camp beautification. They had too much to worry about with their various projects, and for a number of camps in Florida, those projects included beautifying and improving Florida's natural areas.

One of the best examples of park creation was at Greynolds Park, a city park located near the Oleta River in Dade County. The park was designed and supervised by landscape architect William Lyman Phillips, who also designed Bok Tower Gardens and the gardens and arboretum at Highlands Hammock State Park.[22] Working in an abandoned rock quarry, the CCC planted hundreds of trees, created waterways, and erected an artificial "lookout mound."[23] The result was a visually perfect yet completely fabricated forest. At Fort Clinch State Park in Fernandina, the CCC's actions were less drastic, though enrollees still leveled several sand dunes to provide a clear vista of the ocean for the beach casino being built onsite.[24] Several more of the park's massive sand dunes were bisected by the park drive, leading to futile efforts made to stabilize the ever-shifting sand mounds with grass plantings and sand fences.[25] As historian

Phoebe Cutler once described it, the NPS used the CCC to create natural areas that conformed to an idealized version of the "eastern woodlands," creating "an elaborate artifice."[26] Just as with the Progressives in the early twentieth century, Florida Southern College professor Dr. Ludd Spivey argued in 1933 that beautification could be used for positive social engineering. "Man achieves his nature.... Everything that a child does in the way of human behavior has to be taught.... The world out there has been poor, poverty-stricken and it has made us into its image—poor, poverty-stricken, lacking in appreciation of the beautiful things in life."[27] In other words, people must be taught to appreciate beauty. Beautification should be a societal "educational task." Florida Horticultural Society president Taylor even promoted the social implications of beautifying Florida: "There is nothing, in my judgment which stimulated good citizenship more than beautiful homes, particularly their surrounding in the average small urban or country home.... [Beautification] creates loyal, God-fearing, Christian peoples."[28]

For the CCC-built state parks, that beautification process began with a master plan, a practice developed by the NPS. Each park had a master plan, which was a blueprint for the construction and final layout of the park. The master plans for Myakka, Torreya, and Hillsborough state parks reveal that most of the vistas and other natural areas visitors encountered were created from scratch. Trees were planted in layers, foreground and background, with species integrated so that, mindful of the seasons, no area would be bare at any one time throughout the year. As the pictorial review for CCC Company 2444 at Gold Head Branch State Park described that camp's achievements, the men changed "what was once a wilderness into a beautiful scenic recreational area."[29] The finished product in Florida's parks and forest recreation areas was closer to a large garden than to a preserved wild area.

One of the first steps taken at the state parks was a "general cleanup." While the name may conjure images of removing trash and litter from the park grounds, this was not the case. As described by one superintendent in a 1934 narrative report, general cleanups consisted of work crews roaming through the forests removing all dead trees, snags, and stumps.[30] Another superintendent explained that cleanups were undertaken so that "the scars of past fires and timber cutting are obliterated." Often dynamite was used to remove the larger stumps. The idea was to allow the woods to "breathe." The other name used in a few reports for these activities is even more revealing: woods improvement. According to CCC monthly narrative and inspection reports, all state park camps, along with several forest-based camps, devoted a large portion of their work load (tabulated in reports as "man days") to general cleanups.

Because the ideal included only healthy trees surrounded by safe, friendly animals, several plant and animal species were targeted for removal. For the cleanup crews, palmettos, Florida's predominant ground-covering plant, were considered especially undesirable. In another narrative report, progress on a cleanup project was described as slow going "as there is a heavy growth of palmetto on the greater portion of the area."[31] Enrollee Buck Heath described digging up palmettos while stationed at Florida Caverns State Park. "We'd pile them up high, as big as [a] house, and had a bulldozer come get them and put them all in one big pile. . . . While I was there, that was about all I done is dig them palmetto roots."[32] Also considered unacceptable at state parks were gar, catfish, and turtles, which the NPS and FPS believed interfered with sport fishing. Reports from Myakka State Park are filled with photos of enrollees netting and spearing turtles and gar from Myakka Lake.[33] Myakka's project supervisor boasted in a monthly report, "We have been destroying quantities of killer gar, savage catfish, and ferocious turtles. The men have been very interested in this activity."[34] Plant life was also raked out of most freshwater areas. "There would be nothing floating there in all the water," remembered one former enrollee.[35] As he explained further, it was not a problem for the CCC crews to keep out the flora once removed, "'cause we kept it down. The moment [the plants] would start to grow, we'd get it out of there."[36]

In a few cases the CCC would replace what was removed with more desirable species. A June 1935 report from Myakka mentioned that into Myakka Lake "have been transferred thousands of game fish."[37] Deer, another acceptable species, were reintroduced into several parks. After a disastrous deer tick infestation in the mid-1930s, the Florida State Livestock Sanitary Board, partly funded through the Works Progress Administration, paid citizens to kill thousands of deer.[38] Deer populations in several areas, including Myakka River State Park, were wiped out.[39] The CCC camp at Vilas, in the Apalachicola National Forest, raised deer for reintroduction across the state.[40] According one former enrollee from Gold Head Branch State Park, deer were so desirable that bobcats were trapped and removed from park grounds because they were sometimes known to kill deer.[41] At Gold Head Branch as well as Highlands Hammock state parks, feeding deer was a daily activity for enrollees. Enrollees fed deer table scraps, candy, and cigarettes. One deer at Gold Head Branch State Park became so accustomed to his daily tobacco dose that the camp superintendent was treed for several hours when he found himself out of cigarettes.[42]

But the animals that received the most attention were snakes—universally despised by all involved. During off times it was common practice for enrollees to go on snake hunts. Camp newspapers regularly reported the number of snake kills at their camps. One example is found in the Highlands Hammock State Park CCC camp's newsletter *C-bring C-amp C-ourier*, which reported in 1934 that "courageous members of this company" killed three snakes in the past week."[43] The article encouraged more such activity. The *Myakka Rattler* reported that one crew at the park's CCC camp killed over thirty diamondback rattlesnakes in January 1935 alone.[44] "It seems that the survey crew has all the luck with the rattlers," the article opined. "By the time they leave the camp, the palmettos will be hiding nothing but rabbits. Let's hope."[45] The CCC camp at Gold Head Branch State Park held a snake-killing contest, which netted seventeen rattlers.[46] As reported in that camp's newsletter, "taming the woods has become the hobby of many."[47] The Highlands Hammock CCC camp newspaper provided the following advice: "Never disturb a snake—unless poisonous. Most snakes are useful to humanity. They destroy other snakes."[48]

Whether the CCC and the FPS exterminated, removed, or preserved a park's natural fauna, they nonetheless kept detailed records of the wildlife found. An illustrative example is the December 1941 progress report by Wildlife Technician Gus Van Duyn for Myakka River State Park.[49] This was a supplement to an earlier 1940 floral study of Myakka by James McFarlin, botanist for the CCC camp at Matheson Hammock Park, in which he collected 242 plant species that were then, according to Duyn, "identified, mounted, and labeled and [are] now stored in a recently acquired steel herbarium cabinet."[50] Van Duyn rejected an earlier report from 1937, which covered the period of June 4 through September 4, 1937, out of sufficient concerns about "the observer's competence that scant evidence can be accorded any records not otherwise substantiated."[51] It is unclear whether this was a matter of science or race, as the previous report came out of Myakka's original African American CCC camp. Yet even disregarding the earlier report, the amount of wildlife observed from November

1939 to December 1941 is staggering.[52] Covering eighteen pages, ten of which are devoted to birds alone, Van Duyn's report lists sixteen mammal species, eighteen species of amphibians, over thirty species of fishes, thirty-six reptile species, and a whopping 191 varieties of birds.[53] The disputed earlier report lists another forty-six avian species. Twenty-five years later the completeness of the CCC report warranted a republication by the Florida Park Service for sale to park visitors.[54]

Aside from their perceived waste and unproductiveness, wetlands were regarded as problematic: the CCC "improved" wetlands to rid forests and parks of yet another unwanted pest—mosquitoes. At all seven state parks, and most forests, wetlands were drained with ditches and culverts to keep down the mosquito populations. Such drainage altered the surrounding ecosystems, changed the soil composition, and resulted in loss of habitat and species migration. These efforts were not always successful. According to one United States Forest Service inspection of Florida's CCC camps, "drainage is quite a problem in some sections of the state."[55] Nevertheless, truck trails were built up high to facilitate water drainage into the deep ditches dug out on either side of the road.[56] The near universal opinion held by CCC crews and park staff was that Fort Clinch had the most severe mosquito problem. Along with drainage ditches and culverts, pyrethrum spray was used extensively.[57] One former Fort Clinch CCC enrollee remembered their meager defenses against the biting insects. Each man would "take a gallon of citronella and hand pumps" to the work site each day. "We made sure to keep our clothes on."[58]

Although considered routine at the time, general cleanups best reveal the attitude that CCC administrators held about how the wilderness should appear in a perfect world: clean, safe, uncluttered, and picturesque. But these efforts paled in comparison to the time and worrying put into protection of the woods from fire.

Most Americans believed that fire was a destructive force to forests and parks. As famed CCC-promoter Roy Hoyt wrote in the 1930s, "Fire is the great enemy of men in the forest. Protection against fire, and the suppression of fire, are necessary if man is to gain or maintain his control over the natural resources."[59] Fire suppression and prevention was one of the main reasons for the creation of the CCC back in 1933. A 1937 memorandum from Florida Forester Harry Lee Baker to all CCC camp superintendents contained the reminder that firefighting has "priority over all other camp work."[60] That year's instructions on fire control sent out to all Florida camps from the U.S. Forest Service likewise said that fire suppression had priority "over all other jobs, regardless of the day or hour."[61] Similarly, the 1938–39 Florida CCC fire plan stressed "work in firefighting takes precedence over all other work."[62] CCC veteran George LeCouris remembered that his Apalachicola National Forest camp's purpose was to simply "fight fires and build roads."[63] At the camp level such priority was even stressed in the camp-printed newspapers. One example was from Gold Head Branch State Park's newspaper *Tent Town Topics* (later renamed *Pick and Spade* once the company moved into permanent barracks), which mentioned, "It is the work of the camp to fight fires as well as prevent fires."[64]

But for Florida fire played a much different role than it did in other areas of the nation. For thousands of years, fires annually swept across the Florida landscape, shaping ecosystems and providing niches for many species. Native Americans and early settlers were aware of this cycle, and adjusted their lives accordingly, often conducting primitive controlled burns to encourage desirable habitats and species. But by the 1930s, as development increased and natural areas dwindled, most Floridians were unaware of fire's role in the state and followed a strict no–fire tolerance policy. Anti-fire prejudices were fueled further by the U.S. Forest Service's expansive campaign to educate the nation on the benefits of fire suppression.[65] As May Mann Jennings said in a 1934 speech to the State Chamber of Commerce, "Fires in no instance should be allowed."[66] Both the CCC and the Florida Forestry and Park Service held the erroneous belief that 99 percent of all fires in Florida were human-created.[67] In actuality, many biologists and ecologists have concluded in recent years that Florida is annually hit by more lightning strikes than anywhere else in North America, resulting in hundreds of natural fires every year. Nevertheless, many observations of Florida's state park and forest properties by CCC personnel remarked upon the effects of "intentional" fires. CCC state inspector C. R. Vinten described Gold Head as "a scene of desolation which resulted from years of continuous burning."[68] A CCC narrative report from Myakka River State Park remarked that it was "common practice to burn the surrounding country" and therefore "fire breaks around the property . . . were most necessary."[69] CCC fire reports invariably blamed fires upon the local residents. One report mentioned that "the cowboys could not resist the temptation to set the world on fire."[70] The fear of the FPS, CCC, and NPS was that a fire would destroy one of the newly created state parks.

The widespread fear of fires at the time is understandable when viewed from the CCC's perspective. It was not until the 1960s that biologists and ecologists began to understand the role fire played in Florida's ecosystems.[71] Few areas are more desolate than a recently burned forest, with its smoldering black ground and charred trees. May Mann Jennings once described such an area: "Charred wood and smoked choked atmosphere is not inviting to either visitors, nor home folks who travel our splendid highways. We certainly must stop this vandalism."[72] And the State Planning Board declared in 1937, "Another result of unrestrained burning is the destruction of the natural beauty of the State, particularly at a time when winter visitors are present."[73] Yet within weeks—even days—green shoots spring up, flowers blossom, and trees germinate, creating a spring-like atmosphere.[74] As ecologist Ronald Myers wrote in the definitive *Ecosystems of Florida*, many areas "have evolved in response to frequent, low intensity fires."[75] Plants such as turkey oaks, longleaf pines, and wiregrass depend on fire for seed germination and flowering, while animals such as gopher tortoises, red-cockaded woodpeckers, Sherman's fox squirrels, and indigo snakes require it for foraging and habitat maintenance.[76] Without fire, such species would migrate or perish and leave many areas vulnerable to larger, more damaging fires as well as exotic invasion. But in the 1930s little of this was known, and fear of fire as a destructive agent ran unchecked by empirical evidence proving otherwise.

The CCC responded to this fear with extensive fire prevention efforts. Enrollees cut fire lanes fourteen feet wide throughout the parks and forests. Camps made cooperative agreements with local fire agencies, and each enrollee was trained in fire-fighting techniques.[77] Enrollees worked rotating fire shifts, staying in camp every other weekend in case of a fire breakout. At Highlands Hammock Project Superintendent A. C. Altvater required a minimum of seventy-five enrollees present in camp at all times.[78] Other camps had similar policies. Every camp was required to maintain two fire tool boxes, equipped with rakes, flaps, shovels, machetes, and backpack water pumps.[79] Also required at the door of every building were two sand-filled barrels, the CCC equivalent of the modern fire extinguisher.[80]

Once fire was found, the nearest CCC camp was called into action. Fires on state and federal lands, especially within the expensive state parks, took first priority. Below that fell any land owned by a person or group armed with a cooperative agreement with the state. Such agreements required the owner to aid in fire fighting and to follow state standards on forest maintenance. Finally, fires within a fifty-mile radius of the camp that could threaten state or federal lands might be considered for CCC extinguishing. Most of the fires fought were small affairs, few more than a dozen or two acres. However, a few were quite large. CCC veteran George LeCouris recalled working on one fire in the panhandle for two weeks.[81]

Enrollees knew from their training that "in fire control work, speed counts. Travel to a fire is not a pleasure trip. Every single minute counts."[82] Fires were usually fought by hand. "We had shovels, we had flaps, and you'd go beat the fire down," remembered LeCouris. Many carried a knapsack water pump on their backs.[83] "When we'd run out of water, we'd wade out into a pond or a lake, and we'd just sink down, and fill our water up."[84]

On March 3, 1941, everyone's worst fear was realized. That morning recently appointed FPS Director Lewis Scoggin received the following telegram from Gold Head Branch State Park's newly hired park superintendent, L. R. Brodie: "Fire swept through park yesterday, and last night. Buildings all saved. Half of acreage burned. Under control now."[85] It was the beginning of Florida's fire season that year, and the longleaf pine sand hill community was a prime area for forest fires. A fire had begun off park grounds to the south.[86] But as winds blew north, burning leaves were blown into the park. Within minutes dozens of small fires ignited throughout the park. After Brodie shot off the telegram to Scoggin the fire erupted again. By the time the fire burnt itself out, three-fourths of the park was burned, including the picnic area, the ravine, and the land surrounding the spring-fed Sheeler Lake. "There is no doubt but that these fires were deliberately set," concluded Brodie.[87] That June an emergency conference was held between the NPS and the state parks to discuss how to improve fire protection.[88] The general consensus was that too much federal money had been invested to neglect the threat of fire. The worries were misplaced, however. Gold Head Branch's forests rebounded within months.

One activity for which the CCC was most well known—tree planting—was also one of its most ambivalent. In one sense, the CCC replaced thousands of trees in Florida lost to decades of rampant clear-cutting by residents and timber companies. Some scholars calculate that as many as 16 million acres of virgin forestland were lost in the years before 1933.[89] Using two-man crews—one digging with a grub hoe, the other planting the tree seedling—the CCC planted well over three million trees in the Sunshine State from 1933 through 1941.[90] The results were immediate and long-lasting. The work produced expansion of two national forests—the Ocala and Choctawhatchee national forests.[91] It also created two new ones—the Osceola and Apalachicola national forests—as well as several wildlife preserves and state forests.[92] Signs posted across the state and promotional brochures, articles, and radio broadcasts created by the CCC heralded the restoration of Florida's forests.

What the public relations efforts did not mention was what types of forests were being restored. Slash pines, oaks, and even invasive exotics such as Australian pines were planted indiscriminately in the state parks. CCC enrollees planted more than one hundred Australian pines each at Myakka and Highlands Hammock state parks.[93] Natural ecosystems such as wetlands, prairies, and longleaf pine communities were transformed into what both the Florida Forestry Service and the state's promoters believed were the ideal environment: slash pine forests with a clean understory. As CCC Director Fechner once wrote, the CCC grew "fast-growing type trees" for maximum effect.[94] One goal, even within the state parks, was to increase Florida's timber supply. But replacing an area's native flora with slash pine altered not only the soil composition but also the water flow and the type of wildlife the land now supported. In most forests the slash pines were usually planted in close rows that stressed the trees, while the resultant pine needle litter killed the wiregrass and other native grasses. At Myakka enrollees attempted to turn the natural prairie—seen as a wasteland "where there was just palmettos and nothing else"—into a pine forest.[95] Over 100,000 slash pine trees were planted in the prairie, the native habitat to the indigenous crested caracara, the Florida sand crane, the gopher tortoise, and acres of wiregrass and palmettos.[96] (Much modern debate has gone into the origins of dry prairies. Many contend that they were human created, perhaps through repeated burning by indigenous cultures. Therefore, the CCC's assessment may have been partially correct, with the exception of a few centuries.)

Ironically, despite the intense planting of pine trees, many conservationists, as well as some botanists and members of the general public, often considered the pine tree aesthetically unappealing. For state parks and other recreation areas, the CCC often turned to exotic and more tropical species.

One example can be found in a May 1937 communication exchange between the University of Florida's College of Agriculture and the Florida Forest Service. The college sent two hundred African mahogany trees and a thousand Australian pines to Highlands Hammock State Park.[97] Three hundred of the Australian pines were sent to the CCC nursery in the Olustee-based camp, and the rest were spread throughout the state's various parks and forests.[98] Melaleuca were planted to dry out unwanted wetlands.[99] In a similar vein, at Gold Head Branch State Park, the deep ravine at the park's headspring was stripped of much of its native plant life to "improve its attractiveness."[100] "I have a feeling that the dense vegetation on all sides forces a feeling of restricted space," argued Malsberger to Gold Head's landscape architect.[101] "This could be accomplished by the removal of thick growth of vines on trees which do not materially add to the beauty of the ravine."[102] (He also suggested adding briar to keep people off the ravine's "steep bank.") If Florida's natural environment did not match the idealized image held by the CCC, then it would be altered until it did.

As a modern observer looking back at descriptions and depictions of Florida's roadside attractions of the 1930s, one is struck by how quaint and natural they were. Most of the kitschy trappings associated with Florida attractions would not appear until the 1950s or even later. These attractions in the 1930s were largely devoid of plastic flamingos, thrill rides, and flashy shows. The major attractions differed little from the state and national parks. In fact, were it not for the tempering effect of the NPS, the CCC-built state parks would have equaled or even surpassed the shimmer and glitter of many of the other attractions.

These commercialized natural parks were also beautified and improved, albeit in a more obvious fashion than the state parks. Exotic flowers, tropical trees, monkeys, and parrots might be blended in with native flora and fauna. And often it was the native features—cypress and palm trees, alligators, ravines, hammocks, or fish—that served as the main attraction at the sites. The mermaids, water ski shows, Florida-shaped swimming pools, and carnival rides would have to wait until after the Second World War.

The two main types of attractions in Florida in the 1930s were gardens and springs. Springs such Rainbow, Silver, Wakulla, Weeki Wachee, and Homosassa usually featured glass bottom boat rides that, aside from the humorous boat tour spiels, presented unaltered or unimproved springs and fish. Homosassa Springs on the Gulf Coast added a structure called "Nature's Fish Bowl," which allowed visitors to walk below the spring's water surface. And Rainbow Springs in Dunnellon added submarine boats that ran alongside the glass bottom boats, whereby passengers sat below the water line; essentially a vertical glass bottom boat. Silver Springs in Ocala featured the most improvements, with meticulously landscaped grounds, a deer farm, a Seminole Village, and Ross Allen's Reptile Institute. But the main attraction—the spring—was left untouched. And the site's "jungle" tour was nothing more than a river cruise down the undeveloped Silver River. Unlike in the early 1900s, when springs owners marketed their sites to ailing elites looking for health restoration and convalescence, in the Depression era the springs owners targeted middle-class families searching for a day of sightseeing.

Botanical and other gardens (often tantalizingly called "jungles") were usually more "improved" and cultivated than the springs. As Marjory Stoneman Douglas wrote on Cypress Gardens and McKee Monkey Jungle in her 1937 guide: "In both cases, man has capitalized on the beauties of nature and aided in creating places of wonderful interest and beauty."[103] But even here the prime features were often more the native flora, with tropical plants, flowers, and trees blended in. Sometimes the focus was a natural ravine (as at Gold Head Branch State Park), while elsewhere it was a natural hammock (as at Highlands Hammock State Park). While monkeys, orchids, parrots, and exotic flowers and trees provided these "jungles" with the expected tropical flair, more often than not the gardens were simply landscaped Florida hammocks. Among them were Ravine Gardens (Palatka), Orchid Gardens and Parrot Jungle (Miami), Monkey Jungle (Goulds), Eagle's Nest Gardens (Bellaire), and Sunken Gardens (St. Petersburg), Cypress Gardens (Winter Haven), Everglades Wonder Gardens (Bonita Springs), Famous Trees Botanical Gardens (Miami), Jungle Gardens (Brooksville), Moon Lake Gardens (Dunedin), Oriental Gardens (Jacksonville), and Orchid Gardens (Ft. Myers).

To measure the similarities of state parks and other roadside attractions, one can compare how Douglas describes Myakka River State Park with how Florida Horticultural Society member A. H. Andrews describes a visit to McKee's Monkey Jungle. On Myakka, Douglas wrote:

> Have you ever wanted to walk, ride a horse, or drive an automobile through a forest of palm trees? Have you ever wanted to look across the

broad expense of a river or lake and see in the distance waving fronds of sub-tropical palms and other vegetation which ordinarily is only seen in tropical or sub-tropical countries? If you have, in all probability you thought you would have to go to Central America, Hawaii, or perhaps to India. However you can do all of these and many more without leaving the United States. The Myakka River State Park is located on State property of over 26,000 acres.[104]

And Andrews wrote of the McKee's Monkey Jungle:

Comprising some 80 acres of tropical jungle, [it consists] largely of great oaks and native palms, together with varieties of East Coast jungle vegetation.... A semi-circle drive leads in from the Dixie Highway, affording parking space for visitors. In the foreground are slatted plant sheds flanked by a rustic lunch room and souvenir shop.... Entrance to the grounds is a long floral archway.... For the most part only the native forest vegetation prevails in the jungle, though here and there vacant spaces have been filled and woodland paths more definitely outlined by introduction of occasional exotic species which contribute much to the interest of visiting tourists, but blend well with the wild surroundings.... A small stream flows through the jungle.... Everything for the most part is as wild and rugged as nature made it. Lining the exit trail it had two rows of thirty [planted] royal palm.[105]

Of course orange juice was served at the park. For park officials and roadside attraction owners alike, nature, scenic views, and climate were Florida's prime commodities in the 1930s.

In 1932 Marjory Douglas wrote, "Ask any Florida resident where are the parks and playgrounds, and he will hesitate in surprise. To every Floridian all of Florida is one enormous place of rest and recreation.... Florida is essentially a recreational and play state."[106] This assertion would have surprised many Floridians who made their living, often a meager one at that, from this same natural "playground." And to the men serving in the CCC, Florida was not naturally a playground—that required planning, molding, and intense labor. At a CCC reunion at Highlands Hammock State Park in 2002, a CCC veteran remarked before sitting down for an interview that he approved of the park's "beautiful" appearance. He explained that keeping fires out must have done the trick.[107] The following year former CCC enrollee Buck Heath, a veteran of camps at Florida Caverns State Park and the Apalachicola National Forest, hesitated during an oral history recording when asked why the palmettos were removed at the state park. After a moment, incredulous at the question, he answered, "Why? Because we were building a park!"[108] For him, and most of the others involved in Florida's CCC program, parks and managed forests were considered glimpses into paradise, but only after humans had completed the job of nature and improved on it for human consumption.

8

The New Deal in Old Florida

GOVERNOR FRED CONE AND FLORIDA'S WELFARE SYSTEM

Even as late as spring 1937 Florida still suffered from the crippling effects of the Great Depression. The governor's office received daily letters from out-of-work laborers, single mothers, starving children, and elderly dependents pleading for assistance and state action.[1] Faced with the flood of welfare requests, the newly inaugurated governor Fred Cone—elected by what some might call the "cracker" vote—asked the state legislature in May 1937 to abolish the State Board of Public Welfare and replace it with a new State Welfare Board. Citing overblown salaries, mishandled funds, and "foreign" influence (i.e., northern-born appointees), Cone painted a picture of vast corruption and inexcusable government waste. His plan called for a scaled-down, economically minded board run in a businesslike manner. However, Cone's reorganization plan jeopardized millions in federal grants and threatened the entire New Deal program in Florida, including the state's CCC program and the newly created Florida Park Service. It also placed Florida's recent New Deal–dependent advertising campaigns in harm's way. By striking at the state's welfare operation, Cone struck at the nexus of power and money that tied all these elements together. Unknowingly, he was also unintentionally alienating his core political base by essentially attacking the relief upon which so many of them depended.

In many ways Governor Frederick Preston Cone was an odd mix of loyalties and convictions—mirroring to a large degree the conflicting impulses of many in Florida's population that rendered the 1930s era in Florida a contested and ambiguous period. As a former banker and businessman, Cone believed that state government should be run as a business, economically and efficiently. Issues such as conservation and welfare should be handled, if at all, by the private sector. And if government absolutely must deal with these issues, which by the 1930s was so, then he wanted business leaders in charge of those departments. That belief in a small central government was very much a by-product of Cone's experience as a white southerner, growing up in the agrarian postbellum South, of which his native North Florida was very much a part. Yet his business leanings had their limits.

While he supported advertising of the state, as he knew it was good for business for tourism as well as for agriculture, real estate, and banking, he nonetheless detested the social and political changes brought about by too much outside ("foreign") influence. With the mindset of someone who came of age politically at the turn of the century, Cone was very much a man out of step with his times by the 1930s. Florida's political and economic power, in his mind, should rest in the hands of North Florida's agrarian elite with their belief in small government, limited federal influence, low taxes, the primacy of agriculture, the righteousness of the Lost Cause, and of course, the maintenance of the prevailing white supremacist racial customs.

And yet, while the New Deal eroded many of these concerns, Cone rarely opposed outright the liberal policies handed down by Washington, for one simple reason: a Democratic president, Franklin Roosevelt, was the guiding force behind them. And Cone was, almost above all else, a staunchly loyal southern Democrat. Therefore he would always provide obligatory lip service to the goals of the New Deal, and would campaign relentlessly for his party during election years, but often fought the New Dealers behind closed doors. In a few cases his personal hostilities to the changes—changes arising both from the New Deal and from the growing influence of tourism the New Deal helped advance—bled over into the public realm. In summer 1937 Cone announced in front of a reporter that he wished the federal government would cease its relief grants. "They got their foot on our necks right now. It's always a lot of trouble and they always want to boss everything."[2] But usually Cone managed to keep these opinions to himself.

When Cone entered office in 1937, the New Deal was in full force. While many citizens had specific complaints about the welfare program in Florida, and many were fed up with former Governor Sholtz and the corruption that arose from his administration, most did not lose faith in the New Deal. As one politician described it, they were simply "disgusted with the way Sholtz ran it."[3]

Born in 1871 in the North Florida community of Benton in Columbia

County, an area newspaper columnist Allen Morris called the "hog and hominy" part of Florida, Cone's earliest experiences were shaped by memories of Reconstruction.[4] In fact, one of Cone's earliest public acts was when he shot, but did not kill, a Republican. While visiting his uncle Charles Cone, young Fred heard that a former Union soldier and staunch Republican—C. L. Morrison—was about to be named postmaster of White Springs. Taking matters into his own hands, Cone shot Morrison one night. The resulting wound proved painful but not life-threatening. Fred's uncle paid Morrison's medical bills and convinced the Unionist not to press charges. Ironically, soon thereafter, Charles Cone had the sheriff arrest Morrison on charges of concealing a felony: Fred Cone's attempt to murder Morrison! At the trial, the young Cone was the primary witness, and Morrison was convicted.[5]

Cone's low-key image and his rural roots contrasted with Sholtz's urban manners and New York upbringing.[6] As former state senator William Shands explained, "you go from one extreme to another as a rule politically."[7] Cone ran on a plank of small government, no new taxes, and "Florida labor at living wages for all public works"—a none too subtle reference to the New Deal with its high number of non–Florida born administrators.[8] Unlike Sholtz, he believed the best way to advertise Florida was "through good sound government," revealing his banking background. "If the people of the nation find out . . . that we have food, straight honest business administration in our state, where their property will be safe when they move among us, that is the best advertising Florida can have."[9] Not surprisingly, "the tourist areas distrusted him," according to political commentator Morris.[10]

The majority of his support came from politically powerful North Florida, which elected to office Florida's oldest chief executive.[11] Senator William A. Shands called him an "ultra-conservative."[12] The *Ocala Banner* derisively and tellingly described him as "cracker from head to toe."[13] Armed with a booming voice and an imposing figure, Cone walked the Capitol barefoot and kept an oft-used spittoon next to his desk.[14] His manners were as coarse as his language was blunt. Once during a heated exchange at a weekly executive cabinet meeting in the Capitol, Cone shoved a cabinet member back into his chair.[15]

For attentive listeners who supported matters such as relief, Florida advertising, and development, Cone's inauguration speech of January 5, 1937, proved ominous. Cone called for a return to business-minded, smaller government with smaller budgets, abolishing unneeded agencies, and the removal of out-of-state workers in public works programs.[16] Fair commissions, advertising committees, and new park boards, all peopled with recent arrivals to the state, did not seem to fit into Cone's vision for Florida.

When the federal government accused Florida of offering an inadequate financial commitment to its relief program in 1935 the state legislature revamped the State Board of Public Welfare, renaming it the State Board of Social Welfare and giving it more power in handling state relief efforts. While many balked at this increase in power, the Florida Health and Welfare Council—a statewide organization made up of state and private social workers—pointed out that "the power . . . given to the Florida Board is found in most of the more progressive states of the North. It is impossible to have a State Board that can prove at all effective along welfare lines without granting it a good bit of authority."[17] The legislation created twelve districts, each with its own welfare board. The state board enjoyed an annual budget of $100,000 and a mandate both to handle state-sponsored relief and to administer the federal work relief programs through a parallel organization called the Florida Emergency Relief Administration (FERA). At the head of all these operations was the man whom Harry Hopkins personally approved, Commissioner of Welfare Conrad Van Hyning.

Born in Akron, Ohio, in 1900, Van Hyning was schooled in social work at the University of Akron. He graduated with a bachelor's degree in 1922 and moved to New York as a caseworker for the Charity Organization Society. After marrying a fellow social worker, Van Hyning became assistant director of the New York State Emergency Relief Administration under Governor Franklin Roosevelt.[18] Through his New York contacts Sholtz learned of Van Hyning's work and asked him to lead Florida's Emergency Relief Administration and serve as Florida's welfare commissioner. Soon after his arrival, however, Van Hyning found himself in charge of a system with no professionally trained social workers. He worked to set up local training programs for native social workers. In the meantime, he had to hire out-of-state workers to meet immediate needs.[19]

As one might expect, most of those workers were from Ohio and New York. While they were qualified and professionally trained, their presence caused quite a stir throughout Florida's political circles. As Jack Horne—Florida's CCC selection agent who would lead a one-man letter-writing campaign against

Cone's changes to the state's welfare system—explained to federal authorities in June 1937: "Even though Florida spends millions of dollars annually to advertise its attributes and encourage out-of-state people to come here and spend their money, Floridians resent outsiders on public payrolls." Van Hyning and his fellow social workers were "foreigners" in the eyes of many in Florida's government.[20]

Cone had instructed his friend William Wainwright on the State Audit Board to begin investigating the State Board of Social Welfare. Cone then ordered background checks on all welfare employees. In his archived papers is a list of State Board of Social Welfare employees, including information about their places of origin, monthly salaries, where their families lived, what state tags they had on their cars, where they had previously worked, and even notations of which employees were Jewish.[21] Welfare Commissioner Van Hyning received the following notation, for example: "He refuses to consider for positions applicants with endorsements from Florida politicians."[22]

Within days Cone's ally Senator William H. Mapoles of Crestview (where he was editor of the *Okaloosa Messenger*) was in touch.[23] Mapoles asked for and received funding to investigate the State Board of Social Welfare.[24] Aiding him were two recently fired FERA employees, T. J. Fenn and Virgil Riley, and two state auditors.[25] Charged with exploring "rumors" of "excessive expenditures and misadministration of its affairs," the investigation focused on the board's high salaries and operating expenses, sparking a sharp public relations battle that played out across the front pages of the state's major newspapers.[26] Mapoles called the Board "one of the dirtiest, nastiest things you've ever seen," also claiming that Van Hyning was paid $8,000 a year.[27] (The actual figure was $6,000.) A fellow panhandle senator, Pensacola's Philip Beall, invoked Reconstruction-era Yankee interventionist imagery as he remarked that the government should "prevent social workers from coming into our homes and telling the mothers they don't know how to raise their own children."[28] Upon hearing news of the probe's preliminary findings, Cone declared that the board was "a waste of money and an awful expense. I haven't a clue where the money is going."[29]

Timed to coincide with the Senate probe came a bill proposed by Representative Bob Sikes of Crestview, where he edited the *Crestview Journal* and was a friendly rival of Mapoles.[30] The bill would abolish the current State Board of Social Welfare and replace it with a new State Welfare Board.[31] All involved recognized that the bill was ghostwritten by the Cone administration. It called for a state board, twelve district boards, and a commissioner, all to be appointed by the governor. The proposed bill would replace all present members (including Commissioner Van Hyning) and implement a five-year residency requirement for all State Welfare Board employees.[32]

By the spring of 1937 many in the CCC and the FPS realized that the political climate that created them was beginning to change. They also began to wonder if the NPS was no longer an ally, either. For two years the Florida Board of Forestry, led by Harry Lee Baker, negotiated with the city of Pensacola to acquire Santa Rosa Island as a state park. In the 1934 FERA state park surveys, the barrier in the Gulf of Mexico ranked very high for its park potential. Not only did the property feature over thirty miles of undeveloped beaches; it was also the site of some of the Civil War's first military action.[33] The FPS was eager to add the naturally and historically significant site to its park system. But the FPS was not alone in its admiration of Santa Rosa Island. The NPS, which approved all sites chosen by the FPS for CCC work and was involved in the FERA survey, wanted the island for its own park system and was willing to spend whatever money was needed to acquire it. Leading these efforts was C. R. Vinten, the NPS representative in Florida. Back in 1934 Vinten had remarked to the Forestry Board that the property was "the most remarkable park site in Florida."[34] But Baker was not willing to let go of Santa Rosa Island without a fight, angering many in Pensacola who much preferred the idea of having a national park near their city than a mere state park.

Several wrote to Governor Cone in protest, calling Baker "selfish" and accusing him of "interfering" with Pensacola's economic future.[35] Cone responded that Baker "is not authorized by me to take over any park or build any park" and that he knew nothing of the deal.[36] Calling Baker "one of Sholtz's men," Cone claimed "he never talks to me about anything."[37] Cone felt that if the federal government wanted to buy, then he would "not put anything in the way of it."[38] With Cone's help, the NPS acquired their park, and in the process raised the ire and suspicions of the FPS for the remainder of the CCC program. Despite promises by Vinten at the April Forestry Board meeting that the NPS would never acquire another park in Florida without the FPS's consent, relations between the two agencies were never again close.[39]

There is reason to believe that Representative Sikes of Okaloosa County proposed the State Welfare Board bill in order to obtain help with establishing the national park on Santa Rosa Island. Considering that Sikes was privately critical of the new welfare board within weeks of its inception, it seems likely he proposed the bill to gain the governor's favor.[40] All knew that Cone reciprocated political favors, and there would be plenty of rewards if his bill passed. His brother Branch, a small-scale lawyer from Maclenny, was his executive secretary.[41] Known as a "jooker" who was often found fishing in the Gulf, Branch handled much of Cone's political networking.[42] Indeed, Senator William Shands of Gainesville referred to him as Cone's "patronage man."[43] The Cone brothers regularly checked to see who supported them before making appointments. The governor once remarked about a candidate for the State Audit Board, "It is my information that Mr. Coleman did not support me, and I want proof that he did before I do anything about it."[44] Such behavior led to May Jennings's deep dislike for the governor; she once called Cone a "double dealer."[45]

The State Board of Social Welfare would be abolished on June 30, and the new State Welfare Board would take over on July 1, 1937. In the end the new board had essentially the same function and structure as the previous one.[46] The only difference, aside from its name, was that Cone controlled its membership. Board members served at his pleasure, and he could replace them at any time.[47] And Cone wasted little time in choosing his new board. On June 15 he sent telegrams to seven potential members for the new State Welfare Board officially asking for their service.[48] He then chose a new welfare commissioner—Clayton C. Codrington, editor of the *Lake City Reporter* and Cone's gubernatorial campaign manager, which the *Florida Newspaper News* called the "prize political appointment."[49] Although he met the five-year residency requirement, Codrington was originally from Cleveland, Ohio, and was educated in New York City. His salary was $500 a month, only $2.18 less than Van Hyning's.[50]

Elected in a mood of discontent and confusion over changes in Florida, Cone believed that most Floridians shared his agenda, a Depression-era "silent majority." But in his actions with the Welfare Board Cone had misread his constituency. He was supposed to be the Florida official to represent the small farmer, the turpentiner, the cracker. But threatening New Deal relief funds was not what they had in mind. And perhaps many "native" Floridians had changed more over the past decade than they themselves realized. Many Floridians considered the New Deal and its spiritual architect President Roosevelt as godsends. In nearly every oral history conducted with Florida residents of the 1930s, their praise for Roosevelt and the New Deal was unwavering. CCC veteran Paul DeGirolamo of Dade County said of FDR: "He was a great man," and Paul's parents "thought he was God."[51] Another CCC vet, George LeCouris of Tarpon Springs, proclaimed the New Deal as "the salvation of the country."[52] Former citrus sharecropper James Keene remembered how his mother "just loved that man [Roosevelt]."[53] Fatherless Hillary Cowart, who survived on WPA surplus commodities and later by working for the CCC, said that his mother "could not think but one thing, that [Roosevelt] was a wonderful person."[54] Interview after interview contains similar sentiments, as do the hundreds of letters both Cone and Sholtz received throughout the 1930s.[55] When Florida citizens voted for Cone, they were voting against Sholtz and a catering to the needs and desires of non-Floridians, not against the New Deal.

Indeed, when CCC camps (and other New Deal projects) were temporarily stalled in July and August 1937, many of Cone's supporters bolted. He was no longer attacking Yankee state workers and unwanted tourists but rather attacking poor people's checkbooks and employment. One petition that circulated protesting against any change in the welfare board came from Cone's own backyard in Alachua County in North Florida. "Any change in the present Social Welfare Program will cause delay and unnecessary suffering to our folks."[56] Sensing this potential turn in public opinion, departing members of the State Board of Social Welfare added a scathing criticism of Cone and his cronies at their last meeting in June 1937: "Man by nature is cruel—this is the only answer I can find to the debased and unwarranted charges [and] a series of political trickeries to embarrass the Board and the continuance of a non-political program . . . political immorality can never be successfully substituted for a sound business administration."[57]

Never again would Cone be as aggressive. Rather he struck an uneasy and uneven balance between his core agrarian and rural political base and those pushing for expansion, advertising, and beautification of the state. As did Sholtz before him, Cone eyed national office, perhaps even a run for the U.S. Senate in 1940. He could not completely alienate Florida's new economic and political class—hoteliers, attraction owners, race track owners, advertisers, and others backing Florida boosterism. Cone's dilemma in how far to go in either direction mirrored the inherent conflict throughout the state. What was Florida's future, how to get there, and who would control it?

One aspect on which Cone remained unwavering was white superiority and segregation. The governor freely used the terminology of the segregationist South. Even when recommending a young woman from Lake City to an administrator of the all-black Florida A&M College, Cone revealed his stance on racial matters: "Valworth Jenkins is a young darkey of good character."[58] But Florida was no longer the sleepy backwater state to which no one in the nation paid attention.

Thanks to years of advertising and development, how others in the country perceived the state now had economic repercussions for many Florida businesses. And as Cone discovered, often to his dismay, he was the national face for the state. During a cabinet meeting in a discussion over the salary of the president for Florida A&M College, when Cone said, "No Negro is worth $4,000 a year," he caused a firestorm of bad press.[59] For Cone, that such a comment was considered news at all was the truly shocking element, let alone the reaction of many of his fellow Floridians. When crowds lynched two black males in Tallahassee in 1937, "Florida [newspaper] editors expressed concern about the damage to the state's good name."[60] Cone denied that the two murders constituted a lynching, sparking local and national criticism. And on an official visit to New York City that same year, at a meeting with religious leaders and the press in his Waldorf-Astoria room to discuss the lynching of Socialist activist Joseph Shoemaker in Tampa, Cone again dented Florida's neutral public image. After indulging several criticisms regarding Florida's handling of the case, Cone shot back, "You go down there and violate state laws and you'll be punished. . . . I think a man ought to be hung on a tree if he advocates overthrow of the government."[61] Again public criticism and ridicule ensued in the national press, and New York Mayor Fiorello LaGuardia refused to meet with Cone at their previously scheduled appointment.[62]

But not everyone in the state had become a proto–civil rights supporter. Although economics saved the three African American CCC state park camps from removal, the racism that fueled those fights had not vanished. Two years later, as Myakka River State Park was closer to completion, some Sarasota residents again asked Governor Cone to remove the camp from

Myakka and have it replaced with a white camp. His responded with: "I don't have anything to do with the transfer of these camps. Personally I think it would be a good idea to abolish all the colored CCC's and let them work where they belong, but you know these northern people want to see the n[——]s protected."[63] Though no other black CCC camp was publicly contested after 1935, it was obvious that these camps were tolerated only if they proved to be economically useful.

But despite Cone's stance being the antithesis of most of the political and social changes of tourist development that roadside attractions and CCC-built state parks ushered in, he was nonetheless not completely immune to the desire to develop a tourist economy, if under his own terms. Cone was instrumental in creating what would eventually become the Stephen Foster Memorial State Park in White Springs, Cone's boyhood hometown. In 1937 he proposed that a Stephen Foster memorial should be built in Foster's ancestral home on the bank of the Suwannee River in North Florida, and then proceeded to make sure it happened.[64] Cone's enthusiasm was so great that he attempted to arrange both a CCC camp and a PWA crew to construct the memorial.[65] Two years earlier Governor Dave Sholtz, State Senator William C. Hodges, U.S. Senator Claude Pepper, and many others campaigned for the redesignation of Florida's state song, from 1913's "Florida, My Florida"—written by Florida Agricultural College language professor C. V. Waugh in 1898 and sung to the tune of "O Christmas Tree"—to "Old Folks at Home," penned by former minstrel songwriter Stephen Collins Foster.[66] Although the song was originally written about the Pee Dee River in South Carolina, Foster immortalized Florida's relatively meager blackwater river, which the native Pennsylvanian had never laid eyes upon, with one simple word change because the name Suwannee scanned better. By the 1930s popular performers such as Al Jolson often sang Foster's song—as well as other tunes containing the name Suwannee by such luminaries as Irving Berlin and George Gershwin—on stage, in films, and on radio shows. One of the very first talkies was a 1926 Warner Brothers short called *A Plantation Act* that featured a black-faced Jolson signing "Swanee."

Governor Dave Sholtz signed the song change into law on May 28, 1935.[67] In a rare instance of political and cultural unity, nearly everyone—at least white Floridians—supported the change. The song not only celebrated Florida's role in the mythical "Old South"; it was also another uniquely Florida attraction for tourists to visit and state boosters to promote. Everyone was familiar with the song that most mistakenly called "Way Down upon the Suwannee River." How many state songs were played in Warner Brothers cartoons, one could argue. That was free advertising Cone could get behind. And so could many of those Floridians who also felt alienated by the changes over the 1930s—the self-identified Florida crackers.

9

Florida Crackers and Yankee Tourists

CLASS, CONFLICT, AND REJECTION IN PARADISE

On May 24, 1998, at the Florida Folk Festival, a self-identified "Florida cracker" named Bobby Hicks swaggered onstage armed with a guitar and an attitude. This was the forty-fifth year of the festival, a state-funded event cosponsored by the Florida Folklife Program and the Florida Park Service. Starting in 1953, the event was held each May at the Stephen Foster Memorial State Park in White Springs, the Cone-supported tribute to a mystical, agrarian Florida past. So when Hicks decided in 1998 to unleash an impromptu "cracker-style" nativistic rant, he felt he was lecturing to the home crowd: "First of all, those of you that matter, you know how much I love you and you know how much I love this place. And my problem isn't with this place. I think it's important that people come here [to the festival] before their name's in the program. . . . But if this thing ever becomes the Florida Folk Festival where Florida is not the damn exception here, then I'll come back." Hicks then began to sing his signature song, "I am Florida, Need I Say More," a musical Florida history lesson that some in the 1980s and 1990s argued should replace Foster's tune as state song. Toward the song's conclusion Hicks continued his monologue: "Isn't it a little different when you listen to someone sing a song about something they grew up in? I'm not taking away from our new songwriters, but you know, some of us didn't have to read a book to figure out what the hell we're talking about." His voice grew louder and angrier. "Both sides of my family have been on this Florida soil since 1791. There was never anything wrong with my home to leave. So when you're visiting here, you're visiting from someplace else. You moved here from somewhere else. This is sacred ground. This is my home." He finished the song, then offered, "But you all better realize that every time somebody different lands at the airport, that doesn't make them part of the picture. You gotta be here a while before you earn a part in Florida folk culture.... Good night White Springs."[1] Off he went, not to return for several years.[2]

While the anger Hicks displayed was rare for the Florida Folk Festival, the sentiments were not. By the 1960s and 1970s a cracker song tradition arose among Florida songwriters and performers, many of whom played the annual festival, including Will McLean, Don Grooms, Gamble Rogers, Red Henry, Dale Crider, and Jeanie Fitchen. Typical song titles include, "Stop Running My Florida into the Ground," "Cracker Cowman," "Damn the Man Who Says Florida Ain't Part of Dixieland," "Florida Development Blues," and "I Want to Be a Florida Cracker."[3] Even the themes running through many of the songs by southern rock bands in the 1970s, such as Jacksonville-based Lynyrd Skynyrd, can be seen as part of this defiant southern revivalist stance. All these songs exhibit a cultural divide that originated in the debates over tourism and development in the 1930s—a Florida version of the age-old conflicts in the South over urbanization and modernization, tradition versus change. But even the frequent and specific use of the word *cracker* as a badge of defiance, an oppositional label used to identify a native, non-elite Floridian who wanted exemption from the plastic commercialism present in many areas of the state, can also be traced back to events of the 1930s. When people today talk about "cracker Florida," they are conjuring up images created both by non-native writers in Depression-era Florida and by rural natives during their simultaneous clashes with state promoters. And it was not necessarily a continuation of the supposed historic Celtic-Anglo folkways of the state's settlers in the eighteenth and nineteenth centuries that some scholars have identified as cracker.

But whether or not they labeled themselves crackers, hillbillies, hicks, or simply nothing at all, many Floridians in the 1930s felt not only alienated, but at times even under attack, by Florida's growing dependence upon tourism. People whose livelihoods and folkways were threatened by such causes viewed seemingly benign topics such as beautification, fire prevention, fencing of cattle, and wildlife conservation with suspicion. And while these contested topics began in the Depression, they would continue for decades afterward. Political, cultural, and social clashes in Florida in the latter half of the twentieth century originated in the selling of Florida in the 1930s.

In 1933 a new novel called *South Moon Under* appeared in stores across the nation and became an immediate bestseller. The Book-of-the-Month Club chose it as the main selection for March 1933. There was even hopeful talk of a Pulitzer Prize being awarded to its author. Written by a Washington, D.C., native now living in the backwoods of North Florida, the book concerned the lives of two pairs of Floridians. The first were recently transplanted English citrus growers, though theirs was not the story that reviewers and readers remembered. It was the second pair that everyone talked about (based on an actual married couple who worked as tenant farmers on the author's property), people the writer referred to not with sarcasm or derision but rather with respect and admiration—as crackers. Such admiration was rare for the time. For instance, a *New York Herald Tribune* review of the novel referred to the story's cracker characters as "members of the subspecies of the human race."[4] The novel traces the cracker couple as they move from Dixie County to Alachua County and then back again. She presents them as uneducated, primitive in their folkways, and speaking in a dialect that was closer to the land of Appalachia than to the land of Sunshine. But as with Foster's popular song, the novel (and the two that followed) united readers. Rural Floridians felt it was an accurate portrayal by someone who both lived among and understood "native" Floridians, thereby earning the right to employ the word *cracker* by understanding that it was a term of pride as much as insult. But others in both Florida and the nation read with curiosity and amazement of the lives and folkways of a previously unknown group of people. With this novel, writer and former journalist Marjorie Kinnan Rawlings became a celebrity, and *Florida crackers* became a household term in many areas.

A detailed history of the term *cracker* that Rawlings so openly and unashamedly employed in her writings is beyond the scope of this study. The word itself dates back to Elizabethan England and was usually used to describe a braggart or a "wise-ass"; someone who "cracks" jokes.[5] In British North America it was used to describe "backwoodsmen living in the area stretching from Maryland to Georgia."[6] By the late eighteenth century the term *cracker* was synonymous with modern class-based terms such as *hillbilly* or *white trash*. Even Spanish officials had adapted *cracker* from English usage and used it to refer to poor Carolinians and Georgians moving into Florida's hinterlands.[7] By the nineteenth century, the term—still negative in connotation—could also be applied to the men who rustled cattle for the Cuban beef market. But in normal usage, *cracker* was a class-based insult.[8]

Most early uses of *cracker* to refer to Floridians can be found in the *New*

York Times, which from the Civil War to the Depression era often wrote about travels in the peninsular state. The earliest instances of the word are found in two articles from 1861 and 1864, both of which refer to Florida "corn crackers." The 1864 article mentions that such people were "not wholly reliable" and were "poor" and "lazy." *Corn cracker* was also used in an article from 1875 to describe people in Kentucky who possessed a "fondness for fun."[9] One article from 1875 was about a traveler visiting Jacksonville and describes "the ignorant and degraded cracker" of Georgia and Florida who occasionally visited the city. According to the writer, upon seeing the town's progress, these men "merely stare, yawn and go back, apparently contented with their comfortless homes, rude fare, and dense ignorance." In many of these articles, the word seems to be a white version of *darkey*, a term also used liberally in these articles.[10] Historian Anthony Harkins, in his history of "hillbillies," talks of that term as describing what many perceived as a white "other."[11] This analysis could also be applied to uses of cracker in Florida in both the nineteenth and twentieth centuries. (There are exceptions: in one *New York Times* article describing activities in Tampa as the U.S. Army prepared to invade Cuba in 1898, the author mentions one regiment's mascot, a poor, destitute African American nicknamed "Uncle Remus," whom the writer labels a cracker.)[12]

In the early twentieth century, as with many race- and class-based labels whereby the target group appropriates the term as a badge of defiance and resistance, poor white Floridians and Georgians began to do the same. In private circles many poor whites in Florida began using *cracker* as a self-identifier, a label for "us" against "them," much as people were also doing in Tennessee and Arkansas with "hillbilly," and as working-class southerners across the region would do in later decades with "bubba" and "redneck." But as late as the 1930s the word *cracker* was still an insult, a more widely used version of other regional derogatory terms such as *lintheads, clay-eaters, wool hats*, and *briar hoppers*. For instance, a *Time* magazine cover story on the U.S. Senate race in Florida in 1938 featured a negative portrait of candidate James Wilcox, whom the article refers to as "Cracker Boy" because of his rural origins on the banks of the Suwannee River in South Georgia.[13] Interestingly, in a passage that inadvertently harks back to the word's origins, the one positive assessment of Wilcox in the article was "that he made the best wisecrack of the campaign."[14]

But in the 1930s, as regional writing exploded as a distinct genre—over 1,500 regional novels appeared in the 1930s, including several Pulitzer Prize winners—Rawlings fell in love with the neighbors she found at her Cross Creek homestead, which she called Los Hermanos, and where she and her then husband dreamed of becoming rich growing oranges near the banks of nearby Orange Lake, and where she saw literary opportunity. Although she has been described in recent years as a literary ethnographer who often took her fictional descriptions as fact, Rawlings's inclinations and inspiration actually came closer to those of tourists and winter residents, sensing in Florida a tropical "otherness." Crackers—that is, Florida's poor white culture (along with citrus, alligators, mosquitoes, and the warm climate that she also described in meticulous and loving detail)—fascinated Rawlings, just as palm trees, springs, and Seminoles fascinated other tourists. As one literary scholar described it, Rawlings "was amazed at the lavishness of the natural beauty which surrounded her" and which "appealed to her imagination and allowed her romantic sensibilities" to emerge.[15] It was the "American frontier come to life."[16] And instead of taking photographs or buying souvenirs, Rawlings captured her experience in her own way. She wrote about it.

First came the short stories in *Scribner's* magazine in 1931 and 1932: "Cracker Chidlings," "Jacob's Ladder," and "Crop of Beans."[17] Then she published "Gal Young 'Un" in *Harpers* in 1932.[18] And in 1933 she was in the *Saturday Evening Post* with "Alligator."[19] These were popular, but when *South Moon Under* appeared, Rawlings was on her way to becoming a bona fide celebrity. And once she published her Pulitzer Prize–winning *The Yearling* in 1938, both her fame and the cracker image solidified in the public mind. Rawlings, as only an outsider could, had provided an alternative version of commodified Florida, though one just as tropical, exotic, and unique. Crackers, at least as they appeared in Rawlings's novels, were stoic and fiercely independent; Jeffersonian farmers who bore little resemblance to the sharecropper and relief workers in other southern regional works. They became for non-Florida readers another source of fascination and attraction. Primitive, pre-modern, and wholly "other," crackers were like an Anglo version of the Seminoles. (And noticeably, Cross Creek's large African American population—including several families who worked Rawlings's citrus grove—remained relatively invisible in her books, though their lives and folkways differed little from those of their Anglo neighbors. In an early manuscript Rawlings once wrote that while crackers fit their surrounding "like jack pine" the "local Negro . . . is a little alien.")[20] As one scholar pointed out, her work was often more accessible to national readers than were other southern-based writers because she was "not haunted by a specific Southern past with its Lost Cause and 'peculiar institutions.'"[21] Like the national image of Florida, her books were in many ways regionally neutral. And while few travelers actually sought out crackers (although many did visit Rawlings's Cross Creek home, much to her dismay) their presence, like that of alligators, snakes, and panthers, only added to Florida's exotic allure.

When the WPA's Federal Writers' Project published *Florida: A Guide to the Southernmost State* in 1939, they included material on Florida crackers, much of it written by aspiring folklorist and native Floridian Stetson Kennedy. He would expand these descriptions in his book *Palmetto Country*, published in 1942 as part of Erskine Caldwell's American Folkways series.[22] While less fictional than Rawlings's popular novels, both publications nonetheless employed much of her romanticism and uncritical admiration, describing what could be Florida's version of John Steinbeck's dust bowl farmers. In fact, Stetson Kennedy even calls Florida crackers "the Okies of their day (as they have been ever since)."[23] With all this positive press, by the 1940s the *New York Times* could refer to Florida crackers with no malice or ill intent. In a travel article from 1940 about the various less well known sights in Florida, the writer described a romanticized rural evening: "Dancing whiles away the Florida nights. Crackers swing their partners in squares on Saturdays, sometimes in a schoolhouse, sometimes in a rustic pavilion. . . . The old fiddler scrapes his fiddle playing tunes of his own making. . . . These folk dances are like old ballads."[24]

And while Rawlings did not invent the word *cracker*, her writings did bestow it with legitimacy. She provided a romanticized, mythical past that evoked an alternative Florida to the one that chambers of commerce, fair exhibits, advertisers, and state parks offered visitors. Historian James Cobb argued that cultural identity "typically refers to a perception of reality rather than to reality itself."[25] Rawlings's perception of reality in Florida was simultaneously counter-cultural (for some native, mostly rural Floridians) and commercially appealing. To a lesser degree, this was also the perceived Florida of her imitators, such as Theodore Pratt, Bernie Borchardt, Cecile Hulse Matschat, and Stetson Kennedy, among the many others who began to include cracker characters in their writings in the late 1930s and early 1940s.[26]

Therefore by the late 1930s (and increasingly so in the decades that followed), the Florida cracker came to represent an oppositional cultural stance, a rejection of the tropical, commercialized Florida that was found in the popular media at the time. Cracker Florida came to represent "authentic" Florida. Many Floridians were unhappy with the changes in Florida's economy and governmental policies, and though Rawlings avoided these issues in her novels (and to a large degree even fueled those changes with her fame and literary success), her image of honorable, respectable crackers offered a useful unifying mythology of sorts to this "other Florida."[27]

Small farmers' use of fire was becoming less economically useful as the decade progressed. When future state forester Harry Lee Baker published his anti-fire tract *Forest Fires in Florida* in 1927, it marked the escalation of a literal turf war that had been brewing for nearly a decade. Across the state and nation, a rising awareness of forest fires created rifts between land managers, politicians, and native residents. Tensions that stemmed from debates over forest management had by the 1920s erupted into outright hostility. In Florida, foresters and timber men united against turpentiners, cracker farmers, and—most of all—cattle ranchers. Baker wrote what many in the state had been quietly saying for years: cattle ranchers were Florida's largest and most damaging group of woods burners. According to Baker, "Cattlemen have for years been accustomed to burning off dead grass during the winter and spring" in order to provide fresh grass for their roving cattle.[28] Using words such as "apathy," "indifference," and a "need for education," Baker accused cattlemen of fostering an unprogressive and damaging burn culture. For him, cattlemen "had horns and a forked tail."[29]

Former USFS forest ranger Inman Eldredge described the fire situation in Depression-era Florida in a 1959 interview: "In those days, fire was looked on as an aid to living. Turpentiners burned over the woods so that they were open . . . cattlemen burned the woods to fatten his cattle . . . the farmer burned the woods because the turpentine men and the cattlemen were going to burn and it would burn him up to if he didn't burn first."[30] According to Eldredge, and many other observers, fire was an integral part of rural Florida culture. Locals "felt that to kill the boll weevil and get rid of snakes and to take care of cattle ticks, and almost anything else," explained Florida State Forester C. H. Coulter in 1958, "you ought to burn the woods."[31] Land clearing through fire was a common practice for rural farmers and ranchers. This was usually done, according to one rural farmer who also owned cattle, "in the winter when there was plenty of moisture on the ground. Then when the weather warmed the grasses grew tender and nutritious for grazing."[32] For turpentiners, large wild fires were "a constant menace."[33] Not only did uncontrolled conflagrations damage equipment such as the zinc cups and gutters but they also preyed upon the trees covered in a highly flammable gum, the result of the extractive turpentine methods. Anything other than low-intensity ground fires would irreparably damage the resin-rich pines. In addition, turpentiners sought cleared, open forest floors to keep away spiders, snakes, and impassable vegetation from their laborers. Therefore, regularly controlled burns were common in turpentine forests and were usually conducted at night when "the litter on the forest floor was damp" and there was little wind.[34] Ranchers also preferred cleared forest floors as well as the fresh grass shoots that sprang up after a forest fire.

"The way we did it was with dead palm fans," Gilbert Tucker wrote in 1999 to describe how he and his father burned the woods for their cattle. "He would set a palm fan on fire and drag it through the grass to ignite. We boys would hand the fans to him. One day we were burning when a Florida fire control water spray truck from the forestry service came in behind us and started extinguishing our fire. Papa lost his cool, took his pistol from his saddle bag, pointed it at the man, and told him if he did not stop what he was doing it would be the last fire he would ever put out."[35] Contrary to what many contemporary and present observers have argued, fire was considered by rural Florida residents as an integral part of their lives. As Tucker explained, "This is absolutely necessary practice if you grow cattle and wildlife in rough native woods."[36]

The Florida Forest Service labeled such fire customs as "short-sighted," creating "uncontrolled wild fires that stripped much of the timber from the land."[37] The Florida Federation of Women's Clubs in 1932 instituted a series of school lectures and programs warning about the danger of woods burning. This idea was to grab them before their parents infected their woods ethics. "It is believed that they carried home to their parents much of the information."[38] The fear and frustration expressed by the FFS and others originated in the late nineteenth century. Large fires in many major cities, as well as several deadly wildfires out West—such as the Wisconsin fire in 1871 and the Minnesota fire of 1894—were widely reported.[39] In a world built almost entirely of wood, fire was rightly seen as a dangerous and unpredictable force that required eradication in urban areas. And it was not too large a leap in logic to transfer the fear that fire instilled in town dwellers to the uninhabited woods. This new fear of fire coincided—especially in the South—with the growth of the timber industry, in large part fueled by the growth of those wood-built cities. As with many industries, in-house studies, scientific experiments, and resource protection were seen as vital to the timber industry's survival, which led to the emergence of the professional forestry field. Forestry schools developed that were centered primarily in the North, such as in Pennsylvania and Michigan. Soon fire suppression was viewed as the most pressing issue in forest management, and these timber men and professional foresters saw arsonists behind every tree.

Into this mix came the CCC, Roosevelt's "tree army," who not only put out every fire they found but spread the message to an entire nation that fires were destructive and a threat to the nation's future. And federal New Deal support of fire protection was not limited to the CCC. As a WPA Federal Writers' Project publication argued, "Woods burning has become a custom in this State and old residents could not understand why such a practice would impair Florida's resources. . . . Woods burning has been perhaps the greatest single factor in the depletion of Florida forests."[40] After years of lamenting the effect blackened forests and smoke on the highways had upon the state's tourist industry, Florida's promoters were thrilled.

Those concerns appeared to be confirmed in 1940 when John Shea, a psychologist employed by the USFS to study the prevalence of fires in the South and especially Florida, published "Our Pappies Burned the Woods" in *American Forests* magazine.[41] Based on dozens of interviews throughout the region, Shea concluded that the answer resided in the poorer classes' pre-modern customs and their "frustrated lives," in which the only excitement they experienced was in burning the woods.[42] The belief of the crackers (Shea's word) that fire killed ticks and snakes and had other benefits, wrote Shea, was ignorance coupled with outdated folkways. Shea's study only validated how many throughout Florida already felt.[43]

The cattle industry's reaction to these anti-fire campaigns was swift. A series of rebuttal writings appeared after Baker's initial publication. These writings took on Baker, point by point. In one essay entitled "Some Strictly Minor Details of Testimony," the anonymous writer analyzed Baker's illustrations, starting with the cover. "The cover's portrayal of a Florida woods fire being beaten with a pine bough. My, but what a bonehead!"[44] On page four of Baker's booklet, the essay pointed out, the photo showed trees displaying "unmistakable evidence of having been killed by method of turpentining before they were burned."[45] The photo was only captioned with "Destroyed trees," leaving the impression that fire killed them, but never stating that fact overtly. Another photo—on page six—of a "healthy" forest was also clearly a turpentine forest, with a litter-free understory, signifying recent burning.[46] Another essay used deductions analogous to modern historical analysis to dispute Baker's claims. In "Just How Little the Outside Expert Knows," the writer described how explorers Hernando DeSoto and William Bartram both reported—two hundred years apart—plentiful pine forests in North Florida. Furthermore, Bartram "records that the Indians habitually burned the woods—just as they must have been doing for ages."[47] Therefore, the essay asked, why after centuries of uncontrolled burning are pine forests still thriving in North Florida?

Many of the essays took on regional and class connotations. Baker's northern origins were often remarked upon despairingly, as was the Florida Forestry Association's urban membership. In one sentence in an essay called "Something for the Florida Cracker to Think About," the writer managed to invoke racism, regionalism, class, the land boom, states' rights, and a rural-urban dichotomy:

> Certainly as a Democratic State that holds some manner of State Rights against the increasing absorption of power by the federal government, Florida can work out control and development of its own forests for its own people instead of for speculators and boomringers that never get nearer to what the country means than by golfing over forty acres after a little ball in company with a little n[——]![48]

These essays pointed out the power struggles inherent in land management issues, especially as the federal government became more involved.

But many in the cattle ranching industry felt justified in their anger. Ranchers and small farmers saw attacks leveled at them from several fronts. For starters, although the law would not be passed until 1949, many Floridians pushed for a fence law as early as the 1920s. Such a law would restrict the normal practice of allowing branded cattle to roam freely in common forests. This period also saw the emergence of the cattle tick fever that led to Florida's State Livestock Board requirement that all cattle be dipped in an arsenic solution every two weeks. For ranchers who normally let their cattle roam freely, that meant an investment of time and intense labor for rounding up and dipping the cattle in the state-approved concrete vats. For many small-scale ranchers, it meant an exit from the livestock industry as they buckled under the expense involved. Therefore the proposed restriction on range and woods fires was the final straw for many.

In the meantime law enforcement officials were having difficulty actually catching and prosecuting the woods burners and arsonists the foresters so feared. The frustration can be seen in several letters of the period. For instance Florida forester Coulter wrote, "It is extremely difficult to catch woods burners and to get sufficient evidence for conviction."[49] In another letter, Baker explained to the governor: "Even our present rangers, who speed to fires reported by look-outs have difficulty in actually seeing the party who threw away the match."[50] The unspoken explanation was that in many cases the fires were natural in origin and not the work of fellow humans.

Years later in 1962, at a fire ecology conference held at Florida State University, fire ecologist Herbert Stoddard lamented the plight of rural Floridians during the Depression. "Some with no first-hand knowledge of these hardy pioneers would have us believe that they set fires just to see them burn."[51] Through the publications and no-fire campaigns, they were "much maligned"; and they had "valid reasons for burning."[52] And they were correct that fires killed chiggers, ticks, and other pests. Stoddard saw regional bias playing a role in the actions of foresters, most of whom were from the Northeast and had been trained in areas outside Florida. "The liberty-loving natives began to be harassed by an influx of Northerners that neither understood them, nor had much consideration of them."[53] But this was little consolation to those in the 1930s who felt under attack. And if these people felt maligned over their fire practices, that paled in comparison to the reaction to ranchers' and farmers' methods for eradicating cattle ticks, killing deer by the hundreds.

In July 1933 Florida Conservation Commissioner George Davis received a frantic letter from Dorothea Mason of Winter Park asking whether the government was poisoning deer to eradicate cattle tick fever. A concerned Davis forwarded the letter with one of his own to State Veterinarian Jean Knapp. In response, Knapp wrote, "So far as this department is informed, deer are not a factor in tick eradication work."[54] Knapp's response appeared to quash the seemingly conspiratorial rumor. A month later, Florida Governor Dave Sholtz and U.S. Senator Duncan Fletcher both received letters from the president of the Tropical Sportsmen Club, Scott Weaver. "Ticks have already been sent to Washington to convince the Dept. of Agriculture that in order to fully eradicate the fever tick, it will be necessary to destroy all the deer in the lower Everglades," Weaver wrote to Sholtz.[55] To Fletcher's letter he added, "Dr. Knapp denied any knowledge of this," although Weaver claimed to have "reliable" data to back up claims that "such an unbelievable act" was indeed in process.[56] In his response to Fletcher's request for confirmation, Knapp denied all of Weaver's claims.[57] But Knapp was holding back information.

Far beyond the notice of civic boosters and out-of-state tourists, cattle tick fever ran rampant among Florida's cattle throughout the 1930s. Concurrently, other livestock diseases, including hog cholera, brucellosis, tuberculosis, and poultry white diarrhea were also devastating the state's livestock industry. But ticks were what most concerned ranchers, farmers, and regulators, as they were the carrier of cattle tick fever, which rendered cattle lethargic, decreased their milk production, and caused high mortality rates. Known scientifically as *Babesia bovis*, it spread to cattle via the tropical tick (*Boophilus annulatus*). At the time the only effective method to rid the cattle of the dreaded tick, and thereby the economically disastrous fever, was arsenic cattle dips. Begun in the 1920s through the newly created Florida State Livestock Board, these dips were both expensive and potentially fatal for the cattle. State-mandated dipping was a major disruptor in Florida (and elsewhere in the South).[58]

Up to that time Florida had a distinctive, unregulated open-range ranching culture.[59] Former rancher Harris Fussell described Florida's cattle culture in the 1930s: "Open range? It was no definition of where everybody's property was. No fence lines. Everybody's cattle just ran together. They all done community work to get together and have what they called a round-up. They would mark and brand their cattle where they would be identified. . . . Then they'd turn them back out."[60] More than solely an economic pursuit, rounding up and branding cattle was a social event. "That was the biggest picnic—that was the only real picnic that they knew about at that time cause they looked forward every year to catching and wrassling those calves . . . it was a great excitement for the boys. . . . It was just a great holiday time."[61]

Inez Magill (née Hull) also remembers cattle in her native Caloosahatchee Valley, between present-day Okeechobee and Fort Myers: "Pioneer families had cattle, which had free range. While they were scrub cattle, they could take care of themselves in the tick-infested country and could live through the dry winter on the sparse grass. Every owner had his own brand, as that was the only means of identity when they ranged in unfenced territory."[62] She noted: "Practically everyone had a milk cow, they ran loose in the streets."[63] And she repeated that cattle were not restricted to the woods but roamed the town. "We still stumbled over cows in the streets. Soon after the creation of the county, an anonymous writer had a poem in the local paper about cows not knowing they were supposed to stay home."[64]

Ironically, just as with tourism, Florida ranching was an "environment dependent industry," which depended on the ability of "scrub cows"—a Florida-acclimated animal derived from Spanish Andalusia bred with English-stock cattle—to survive Florida's sandy environment.[65] These Florida bovines were smaller and hardier than the "pure-breds" of western America. The Florida cattle could live on the nutrient-deprived wiregrass and other native grasses in Florida's sandy flatwoods and vast longleaf pine forests.[66] Ranchers, who used cow dogs and cattle whips instead of lassos and fences to control cattle, never had to feed their cattle.[67] Unlike other cattle common in the United States, the scrub cattle could survive on native forage alone. Once, perhaps twice, a year the cattle were rounded up—identified by either brands or owner-specific ear cuts—for selling at market.[68] The rest of the year ranchers and small farmers did nothing for the cattle. And because they roamed the open territory, owners could enter the livestock trade with very little investment: feed, extensive land holdings, and large staffs were unnecessary. And unlike in the rest of the nation, Florida ranchers sold meat either locally in the state or, more commonly, to Cuba.[69]

The net result of the tick eradication program was that by the mid-1930s many small farmers quit the business altogether. Large cattle owners, able to withstand the occasional dip-related deaths as well as afford to hire staff to gather cattle every other week, prospered as they consolidated their control over the industry. And even though the law did not require it, many of the well-to-do ranchers began fencing in their property. Not only was this more efficient for their operations, further boosting their control, but it removed those specific grazing lands from use by other smaller farmers not able to afford their own land or fencing. By the 1930s there was already talk of improving the industry by bringing in pure-bred cattle to allow Florida ranchers to compete on the national market. With fenced areas that could be stocked with adequate feed, coupled with the increased infrastructure of the larger ranches, imported cattle could now be a profitable endeavor in the Sunshine State. Such a development would further erode the small rancher's stake in the trade. But forces outside the industry were about to emerge that would affect not only the small farmer and rancher but also the cattle industry as a whole.

As discussed in previous chapters, by the 1930s all of Florida had become a tourist attraction. Beaches, citrus farms, forests, lakes, and even alligators became selling points. Therefore all of Florida had to be presentable. As with farmer-sparked fires that caused smoke on the highways and left behind charred trees and blackened ground, promoters scrutinized the actions of cattle owners, large and small. And the top issue these state promoters focused upon was the paving and improving of the state's roads. And in doing so, they struck directly at the heart of the now beleaguered open-range ranching culture. Despite the increase in the amount of fenced-in lands, the central feature of the Florida ranching industry was free-range cattle. Even some of the larger landowners viewed fencing as a temporary fix, only valid until the tick eradication program ended. But as early as the 1910s, a small but influential segment of Floridians demanded what they termed No-Fence laws that would require all livestock owners to keep their animals fenced off. There was even a No-Fence League formed by members of the Florida Federation of Women's Clubs (FFWC).[70]

But the movement did not pick up steam until the 1930s. By then too many accidents were occurring on the state's highways, advocates of fencing argued. One supporter called the open-range ranching "a relic of near Civil War times."[71] Journalist and owner of the Florida Clipping Service (and future gubernatorial candidate in 1940) Russell Kay began to write searing opinion pieces against open-range cattle. Originally from Los Angeles, California, and one of the original "Tamiami Trail Blazers" (a group of men who drove the proposed Tamiami Trail between Fort Myers and Miami in 1923 to raise publicity for the need for good roads), Kay was a major player in the creation of the Florida Exhibition at the Century of Progress and Great Lakes Exposition and later at the 1939 New York World's Fair.[72] Convinced that cattle were a threat to Florida tourism, he even wrote a poem in 1934 about the issue called "Clear All Roads":

In all of our Zephyrs
The folks from other states do like
Our winds but not our heifers

So kick the scrubs right off the roads
And shut them up by heck!
And we'll be rid of those darn things
That often cause a wreck

For when you bump right into one
The owner set up a holler
He swears the cow would bring ten bucks
When she ain't worth a dollar

Besides all this, I'm afraid to say
I've more to tell of heifers
If they would stay from off our roads
Purer'd be our Zephyrs[73]

The cattle industry, in the guise of the Florida Cattlemen's Association (FCA), responded with a vengeance. In a lengthy series of editorials in the *Florida Cattleman*—many of which were reprinted in various newspapers—the president of the FCA argued for retention of open-range ranching. In one piece he argued that cattlemen paid gas taxes—the main revenue for highway construction—just as every other Floridian did, as well as paying the gas tax for tractors "that never touch the highway."[74] In another he argued that cattle were not as dangerous as advertised. He pointed out that only twenty-seven deaths resulted from cattle on the highways, while thousands were caused by "driver error."[75] Finally he mentioned that ranchers pre-dated cars by nearly three hundred years. "Cattle were not put on the highway; but rather the highways were put on the cattle, so to speak."[76] One cattle owner in the 1930s developed a way to let out his frustrations with the tourists affecting his livelihood. After the bridge was built across the St. Johns River, "We used to go there when working cattle along the river. . . . When a car went over the bridge someone would pop his whip real loud. The driver would think he had a flat and stop to get out and look at his tires. Everyone thought this was a big joke except the driver of the car."[77]

Even Gold Head Branch State Park had to contend with fencing issues. In

1942 the park's superintendent wrote to FPS director Scoggin that free roaming hogs were invading the park. "Damage to park property has now reached a point of several hundred dollars to turf alone and is continuing at an appalling rate.... We have contacted the owner many times and they merely quote the open-range law." Park staff even resorted to firearms, "but the in-coming herd is far above the mortality rate."[78]

But for small farmers, the refusal to fence was more than mere cracker contrariness. In 1937 one economic study of Florida put the cost at between $400 and $800 per mile.[79] "Many small cattle raisers—and they are the main offender—do not make that much profit a year from their cattle."[80] Most cattle raisers who had not fenced by the 1930s argued that if people "want the highways fenced, then the State Road Department should stand the cost."[81] The Florida Research Bureau concluded in 1938: "Little can be accomplished in the way of highway fencing unless, as happened in Texas, the cattle and hogs become too valuable to allow them to roam at large."[82]

In this debate over highways and cattle, a fissure had opened up between two visions of Florida: one that pushed for agricultural and traditional agrarian values; and another that saw tourism, development, and order in Florida's fortunes. It was an issue of land use and, ultimately, control over Florida's future. And with millions in public funds pouring into both highway construction and tick eradication and other livestock disease control, parties that might otherwise have kept quiet felt empowered to speak out.[83] During the span of its first decade, the Livestock Board used science and empirical evidence to justify its actions, usually in the face of what many considered "backwoods" and pre-modern ranchers. In fact, the board was in many ways part of the modernizing force that brought order, control, and cleanliness to Florida's physical and cultural landscape. But by the mid-1930s many questioned whether the board was even necessary if Florida was indeed moving to be a tourism-centric state. Why spend public funds on an increasingly archaic industry that neither had much tangible value for tourists nor contributed, as did the citrus, shrimping, or sponge-fishing industries, to the beauty and uniqueness of the state? The board found itself on the same side of the political fence as the "backwoods" ranchers. The grumbling between these two factions would deviate into a wide, impassable gulf once the Livestock Board began what many might consider a public relations suicide mission. They began killing deer by the thousands.

Three days after writing to Fletcher, Knapp came clean. In a letter to Conservation Commissioner Davis, Knapp admitted that a "most unusual" discovery had been made.[84] While in the past the "presence of deer has never been a factor in tick work," it appeared that heavy concentrations of deer in South Florida had prolonged the presence of the Texas cattle tick fever in that region.[85] He requested assistance from Davis in "handling the deer question without exciting the cattlemen on one side and the sportsmen on the other."[86] Finally in September, Knapp revealed the news to Governor Sholtz. In early summer, ticks had been found in Volusia County on the McCrory Ranch, Orange County at the Tosahatchee Game Preserve, Broward County in the Jane Green Swamp, St. Lucie County in the Allapattah Flats swamp, and Polk County on Johnston's Island Game Preserve.[87] By that date, those areas had been declared tick-free. USDA Chief Entomologist Dr. F. C. Bishopp discovered that the ticks found on the deer were actually *Boophilus annulutus v. australis*, a tropical variety of the Texas fever tick; and it appeared these ticks were thriving on deer as well as cattle, only the deer did not grow sick as a result of the ticks.[88] Knapp then revealed his plan: "It is believed that if the deer could be reduced to a degree in these areas . . . [over] eighteen months to two years the terrain . . . would all be tick free."[89] He then attempted an explanation of his earlier denials: "We have never indicated that it was necessary to destroy all the deer. . . . It is our opinion that if deer could be reduced in numbers," then that would suffice in successful tick eradication.[90] He pondered allowing hunters to perform this work through an "open season." This letter would be the start of a public relations disaster.

The ensuing deer reduction program—begun in earnest after a state law was passed in 1937 setting a bounty for killed deer in the infected area—has been written about elsewhere regarding the highly publicized battle with the Seminole Tribe of Florida over rights to eradicate reservation-based deer.[91] All these works address the issue either from a proto-conservation angle or as a case study in Native American–U.S. government relations. What is of interest here, however, is the small window it provides into the different versions of Florida that many citizens harbored.

While cattle owners may have bristled at (and occasionally violently opposed) the increased regulations and modernizing efforts of the state veterinarians, ultimately both groups shared a common vision. The State Livestock Board and the cattle ranchers and small farmers saw Florida's future in the state's still-profitable agrarian fields. In fact, with the changes in recent years, along with the possibility of a tick-free cattle industry, they felt that Florida could finally begin to compete on a national level in the livestock industry. As fences were erected and farms mechanized through the federal New Deal, Florida's ranchers and farmers were poised to uplift their industry. They resented the focus many in Florida were placing upon recreation, road construction, and tourism. As the FCA president, a Livestock Board member, wrote in 1937: "I am sure you are familiar with the effort of a small group of so-called sportsmen to defeat the completion of tick eradication in Florida while in effect . . . denying Florida's great cattle industry."[92] Cone agreed: "I am in sympathy with the cattlemen of Florida . . . [tick eradication for] the small farmer owning a small herd of cattle [is] a necessity in the support of his family and their continued existence in this state. . . . [I] do not think the protection of a few deer that can be replaced or restocked" should stop the tick program.[93]

But the opponents to deer eradication saw the board's actions as a throwback to the Old South by people who lacked vision. Their actions were not consistent with the direction in which Florida was now heading. And at the program's foundation, they felt, was bad science. One *Miami Herald* editorial argued: "All the scientists opposing [deer reduction] cannot be wrong. Also there is a distinct possibility that the scientists supporting it may not be right."[94]

But science was rarely the main topic of concern. One writer to the governor mentioned that "deer is one of the attractions of Florida . . . the cattle are of less value than the deer. Cattle can be purchased anywhere. Where can you obtain our deer?"[95] She blamed what she perceived as outdated management of livestock for the tick outbreaks: "A healthy person can soon forget mosquitoes biting, and learn to keep them away. A healthy cow will not show disease from ticks."[96] Another writer shared the sentiment: "The cattle owners should take care of their stock and keep them fenced in and healthy. Would keep them off the highways[. Killing] the innocent deer will do none of these things."[97] A member of the Daytona Humane Society argued that "the wildlife belong to the people of the State and not a small minority of Cattle men who refuse to protect their livestock and permit them to roam at large, inbreed [and] suffer from lack of proper food, thus making them ready prey to insects and disease.[98] . . . One could not expect them to regard the deer of this State, who lend great beauty and certainly are more pleasant to see than the emaciated herds of scrub cattle one is forced to look at on our highways."[99] Betty Stokes of Ormond Beach, in a letter to Cone, invoked God's wrath upon the deer killers: "I would greatly appreciate if you would save these innocent gentle deer.... If it [deer killing] does take place, those who take part in the killing will be punished. A Greater Power always sees to that."[100]

Deer added to Florida's safe image as a natural playground. State parks commonly featured deer on their promotional materials, as did other attractions such as Silver Springs, Homosassa Springs, and McKee's Monkey Jungle. CCC crews often introduced deer to areas of state parks with low populations. One of the most common images for Myakka River State Park was that of visitors feeding tame deer. Even Marjory Stoneman Douglas, in her popular guide *Parks and Playground of Florida*, explained that "Florida deer become very tame quickly and they make most lovable pets, particularly the female." And of course, Marjorie Rawlings's Pulitzer Prize–winning popular novel *The Yearling* featured the story of a cracker boy and his pet deer in the Florida wilderness.[101]

Keeping deer alive and plentiful was good business. As sports writer and recent Cleveland transplant Morris Ackerman once explained to Sholtz: "Give Highlands County some protection that keep[s] these 'Yankees' coming."[102] But by August 1937 news of the deer killing had reached the *New York Times*, which stated that between 500 and 700 deer would be killed in Orange and Osceola counties to save "the 'scrub' cattle."[103] What would Florida's greatest pool of visitors think about this new policy? Would it deter them from visiting? Cause them to go to California instead? Boosters had cause to worry, as Florida's wildlife was a major draw. As one Cleveland native wrote in 1933: "Of all the great assets of a great state, none are more valuable to you, to your people and to the guests of Florida than its wildlife. Take from Florida its inland game fish and its quail and other attractions to sportsmen ... and Florida no longer would hold the lure of its now proud position of a sportsmen panacea."[104] The Florida State Planning Board clearly stated in its biennial report for 1934 to 1936 that "the proper conservation of our wildlife will add to the State's attractiveness from the standpoint of those who like to hunt and fish, as well as those who like to use the camera for the shooting of wild life ... such a program would more than pay for itself by the increase in revenue brought into the State by visitors to enjoy hunting."[105]

Much of the concern over tick eradication was not about the lives of the deer but rather who got to hunt the deer. Upper- and middle-class hunters and sportsmen have always been seen as possessing wilderness ethics and employing "fair" tactics in the wild.[106] It was such hunters who pushed for the first conservation laws, asked for bag limits, and pushed governments to create nature preserves. And as many argued in the 1930s, these hunters spent their time and money in the Sunshine State. Not only did placing bounties on deer violate the sportsmen's code hunters pledged to follow, but it removed the very attraction that brought hunters as well as sightseers to Florida in the first place. And it was that inherent bias to which many native Floridians objected: that "foreign" visitors should enjoy more rights than local people did. As the Junior State Chamber of Commerce stated bluntly, "Improve fishing. Tourists are our cash customers and our greatest source of revenue, therefore we should cater to their wishes."[107] And not cater to natives' wishes, the statement implies.

Another example of this conflict over wildlife concerned Florida's native black bass, commonly found in lakes, streams, and rivers. For decades, bass were locally harvested by freshwater commercial fishers for sale in local and national markets. In March 1933 alone, three million pounds of black bass were sold.[108] But by 1934 many boosters, tourists, and conservationists began arguing for restriction of the catching of bass to recreational fishers only. "It has been said the black bass fishing attracts to the state as many tourists who freely spend their money as any other Florida sport. . . . Every black bass under a lily pad in Florida is worth $5 to the state," argued one writer.[109] The sale of bass should be prohibited. Another claimed that "30% of the inquiries in Central and South Florida from tourists bear directly on fishing. . . . The hotels, sporting goods dealers, gasoline stations, clothing stores, grocery stores all profit by it. . . . It is high time that we go to bat and fight our seed stock so that we may have a few fish."[110] One tourist from White Plains, New York, complained that unless Florida protected the bass as a game fish, "You are going to lose a great many of we sportsmen who enjoy your climatic conditions in the winter but we also expect a little pleasure and are willing to pay for the same but we are not going to come if you still persist in allowing this wholesale slaughter to continue." He closed with: "Your fish are one of your chief assets and should be amply protected . . . you cannot afford to lose this asset."[111]

Marjory Stoneman Douglas wrote in 1938 that "the greatest single recreation which the whole state offers is fishing. . . . Fish in the millions teem in all the salt waters . . . and all its 30,000 fresh water lakes and many thousands of miles of rivers."[112] The Junior State Chamber of Commerce asked readers in another article, "Does Florida want the tourist fisherman's dollar or will she continue to be satisfied with selling bass in the open market along with catfish and mullet at a few cents per pound?"[113] The answer came during the 1935 legislative session when the Black Bass Bill was passed, prohibiting the sale or purchase of black bass as well as the shipping of the fish out of state. Many native Floridians felt the State of Florida was still selling bass, only now to tourists through the widespread use of bass on brochures, posters, and press releases (including for all the state parks), while they were prohibited from doing so.

Other laws passed in 1935 and 1937 restricted the use of stop-nets and seine nets in fresh and salt waters, placed catch limits on certain species, and established harvesting seasons. One fish market owner in Panama City complained to Conservation Commissioner Dowling, "The non-resident coming to Florida paying no license, the fools of Florida closing the waters to [seines] and nets, prohibiting them making a living where they own homes, pay taxes, try to be a law abiden [sic] citizen."[114] Another fish market owner from Tarpon Springs wrote about a young boy arrested for fishing. "The boy had violated a law and of course Mr. Booth [the warden] had to do his duty," and confiscated the boy's nets and skiff. "This boy hasn't asked any relief yet from the government and he was trying to make a living for his family. If he loses his nets and skiffs it will cause his family to suffer. . . . He hasn't committed a serious crime."[115]

But even the enforcement of conservation laws, many of which had been created and justified as ways to support tourism, sparked debates over their bias. Many argued that they should not be enforced too strongly lest they deter visitors. One West Palm Beach resident complained of overzealous game wardens and told the story of a "millionaire sportsman of Atlanta" who felt harassed by a Game and Fresh Water Fish employee. "Are they [the wardens] the type of men to induce sportsmen to come to Florida's great hunting and fishing grounds? If the Game Department persists in keeping this type of man as warden how long do you think we will enjoy the revenue that thousands of sportsmen bring to all the business people of Florida every year? How many thousands of dollars worth of advertising do you think it will take to begin to offset what this one sportsman will tell his friends."[116] He closed with: "Yours for more GAME CONSERVATION and less hounding of the sportsmen." The Fort Pierce Chamber of Commerce wrote to Cone that "the activities of State

Conservation Officer Simms in arrests of Fort Pierce anglers fishing from boats are running our winter visitors off by the drove.... Our state must protect its four hundred million dollar tourist industry."[117]

But aside from the destruction of deer or black bass, many boosters and conservationists implied that it was the behavior of native residents—the crackers—that was the larger problem. In regard to the passage of a series of conservation laws in 1937, several middle-class residents of Volusia County (including the FNE's Earl Brown) sent a telegram to their legislator urging the bill's passing as "our fish and game are becoming very scarce due to lack of legal protection."[118] J. E. Knight of Plant City wrote in 1938 that "there should be an abundance of game, but I find that in most places it is being rapidly depleted. The reason for this is that the number of Game Wardens is not sufficient during the closed season."[119] Areas where locals had been kept out during the off-season had become "Paradises regained."[120] The principal of the Clewiston High School offered the following reason for increased game protection: "The summer here is the time when so many people are idle due to the closing of the sugar mill and there is a great tendency in this county to hunt out of season, and unfortunately many DO IT and will continue to do it unless they know that the law will be enforced by a game warden who STAYS in the fields and woods" (emphasis in original).[121]

A bounty placed upon "hawks, crows, and wildcats" by the legislature in 1937 to aid livestock owners also raised similar ire. "The type of hunter who would take advantage of this proposed legislation is the type who would be uninformed, careless and indifferent in discriminating one bird from another.... It is detrimental to the interests of sportsmen since it would attract to the field the most lawless and indiscriminate type of gunner who would use the bounty law as an alibi for hunting out of season."[122] Such behavior would remove "a source of attraction to ... the tourist population who love and value wild life solely because of its scenic and educational value. . . . [Removing this law would] confer a very great favor upon the true conservationists, the true sportsmen, naturalists and lovers of the scenic natural resources of our state."[123] Another writer asked for a bill to prevent alligator hunting for similar reasons.[124]

Birds were a special concern for conservationists and boosters. "Our wild life," wrote R. L. Longstreet, conservation chairman for the State Chamber of Commerce, "has been subject ... to the depredation of the native population."[125] In an attempt to transform birds into economic commodities, Longstreet pointed out that "some people are thrilled by the sight of an American egret in a roadside ditch or a cardinal in an orange tree.... Let us consider the value of birds from a purely economic point of view [because] they make the state more attractive to the tourist upon whose presence and expenditure so many of us are dependent for a living."[126] And unlike the local hunters, "Every northern hunter coming here leaves not only his cash for a hunting license, but also a very considerable sum by way of hotel bills, payments to guides, and for many other necessary costs of living.... Every year many people from the North come here just to see these famous water birds. And those people leave money with us when they come."[127]

Such concerns by boosters regarding the hunting habits of locals did indeed have some basis in reality. For instance, in 1935, the *Florida Conservator*, the short-lived public journal for the Florida Department of Conservation, reported that two bowhead whales were killed for sport near Hillsborough Lighthouse at Pompano on March 25, 1935.[128] The whales, "one monster at least seventy-five feet in length and a smaller one thirty feet or so," were harpooned at least seven times by a local fisher who happened upon them one afternoon. It took seven hours to get the whales ashore. Before being harpooned itself, the larger whale even at one point lifted the fishing boat into the air, refusing to leave the smaller injured whale. "Boats of all sizes and descriptions attracted by the sea battle joined the procession. They sounded their horns and sirens. There was bedlam from thousands of people lining the banks and from automobiles."[129] A Fox Movietone News crew, which happened to be in the area, even caught the event on film. Eventually that evening, the impromptu whalers dumped the carcasses into Port Everglades, where local "sight-seeing parties were taken out to view the spectacle of hundreds of ravenous sharks."[130] At that point, more locals began hunting the sharks: "Several 14-foot tiger sharks weighing from 800 to 1000 pounds, their bellies gorged with whale meat, were harpooned, shot, and brought to the city docks, some of them still alive and kicking."[131]

In late October 1940, NPS staff reported to the conservation commissioner a similar occurrence in St. Augustine in the waters near Castillo de San Marcos National Park. A porpoise was shot by locals, while a state conservation officer looked on, "within full sight and hearing of indignant citizens and visitors to the city."[132] It was the second such killing in less than two weeks.[133] As the ranger explained, "Our situation in St. Augustine is somewhat different than it is in industrial or commercial fishing towns. We have one principle item to sell and anything that interferes with that commodity does us a grave wrong indeed. We are rightfully proud in being a city which affords to the visitor an unparalleled vista of scenic and historic beauty."[134] He further pointed out that dolphins and porpoises were popular with tourists. "Your office might have consulted the world famous staff of the Martine Studios who report that their porpoises are one of their greatest attractions."[135] Cone and the commissioner, Robert Dowling—a Cone appointee and a North Florida native—never responded.

State parks and forests helped by not only providing protected areas in which birds, animals, and plants were protected from local hunters and fire starters, but where tourists could easily access these natural areas. As the chair for the Division of Birds, Flowers and Wildlife for the Florida Federation of Women's Clubs (FFWC) stated in their annual report in 1938, "Recent developments in the Federal State Forest program throughout had lessened the loss of wildflowers by fire."[136] In their annual report for 1933, the FFWC argued for preventing "forest fire to save not only our forest and plant life but to save the bird and animal life so cruelly destroyed."[137] And many organizations called for increased wildlife refuges, preserves, parks, and forests. One such area was Sanibel-Captiva Island in southwest Florida. As the secretary for the Inter-Island Association for Conservation explained, the natural resources must be protected "against the distinctive abuses and law violations which are reducing the various species to the point of extinction."[138] The culprits, not surprisingly, were the local residents, who "go out to raise whoopee, invade the lagoons and adjacent waters of Sanibel, Captiva and Pine Island and make targets of anything in sight including Ibis, pelicans, greater and lesser white herons and song birds, gulls and ducks. Their shooting is obviously without object since they do not even stop to pick up the dead birds."[139] The organization wanted it to be designated a state refuge so that recreation in such a "wasteful and useless manner which threatens complete elimination of our most interesting and spectacular exhibits value[d] by our winter residents and visitors to this region" could be halted.[140] Even the Leesburg chapter of the Daughters of the American Revolution wrote to Governor Cone, calling for greater fire protection and an increase in protected wildlife areas.[141]

In the end only 8,874 deer were killed for cattle tick eradication.[142] While a high number for conservationists, it was nowhere near the number many had feared. The last ticky deer on non-Seminole land was killed in March 1939; and the last non-ticky deer was killed in December 1939. In September 1944 the USDA and Livestock Board declared Florida to be tick-free.[143] But ultimately the main issue had little to do with ticks and cattle fevers and everything to do with which economic, social, and political path would Florida follow. Historian Neil Maher recently argued that the modern environmental movement arose out of the CCC bringing awareness to the American public through its forests, parks, enrollees, and publicity.[144] But in Florida, there was an extra step. Early environmental stirrings were brought about by the realization by the civic elite of the economic benefits that an improved nature could offer, such as those areas created and maintained by the CCC, including state parks. Nature should be preserved (or at least, the attractive aspects of nature) because it sells. Green equaled green.

And while ranching remained a vital part of Florida's economy, and would for many more decades, Florida was urbanizing with new roads, bridges, and highways, increased national media attention, numerous tourist attractions, hotel chains, and natural parks. Florida's economy became increasingly dependent upon the whims and desires of people living and working thousands of miles away, who expected to see cattle in the West, not in sunny, sandy Florida. While the future of Florida never hung on the fate of the *Boophilus* tick, the effort to eradicate it clarified and crystallized the debate that began in the 1930s over control of Florida's land use and development. The primacy of Florida's scrub cow, cracker cowboys, and cattle dips would eventually yield to Mickey Mouse, snowbirds, and protected lands.

10

The Sunshine State Emerges on the World Stage

FLORIDA AT THE NEW YORK WORLD'S FAIR

Long before Florida was a home to Mickey Mouse, Harry Potter, and Shamu, though, it was first home to mermaids, Tarzan, and monkeys at sites such as Silver Springs, Marineland, and Parrot Jungle. By 1939 Florida's tourism business was booming. And while estimates over the decades had varied wildly as to numbers of visitors and amounts spent, by the end of the 1930s Florida enjoyed some hard numbers, which sealed its fate for the foreseeable future.

One of the first studies of Florida tourism began in 1936 with the passage of the Federal Park, Parkway, and Recreation Study Act on June 23. To be conducted at the state level as an aid to state planning, the study would look at the conservation, park, and recreation efforts in each state. The idea was to identify activities prevalent in a state and to provide an inventory of possible properties for park, forest, and recreational development. Completed in Florida as a WPA project (Project #665-35-3-6) between 1937 and 1939, the Florida State Planning Board and the Florida Forestry and Parks Board were the supervising agencies for the state. The focus for the Florida study was how to develop the state's "potential natural resources" for tourism. By the time of the study's completion, there were 15,774 acres in state parks and 29,713 acres in state forests. The report found that fishing, hunting, and sightseeing were three of the top reasons people visited Florida.[1]

In September of that year the Florida WPA, in cooperation with the Florida State Chamber of Commerce, released *The Florida Tourist: A Preliminary Report of the Florida Tourism Survey Project*. Directed by WPA worker Thomas P. Denham, the study tried to provide some quantification of the tourism industry, as "there is little definitely known, though many guesses and estimates have been made."[2] The guiding problem propelling the study was "Why People

Come to Florida." The study involved 53,000 questionnaire cards given to passengers on trains, buses, and planes. The study also incorporated a 1937 highway survey by the State Road Department, conducted by setting up random stops at road arteries into the state and asking drivers to fill out cards explaining why they came to Florida, what they were planning to do, how long they would spend, etc. Both studies found that climate, natural recreation, and parks were the major attractions for Florida visitors. Among the findings were that 20 percent of tourists came for fishing, 28 percent for bathing and swimming, and 21 percent for motor sightseeing.[3] Most stayed at hotels (43 percent), followed by apartments, friends, and rental homes.[4] News media and newspaper ads accounted for over 20 percent of the ways tourists learned about Florida, while word of mouth counted for a whopping 42 percent.[5] Not surprisingly to anyone in Florida in 1939, the majority of tourists hailed from New York, New Jersey, and Ohio, followed by Illinois, Pennsylvania, and Wisconsin.[6] The only states contributing no tourists were Wyoming, Oregon, Arizona, and Nevada.[7] Tourists staying between two and three months in the winter numbered higher, followed by those staying between two and three weeks.[8] Most spent between $2.50 and $4.99 a day.

Echoing those Floridians protesting deer eradication, the report concluded that "the wildlife resources of Florida constitute one of the state's greatest and most valuable assets. . . . Florida is preeminently an outdoor state. To the sportsmen who likes his nature in the raw, Florida offers vast acres of wilderness forest and swamplands."[9] In addition to hunting and fishing, parks (city, county, and state) were "the center of action for many tourists," valued at $11 million in revenue.[10] Each community should build parks to "provide them [tourists] with recreation and amusement . . . to enjoy themselves and to return to Florida for subsequent visits and bring others with them."[11] Over 1.5 million tourists played shuffleboard in 1938—500,000 in Palm Beach and Pinellas counties alone.[12] Twenty-nine counties sported over 800 shuffleboard courts. Other popular park activities were horseshoes, checkers, and lawn bowling. All three studies validated the state government's efforts in building a state park service.

In 1939 the Florida Hotel Commission, charged with inspecting hotels, rooming houses, restaurants, and apartment buildings, reported that Florida housed 16,396 hotels and 8,079 restaurants.[13] Back in 1933 they had issued 289 building permits for new hotels. By 1939 that figure had quadrupled.[14]

According to their biennial report, "The Florida Hotel Commission issued more permits for operation under state supervision of hotels, apartments, rooming house and restaurants than FOR ANY OTHER YEAR IN THE HISTORY OF THE COMMISSION" (emphasis in the original).[15]

Safe from Cone's government-trimming axe after his welfare board fiasco, many of the state's New Deal programs continued to expand the efforts to sell Florida to the nation in the late 1930s. Top among these was the Florida Federal Writers' Project (FWP), which operated as a section of the state's WPA program. Based out of Jacksonville, and under the active guidance of local historian and writer Carita Doggett Corse as state director, the FWP churned out numerous travel guides and tourist brochures. While often focusing upon culture and history, nearly all the publications completed by the FWP assumed the reader to be a tourist.[16] Briefly assuming primacy over the State Department of Agriculture's Bureau of Immigration (although they collaborated on several publications), the FWP created numerous booklets on Florida towns, highways, nature, and travel, including:

1936	*History of Broward County*
1937	*Seeing St. Augustine*
1938	*The Intracoastal Waterway: Norfolk to Key West*
	The Ocean Highway: Brunswick New Jersey to Jacksonville, Florida
1939	*Florida: A Guide to the Southernmost State*
	U.S. One: Maine to Florida
1940	*Seeing Fernandina: A Guide to the City*
	Spanish Missions of Florida
1941	*Birds in Florida*
	Florida: Facts, Events, Places, Tours
	A Guide to Key West
	Pensacola Recreation Handbook
	Planning Your Vacation in Florida: Miami and Dade County
	Seminole Indians in Florida
	Tropical Fruits in Florida[17]

But the FWP's main project, toward which it spent most of its energies, was *Florida: A Guide to the Southernmost State* (sometimes referred to as the *WPA Guide to Florida*), published in November 1939 by Oxford University Press, the first of thirteen they would eventually release. Using the Baedeker series of travel books as a model, the national director for the Federal Writers' Project, Henry Alsberg, hoped to produce such a guide for every state and territory. Florida's mammoth guide was over six hundred pages with more than one hundred illustrations and images. Although some social commentary creeps into the text at times—folklorist Stetson Kennedy and anthropologist-novelist Zora Neal Hurston were among the two hundred Florida writers who worked on the project—the guide was primarily a state advertisement, under the guise of an educational publication. Divided into a series of driving tours, the book completed the goal begun in 1933 of marketing Florida as an attraction unto itself. The book discussed everything from roadside attractions, beaches, and restaurants to Spanish history, turpentine stills, and Florida crackers. But for the most part, in its overall effect, it followed the lead of advertisers within the state's government. As in all New Deal programs, the local leaders and workers peopled the FWP program, with oversight and guidance from the national office. And by the time the book appeared in 1939, the State of Florida had been selling the state for over six years through fairs, brochures, booklets, speeches, and the Florida Park Service. While this was the largest federal effort at promoting Florida, *Florida: A Guide to the Southernmost State* seemed almost repetitive when it was finally published.

Florida's tourism still had problems, however. Roads and accommodations were still needed, especially in North and West Florida. And while there were strong efforts made to tone down the claims made in advertisements as well as curbing the behavior of business involved—no one wanted a return to the binder boys and "water-front" realtors of the 1920s—occasional promotional problems arose nonetheless. Reports began pouring in to the governor's office that some hotel operators of the East Coast "would toss their circulars into moving cars, thereby distracting the attention of the drivers."[18] Sometimes they were "thrown into moving automobiles in bunches," and one person reported: "We had one car concession come through and while in motion one of these cardboard circulars was thrown in and the woman's glasses were knocked off."[19] As the *Miami Herald* reported, the flyers generally advertised beachfront hotels at cheaper rates ($1.00 to $1.50 a night) than those that predominated on the East Coast, usually $4.00 a night.[20] Often these claims were fraudulent. Cone ordered the Florida Highway Patrol to step up their efforts.

But during the 1937–38 season, more than 2 million people came to Florida. By winter of 1938–39, that figure was up to 3 million, with spending at nearly

$300 million.[21] For a state with only 1.7 million permanent residents, this was a significant influx of both people and dollars. Some estimates were that by 1946 Florida might receive more than a half billion in revenue from tourism.[22] To fulfill such a prophecy more publicity was needed. That conveniently arrived in the form of another fair.

To celebrate the 150th anniversary of George Washington's presidential inauguration New York Mayor LaGuardia began planning for a New York World's Fair in 1935. Grover Whalen directed the fair, which was designed with seven themed areas (Transportation, Food, Government, Amusements, Industry, Communication, and Community) all tied together at the fair's center with the statue of George Washington and the fairs' architectural trademark, the Trylon and Perisphere.[23] Located at Flushing Meadows in Queens, it proved to be one of the world's largest and most influential fairs. Over 44 million visitors passed through its gates to witness such wonders as the public premiere of the television set, a robot that could count to five, the 36,000-square-feet Futurama exhibit, and the Aquacade water show. Although designed to be educational in nature, the Amusement area was by far the most popular feature, and that was where the Florida Pavilion wound up. For the fair's planners, Florida was a highly sought-after participant. Fair administrator Dennis Nolan wrote to New York Representative A. E. MacKinnon that "we must and will have Florida. . . . They have been key features at the [Cleveland] show and in matter of the attendance of exhibits they have smashed all records, as they did at Chicago, even beating out Ford and GM presentations."[24]

After two international fairs and a stint at the Rockefeller Center, the Florida National Exhibits were becoming quite adept at pulling off major exhibitions. For the 1939 New York World's Fair they created their largest exhibit yet, with three levels that housed over 350,000 square feet of exhibit space and required over one hundred train car loads of equipment. While recycling much of the material from previous exhibits—Gauniere's "Ponce De Leon" and "Spirit of Florida" statues, most of the dioramas, and another live citrus grove (again designed by Foster Barnes)—they also added much more. For one thing, they created their own building. It was located in the Amusements zone on the shores of Fountain Lake—sending the message that Florida officials were glad to convey that Florida was an attraction and not merely a state. Because of both its size and the public anticipation, FNE created a faux Spanish Mission (albeit one based on the grander eighteenth-century California mission style, not the humbler wattle-and-daub version found in seventeenth-century Florida) in order to "convert" fair visitors to Florida. For the mission's bell tower, the FNE installed what at the time was billed as the world's largest carillon bell tower, with seventy-five bells. Created by J. C. Deagan Company of Chicago, the carillon would be installed at the Stephen Foster Memorial in White Springs, Florida, upon the fair's completion. At the fair it played a record number of 14,167 times in six months.[25] The Aquacade show, featuring Johnny Weismuller and other stars, was located nearby, and at the conclusion of each performance the carillon played a Stephen Foster tune to attract a large portion of each show's audience. There was also a seventy-one-foot orange juice bar made of "Georgia marble with twenty attendants serving Florida orange juice, orange sherbet and canned grapefruit juice"—along with six more located throughout the park, one in each zone.[26] "Each of the new [juice] concessions will consist of a juice bar, painting, and dioramas for Florida, and a comfortably furnished lounge," for a total of 5,000 square feet.[27] The theme was "Florida: Where Dreams Come True."[28] Throughout the entire exhibit wafted the scent of orange blossoms.

Among the new dioramas were one of Tampa and its Gasparilla festival, of Daytona's hotels and beach, and a citrus farm, with 10,000 handmade oranges and blossoms. But the most impressive diorama (referred to by the FNE as a "spectorama") was a life-size fishing boat in Tarpon Springs. The magazine *Great Outdoors* described it: "Looking through the open doorway of the cruiser the spectator sees a tarpon leap from the water nine feet in perspective while the fisherman reels in the slack of the line. The boat rocks on the waves. Boat, figures, and all equipment are life size. A Florida sunset with drifting purple clouds brightens the scene."[29]

Another new diorama was "Florida Seen through a Windshield," which the *Florida Grower* described as "a citrus grove as seen through the windshield of an automobile. The spectator appears to be sitting in a car. On the right a packing house shows workers in action. Every few minutes rain beats against the windshield to illustrate the fact that Florida oranges contain more juices because of frequent summer showers."[30] Another for Wakulla Springs "faithfully reproduces the color and flow of water of the world's largest spring while onlookers can see, through panels, underwater scenes such as 'Henry the pole-vaulting black bass.'"[31] And *Florida Highways* wrote of the entire exhibit: "The visitor walks beneath moss-hung oaks, among orange trees hung with ripe fruit and looking upon vistas of Florida. All around him in movement and animation, dioramas, spectoramas, and rotoramas depict scenes in Florida.... [Visitors view] such oddities as live parrots and macaws who say 'Come to Florida,' Henry the Pole Vaulting black bass of Wakulla Springs, the catfish parade and a mechanical mocking bird."[32]

FNE president Earl Brown announced in April 1939 that there would be an area for Florida's African American population with "free exhibit space ... including exhibit cases for Florida A&M College and the Negro citizens of the state in which to display samples of manufactured articles ... made from native materials ... including hook rug weaving, tables and chair bottoms."[33] But despite these assurances, African Americans representation in Florida differed little from that in earlier incarnations, such as the "happy slaves" imagery in both the Suwannee River and turpentine displays. Most prominent was a janitor for the exhibit, from Sanford, Florida, named Whistling Willie Williams, who could imitate over thirty bird calls. According to an extensive feature story on Williams in the *New York Times*, which referred to him as "a shrimp-sized edition of Stepin Fetchit," he was discovered in the tropical gardens section of the Florida exhibit giving voice to the unexpectedly mute parrots with "Come to Florida."[34] When asked by NBC radio about being a janitor, he supposedly responded, "When the company smokes a cigarette, its theirs, and when it's a butt, it's mine."[35] By the end of the fair he was featured in his own shows, imitating birds, rattlesnakes, and other Florida animals. (A related—and more than likely fictional—press story concerned a parrot named Cracker, which once said, "Hello Cracker" to a passerby. She responded, "I know I am from the backwoods of Florida but I didn't think even the birds would notice.")[36] But otherwise, Florida promoters for the most part chose to ignore African Americans, lest their presence turn off white, middle-class tourists and brand Florida as "too southern," with all the social and racial baggage that entailed.

Probably the toughest hurdle for the FNE in 1938 and 1939 was not keeping race out but keeping Governor Fred Cone on board. When Cone first entered office, he essentially ended the All-Florida Advertising Campaign. While he agreed that advertising "should continually and constructively tell the world of our agricultural, industrial and tourist possibilities," Cone felt "the Legislature was wise in their refusal to appropriate a fund for advertising."[37] He even told the committee to "stop this advertisement matter" and ordered it "not to spend any of this money and to make no contracts to spend it."[38] When the legislature passed an appropriations bill for $250,000 for FNE and its exhibit for the New York World's Fair, it went into law without Cone's signature.[39] But the FNE discovered in 1937 that the best way to achieve their goals was to play upon his ego, usually a healthy component of any governor's make-up, and Cone was no exception. They dreamed up "Governor Fred Cone Day" at the Florida Exhibit during the Great Lakes Exposition in Cleveland in summer 1937. As banker and FNE vice-president Ed Ball explained to Cone, the day would play out on a national radio hook-up. "It is essential that at one of the great halls of the Florida Exhibit building we have a portrait of you . . . after your inauguration we would like to have some prominent artists come to Tallahassee and paint your portrait."[40] They would also print a brochure for the exhibit with both his and Roosevelt's portraits and a brief statement, which Ball pre-wrote and enclosed with the letter.[41] In March 1937 FNE also made Cone an honorary chairman.[42] Cone, who made special trip to the Cleveland fair, even wrote a letter of introduction to the director of the 1939 New York World's Fair, Grover Whalen, on behalf of Earl Brown and the FNE, beaming: "You will find him a master showman and Florida is proud of his many accomplishments."[43]

Two years later a second Fred Cone Day, designated as August 29, 1939, was devised during the FNE's largest accomplishment—a "Florida Week" at the New York World's Fair.[44] No other state was honored at the fair in such a way. Cone made plans early to attend. In early summer he began inviting his friends in North Florida to come the fair and to bring their colonel's uniforms. They rode the Seaboard Air Line Railway, which offered a Governor's Special rate so that any Floridian could "ride with the governor" to New York. The passenger trains had "air conditioned, deluxe, reclining seat coaches," with prices running from $23.15 for coach to $59 for lower berth, Pullman class.[45] Although Cone publicly declared that all should pay their own way, FNE official Ed Ball sent Cone and his wife two free tickets, which he put to use.[46] At the fair Cone would review the military guard complete with a gun salute, dine with fair president Grover Whalen, inspect the Florida exhibit, dedicate the Florida Building with Ed Ball, and finally enjoy a special fireworks presentation.[47] And between 4:00 and 4:30 p.m., NBC Radio would cover Cone presenting the exhibit to Whalen.[48] Unfortunately once he arrived, Cone fell ill—his health would plague him throughout his gubernatorial term—and never left his hotel room.[49] But even with the governor laid up in his hotel room, the Florida exhibit attracted 230,000 that day, while several newsreels and radio programs covered Florida Week in their weekly presentations.[50]

By the end of the New York World's Fair on October 31, 1939, Florida promotional efforts were at a peak to which they would not return until the 1950s. By August 6, 1939, four million visitors passed through the exhibit, with another 3 million expected before the end of the fair, which itself attracted 26 million in 1939.[51] Not only was Florida invited back to the 1940 version of the fair, but news coverage of the exhibit could be found in *Time*, the *New York Times*, *New York Herald Tribune*, several radio programs, and numerous newspapers in Pennsylvania, California, New Jersey, Connecticut, and of course Florida.[52]

In the midst of all this sat an unobtrusive exhibit for a small state agency that was originally created to spur on Florida tourism but was—with the success of this and other fairs—already overshadowed and overlooked as an effective source for attracting visitors to Florida even before all of its properties were completed and opened to the public. Although featured several times in the 1940 souvenir booklet for Florida's exhibit at the fair, the Florida Park Service's moment to shine was passing, and this was its last hurrah before dramatic changes in the ever-expanding and dynamic world of Florida tourism.[53]

11

The End of the Beginning

In January 2008 Florida's Department of Environmental Protection announced that the ailing roadside attraction Weeki Wachee on the Florida Gulf Coast would become a state park at the end of the year. Other state park additions since the 1980s have included Wakulla Springs, Rainbow Springs, Ravine Gardens, Homosassa Springs, Gamble Plantation (formerly known as the Judah P. Benjamin Memorial), Silver Springs (under lease by a private corporation), and Cypress Gardens (also under private lease). Marineland, one of the earliest seaquariums, just missed becoming a state park in 2003. The Stephen Foster Memorial, with its 1939 New York World's Fair carillon, joined the FPS in 1979. While state parks were first created to become tourist attractions, they have since become living history museums for Florida's golden age of roadside attractions. It is also a sign of how Florida tourism has both changed and also remained the same. While the industry still targets middle-class families, these early attractions have become too quaint to appeal to today's visitors, who are offered thrill rides, fairytale castles, and performing orca whales. What seemed exotic and unique in 1937 now seems mundane. Palm trees, alligators, flowers, and natural springs no longer excite or attract the average visitor. In fact, despite the introduction of exotic fauna and flora, intricate landscaping, and hyperbolic promotions, many of these sites are often considered almost "second nature." The ease with which these sites fit in with the other natural and historical properties of the Florida Park Service reveals both how natural the roadside attractions were in the 1930s and, at the same time, how manufactured were many of the state parks. Both types of sites simply repackaged native Florida environments (a natural spring, a native hammock, a ravine) with varying degrees of landscaping and introduced exotics, romantic names, and attractive brochures. It was a time of truly Florida-oriented tourism.

Other sites from this era have also become state park properties, including the homes of writers Marjorie Kinnan Rawlings and Marjory Stoneman Douglas; the latter has been an out-parcel of Cape Florida State Park since 2009 and is used as a private ranger residence. And the Florida cracker culture described by Rawlings, Douglas, and others has become an alternative Florida image, now just as packaged and commodified as "tropical Florida" was in the 1930s. One can find several cracker historical sites, such as the cracker cowmen camp at Lake Kissimmee State Park, Forest Capital State Park's cracker home in Perry, the cracker homestead and festival at Silver River State Park in Ocala, and numerous exhibits and buildings at local museums and historical societies. What was once merely an oppositional stance has now become official heritage. An entire cracker cottage industry has emerged, through books on cracker humor, food, history, and architecture (though on closer inspection these buildings differ little from poor vernacular homes in Georgia, Alabama, and the Carolinas); and through cracker festivals, clothing stores, log cabin construction companies, themed restaurants, novels, and music. Interestingly, the bulk of these companies and items are found in tourist-heavy Central Florida. But the larger irony is that the agency created to aid tourism, and that then led to the emergence of the defiant cracker culture, has today done more than anything else to preserve that culture.

In the early 1940s the FPS felt it needed preserving. In September 1942 the National Conference of State Parks—the organization created by NPS director Stephen Mather in 1921 to promote state park development—met in Chicago. This was not its usual annual meeting, however, but rather was a special roundtable discussion. The meeting's topic was the "Wartime Uses of State Parks," and its poor attendance and pessimistic tone reflected how severely World War II had curtailed state park operations. Sessions on themes such as "How to operate state parks on reduced budgets," and "Loss of experienced workers to armed forces" gave hints of the problems faced by state parks since the surprise bombing of Pearl Harbor by Japanese forces nine months earlier.[1] According to conclusions of the conference, park attendance was down 40 percent, with the East Coast parks reporting even higher percentages.[2] Camping had virtually disappeared from state parks, and many parks had been requisitioned by the military.[3] The worst culprit for the decrease in state park usage, it was decided at the conference, was tire and gas rationing, which was particularly prevalent on the East Coast.⁴ While the conference's conclusions were applicable to nearly every state park service, the issue not dealt with at the conference was the one that most affected attendee Lewis Scoggin's Florida Park Service: the loss of CCC labor and funds earlier that year.

The Second World War transformed the South as nothing else had since the Civil War. Federal dollars poured into the southern states as bases, airfields, and training camps were built to take advantage of the South's cheap land and temperate climate. The war accomplished something, both regionally and nationally, that the New Deal after nine years never could: ending the Great Depression by putting people to work. World War II has even been credited with supplying the catalyst finally ending Jim Crow segregation and reigniting the women's rights movement. But for Florida, the changes brought on by the war were something of a trade-off. Tourism was down—pushed out by gas shortages, tire rationing, and shifting of priorities. But the defense spending in the state by the United States government far exceeded the lost tourist dollars. The state also lost its New Deal programs, signaled by President Roosevelt's switch from Dr. New Deal to Dr. Win-the-War. While the military draft and defense jobs eased the transformation of federal and state aims for most Floridians, these changes were detrimental to the Florida Park Service (finally facing the obsolescence it had so long feared) and meant the end of the Civilian Conservation Corps.

Even before Roosevelt announced that a "state of war" existed between Japan and the United States, the nation was already preparing for possible war in Europe and the Pacific. New Deal programs shifted their focus from relief and the restructuring of society to building up the nation's resources and defenses. The Civilian Conservation Corps was no exception, as CCC director James McEntee stated bluntly.⁵ In a 1940 article for *American Forests* he wrote: "The Civilian Conservation Corps has a new objective as it marches forward in its eighth year. It is national defense."⁶ In 1941 the CCC produced a brochure entitled "Civilian Conservation Corps Contributing to National Defense," which linked conservation with victory.⁷ In a reversal from its earlier positions, the CCC also played up its connections with the U.S. Army. "Many of the types of work in the conservation program parallel that done by engineer corps," it explained. The corps was in fact "a reserve of trained men" ready for war.⁸

Priorities in Florida had changed as well. Assisted by yet another year at the

New York World's Fair, plus a specially designed Florida Exhibit Highlights that toured the Midwest, including stops in Detroit, Cleveland, Cincinnati, and Milwaukee, Florida was increasingly dependent upon tourism.[9] Throughout 1939 and 1940, no doubt a by-product of the world's fair, the *New York Times* ran numerous stories on Florida travel and attractions.[10] George Gross of the Florida State Planning Board announced at the Southeastern Regional Planning Commission in Atlanta that Florida's tourist industry was at $350 million a year, "a sum greater than the total farm and forestry production."[11] Florida was the only state at the conference even to mention tourism. But that newest priority was soon to be jeopardized.

By 1940 state legislator Spessard Holland won election as governor and spent the majority of his term wooing the military to Florida and building up the state's defenses and industries. Florida boasted 172 military installations by war's end.[12] Relief was no longer on the minds of Florida's leaders, despite the fact that the need for it still existed. In 1941, 72,464 people were eligible for welfare assistance, and in 1942—the year Florida's remaining New Deal programs ended—over 43,000 families were still on the relief rolls.[13] But just as national enthusiasm for maintaining the New Deal relief programs faded by the early 1940s, so did it in Florida.

The first state park camp closings in Florida happened long before the U.S. Congress ordered the liquidation of the CCC in July 1942.[14] Three camps closed in 1940: Hillsborough River State Park (P-71), Highlands Hammock State Park (SP-10), and Gold Head Branch State Park (SP-5).[15] For the spring of 1942, nearly two years after CCC veteran company 2444 had abandoned the barracks, Gold Head housed CCC camp AF-5, a defense CCC camp that worked at nearby Camp Blanding.[16] Oleno State Park's CCC camp completed its tasks long before the Forestry Board transferred it to the State Park Branch.

The remaining three camps closed in spring 1942. The National Park Service sent out special investigator J. S. Billings in early 1942 to visit the remaining camps in the Southeast to offer suggestions for closings and set priorities for which jobs should be completed. At Fort Clinch State Park, Billings found the camp "under hardships," and "practically dismantled."[17] Only fifty-nine enrollees remained, of whom twenty-five were at a side camp in Lake City working on a defense project.[18] The camp was scheduled for abandonment on February 15, 1942.[19] Billings next visited Florida Caverns State Park, and its side camp at Torreya State Park, and recommended immediate closing.[20]

When this was reported in the Marianna paper on February 27, FPS director Lewis Scoggin—who at the time was trying to secure an extension for the camp—exploded.[21] He wrote to the NPS regional office explaining that "such half-truths does the Florida Forestry and Park Service incalculable damage" by giving the impression that the FPS is abandoning the park.[22] Scoggin tried to calm local fears by assuring the president of Marianna's First National Bank that with the CCC camps out of the way, "we shall be able to hire local skilled help, and push jobs to completion faster than would have been possible under CCC regulations."[23] Scoggin failed to explain how he proposed to pay for these job completions, however. On February 28 all work at Torreya and Florida Caverns ceased.[24] Billings found the last camp, Myakka River State Park, also depleted, with its newly created side camp working five hours away in Jacksonville on an army recreation center.[25] That camp also soon closed.

With the CCC enrollees gone, the FPS had to depend upon its own resources to run the parks, a task it found increasingly difficult to accomplish as it began losing its staff to the war effort. Roughly one-third of the FPS staff had joined the military by June 1942.[26] Several others left for the growing defense industries.[27] M. B. Green, the superintendent of Fort Clinch State Park, resigned in 1942 to join the U.S. Navy. His sentiments probably echoed those of most FPS employees who left during the war: "I felt that my first duty is that of doing what I can to help win this war."[28] Green had also served as the superintendent of Gold Head after that park's superintendent, Clayton Perreault, resigned to join the U.S. Navy.[29] Former enrollee B. H. Griffin was hired to replace Perreault (and relieve Green at Gold Head), while the German showman who was contracted to run Fort Clinch's museum was made the park superintendent, replacing Green. Across the FPS, hired help was "as rare as hen's teeth."[30] Even NPS inspector C. R. Vinten was promoted to coordinating superintendent of the southeastern national monuments in late 1941, which removed him from state park matters.[31] Slowly but steadily, the war was carving away at the FPS's pool of managers and workers.

As Florida transformed from a tourist destination to a military training post and gas and tire rationing hindered tourism, the state parks became the servicemen's personal playgrounds. As one employee at Fort Clinch observed, "gas rationing has killed everything."[32] Several roadside attractions closed.

Some, such as Marineland south of St. Augustine, were leased to the military.[33] Defense workers and servicemen became the state's main visitors. State parks were often the sites for military social events. But problems soon arose, as the "beer parties" the servicemen threw in the parks often became rowdy. At Florida Caverns State Park, one rowdy party led FPS director Scoggin to demand that no more beer parties be allowed in state parks.[34] (Major Samuel Gormes at Marianna Air Base remarked upon hearing this, "I am the only one here who runs anything public that they haven't had a row with, so I guess it's my turn.")[35] But just a couple of weeks later when Gold Head Branch State Park superintendent Griffin echoed the call for banning beer parties because of problems at his park, Simpson wrote in a note at the bottom of the letter: "This would prevent temperate men from taking a beer."[36] Scoggin finally settled on a solution dreamed up by Hillsborough superintendent Oscar Baynard: servicemen would be allowed only two bottles of beer per party; no more unlimited draft beer.[37]

The influx of war workers to Florida also meant a new type of visitor to Florida's state parks: African Americans. Before World War II, just as with most roadside attractions, the state parks served white visitors. The entrance fees were an economic barrier to African Americans, just as were admissions for other roadside attractions. But as African Americans found better paying jobs in war plants and in the military, that financial situation changed. One letter from Florida Caverns superintendent Clarence Simpson illustrated this unexpected dilemma for the FPS. "We are beginning to have parties of negroes coming to go through the caves," Simpson explained.[38] "I think we may expect more and more of them."[39] While Simpson believed "they should be given the same service that we accord to anyone else," he argued that "we will make a grave mistake if we allow them to use the same rest rooms."[40] New facilities must be built, Simpson argued, for "if we set aside a separate day for negroes, it would still be apparent to our white visitors that they were not segregated, and that they were using the same facilities."[41] This should not have surprised the FPS, as there were already a few tourist attractions catering to Florida's black residents and visitors, such as American Beach near Fort Clinch State Park in Fernandina and Paradise Park, a black-only version of Silver Springs, in Ocala, Florida. Not until the 1950s would the Florida Park Service open parks specifically for African Americans, including South Little Talbot Island in Jacksonville and St. Andrews State Park in Panama City Beach. Scoggin's handwritten note on the letter mentioned that he instructed the park to build "privies for coloreds" until "permanent facilities" could be built.[42]

Despite the use of the parks by the military, it was soon clear that the budget cuts and the drop in tourism caused by the war were too much for the state to sustain the parks for much longer. Even attempts to keep many of the temporary CCC buildings, such as oil sheds, garages, barracks, and storehouses, usually failed. As one army authority wrote to Scoggin, "All surplus buildings go to the war effort."[43] As a way to combat the restrictions on "pleasure driving," many in the FPS tried to reenvision state parks as educational centers—an idea that ironically caught on during the postwar years, when Florida's tourism returned more strongly than ever.[44] But in the 1940s, the link between Florida's state parks and tourism was too strong for that ploy to work. Therefore by 1942 parks began closing.

The war's first casualty in the FPS was the Florida Garden and Arboretum at Highlands Hammock State Park. The expensive gardens were closed because of slashed budgets in 1941, and their upkeep was neglected. Theft of the garden's plants by staff, citizens, and servicemen was common during the war.[45] When the war ended, the "park officials were so busy patching up the state park system that they ignored the Botanical garden entirely."[46] Highlands Hammock State Park itself closed the following year. At the same time, Hillsborough River State Park was leased out to the Army's Third Fighter Command.[47] A rumor began among Gold Head's staff that the army would use their park as an "isolation camp for diseased prostitutes."[48] The rumor was only partially correct: Myakka River State Park would be used as the isolation camp. But eventually, the army also leased Gold Head for training exercises. The state then shut down Fort Clinch, Oleno, Florida Caverns, and Torreya state parks completely by 1943, and they remained closed for the war's duration.

The closing of the eight Florida state parks demonstrated how dependent upon both the Civilian Conservation Corps and tourism the parks actually were. Without enrollee labor and NPS supervision, the FPS proved inadequate to managing the parks on its own. Even more damaging was the loss of out-of-state visitors. Despite Scoggin's claims to the contrary—both before and after the war—the FPS would not have been built, nor would it have survived as long as it did, without the CCC. And the FPS itself recognized its dependence on tourism when it predicted—and hoped—that after the war, when the young servicemen returned, they would remember Florida, and "an unprecedented tourist business is anticipated in the post-war period."[49] But for the time being, as Florida historian Gary Mormino once wrote, "News of Pearl Harbor shattered the dream of Florida beaches filled with tourists in swimsuits."[50]

From 1941 to 1945 Florida did not need tourism. It had the military and national defense to fill that economic void. Men in olive drab and combat boots replaced tourists in swimsuits and sandals. Therefore, the FPS could be terminated—if only temporarily—without damaging Florida's tourist industry. In fact, the land of the FPS was more valuable as property for the military to use than it was as a tourist destination. The same was true for the federal government and its New Deal programs. The war was putting people back to work. Enrollees, trained by the U.S. Army and well adjusted to regimented life, were valuable commodities to the military. Those too old for service could put their job skills learned in the corps to work in the defense plants. While in a broad sense the agendas of the federal government and of the enrollees remained the same, the avenues for achieving them had changed. The Florida Park Service was created as a product of the New Deal to put young men to work and to revive Florida's tourism. With the country at war, those reasons had become null and void. In fact, the only ones wanting to keep the FPS alive were its few remaining employees.

In 1943 frustrated Florida Caverns superintendent Clarence Simpson wrote to FPS director Scoggin about his complaints on the pleasure driving restrictions that the federal government had recently put into effect. He argued that while circuses and theaters were indeed for pleasure, state parks were instead educational. People must be allowed to visit them, or else the FPS would be soon "out of business."[51] Scoggin replied that he felt the same, but there was nothing he could do. There was a war on. "I feel that before the war is over, we can expect further setbacks, but there will come a day when what we have to offer will again be in demand and to a much greater extent than it has ever been before."[52] Simpson's suggestions foreshadowed the modern image of Florida's state parks as sites of education and recreation rather than as roadside attractions.

By 1947 the Florida Park Service was picking up the pieces left scattered by the Second World War. Scoggin wrote proudly in the 1946 annual report that his "predictions of attendance during the post-war period have come true."[53]

That year Florida's state parks welcomed 125,029 visitors. The park service was entering a period of massive expansion as Florida's tourist business rose to astronomical heights resulting from an ever-expanding postwar economic boom. For Scoggin it was a time to look back upon the past twelve years and assess the progress made. In the inter-agency newsletter, the *Florida Park Service News*, Scoggin sketched the FPS's history, praising the efforts of past directors, of forester Harry Lee Baker, and even of May Mann Jennings (perhaps the last time she would be credited with helping to create the FPS). But missing from this praise were the Civilian Conservation Corps and its representative agency in state park work, the National Park Service. Scoggin wrote that if the FPS had begun with Royal Palm State Park back in 1915, then perhaps the CCC could have been helpful to the parks. But as it played out, according to Scoggin, the CCC was nothing more than "a haphazard program of keeping men at work on virtual leaf-raking jobs in the parks."[54] Only now, with war victory in hand and the CCC out of the way, Scoggin contended, could the Florida Park Service complete and professionally run its state parks. But Scoggin's assessment in 1947 of the CCC and NPS roles in the creation of the FPS badly missed the mark. Without the CCC and NPS, the FPS would have been stillborn.

In 1930 Florida's southern and Confederate heritage was still very much on display. But the state parks, the major tourist attractions, and all the world fair exhibits throughout the decade presented a regionally neutral Florida, devoid of any mention of the Civil War, slavery, or the Lost Cause. Yet this was not for lack of trying by some organizations, including the Florida Chapter of the United Daughters of the Confederacy (UDC). The struggles the UDC faced in attempting to maintain and exploit Confederate Florida illustrate the social and cultural changes brought about through tourism.

Though the sites were owned by the state, the UDC managed several of Florida's antebellum and Civil War historic sites, including the Olustee and Natural Bridge Battlefield Memorials as well as Dade Battlefield Memorial, all of which would become state parks in the 1950s. But the site and UDC experience most indicative of the changing image of Florida was the Judah P. Benjamin Memorial at Gamble Plantation near Sarasota in Manatee County. In 1930 the UDC received $20,000 from the state legislature for restoration and maintenance of the former plantation, plus funds to hire a caretaker at

$50 a month.⁵⁵ And when some of the funds did not come through, a quick call to State Comptroller Ernest Amos freed them up—nearly $5,000—within a day.⁵⁶ The memorial was designed as "a shrine . . . to the brave men and women of our beloved Southland, who gave their all for the cause they loved so well."⁵⁷ In 1933, as tourism began to take off, the UDC hoped that the memorial would be a site to which "thousands of winter visitors will pay homage. Thus we could place before them much valuable and true history of the War Between the States."⁵⁸ But over the decade, visitation at the historic sites remained low, and the group had a hard time interesting civic and government leaders in their properties. Few guidebooks even mentioned the historic sites, preferring the more exotic Spanish colonial sites in Pensacola and St. Augustine. By 1935 the local UDC "planted tropical fruit trees [at the site] which will be of interest to the thousands of Northern people."⁵⁹ While the state funded exhibits in Chicago and Cleveland, the UDC could not even acquire $100 to fix the plantation's roof.⁶⁰ In 1937 the state promised $2,500 to the site but then rescinded the offer at the last moment.⁶¹ And while in 1939 they succeeded in having Governor Fred Cone proclaim the portion of U.S. 19 that ran from Monticello to St. Petersburg as the "Stonewall Jackson Memorial Highway," the state erected no signs for it, and no major guidebooks mentioned it.⁶² In January 1940 the UDC placed a marker in Monticello and later a terminal boulder made of native travertine rock at a cost of $100.⁶³ Even complaints of the exclusion of the Confederate flag from a WPA-built decorative grill of Florida flags over the entrance to the Pensacola Post Office were ignored.⁶⁴ And in the 1930s the Florida UDC lost over one thousand members as well as six state chapters.⁶⁵ More and more, if it was not tropical, exotic, or natural, then Florida and its visitors were no longer interested.

Such was the change that the CCC, the FPS and the rest of the New Deal brought to Florida. But the New Deal, for once, was not the catalyst in these changes but rather the main tool used by Florida's civic elite to develop and expand the state's tourist industry. State parks, funded, staffed, and planned by the CCC (under the NPS), were developed as tourist attractions, in part leading to the development of other attractions in the mid- to late 1930s. While the planning and standards demanded by the NPS and the CCC slowed down the parks' development, the parks still offer an insight into how Floridians developed and altered their environment as a commodity to promote and sell Florida to the national public.

For decades scholars have argued over whether Florida was even a part of the South culturally. Had the state's history ended in the 1920s, these debates would not have taken place. But the 1930s, more than any other time period, transformed the outward appearance of Florida, both physically and metaphorically. While much of the essence of the state—its people and their private culture and economic status, its racism, conservative politics, and even most of its industries—remained intact, Florida appeared differently in the eyes of both its own citizens and the rest of the nation after this period. Numerous histories of Florida have described it just prior to the Second World War as a "sleepy, backwater" state. The following quote from a recent study on public policy sums up this scholarly misperception the best: "A snapshot taken in 1940 of a Florida town would simply be a 'mirror image' of a typical Bourbon-era town.... The major technological change, besides electricity, was the automobile or pickup parked in front of the feed store."[66] But as we have seen, whether it was as a climatic paradise and a natural Eden, or as the home to the Florida cracker bravely facing the onslaught of a second northern invasion, Florida was not the same place in 1940 as it was in 1930.

In 1940 Florida elected Spessard Holland governor: an urbane young lawyer who regularly supported Florida's development and tourism. As a legislator Holland had supported the FNE, the 1939 World's Fair, conservation, and the elimination of the state's poll tax. Later as governor he even pushed for the establishment of the Everglades National Park. Also in 1940 outgoing governor Fred Cone suffered a humiliating defeat in the race for the U.S. Senate, coming in last in a field of six. (In contrast, Holland would be elected U.S. senator in 1946.) And finally, on June 17, 1940, Tallahassee suffered the death of another prominent resident. State Senator William Cabot Hodge died at his Goodwood Plantation home.[67] Although born and raised in Ashton, Illinois, with degrees from the Universities of Illinois and Indiana, Hodge found political success in North Florida starting in the 1910s. A well-respected defense lawyer—the *Tallahassee Democrat* compared him to Clarence Darrow—with "stooped shoulder and flowing gray hair," Hodge joined the State Senate in 1922.[68] While he took care of his local constituents who kept him office for two decades, Hodge was a major mover and shaker in Florida's tourism industry. He helped create and fund both the Century of Progress Commission and the Florida National Exhibits Corporation, pushed for appropriations for exhibits in Cleveland and at the 1939 New York

World's Fair, and was "keenly interested in real estate development."[69] Hodge had no Confederate or Old South heritage to cling to and flaunt, nor did he fabricate any. Yet when he passed away, the state mourned, just as it had ten years earlier when Confederate veteran Thomas Appleyard died. Flags were flown at half-mast and the state's leaders attended the funeral. But unlike for Appleyard in 1930, draped upon Hodge's casket as he lay in state was an American flag. Florida had begun to move on.

Notes

Introduction

1. Rowe, *The Idea of Florida*, 9.

Chapter 1. A Tropical Depression: A Tale of Two Floridas

1. "Gen. Appleyard Suddenly Dies of Pneumonia," *Pensacola News Journal*, January 5, 1931.
2. *Tallahassee Democrat*, January 5, 1931.
3. *Tallahassee Democrat*, April 30, 1931.
4. United States, *Fifteenth Census*, 338.
5. McElvaine, *The Great Depression*, 46; Allen, *Since Yesterday*, 22.
6. Allen, *Since Yesterday*, 10.
7. Leuchtenburg, *Perils of Prosperity*, 243.
8. Watkins, *Hungry Years*, 25; Danese, *Claude Pepper and Ed Ball*, 4.
9. Watkins, *Hungry Years*, 27.
10. Leuchtenburg, *Perils of Prosperity*, 242.
11. Ibid.
12. Watkins, *Hungry Years*, 25.
13. McElvaine, *Great Depression*, 46–47.
14. McElvaine, *Great Depression*, 47.
15. Kennedy, *Freedom from Fear*, 38.
16. Allen, *Since Yesterday*, 26.
17. Watkins, *Hungry Years*, 54.
18. Watkins, *Great Depression*, 55. Kennedy makes a similar argument in *Freedom from Fear*, 38–39.
19. McElvaine, *Great Depression*, 49.
20. For a discussion of southern poverty in the 1920s, see Mertz, *New Deal Policy*.
21. Rogers, "Paradoxical Twenties," 305–6.
22. Rogers, "Paradoxical Twenties," 298.
23. For information on sharecropping in the 1920s and 1930s, see Conrad, *Forgotten Farmers*; Mertz, *New Deal Policy*; and Patterson, *America's Struggle*.
24. Conrad, *Forgotten Farmers*, 15; Rogers, "Paradoxical Twenties," 300.

25. Conrad, *Forgotten Farmers*, 11.
26. Ibid., 2.
27. Reporter Lorena Hickok, while on a fact-finding mission for Harry Hopkins's Federal Emergency Relief Administration (FERA) in 1934, wrote the following about citrus grove owners and their resistance to work relief efforts: "Now I'll tell you right off the bat, for being mean-spirited, selfish and irresponsible, I think Florida's citrus growers have the got the world licked." Hickok to Hopkins, January 29, 1934, in Lowitt and Beasley, *One Third of a Nation*, 164.
28. Mertz, *New Deal Policy*, 12.
29. Hickok to Hopkins, January 29, 1934, in Lowitt and Beasley, *One Third of a Nation*, 164.
30. Mertz, *New Deal Policy*, 14.
31. Rogers, "Paradoxical Twenties," 298.
32. Mertz, *New Deal Policy*, 15.
33. George LeCouris, interview by Dave Nelson, November 2, 2002, Reichelt Oral History Program (ROHP), Florida State University.
34. Fred Williams, interview by folklorist Doris Dyen, April 16, 1983, Recording of the Florida Folklife Program, 1936–2006, box 5, tape C83-104, Florida State Archives (FSA).
35. Ibid.
36. Ansley Hall, interview by Dave Nelson, November 2, 2002, ROHP.
37. Albert Gufford, interview by folklorist David Taylor, August 8, 1986, Maritime Heritage Survey files, 1986–1987, box 7, tape 16, side A, FSA.
38. Buck Heath, interview by Dave Nelson, July 12, 2003, ROHP.
39. Tucker, *Before the Timber Was Cut*, 40.
40. Derr, *Some Kind of Paradise*, 319.
41. McGovern, *Anatomy of a Lynching*, 29.
42. Anonymous, "A Bus Americus," in *Veterans Viewpoint (Co. 2445)* (July 1939): 8.
43. Ibid.
44. The article recounted an anecdote involving some of the passengers loudly complaining of the federal government, FDR, and the rich.
45. For the turpentine industry and its working conditions, see Derr, *Some Kind of Paradise*, 117–20.
46. Quoted in Derr, *Some Kind of Paradise*, 120.
47. The phrase "dress rehearsal" was used in McElvaine, *Great Depression*, 43.
48. The best source on Carl Fisher is Mark Foster's *Castles in the Sand*.
49. Danese, *Claude Pepper and Ed Ball*, 17.
50. Ibid., 15.
51. Ibid.
52. Weigall, *Boom in Paradise*, 44.
53. Rogers, "Paradoxical Twenties," 293.
54. Foster, *Castles in the Sand*, 214.
55. Rogers, "Paradoxical Twenties," 294.
56. Bryan died in 1926 worth $860,000; Vickers, *Panic in Paradise*, 19.
57. Nolan, *Fifty Feet in Paradise*, 186.

58. Rogers, "Paradoxical Twenties," 291.
59. Ibid., 293.
60. Danese, *Claude Pepper and Ed Ball*, 20.
61. Rogers, "Paradoxical Twenties," 291; Dunn, "New Deal and Florida Politics," 21; Derr, *Some Kind of Paradise*, 184, 312–13.
62. Barnes, *Florida's Hurricane History*, 112. For Florida's hurricane history, see Barnes and also Attevy, *Hurricanes and Florida Agriculture*. For the 1926 hurricane, see Barnes, *Florida's Hurricane History*, 111–26; Attevy, *Hurricanes and Florida Agriculture*, 82–93.
63. Nolan, *Fifty Feet in Paradise*, 221.
64. Barnes, *Florida's Hurricane History*, 86–89.
65. Barnes, *Florida's Hurricane History*, 89.
66. Rogers, "Paradoxical Twenties," 297, Dunn, "New Deal and Florida Politics," 9.
67. For an explanation of the banking crisis, see Vickers, *Panic in Paradise*, 9–13. Vickers's work is the first history based on primary regulatory banking records. The majority of banking records of the 1920s and 1930s across the nation have been either been destroyed or permanently sealed. Vickers, along with Florida State University professor Edward Keuchel, fought successfully for the Florida government to make public the state's banking records.
68. Dunn, "New Deal and Florida Politics," 4; Vickers, *Panic in Paradise*, 5; Tebeau, *History of Florida*, 394.
69. Fred White, interview by Dr. Donald Pleasant, March 16, 1998 (Oral History, CCC-1), 1, Samuel Proctor Oral History Program (SPOHP), University of Florida, Gainesville.
70. Dunn, "New Deal and Florida Politics," 4.
71. Danese, *Claude Pepper and Ed Ball*, 25.
72. Shofner, *Jackson County*, 476.
73. Cox, "David Sholtz," 146.
74. Dunn, "New Deal and Florida Politics," 19; Tebeau, *History of Florida*, 394.
75. "Florida Hails Tax Plan to Lower Tax Rate," *New York Times*, July 24, 1932.
76. Dunn, "New Deal and Florida Politics," 12.
77. Mertz, *New Deal Policy*, 3.

Chapter 2. A New Deal for Florida

1. Much of the information for the Roosevelt assassination attempt comes from Frank Friedel's *Franklin D. Roosevelt: Launching the New Deal*, 168–73; and from the Joseph Zangara Case File, Series LR 47, FSA. See also Kennedy, *Freedom from Fear*, 116–17.
2. "Stubby, curly-haired man" is from Friedel, *Franklin D. Roosevelt: Launching the New Deal*, 170. The three other people wounded were Margaret Kruise, Russell Caldwell, and Willis Scott; Joseph Zangara case file, FSA.
3. *Chicago: A Century of Progress, 1833–1933*, 6.
4. Friedel, *Franklin D. Roosevelt: Launching the New Deal*, 172. Zangara formally pled guilty to the incident on February 20, in Dade County Court. He was labeled a "perverse character" and "psychopathic" in a psychiatric exam by Dr. I. H. Agoson. Agoson's Examination Report, February 18, 1933, Joseph Zangara case file, FSA.

5. Dunn, "New Deal and Florida Politics," 103.

6. Rogers, "Great Depression," 309.

7. Friedel, *FDR and the South*, 1.

8. The best source for Roosevelt's experiences with polio is Hugh G. Gallagher's *FDR's Splendid Deception*.

9. That friend was George Foster Peabody. For information on Roosevelt's Warm Springs experiences see Lippman, *Squire of Warm Springs*.

10. Friedel, *FDR and the South*, 8. Today this property is encompassed within Georgia's FDR State Park.

11. Schlesinger, *Age of Roosevelt*, 337.

12. Watkins, *Hungry Years*, 156.

13. Ibid.

14. Leuchtenburg, *Franklin D. Roosevelt and the New Deal*, 43–44.

15. The origin of the term "New Deal" can be traced to an FDR campaign speech from 1932: "I pledge you, I pledge myself, to a new deal for the American people." Maney, *Roosevelt Presence*, 40.

16. Mertz, *New Deal Policy*, 234.

17. The term "-inspired" was used instead of "-led" because, as Patrick Maney points out, only two of the fifteen bills passed were directly attributable to Roosevelt. Maney, *Roosevelt Presence*, 50.

18. Patterson, *America's Struggle*, 60.

19. Mertz, *New Deal Policy*, 23.

20. Perkins, *The Roosevelt I Knew*, 177.

21. Schlesinger, *Age of Roosevelt*, 336; Watkins, *Hungry Years*, 160.

22. Perkins, *The Roosevelt I Knew*, 177.

23. Salmond, *Civilian Conservation Corps*, 6.

24. Paul Conkin, *The New Deal*, 45–46.

25. Hill, *In the Shadow of the Mountain*, xiv–xv.

26. Ibid., xv; Walston, "A Case for the Revival of the CCC," 3; Salmond, *Civilian Conservation Corps*, 6; Lacy, *Soil Soldiers*, 18.

27. Salmond, *Civilian Conservation Corps*, 6, 86.

28. Walston, "A Case for the Revival of the CCC," 3; Paige, *The Civilian Conservation Corps and the National Park Service*, 3–4.

29. Paige, *CCC and NPS*, 4; Cole, *African-American Experience in the CCC*, 5.

30. Paige, *CCC and NPS*, 5.

31. Reiman, *New Deal and American Youth*, 18; Betty and Ernest Lindley, *A New Deal for Youth*, 8. The terms "teens" and "teenagers" were not used in the 1930s. Ware, *Holding Their Own*, 56.

32. Lindley and Lindley, *A New Deal for Youth*, 8.

33. Ibid., 7.

34. Reiman, *New Deal and American Youth*, 32; Kenneth S. Davis, *FDR: The New York Years*, 361.

35. Rawick, "New Deal and Youth," 178.

36. Jack Baker to Hopkins, December 2, 1934, quoted in Leuchtenberg, *Franklin D. Roosevelt and the New Deal*, 129.

37. Watkins, *Hungry Years*, 26.

38. For more on William James and his influence on FDR, see Salmond, *Civilian Conservation Corps*; Reiman, *New Deal and American Youth*, 33.

39. Reiman, *New Deal and American Youth*, 14–15.

40. Ibid., 45.

41. Ibid., 4.

42. Ibid.

43. Ibid., 49.

44. Watkins, *The Hungry Years*, 269.

45. Quoted in Watkins, *Hungry Years*, 158.

46. Ibid.

47. Paige, *CCC and NPS*, 12; Salmond, *Civilian Conservation Corps*, 27.

48. Secretary of the Interior Harold Ickes and Labor Secretary Frances Perkins also disliked the army's involvement, though logistically each knew it was unavoidable. Watkins, *Hungry Years*, 161; Perkins, *The Roosevelt I Knew*, 178.

49. Schlesinger, *Age of Roosevelt*, 337; Lacy, *Soil Soldiers*, 29.

50. Watkins, *Hungry Years*, 161.

51. Salmond, *Civilian Conservation Corps*, 27.

52. Kennedy, *Freedom from Fear*, 146.

53. Salmond, *Civilian Conservation Corps*, 28.

54. Ibid., 42.

55. For the sake of clarity, the abbreviation CCC is used throughout this book. Watkins, *Hungry Years*, 158; Kennedy, *Freedom from Fear*, 144.

56. Paige, *CCC and the NPS*, 15; Salmond, *Civilian Conservation Corps*, 36. For more on WWI veterans' bonus marches, and their entrance into the CCC, see Keene, *Doughboys*.

57. Paige, *CCC and the NPS*, 13; Salmond, *Civilian Conservation Corps*, 45.

58. As for who was the first enrollee, there is some confusion among scholars. Sometimes Fiore Riozzo of New York is credited, while at other times, it is said to be Henry Rich of Virginia. Hill, *In the Shadow of the Mountain*, xv; Watkins, *Hungry Years*, 162; Lacy, *Soil Soldiers*, 20.

59. Salmond, *Civilian Conservation Corps*, 45.

60. "With the Civilian Conservation Corps," *American Forests* 39 (July 1933).

61. Buhite and Levy, *FDR's Fireside Chats*, 21.

62. Salmond, *Civilian Conservation Corps*, 47; Ickes, *Secret Diaries*, 78–79.

63. Salmond, *Civilian Conservation Corps*, 63; Lacy, *Soil Soldiers*, 65.

64. Watkins, *Hungry Years*, 162.

65. Leuchtenburg, *Franklin D. Roosevelt and the New Deal*, 174.

66. Watkins, *Hungry Years*, 163.

67. Leuchtenburg, *Franklin D. Roosevelt and the New Deal*, 174.

68. Clarke, *Roosevelt's Warrior*, 172–73, 259; Lacy, *Soil Soldiers*, 68–69.

69. The agrarian aspects of the CCC were explored by Maren Starge in "Publicity, Husbandry and Technocracy."

70. Patterson, *America's Struggle*, 76.

71. Ibid., 61.

72. Tebeau, *History of Florida*, 395; Rogers, "Paradoxical Twenties," 298; Dunn, *New Deal and Florida Politics*, 10–11.

73. Biles, *South and the New Deal*, 4.

74. Rogers, "Great Depression," 306.

75. Tebeau, *History of Florida*, 401.

76. "Report on Social Security in Florida," State Welfare Board, Administration files, S 871, RG 897, FSA.

77. Dunn, "New Deal and Florida Politics," 161.

78. Rogers, "Great Depression," 306.

79. Dunn, "New Deal and Florida Politics," 5.

80. Breslauer, *Roadside Paradise*, 23.

81. Doyle, *Government and Administration of Florida*, 114.

82. Ibid., 231.

83. Ibid.

84. Ibid.; Gray, *The Government of Florida*, 125.

85. Key, *Southern Politics*, 82; Colburn and Scher, *Florida's Gubernatorial Politics*, 22–23.

86. Key, *Southern Politics*, 85–87; Colburn and Scher, *Florida's Gubernatorial Politics*, 22–23.

87. Dunn, "New Deal and Florida Politics," 26.

88. Doyle, *Government and Administration of Florida*, 238.

89. "State Board of Public Welfare First Annual Report, 1927–1929," p. 1, State Welfare Board files, S 1871, RG 897, FSA.

90. Tebeau, *History of Florida*, 401.

91. "State Board of Public Welfare First Annual Report, 1927–1929," 1.

92. Patterson, *The New Deal and the State*, 48.

93. Dunn, "New Deal and Florida Politics," 26, 36, 42.

94. Dunn, "New Deal and Florida Politics," 39; Rogers "Great Depression," 305.

95. Rogers, "Great Depression," 304.

96. Rogers, "Great Depression," 306; Tebeau, *History of Florida*, 398–99.

97. Rogers, "Great Depression," 306.

98. In the 1910 census Sholtz is listed as a "mulatto," and his parents, Michael and Amie, as Russian immigrants. United States, *Thirteenth Census*, Brooklyn Ward 29, Kings, New York, roll T624-982, p. 4A.

99. "Pepper v. Sholtz v. Wilcox," *Time*, May 2, 1938; "Florida Hails Plan to Lower Tax Rate, *New York Times*, July 24, 1932.

100. Cox, "David Sholtz," 143; Dunn, "New Deal and Florida Politics," 76; Colburn and Scher, *Florida's Gubernatorial Politics*, 35, 40; Tebeau, *History of Florida*, 399.

101. Cox, "David Sholtz," 145; Dunn, "New Deal and Florida Politics," 73, 76; Tebeau, *History of Florida*, 399.

102. "Florida Hails Plan to Lower Tax Rate," *New York Times*, July 24, 1932; Cox, "David Sholtz," 147; Dunn, "New Deal and Florida Politics," 77; Tebeau, *History of Florida*, 399–400; *Florida Times-Union (FTU)*, June 16, 1932.

103. Dunn, "New Deal and Florida Politics," 78.
104. Vickers, *Panic in Paradise*, 212.
105. Rogers, "Great Depression," 307.
106. "Names Make News," *Time*, February 24, 1936.
107. "Florida Hails Plan to Lower Tax Rate."
108. Dunn, "New Deal and Florida Politics," 128.
109. Gray, *The Power and the Glory*, 46.
110. Flynt, *Duncan Upshaw Fletcher*, 166–68, 179, 182.
111. Cox, "David Sholtz," 148.
112. Ibid.
113. Daniel, "The New Deal, Southern Agriculture and Economic Change."
114. Tebeau, *History of Florida*, 402. John Sweet identifies Eastport camp (P-54) in Duval County as the first CCC camp in Florida; Sweet, "CCC in Florida," 79.
115. This included camps in one state forest, fourteen private forests, six national forests, and one biological survey; folder 5, box 10, entry 13, RG 35, National Archives (NARA).
116. Ibid.
117. Folder: "Minutes," State Welfare Board files, S 367, RG 897, FSA.
118. Sholtz to Charles Lanthrop Peck, American Tree Association, February 10, 1934, box 46, Sholtz papers, FSA.
119. Sholtz to Movietone News, February 13, 1934, folder: "Florida Forestry," box 46; Sholtz to Pathe Exchange, February 4, 1934, folder: "Forestry," box 46, Sholtz papers, FSA.
120. Sweet, "CCC in Florida," 83; Sholtz to George A. Kanser, November 28, 1934, brochure "Forest Fire Prevention Week," folder: "Forestry 1934," box 45, Sholtz papers, FSA. Photos of some of the Fire Prevention Week parades in southwest Florida can be found in Sebring Historical Society's CCC photo collection in Sebring, Florida.
121. Merlin Cox calls Dave Sholtz Florida's New Deal governor and wrote an adulatory article on the governor in 1964 for the *Florida Historical Quarterly* fall issue. In the meantime Florida gubernatorial historian David Colburn describes Sholtz as conservative in his politics and attributes few progressive programs to him. And in his dissertation on the New Deal in Florida politics, James William Dunn found Sholtz to be purely politically motivated in his actions, not relief minded.
122. Newell would later become the Washington campaign headquarters chief for the 1940 presidential candidate Paul McDutt. He died on May 18, 1940. *New York Times*, May 19, 1940.
123. An example is seen in Baker to Newell, June 4, 1934, folder: "Reforestation Applications," box 46, Sholtz papers, FSA.
124. Fills to Newell, June 1, 1934, folder: "Reforestation Applications," box 46, Sholtz papers, FSA.
125. Lundy to Newell, June 11, 1934, folder: "Reforestation Applications," box 46, Sholtz papers, FSA.
126. Hickok to Hopkins, January 28, 1934, in Lowitt and Beasley, *One Third of a Nation*, 164.
127. Hickok to Hopkins, January 28, 1934, in Lowitt and Beasley, *One Third of a Nation*, 163.
128. Ibid.

Chapter 3. Tourism, Conservation, and State Parks

1. Lombard, "Memorable Landscapes of William Lyman Phillips," 266.

2. "Hammock" is of Native American derivation and meant "shady place." Today it is generally used in Florida to refer to an area of hardwood trees, both temperate and tropical.

3. Tilden, *The State Parks*, 207. Tilden was an NPS writer who set out in the 1950s and 1960s to popularize parks and recreation in a series of books and guides.

4. Accounts of the Roeblings' flight over Highlands Hammock are found in Tilden, *The State Parks*, 207, and Sebring Historical Society, *Highlands Hammock*, 6–13.

5. For the records of Highlands Hammock, Inc. and the park's pre–Florida Park Service activities, see FPS Public Relations and Historical Files, 1934–1964, box 4, FSA. This box contains records discovered by author in 2003 at the Highlands Hammock State Park.

6. For more on Highlands Hammock acquisition, see Sebring Historical Society's *Highlands Hammock*, 6–13; *Highlands Hammock State Park* brochure (Tallahassee: Florida Forest and Park Service, 1940); Rex Beach, "Paradise in Florida."

7. *Highlands County News*, July 10, 1930, September 4, 1930.

8. *Highlands Hammock State Park* brochure. The work was done by Ross Farrens Tree Service in Clearwater. Blair to Farrens, December 22, 1933, S 1951, box 4, FPS Public Relations and Historical Files, 1934–1964, FSA.

9. Bailey to Alexander Blair, December 26, 1934 box 4, FPS Public Relations and Historical Files, 1934–1964, FSA. Bailey was the chairman of Highlands Hammock, Inc. Citrus Commission. He was also the superintendent of public instruction for Highlands County.

10. Blair to R. N. Durrance, Secretary for Highlands Hammock Inc., December 14, 1934, box 4, FPS Public Relations and Historical Files, 1934–1964, FSA.

11. Ibid. Due to unexpected freezes in late winter, the following year's yield was decidedly lower. To make up the difference, the park planted Hamlin Sweet Orange, tangerine, and lemon trees in the park grove.

12. Tilden, *The State Parks* 207; Rex Beach to Dave Sholtz, April 27, 1933, folder: "Highlands Hammock," box 46, Sholtz papers, FSA.

13. Note from Gadsby, November 19, 1934, box 4, FPS Public Relations and Historical Files, 1934–1964, FSA.

14. Rex Beach to Dave Sholtz, April 27, 1933; Alexander Blair to Sholtz, May 23, 1933; Raymond Green to Sholtz, April 24, 1933, folder: "Highlands Hammock," box 46, Sholtz papers, FSA.

15. Sholtz to Beach, May 1, 1933, folder: "Highlands Hammock," box 46, Sholtz papers, FSA.

16. Baker to Sholtz, May 23, 1933, folder: "Highlands Hammock," box 46, Sholtz papers, FSA.

17. Sholtz to Baker, May 1, 1933, folder: "Highlands Hammock," box 46, Sholtz papers, FSA.

18. Schedule of the Governor's Visit, February 15, 1935, box 4, FPS Public Relations and Historical Files, 1934–1964, FSA.

19. Blair to Sholtz, April 10, 1934; Mrs. Arthur Cummer to Sholtz, January 28, 1935, folder: "Highlands Hammock," box 46, Sholtz papers, FSA.

20. Blair to Durrance, December 12, 1934, box 4, FPS Public Relations and Historical Files, 1934–1964, FSA.

21. April 18, 1934, "Minutes," Volume 14, Trustees of the Internal Improvement Fund, FSA. See also Resolution of Highlands Hammock, Inc., dated January 7, 1935, box 4, FPS Public Relations and Historical Files, 1934–1964, FSA.

22. For an explanation of the trust fund, see Highlands Hammock Inc., Minutes for November 24, 1935, box 4, FPS Public Relations and Historical Files, 1934–1964, FSA.

23. Wand to Sholtz, May 3, 1935, Sholtz papers, box 2, folder: "Agriculture, Dept. of," FSA.

24. Sholtz to Wand, May 3, 1935; Sholtz to Mayo May 3, 1935, Sholtz to Willis, May 3, 1935, Sholtz papers, box 2, folder: "Agriculture, Dept. of," FSA.

25. Mayo to Sholtz, May 4, 1935, Sholtz papers, box 2, folder: "Agriculture, Dept. of," FSA.

26. Ibid.

27. *Winter Haven Chief*, November 1, 1940.

28. *Marion County Historical Bulletin* (December 1963).

29. Ibid.

30. Chapter 10029, *Laws of Florida*, 1925, copy included in Mayo's letter to Sholtz, May 11, 1933, Sholtz papers, box 2, folder: "Agriculture, Dept. of," FSA).

31. Mayo to Sholtz, May 12, 1935, Sholtz papers, box 2, folder: "Agriculture, Dept. Of," FSA.

32. Florida Department of Agriculture, *24th Biennial Report*, 44.

33. Rogers, "Florida in World War II," 35.

34. Dawes to Carlton, December 27, 1930, Doyle Carlton Papers, box 14, folder: "Century of Progress," FSA.

35. Ibid.

36. For a more complete history of world fair's (a surprisingly neglected topic in historical academia), see Kulterman, "Anticipating the Future," 9–27; and Rydell, *World of Fairs*.

37. Carlton to Dawes, January 7, 1931, Carlton papers, box 14, folder: "Century of Progress," FSA.

38. Senate Concurrent Resolution #9, C. Van Deventer to Carlton, June 9, 1931, Carlton papers, box 14, folder: "Century of Progress," FSA.

39. Hodges to Carlton, August 10, 1931, Carlton papers, box 14, folder: "Century of Progress," FSA.

40. Commission Minutes, August 29, 1931, Carlton papers, box 14, folder: "Century of Progress," FSA.

41. Ibid.

42. Press release, COP Commission, November 1931, Carlton papers, box 14, folder: "Century of Progress," FSA.

43. Press release, COP Commission, January 1932, Carlton papers, box 14, folder: "Century of Progress," FSA.

44. Hodges to R. G. Patterson (president, N. W. Florida Assn., Pensacola), March 21, 1933, Carlton papers, box 14, folder: "Century of Progress," FSA.

45. Press release, COP Commission, January 1932, Carlton papers, box 14, folder: "Century of Progress," FSA.

46. Hodges to Paul Eddy, March 22, 1932, Carlton papers, box 14, folder: "Century of Progress," FSA.

47. *National Cyclopedia American Biography*, vol. 36, 1950, 306–8.

48. Jack Davis, "Alligators and Plume Birds," 235.

49. Antonelli, "Of Imagination and Concrete Fantasies," 6.

50. Mayo to Sholtz, May 11, 1933, Sholtz papers, box 2, folder: Agriculture, Dept. of," FSA. Unfortunately no financial or budgetary records of the FNE or COP survive.

51. Earl Brown (COP circular letter), "To Newspaper and Magazine Editors of Florida," Carlton papers, box 1, folder: "Century of Progress," FSA.

52. Ibid.

53. COP press release, n.d. [1932], Carlton papers, box 14, folder: "Century of Progress," FSA.

54. Ibid.

55. Ibid.

56. COP press release, December 1, 1931, Carlton papers, box 1, folder: "Century of Progress," FSA.

57. COP press release, n.d. [November 1931], Carlton papers, box 1, folder: "Century of Progress," FSA.

58. Ibid.

59. In 2018 this diorama could be found on display at the Stephen Foster Memorial State Park.

60. COP press release, November 2, 1932, Carlton papers, box 13, folder: "Century of Progress," FSA.

61. COP, *Florida in the Court of States* brochure (Deland, n.d. [1933]), available in the State Library of Florida's Florida Room.

62. COP press release, n.d. [November 1931], Carlton papers, box 1, folder: "Century of Progress," FSA; COP, *Florida in the Court of States* brochure; COP, *A Century of Progress; Florida's Part in the International Exposition* (Tallahassee: Florida Commission, 1933).

63. Wilson, "Florida at the Century of Progress Exposition," 60.

64. Ibid.

65. Ibid., 61.

66. Dunn, "New Deal and Florida Politics," 171. Dunn in his recounting of the return of tourists never mentions the Century of Progress nor offers any other rationale for the increase in tourism revenue.

67. Ibid.

68. Ibid., 172.

69. Press release, June 26, 1935, Florida State Chamber of Commerce, Sholtz papers, box 4, folder 4: "Advertising," FSA.

70. Ibid.

71. Earl W. Brown to Sholtz, September 19, 1935, Sholtz papers, box 44, folder: "Florida National Exhibits," FSA.

72. George, "Passage to the New Eden," 440; Tim Hollis, *Dixie Before Disney*, 3.

73. Brundage, *The Southern Past*, 185–86.

74. Mackle, "Eden of the South," 43, 50; Brundage, *The Southern Past*, 187.

75. George "New Eden," 441; Mackle, "Eden of the South," 88. Another popular Florida guide was Harriet Beecher Stowe's *Palmetto Leaves*.

76. Mackle, "Eden of the South," 441.

77. For a discussion of Florida's steamboats, see Edward Mueller's *Along the St. Johns and Ocklawaha Rivers*; Derr, *Some Kind of Paradise*, 65–80.

78. For more on Flagler, see Derr, *Some Kind of Paradise*, 17–56; Chandler, *Henry Flagler*; Standiford, *Last Train to Paradise*.

79. Reynolds, *The Story of Ask Mr. Foster*, 30, 3.

80. For more on the heliophilic craze, see Lancek and Bosker, *The Beach*.

81. Brundage, *The Southern Past*, 184.

82. The nickname has also been attributed to the can-like cars they drove and lived in while visiting.

83. For further explanation of "tin can tourists" see Nick Wynne's *Tin Can Tourists in Florida*.

84. Cutler, *Public Landscape*, 84.

85. Arsenault, *St. Petersburg and the Florida Dream*, 189.

86. Lancek and Bosker, *The Beach*, 207–8.

87. Lorena Hickok wrote to Harry Hopkins in 1934 that Florida's roads were full of cattle. Lowitt and Beasley, *One Third of a Nation*, 167.

88. Rogers, "Paradoxical Twenties," 299; Breslauer, *Roadside Paradise*, 24.

89. Albert Gufford OH, FSA.

90. James, *Alfred I. Dupont, Family Rebel*, 399.

91. Rogers, "Paradoxical Twenties," 293; Breslauer, *Roadside Paradise*, 23.

92. Breslauer, *Roadside Paradise*, 24.

93. Ibid.

94. Rogers, "Paradoxical Twenties," 293.

95. Brundage, *The Southern Past*, 191. For more on the Dixie Highway and other southern road building, see Ingram, *Dixie Highway*, and Preston, *Dirt Roads to Dixie*.

96. Breslauer, *Roadside Paradise*, 25–26; Hollis, *Dixie Before Disney*, 7; Rogers, "Paradoxical Twenties," 293.

97. Garrett, "Blasting through Paradise," 261, 268.

98. Weigall, *Boom in Paradise*, 27–28.

99. Brundage, *The Southern Past*, 192.

100. Hollis, *Dixie Before Disney*, 132; Breslauer, *Roadside Paradise*, 6.

101. Bauer, "Sarasota," 138.

102. Cox, "David Sholtz," 150.

103. Hickok to Hopkins, January 31, 1934, Lowitt and Beasley, *One Third of a Nation*, 167–68.

104. Leslie, "The Great Depression in Miami Beach."

105. Derr, *Some Kind of Paradise*, 318.

106. Hollis, *Dixie Before Disney*, 21.

107. Rogers, "Paradoxical Twenties," 292.

108. Rogers, "Great Depression," 319.

109. This claim could be found in much of the literature about Florida during the Depression. This quote came from a speech by L. M. Rhodes (Florida Marketing Bureau) to the Associated Chambers of Commerce of Polk County, Davenport, Florida, February 15, 1937, Governor Fred Cone Papers, box 57, folder: "Marketing Bureau, 1937."

110. Baker, *Forest Fires in Florida*, 1.

111. Ibid.

112. Ibid.

113. Ibid., 1, 7.

114. Ibid., 6–9.

115. Pyne, *Fire in America*, 171.

116. Ibid., 102–6; Arno and Allison-Burnell, *Flames in Our Forest*, 17.

117. See Pyne's *Fire in America* for more on the "light burning" controversy, 100–12.

118. Their first publication was *The Common Forests Trees of Florida* in 1925. Clinton H. Coulter, interview by Elwood Maunder, February 6, 1958, Forest History Society Papers, Duke University, 213.

119. Wand would only serve one term, 1933. Florida House of Representatives, *People of Lawmaking in Florida*, 163.

120. Vance, *May Mann Jennings*, 119.

121. Pyne, *Fire in America*, 115; Arno and Allison-Burnell, *Flames in Our Forest*, 19.

122. Pyne, *Fire in America*, 115; Arno and Allison-Burnell, *Flames in Our Forest*, 19.

123. Inman Eldredge, interview by Elwood Maunder, February 3, 1959, 47, Forest Society History Papers, Duke University, Durham, N.C. https://foresthistory.org/wp-content/uploads/2016/12/Eldredge.pdf.

124. Kiwanis Club of Tallahassee, *Who's Who*, 26; Florida Society of American Foresters, Hall of Fame 2003 Inductee Biography, http://www.flsaf.org/hof/hof-baker.htm.

125. Kiwanis Club of Tallahassee, *Who's Who*, 26; Florida Society of American Foresters, Hall of Fame 2003 Inductee Biography, http://www.flsaf.org/hof/hof-baker.htm.

126. Florida State Board of Forestry, *First Biennial Report, 1927–1930*, 7.

127. Ibid., 1, 8.

128. Baker was hired at $4,200 a year. Minutes of the Board of Forestry, February 23, 1928, 5.

129. Florida State Board of Forestry, *First Biennial Report, 1927–1930*, 14.

130. Ibid.

131. Pyne, *Fire in America*, 170.

132. Florida State Board of Forestry, *First Biennial Report, 1927–1930*, 14.

133. Baker to Ed Ball, Chairman of the Florida State Planning Board, July 22, 1934, RG 510, Series 1351, Florida State Park Survey 1934–1935, box 1, folder: "Proposed surveys," FSA.

134. Ibid.

135. Ibid.

136. Baker to William L. Wilson, chairman, Florida Agricultural and Industrial Relief (FAIR) Commission, June 27, 1933, Sholtz papers, box 44, folder: "Florida Agricultural and Industrial Relief (FAIR) Commission," FSA.

137. Ibid.

Chapter 4. The Mother Who Birthed the Florida Park Service

1. Gifford Pinchot was Theodore Roosevelt's chief forester as well as a leading member of the Progressive movement. He is also the American most closely linked to the concept of conservation. For more on Pinchot see Martin Fausold's *Gifford Pinchot: Bull Moose Progressive*.

2. McCally, *Everglades*, 86.

3. Historian and Jennings biographer Linda Vance called her the most powerful woman in Florida during the early 1900s. Vance, *May Mann Jennings*, 79.

4. Vance, *May Mann Jennings*, 1–8.

5. Vance, *May Mann Jennings*, 1, 14–18; Florida House of Representatives, *People of Lawmaking in Florida*, 98.

6. Vance, *May Mann Jennings*, 37.

7. Vance, "May Mann Jennings and Royal Palm State Park," 4–5.

8. Vance, *May Mann Jennings*, 58.

9. Ibid.

10. McCally, *Everglades*, 86.

11. Vance, *May Mann Jennings*, 80.

12. McCally, *Everglades*, 74.

13. Kirk Monroe was a famous novelist who lived in South Florida and owned a portion of Paradise Key. Vance, *May Mann Jennings*, 81–83.

14. Scoggin, "History of the Florida State Parks," 16; Doyle, *Government and Administration of Florida*, 285.

15. Some people may identify Olustee Battle Memorial, created in 1909 by the State Legislature, as Florida's first state-funded park. But along with other Confederate and early statehood memorials cared for by the legislature, including Natural Bridge, Benjamin Judah Memorial, and Confederate Park in Marianna, Olustee Battle Memorial was not at that time an actual state park. These "parks" consisted of nothing more than a plaque and a stone memorial commemorating the historic event. The confusion rests in the fact that today these memorials are encompassed within state parks, a development that occurred in the 1950s.

16. Vance, *May Mann Jennings*, 92.

17. Though copyrighted with Douglas as the author, the book was actually written by John Rothchild, culled from more than two hundred hours of audiotapes of Douglas recounting her life story. Douglas, *Voice of the River*, 136.

18. Jackson, *Pioneer of Tropical Landscape Architecture*, 127.

19. Derr, *Some Kind of Paradise*, 166.

20. Landrum, *Southeastern State Park Systems*, 26; Linley, "History of the Florida Park System."

21. Florida, Trustees of the Internal Improvement Fund, Minutes, February 8, 1934, vol. 15, p. 338, RG 194, FSA.

22. "Parks and Natural Scenery, 1/19/1933," folder: "Correspondence: 1934—June–December," box 19, Jennings Papers, University of Florida (UF).

23. Doyle, *Government and Administration of Florida*, 278.

24. Ibid., 275, 278; Gray, *The Government of Florida*, 63; McCally, *Everglades*, 88. In 1934 the board consisted of Dave Sholtz (governor), Nathan Mayo (commissioner of agriculture), William V. Knott (treasurer), Cary Landis (attorney general), and J. M. Lee (comptroller).

25. Florida, Trustees of the Internal Improvement Fund, Minutes, February 8, 1934, vol. 15, p. 338, RG 194, FSA.

26. Each camp had a designation that included a letter followed by a number. The letter represented the type of work the camp conducted, and the number was sequentially the next camp in that line of work for a particular state. "SP-2" was the second state park CCC camp for Florida. Other camp types included forestry work (F), forestry work on privately owned land (P), National Park work (NP), Soil Conservation Service (SCS), and Military Park construction (MP).

27. "Report: Exploring for Torreya Trees in the Apalachicola Bluff Country," Public Relations and Historical Files, 1934–1964, box 1, folder: "Torreya—history," FSA.

28. Ibid.

29. Wirth, *Parks, Politics and the People*, 88.

30. Paige, *CCC and the NPS*, 16.

31. Paige, *CCC and the NPS*, 19.

32. Heinemann, *Depression and New Deal in Virginia*, 65; Humphrey, "In a Sense Experimental," 28.

33. Cutler, *Public Landscape*, 10.

34. United States, Civilian Conservation Corps (US CCC), *CCC and Public Recreation*, 23.

35. Ibid., 3.

36. Black, *Courage in a Dangerous World*, 38.

37. Cutler, *Public Landscape*, 78.

38. Woodward, "Recreation: A Philosophy of Joyful Living," 43.

39. "Recreational Industry in Florida," 47.

40. Everhart, *National Park Service*, 8.

41. McClelland, *Building the National Parks*, 53.

42. Wirth, *Parks, Politics and the People*, 17.

43. Everhart, *National Parks Service*, 13–14.

44. Everhart, *National Parks Service*, 16.

45. Wirth, *Parks, Politics and the People*, 21.

46. McClelland, *Building the National Parks*, 53.

47. Ibid.

48. McClelland, *Building the National Parks*, 54–55.

49. Ibid. Olmsted was very involved in park developments, sitting on the NPS commission, active in the National Conferences on State Parks, and conducting lobbying efforts for other states.

50. Wirth, *Parks, Politics, and the People*, 75.

51. Paige, *CCC and the NPS*, 39; Wirth, *Parks, Politics, and the People*, 72. John Coffman was in charge of National Parks CCC work.

52. Everhart, *National Park Service*, 24.

53. Florida State Planning Board, *Summary Report, March 1934–December 1936*, 6, Cone papers, box 71, folder: "Planning Board, State 1937," FSA.

54. Ball to Baker, July 27, 1934, State Park Survey files, box 1, folder: "Proposed Survey," FSA.

55. Ball to Fred Cone, December 28, 1936, Fred Cone Papers, box 33, folder: "Florida National Exhibits," FSA.

56. Ibid.

57. By 1938 forty-five states had planning boards. National Resources Committee, "The States and Planning," 35. For more on the origin of the planning boards, see Reagan, *Designing a New America*.

58. Merrian, "The Spirit of Planning," 46.

59. Sholtz to Harold Ickes, January 14, 1935, Sholtz papers, box 90, folder: "Planning Board, State."

60. Florida State Planning Board, *Summary Report*, 3.

61. In a WJAX broadcast on January 11, 1939, of the program *U.S. Government Reports*, Planning Board executive secretary George Gross described the board as "purely a study and advisory organization. It advises the Governor and State Legislature." Florida Statewide Library Project, *WJAX Radio Broadcast: U.S. Government Reports*, 6; Florida State Planning Board, *Summary Report*, 56.

62. For Ball's attitudes toward the New Deal, see Danese, *Claude Pepper and Ed Ball*.

63. Florida State Planning Board Minutes, April 5, 1934, box 1, folder: "Official Minutes, 1934–1944," FSA. Other committees of the board included State Tax Problems, Public Works Committee, Public Health, and Improvement of Public Buildings.

64. Baker to Ball, July 22, 1934, State Park Surveys files, box 1, folder: "Proposed survey," FSA.

65. Ibid.

66. Untitled document, State Park Survey files, box 1, folder: "General Explanation and Maps," FSA; State Planning Board Minutes, September 24–25, 1934, box 1, folder: "Minute, 1934–1944," FSA; minutes, July 23, 1934, Sholtz papers, box 90, folder: "Planning Board," FSA.

67. Untitled document, State Park Survey files, box 1, folder: "General Explanation and Maps," FSA.

68. Ibid.; Baker to Ball, July 22, 1934, State Park Survey files, box 1, folder: "Proposed survey," FSA.

69. Florida State Planning Board, *Summary Report*, 24.

70. Walter Coldwell to Jennings, October 8, 1934, folder "Correspondence: 934—Jan–Dec," box 19, Jennings Papers, UF.

71. For copies of both surveys, see State Park Survey files at the Florida State Archives. All three of these sites eventually were acquired by the State as state parks.

72. For the era of Wakulla Springs as a tourist attraction, see Revels, *Watery Eden*.

73. Fechner to Sholtz, May 5, 1933, Sholtz papers, box 46, folder: "Forestry, Reforestation," FSA.

74. Wilson to Fechner, May 30, 1935, RG 35, entry 300, box 607, folder: "Florida: State and Private Lands," NARA.

75. Fechner to Sholtz, October 9, 1934, Sholtz papers, box 46, folder: "Forestry, Reforestation," FSA.

76. Roosevelt to Sholtz, January 8, 1935, RG 35, entry 9, box 1, folder: "Florida," NARA.

77. Ibid.

78. *Tampa Tribune*, December 11, 1934, State Welfare Board Administrative files, box 1, folder: "Clippings, December 1934–July 1935," FSA.

79. *Jacksonville Journal*, March 22, 1935, State Welfare Board Administrative files, box 1, folder: "Clippings, December 1934–July 1935," FSA.

80. Several newspapers opposed the plan, including the *Florida Times-Union* and *Tampa Tribune*.

81. After Representatives Fred Ward and James Banks.

82. *Ocala Star*, May 20, 1935, State Welfare Board Administrative files, box 1, folder: "Clippings, December 1934–July 1935," FSA.

83. *Pensacola News*, May 28, 1935.

84. Gray, *The Government of Florida*, 126.

85. Tebeau, *History of Florida*, 402.

86. Dunn, "New Deal and Florida Politics," 145–47; Cox, "David Sholtz," 151.

87. Tebeau, *History of Florida*, 141–42.

88. Fechner to Sholtz, February 20, 1935, RG 35, entry 9, box 1, folder: "Florida," NARA.

89. Fechner to Sholtz, February 25, 1935, RG 35, entry 9, box 1, folder: "Florida," NARA.

90. Scoggin, "History of Florida State Parks," 16.

91. The rest of the Board of Forestry were John Glen (vice-president), Stanley Sheip (secretary), Harold S. Foley, and Susan Fort Jeffreys (Mrs. Linwood Jeffreys). Untitled document, Sholtz papers, box 45, folder: "Forestry 1932–1934," FSA.

92. Acts of the Legislature, vol. 91: 1935 Acts, FSA.

93. Ibid.

94. Ibid.

95. Baker to Sholtz, May 27, 1935, Sholtz papers, box 105, folder: "State Parks," FSA.

96. Ibid.

97. Ibid.

98. Acts of the Legislature, vol. 91: 1935 Acts, S222, FSA.

99. Jennings to E. E. Atkinson, October 28, 1933. folder: "Correspondence: 1934—June–December," box 19, Jennings Papers, UF; Florida Federation of Women's Clubs (FFWC), *Year Book, 1932–1934*, 278; Lombard, "Memorable Landscapes of William Lyman Phillips," 271; Jackson, *Pioneer of Tropical Landscape Architecture*, 123.

100. FFWC, *Year Book, 1932–1934*, 278–79.

101. Jennings to W. F. Coachman, February 9, 1934; Baker to Jennings, February 31, 1934; Raymond Green to Jennings, February 10, 1934; Jennings to F. C. Elliot, May 10, 1934; Jennings to H. E. Weatherwax, March 14, 1934, folder: "Correspondence: 1934—June–December," box 19, Jennings Papers, UF; FFWC, *Year Book, 1932–1934*, 279–80.

102. FFWC, *Year Book, 1932–1934*, 279–80; Meyer, *Leading the Way*, 115.

103. Sholtz to Jennings, May 12, 1934, May 30, 1935, folder: "Correspondence: 1934—June–December," box 19, Jennings Papers, UF.

104. Jennings to Herbert Evison, May 26, 1934; Sholtz to Jennings May 30, 1935, folder: "Correspondence: 1934—June-December," box 19, Jennings Papers, UF.

105. Baker to Jennings, February 3, 1934; Jennings to Elliot, February 16, 1934, Jennings to McQueen Chaires, February 9, 1934, folder: "Correspondence: 1934—June-December," box 19, Jennings Papers, UF.

106. Jennings to Chaires, February 28, 1934, folder: "Correspondence: 1934—June-December," box 19, Jennings Papers, UF.

107. Jennings to Evison, May 26, 1934, folder: "Correspondence: 1934—June-December," box 19, Jennings Papers, UF.

108. William C. Hodges to Sholtz, July 12, 1934; Mrs. Murray Stanley to Sholtz, July 25, 1934; P. M. Ulsch to Sholtz, April 30, 1935; Senator Duncan Fletcher to Sholtz, June 20, 1935, Sholtz papers, box 105, folder: "State Park Director," FSA.

109. Sholtz to Jennings, May 25, 1934, Sholtz papers, box 105, folder: "State Park director," FSA.

110. Sholtz to Jennings, May 30, 1934, Sholtz papers, box 105, folder: "State Park Director," FSA.

111. See folder "Correspondence: 1934—June-December" in box 19 for dozens of these letters. Jennings Papers, UF.

112. Jennings to Sholtz, July 12, 1934, Sholtz papers, Box 105, folder: "State Park Director," FSA.

113. Jennings to Sholtz, September 17, 1934, Sholtz papers, box 105, folder: "State Park Director," FSA.

114. Jennings to W. T. Edwards, May 8, 1935, folder "1935," box 20, Jennings Papers, UF.

115. Ibid.

116. Ibid.

117. Jennings to Sholtz, June 21, 1935, Sholtz papers, box 105, folder: "State Park Director," FSA.

118. Jackson, *Pioneer of Tropical Landscape Architecture*, 138–39.

119. Oleno State Park, near Lake City, which is usually included as one of the original CCC state parks, would not be added to the FPS until 1941. It was initially created as a forestry training camp.

Chapter 5. State-Sponsored Tourism and the Building of Florida's State Parks

1. Pantzer was stationed "at the shelter at the fork of the roads at the Hammock entrance." *The American*, May 17, 1935, clipping found in box 4, FPS Public Relations and Historical Files, 1934–1964, FSA.

2. Scoggin, "History of Florida State Parks," 16.

3. *New York Times*, October 10, 1935, December 2, 1935, December 3, 1935; Remarks by FDR at the Great Lakes Exposition, Cleveland Ohio, August 14, 1936, John T. Wooley and Gerhard Peters, University of California–Santa Barbara, American Presidency Project.

4. "Reaping Rich Harvest," *Southern Advertising and Publishing* (March 1936), 17.

5. American studies scholar Stephen J. Whitfield once wrote that considering its envy and

imitative efforts regarding California, the State of Florida made an apt choice when it named the mockingbird as its state bird in 1927. Whitfield, "Florida's Fudged Identity," 416.

6. Handout for the July 11, 1935, meeting, Sholtz papers, box 4, folder: "All Florida Advertising Committee—Misc.," FSA.

7. For instance, Sholtz to R. J. Binnecker (of Tampa), July 25, 1935, Sholtz papers, box 2, folder: "Advertising Campaign," FSA.

8. "A Meeting of an Organization Committee Appointed by Governor Sholtz to Discuss Plans for Raising an Advertising Fund," July 11, 1935, Sholtz papers, box 4, folder: "All Florida Advertising Campaign," FSA.

9. Ibid.

10. Minutes, July 22, 1935, All-Florida Advertising Campaign, Tallahassee, Sholtz papers, box 4, folder: "All Florida Advertising Committee—Misc.," FSA.

11. Hamburger, "And They're Off!" 114.

12. Ibid., 140.

13. Ibid., 143.

14. Mayo to G. C. Blume (of Jacksonville), n.d. [1935], Sholtz papers, box 2, folder: "Agriculture, Dept. of," FSA.

15. Mayo to Sholtz, June 18, 1935, Sholtz papers, box 2, folder: "Agriculture, Dept. of," FSA.

16. "Reaping Rich Harvest," *Southern Advertising and Publishing* (March 1936), 18.

17. Many of these inquiries can be found in Sholtz papers, box 5, folder: "All Florida Advertising Campaign," FSA.

18. Alvin P. Dearing (of Eastman, Scott & Company) to Sholtz, December 12, 1935; Sylvan Cox (of the *Christian Science Monitor*) to Sholtz, February 17, 1936, Sholtz papers, box 5, folder: "All Florida Advertising Committee," FSA.

19. The figure is quoted in Dearing to Sholtz, October 26, 1935, Sholtz papers, box 5, folder: "All Florida Advertising Committee," FSA.

20. H. Scott (of Eastman, Scott) to Sholtz, November 22, 1935, Sholtz papers, box 5, folder: "All Florida Advertising Committee," FSA.

21. Dearing to Newell, October 26, 935, Sholtz papers, box 5, folder: "All Florida Advertising Committee," FSA.

22. Cartoon found in *New York News,* March 1, 1936, clipping in Sholtz papers, box 5, folder: "All Florida Advertising Committee," FSA.

23. Scott to Sholtz, March 21, 1936, Sholtz papers, box 5, folder: "All Florida Advertising Committee," FSA.

24. An example is "Florida's Season Lengthens," *New York Times*, March 22, 1936.

25. Summary of Objectives and Results of Governor's All Florida Advertising Committee, n.d. [1936], Sholtz papers, box 3, folder: "Advertising," FSA.

26. Ibid.

27. William Wilson (acting director, Florida Professional Service Projects, WPA, Jacksonville) to Ralph Nicholson (All Florida Advertising Committee), July 13, 1936, Sholtz papers, box 3, folder: "Florida All State Advertising Committee," FSA.

28. Ibid.

29. Ibid.

30. Memorandum, December 20, 1935, Sholtz papers, box 4, folder: "All Florida Advertising Committee," FSA.

31. H. Overman to H. L. Flowers, July 16, 1936, Sholtz papers, box 3, folder: "All Florida Advertising Committee," FSA.

32. Rankin to Sholtz, September 17, 1936, Sholtz papers, box 2, folder: "Advertising," FSA.

33. The Cunard White Star Line—most famous for its ship the *Titanic*—was a British passenger ship company that ran out of Liverpool. Ibid.

34. See for instance Sholtz to Cooks Jones, December 12, 1936, Sholtz papers, box 2, folder: "Advertising," FSA.

35. Rankin to Sholtz, September 17, 1936, Sholtz papers, box 2, folder: "Advertising," FSA.

36. Ibid.

37. These letters can be found in Sholtz papers, box 2, folder: "Advertising," FSA.

38. Sholtz to Jones, December 12, 1936, Sholtz papers, box 2, folder: "Advertising," FSA.

39. Ibid.

40. Rankin to Sholtz, November 20, 1936, Sholtz papers, box 2, folder: "Advertising," FSA.

41. Rankin to Sholtz, October 23, 1936, Sholtz papers, box 2, folder: "Advertising," FSA.

42. Rankin to Jim Newell, December 7, 1936, Sholtz papers, box 2, folder: "Advertising," FSA.

43. J. Walker (Walker & Company, New York City) to Sholtz, December 18, 1936, Sholtz papers, box 2, folder: "Advertising," FSA.

44. Fred Lawson (London's *Daily Telegraph*) to Sholtz, November 12, 1936, Sholtz papers, box 2, folder: "Advertising," FSA.

45. State Planning Board minutes, June 13, 1940, box 192, folder: "Official minutes," FSA.

46. Staff circular, September 6, 1935, Sholtz papers, box 4, folder: "All Florida Advertising Campaign," FSA.

47. Typescript for the WTAL radio broadcast, January 10, 1936, in Chief of Education and Information Charles H. Schaeffer's administrative and reference files, 1936–1959, box 2, folder: "Radio scripts, 1935–1958," FSA.

48. John H. Stone to ECW Regional Supervisor, November 27, 1936, RG 95, entry 52A004, box 28, folder: "ECW Supervision—Inspection reports—Florida FY1937," NARA.

49. *Jackson County Floridian*, February 14, 1936.

50. Ibid.

51. *Jackson County Floridian*, February 21, 1936.

52. *Jackson County Floridian*, December 3, 1937.

53. Ibid.

54. Program of the Dedication of Myakka River State Park, Public Relations and Historical Files, 1934–1964, box 2, folder: "Myakka history," FSA.

55. Lewis Scoggin to Senator Dewey A. Dye, February 25, 1941, Public Relations and Historical Files, 1934–1964, box 1, folder 34: "Myakka-history," FSA.

56. "Report to Accompany Master Report, FL SP-6," March 22, 1937, State park project files, 1933–1942, 1988–1989, box 1 folder: "Torreya general files"; "On the Trail of Natural Beauty in Florida" (undated FPS brochure), Spessard Holland papers, box 39, folder: "Forest Park Service, FL 1941," FSA. The Torreya tree, named for discoverer botanist John Torreya, is a very rare tree, found only along a twenty-mile stretch of the Apalachicola River.

57. "Torreya State Park" brochure, Public Relations and Historical Files, 1934–1964, box 1, folder: "Torreya—history," FSA.

58. Map located in Public Relations and Historical Files, 1934–1964, box 1, folder: "Torreya—history," FSA.

59. Douglas, *Parks and Playgrounds of Florida*, 34.

60. *Highlands Hammock State Park*, undated park brochure; *Florida State Parks Invite You* (Tallahassee: Florida Park Service, 1940), Highlands Hammock files, box 1, Sebring Historical Society.

61. *Florida State Parks Invite You*. Fort Clinch often claimed that its fort was a common rendezvous for pirates.

62. Douglas, *Parks and Playgrounds of Florida*, 39.

63. Ibid., 35.

64. *Jackson County Floridian*, October 22, 1937.

65. S. Ladd to Assistant Regional Officer, November 29, 1936, RG 79, entry 91, folder: "Fort Clinch SP-12," NARA.

66. *Florida State Parks Invite You*, Highlands Hammock files, box 1, Sebring Historical Society. Tomoka River State Park was the other property purchased by the FPS in 1939, also not developed until after the war.

67. Ibid.

68. *Pictorial Review, District I, Company 2444, SP-5 Starke, Florida* (1939), n.p. A copy can be found in Gold Head Branch State Park files.

69. Undated notes (ca. 1935) from a meeting between the FPS and Florida Caverns, Inc., a citizens' group organized to promote the development of the park, State park project files, 1936–1945, box 1, folder: "Florida Caverns State Park Misc. Correspondence, 1938–1940," FSA.

70. Copies of these and other publications by Baynard can be found in Chief of Education and Information Charles H. Schaeffer's administrative and reference files, 1936–1959, passim, FSA.

71. Scoggin to Vinten, January 10, 1941. RG 79, entry 92, folder: "Florida Caverns—general," NARA.

72. H. Schaffer to Sholtz, January 4, 1936, Sholtz papers, box 105, folder: "Forestry, 1936," FSA.

73. Harold Foley, "The Florida Park Service" (WTAL radio broadcast), January 10, 1936, in Chief of Education and Information Charles H. Schaeffer's administrative and reference files, 1936–1959, box 2, folder: "Radio scripts, 1935–1958," FSA.

74. Malsberger to A. B. Weissinger, February 19, 1938, State park project files, 1936–1945, box 3, folder: "Gold Head supervision 1938–1941," FSA.

75. H. Jacobs to Simpson, December 14, 1941, W. F. Jacobs to S. W. Hiatt 28 January 1942, State park project files, 1936–1948, folder: "Florida Caverns State Park Miscellaneous correspondence 1941–1942," FSA.

76. Florida State Board of Forestry, *Fifth Biennial Report of the Florida Forest and Park Service, July 1, 1936–June 30, 1938*, 57.

77. Florida State Board of Forestry, *[Fourth] Biennial Report of the Florida Forest and Park Service, July 1, 1934–June 30, 1936*, 2.

78. Florida State Board of Forestry, *Fifth Biennial Report*, 48; Schaeffer to Col. S. C. Garling, May 15, 1937, State park project files, 1936–1945, box 2, folder: "Fort Clinch Park Use," FSA.

79. *Roger's Post*, November 6, 1935.

80. Scoggin, "History of Florida State Parks," 21. It is unclear why Baker left the FPS, but there are hints that it was not on amicable terms.

81. Glisson remained with the FPS well into the 1950s. The position of FPS architect was abolished in 1941, though reinstated in 1945, with future FPS director Emmet L. Hill assuming the position. Finlayson to Harold Ickes, July 12, 1941, State park project files, 1933–1942, 1988–1989, box 1, folder: "Torreya general files," FSA; Annual Report of the Park Director, July 1, 1945 to June 30, 1946, 1, Chief of Education and Information Charles H. Schaeffer's administrative and reference files, 1936–1959, box 2, folder: "Radio, 1936–1958," FSA.

82. Bird plumages were fashionable accessories in the early 1900s. "Oscar Baynard," undated manuscript, State park project files, 1933–1942, 1988–1989, box 1, folder: "Hillsborough Misc. Mss.," FSA.

83. Minutes of the Trustees of the Highlands Hammock, Inc., November 21, 1940, Highlands Hammock State Park files; A. C. Altvater to T. V. Conway, December 11, 1940, State park project files, 1936–1948, box 4, folder: "Plants and planting," FSA. Park naturalists were simultaneously park curators and interpreters, creating brochures, signs, programs, and exhibits, among other informational duties.

84. *Jackson County Floridian*, July 4, 1941; Scoggin to Sam Ellis, July 9, 1942, State park project files, 1936–1948, box 1 folder: "Florida Caverns Publicity," FSA.

85. Scoggin to Hayden William, April 28, 1942, State park project files, 1936–1945, box 1, folder: "Florida Caverns Supervision, 1941–1943," FSA. Giovanoli, who briefly taught biology at the University of Florida, would later work with herpetologist Archie Carr on Florida's first sea turtle tagging program in the 1950s. Carr, "A Century of Sea Turtles," 1.

86. *Florida Times-Union*, February 20, 1941.

87. McClelland, *Building the National Parks*, 381, 400.

88. Allen C. Altvater, interview by Herbert Evison, Spring 1971, Altvater papers, Sebring Historical Society, 17.

89. Wirth, *Parks, Politics and the People*, 11.

90. "Report on the School for Project Clerks," May 13, 1939, Highlands Hammock files, Sebring Historical Society; "Inspection Report, State of Florida," by John H. Stone, August 16, 1937, RG 95, entry 52A004, folder: "CCC Inspection—Florida FY1938 (2 of 2)," NARA.

91. McClelland, *Building the National Parks*, 434.

92. Ibid., 429–32; Cutler, *Public Landscape*, 91–92. We know the FPS had access to Good's book, as a copy can be found in the State park project files, 1936–1945, box 3, FSA.

93. McClelland, *Building the National Parks*, 280.

94. Ibid., 276–78.

95. See copy of Forestry Board Minutes in box 4, FPS Public Relations and Historical

Files, 1934–1964, FSA. The originals are housed in the Florida Forest Service director's office in Tallahassee.

96. "Supplement to Special Report of Highlands Hammock dedication on March 31, 1936 by A. C. Altvater," Highlands Hammock State Park files.

97. Ibid.; "Highlands Hammock work accomplished under the supervision of NPS from June 12, 1934 to December 31, 1940," State park project files, 1936–1945, box 4, folder: "Reports—General," FSA.

98. Admission charges and Policy for Highlands Hammock State Park, n.d. [1936], box 4, FPS Public Relations and Historical Files, 1934–1964, FSA.

99. Ibid.

100. Highlands Hammock, Inc. Minutes, November 4, 1935, box 4, FPS Public Relations and Historical Files, 1934–1964, FSA.

101. Forestry Board Minutes, box 4, FPS Public Relations and Historical Files, 1934–1964, FSA.

102. See copy of trust fund agreement in box 4, FPS Public Relations and Historical Files, 1934–1964, FSA.

103. See correspondence in box 4, FPS Public Relations and Historical Files, 1934–1964, FSA. The film was created by subcontractor Jack Campbell, also of Tampa. Unfortunately, the film has not survived.

104. Proposed Advertising, Highlands Hammock State Park, n.d. [1936], box 4, FPS Public Relations and Historical Files, 1934–1964, FSA.

105. *Florida State Park News* 1, no. 1 (1936). This was the only issue published, and the entirety of the four-page publication dealt with Highlands Hammock State Park.

106. Ibid.

107. See correspondence in FPS Public Relations and Historical Files, 1934–1964, box 1, folder: "Myakka River State Park—History (CCC files-1935)," FSA.

108. E. Weatherwax, NPS Regional Director, to Harry Lee Baker, November 10, 1935, in FPS Public Relations and Historical Files, 1934–1964, box 1, folder: "Myakka River State Park—history (CCC files-1935)," FSA.

109. Camp Inspection Report SP-4, January 9, 1935, RG 35, entry 10, folder: "FL SP-4, Myakka," NARA.

110. Camp Inspection Report SP-4, March 18, 1940, RG 35, entry 10, folder: "FL SP-4, Myakka," NARA.

111. Hillsborough CCC was primarily a forestry camp, with only 40 percent of its efforts directed to state park work—hence the designation P-71. The project was considered "idle" by 1938. Report of Typemapping Activities in Florida, June 1–18, 1938, by W. H. Thompson, RG 95, entry 52A004, box 11, folder: "CCC Inspection—Florida, FY1938 (1 of 2)," NARA.

112. *Tampa Tribune,* November 5, 1936, November 29, 1936.

113. "Inspection Report, State of Florida" by John H. Stone, August 16, 1937, 54, RG 95, entry 52A004, folder: "CCC Inspection—Florida FY1938 (2 of 2)," NARA.

114. See land records in FPS Public Relations and Historical Files, 1934–1964, box 2, folder: "Gold Head Branch State Park," FSA.

115. *Pictorial Review, District I, Company 2444, SP-5 Starke, Florida* (1939), n.p., copy in Gold Head Branch State Park files.

116. Camp Application SP-5, May 15, 1939, State park project files, 1936–1945, box 2, folder: "Gold Head Camp Applications," FSA.

117. *Pictorial Review, District I, Company 2444, SP-5 Starke, Florida* (1939), n.p., copy in Gold Head Branch State Park files.

118. National Register of Historic Places Inventory Application, March 9, 1971, State park project files, 1933–1942, 1988–1989, box 1, folder: "Fort Clinch—general," FSA.

119. Ibid.

120. The lodge was more akin to an enclosed picnic area than to a traditional NPS lodge. Vinten to Regional Director, July 31, 1940, State park project files, 1936–1945, box 1, folder: "Fort Clinch Accomplishment Reports," FSA.

121. "Report to Accompany the Layout Plan, Beach Area, Fort Clinch State Park, February 10, 1939, State park project files, 1936–1945, box 2, folder: "Fort Clinch—Plans/Layout," FSA.

122. "Report on expedition and survey of caves at Florida Caverns State Park by O. A. Challifeux," April 1937, RG 79, entry 91, folder: "Florida Caverns State Park, SP-12," NARA.

123. S. Ladd to Asst. Regional Officer, June 30, 1937, RG 79, entry 91, folder: "Florida Caverns State Park, SP-12," NARA; "CCC work accomplished under supervision of NPS 9-1-1938 to 6-30-1941," State park project files 1936–1942, box 1, folder: "Florida Caverns State Park—CCC," FSA.

124. Vinten to Scoggin, December 30, 1940, State park project files, 1936–1948, box 1, folder: "Florida Caverns State Park—work plan," FSA.

125. "CCC work accomplished under supervision of NPS 9-1-1938 to 6-30-1941," State park project files 1936–1948, box 1, folder: "Florida Caverns State Park—CCC," FSA. Simultaneously, the WPA built an adjoining golf course that today is located on state park property. Florida Department of Environmental Protection, *Florida Caverns State Park Unit Management Plan*, 76.

126. Thor Borresen to Fred John, NPS Regional Supervisor of Historic Sites, July 24, 1940, box 1, folder 61: "Florida Caverns State Park—history (cave exploration)," FPS Public Relations and Historical Files, 1934–1964, FSA (hereafter cited as Caverns SP history, FSA).

127. Ibid.

128. Ibid.

129. R. Kelly, Chief, Archaeological Sites Division, to Regional Director, August 19, 1940, Caverns SP history, FSA.

130. Thor Borresen to Fred John, NPS Regional Supervisor of Historic Sites, July 24, 1940, Caverns SP history, FSA.

131. Lowrie to Scoggin, July 29, 1940; W. J. Winter to Scoggin, August 3, 1940; John Goggin to Scoggin, September 9, 1940, Caverns SP history, FSA.

132. Job completion report (#147), June 1, 1941; Clarence Simpson, "A Report of an Archaeological Investigation at Caverns State Park, Marianna, Florida," Caverns SP history, FSA; George Davis, "Achievements of the Conservation Dept.," Cone papers, box 19, folder: "Conservation, Dept. of 1937," FSA.

133. Simpson, "Report of an Archaeological Investigation," Caverns SP history, FSA.

134. Simpson to Scoggin, August 5, 1941, Caverns SP history, FSA. Dr. Granberry would later became prominent for his linguistic work on the extinct Timucua language.

135. Ibid.

136. Fairbanks and Milanich, *Florida Archaeology*.

137. Charles Fairbanks, "Report of Collections from Florida Caverns State Park, Marianna, Florida," November 1941, Caverns SP history, FSA.

138. Ibid.

139. Ibid.

140. Simpson to Scoggin, June 3, 1944; Scoggin to Supt., Ocmulgee National Monument, June 7, 1944, Caverns SP history, FSA.

141. William Luckett to Scoggin, June 8, 1944, Caverns SP history, FSA.

142. Goggin to Scoggin, August 6, 1948; Simpson, "Report of an Archaeological Investigation," Caverns SP history, FSA.

143. Buck Heath OH, ROHP.

144. Simpson to Harry Lee Baker, November 29, 1941, Caverns SP history, FSA.

145. Herman Gunter to Scoggin, December 1, 1941, Caverns SP history, FSA. Gunter was also involved in the discovery of a large fossil tortoise in 1935 at Highlands Hammock, which as late as 2018 was still on display at the Hammock Inn on park property. Gunter to Alexander Blair, June 26, 1935, Caverns SP history, FSA.

146. Scoggin to Vinten, December 4, 1941, Caverns SP history, FSA.

147. Scoggin to Simpson, December 20, 1941, Scoggin to Baker, January 10, 942, Caverns SP history, FSA.

148. Ibid.

149. Scoggin to A. S. Romer (Curator of Vertebrae Paleontology, Harvard Museum of National History), March 22, 1946, Caverns SP history, FSA.

150. Asst. regional historian C. L. Johnson (NPS) to Regional Officer R. R. Appleman (NPS), May 10, 1937, FPS Public Relations and Historical Files, 1934–1964, box 1, folder: "Ft. Clinch—history," FSA.

151. Alexander Blair to Col. F.N.K. Bailey, February 3, 1937, box 4, FPS Public Relations and Historical Files, 1934–1964, FSA.

152. Vinten to Malsberger, January 19, 1939, January 23, 1939; Malsberger to Vinten, January 23, 1939, State park project files, 1936–1945, box 2, folder: "Gold Head misc. correspondence, 1937–1940," FSA.

153. Malsberger to Vinten, February 2, 1940, State park project files, 1936–1948, box 2, folder: "miscellaneous correspondence 1937–1940," FSA.

154. Vinten to Malsberger, February 7, 1940, State park project files, 1936–1948, box 2, folder: "miscellaneous correspondence 1937–1940," FSA.

155. Malsberger to Project Superintendent Tom Baker, February 15, 1940, State park project files, 1936–1948, box 2, folder: "miscellaneous correspondence 1937–1940," FSA.

156. Malsberger to Vinten, September 21, 1940, Florida State Park files, 1933–1942, 1988–1989, box 1, folder: "McClary file," FSA.

157. C. Alvater oral history, Highlands Hammock files, Sebring Historical Society, 15.

158. Scoggin to Vinten, August 13, 1941, State park project files, 1936–1948, box 1, folder: "Florida Caverns State Park work program," FSA.

159. Vinten to Malsberger, August 15, 1941, State park project files, 1936–1948, box 1, folder: "Florida Caverns State Park work program," FSA.

160. Scoggin to Vinten, October 13, 1940, State park project files, 1933–1942, 1988–1989, box 1, folder: "Florida Caverns State Hatchery," FSA.

161. Malsberger to Vinten, September 19, 1940, State park project files, 1933–1942, 1988–1989, box 1, folder: "Florida Caverns State Hatchery," FSA.

162. "Record of Conference Held at Camp FL SP-12 on January 3, 1941," State park project files, 1933–1942, 1988–1989, box 1, folder: "Florida Caverns State Hatchery," FSA.

163. Malsberger to M. B. Green, April 10, 1940, State park project files, 1936–1945, box 3, folder: "Fort Clinch—permit use," FSA.

164. Vinten, "An Analysis of Values of the State Park System of Florida," June 11, 1941, Director Emmet Hill's Administrative files, 1934–1960, box 1, folder: "NPS Planning—general," FSA.

165. Ft. Clinch formally opened on November 16, 1940. Scoggin, "History of Florida State Parks," 18; Sullivan, "The CCC and the Creation of Myakka River State Park," 14.

166. Malsberger to *Florida Times-Union*, April 21, 1939, State park project files, 1936–1945, box 1, folder: "Gold Head grand opening," FSA; *Pick and Spade* 3, no. 2 (March 1939); "Florida Park Opened to Public," *NPS Regional Review* (April 1939).

167. *Pick and Spade* (March 1939); *Florida Times-Union*, April 16, 1939.

168. Breslauer, *Roadside Paradise*, 13.

169. Highlands Hammock guest book, 1940, Highlands Hammock State Park files.

170. *Pick and Spade* (July 1939).

171. Vinten to Region One Director (NPS), September 10, 1940, State park project files, 1936–1945, box 2, folder: "Gold Head Camp Applications," FSA.

172. R. Brodie to Florida State Board of Health, June 13, 1939; Malsberger to State Health Officer, June 30, 1939, State park project files, 1936–1945, box 3, folder: "Gold Head Supervision, 1938–1941," FSA.

173. B. Green to Vinten, October 20, 1939, State park project files, 1936–1945, box 2, folder: "Fort Clinch—Park use," FSA.

174. See Scoggin to Clarence Simpson, August 25, 1942, for a copy of the FPS rules. State park project files, 1936–1945, box 1, folder: "Florida Caverns, Supervision 1941–1942," FSA.

175. Ibid.

176. Ibid.

177. Ibid.

178. Douglas, *Parks and Playgrounds of Florida*, 36.

179. Ibid., 42.

180. Lawson to Scoggin, May 17, 1941, State park project files, 1936–1945, box 1, folder: "Florida Caverns State Park, Supervision 1942–1943," FSA.

181. Ibid.

182. Malsberger to Carlos Maxwell, June 4, 1941, W. F. Jacobs to Malsberger, October 19, 1940, State park project files, 1933–1942, 1988–1989, box 1, folder: "Oleno—General files," FSA.

183. Malsberger to Hulan Whitehead, April 3, 1935, State park project files, 1933–1942, 1988–1989, box 1, folder: "Oleno—General files," FSA.

184. F. Jacobs to Camp Oleno Caretaker, July 13, 1941, State park project files, 1933–1942, 1988–1989, box 1, folder: "Oleno—General files," FSA. Carlos Maxwell would serve for thirty years with the FPS, longer than any other employee, and is often erroneously considered the first FPS park ranger.

185. Harold Foley, "The Florida Park Service" (WTAL radio broadcast), January 10, 1936, typescript in Chief of Education and Information Charles H. Schaeffer's administrative and reference files, 1936–1959, box 2, folder: "Radio scripts, 1936–1958," FSA.

186. Green to Scoggin, November 6, 1939; Malsberger to Administration Branch, February 1, 1940, State park project files, 1936–1945, box 3, folder: "Fort Clinch—Permit Use," FSA.

187. Barbara Baynard Palmer to Hillsborough River State Park, July 16, 1985, Hillsborough River State Park files.

188. Her start date was June 6, 1942. Beck to Ney Landrum, December 15, 1970, Chief Naturalist Jim Stevenson's administrative files, 1967–1983, box 1, folder 1, FSA.

189. Beck to Senator Lawton Chiles, March 7, 1969, Chief Naturalist Jim Stevenson's administrative files, 1967–1983, box 1, folder 1, FSA.

190. Jim Stevenson OH, 2, ROHP.

191. Ibid., 4. For more on Stevenson's activities as chief naturalist, see series 1956, Chief Naturalist Jim Stevenson's Administrative Files, and series 1952, Chief Naturalist Jim Stevenson's Interpretive and Research Files. Both collections are housed at the Florida State Archives.

192. Jim Stevenson OH, ROHP, 17.

193. Twenty years after Stevenson joined the FPS, little had changed at some of the parks. Dan Trescott, who began his career as a ranger in 1971 at Highlands Hammock State Park, described his first day at Florida Caverns State Park in the early 1980s in a 2003 interview with the author: "My training at the cave consisted of going on three different tours, then they said, 'Here's a flashlight and there's the tour, go.' . . . I get down to the door and tell everyone that this is my first tour. Don't expect too much. And if the lights go out, just stand still. I'll get them back on. Sure enough they went out several times. I was just mashing buttons. Absolutely no idea what I was doing down that hole." Dan Trescott OH, ROHP.

194. Foley, "The Florida Park Service," January 10, 1936, typescript.

195. Ibid.

196. Suwannee River State Park Management Criteria Statement, box 2, folder: "Suwannee River State Park," State park management criteria statements, 1970–1992, FSA.

197. Ibid.

198. Florida Department of Environmental Protection, *Tomoka State Park Unit Management Plan*, 1.

199. Florida State Planning Board, *Summaries of the Park, Parkway, and Recreational Areas Study*, 41; *The Regional Review* (NPS), (April 1939).

200. Proposed bill for Pan-American State Park, March 10, 1951, box 1, folders: "Bills, 1951–1953," Chief of Education and Information Charles H. Schaeffer's administrative and reference files, 1936–1959, FSA.

201. Florida State Planning Board, *Summaries of the Park, Parkway, and Recreational Areas Study*, 41.

202. Proposed bill for Pan-American State Park, March 10, 1951.

203. Florida State Planning Board, *Summary Report, March 1934–December 1936*, 22, Cone papers, box 71, folder: "Planning Board, State 1937," FSA.

204. B. Edwards to Holland, October 7, 1943, box 4, folder: "Florida Forest and Park Service, 1943," Holland Papers, FSA (hereafter cited as FPS 1943, FSA).

205. Ibid.

206. Holland to Edwards, October 12, 1943, FPS 1943, FSA.

207. Charles Bennett to Holland, March 17, 1941; Scoggin to Bennett, 25 March 1941, FPS 1943, FSA.

208. Scoggin to Bennett, March 25, 1941, FPS 1943, FSA.

Chapter 6. Florida's Welfare State Parks: The CCC at Work and at Play

1. James Keene, interview by Dr. Julian Pleasants, May 5, 1998, SPOHP, 6.
2. Ansley Hall OH, ROHP.
3. Ibid.
4. Buck Heath OH, ROHP.
5. The Government Printing Office published both brochures in 1941.
6. United States, Civilian Conservation Corps (US CCC), *Work Experience That Counts*, 2.
7. Ibid.
8. World War I vets were an exception to these rules—they only had to be unemployed. *CCC Standards of Eligibility for Enrollment*, 1–3, 5–6.
9. *CCC Standards of Eligibility for Enrollment*, 3.
10. Ibid.
11. Sam Thompson, interview by Ben Houston, June 19, 2000, SPOPH, 5.
12. A blank application from Florida State Welfare Board can be found in RG 35, entry 32 "State Procedural Records," box 1, folder: "Florida." Untitled document written by CCC Company 435, March 10, 1940, in State park project files, 1936–1945, box 3, folder "Highlands Hammock CCC," FSA.
13. There were nineteen periods in total.
14. Paige, *CCC and the NPS*, 74; Untitled document written by CCC Company 435, March 10, 1940, in State park project files, 1936–1945, box 3, folder: "Highlands Hammock CCC," FSA.
15. Jack Horne, interview by National Emergency Council state director Jack Guthrie, October 21, 1938, in National Emergency Council, *WJAX Radio Broadcast Transcripts*, Jacksonville, 1939, 3.
16. Ibid.
17. Untitled document written by CCC Company 435, March 10, 1940, State park project files, 1936–1945, box 3, folder: "Highlands Hammock CCC," FSA; Hillary Cowart, interview by Julian Pleasants, November 10, 1998, SPOHP, 3.
18. Wandall, "A Negro in the CCC," 254.

19. Keene OH, SPOHP, 9.
20. Ibid.
21. Paul DeGirolamo, interview by Dave Nelson, November 2, 2002, ROHP.
22. The New York CCC company stationed at Highlands Hammock State Park in 1934–35 was conditioned at Fort Dix, New Jersey. Narrative Report, SP-3 Supt. C. R. Vinten, June 1934, Highlands Hammock State Park files; *C-bring C-amp C-ourier,* October 15, 1934.
23. George LeCouris OH, ROHP.
24. Ibid.
25. Three of these projects, all in South Florida, were for parks not under the state's jurisdiction: Royal Palm State Park, Greynolds Park, and Matheson Hammock. Terence Nolan to Jim Stevenson, Chief Naturalist, January 27, 1975, State park project files, 1933–1942, 1988–1989, box 1, folder: "DNR correspondence," FSA.
26. Fred White OH, SPOHP, 1.
27. Talmadge Holmes, interview by Dr. Donald Pleasant, May 5, 1998, SPOHP, 2.
28. James Keene OH, SPOHP, 1; Hillary Cowart OH, SPOHP, 1.
29. Persons, "Human Resources in the Civilian Conservation Corps," 323.
30. Hillary Cowart OH, SPOHP, 4.
31. Paul DeGirolamo OH, ROHP.
32. Ibid.
33. Talmadge Holmes OH, SPOHP, 6.
34. Oleno State Park was originally a forestry training camp that the FPS acquired in 1941.
35. Salmond, *Civilian Conservation Corps*, 36.
36. Ibid., 34.
37. For the number of enrollees, LEMs, and staff per camp, see RG 35, entry 10, "Camp Inspection Reports," box 1, NARA. Salmond, *Civilian Conservation Corps,* 34.
38. Harry Bush OH, SPOHP, 6.
39. Ibid.
40. Paige, *CCC and the NPS,* 70–71.
41. Richard Ives, interview by Ben Houston, June 19, 2000, SPOHP, 17.
42. B. Edwards to Baker, August 15, 1934, in FPS Public Relations and Historical Files, 1934–1964, box 1, folder: "Myakka River State Park—history (CCC files-1935)," FSA.
43. Bohleber to Baker, August 10, 1934, in FPS Public Relations and Historical Files, 1934–1964, box 1, folder: "Myakka River State Park—history (CCC files-1935)," FSA.
44. Fred Thompson, interview by Ranger Paula Benshoff, n.d., Myakka River State Park files.
45. Sullivan, "The CCC and the Creation of Myakka River State Park," 8.
46. *Tent Town Topics* 1, no. 10 (December 7, 1934).
47. Ibid.
48. See, for example, *Myakka Rattler* 2, no. 18 (February 18, 1935). The *Myakka Rattler* was the new name of the *Tent Town Topics.*
49. *Pictorial Review, CCC Company 5430, SP-4,* n.d., Myakka River State Park files.
50. Untitled document written by CCC Company 435, March 10, 1940, in State park project files, 1936–1945, box 3, folder: "Highlands Hammock CCC," FSA.
51. DeGirolamo OH, ROHP.

52. Ansley Hall, OH, ROHP.

53. *Tent Town Topics* 1, no. 10 (December 7, 1937).

54. Tracy Baker, interview by Capt. Alogna and Ranger Worthington of Gold Head Branch State Park, November 26, 1977, State park project files, 1933–1942, 1988–1989, box 1, folder: "Gold Head Misc. Collections," FSA.

55. Paige, *CCC and the NPS*, 66, 68.

56. Hoyt, *We Can Take It*, 28. Hoyt was the editor of *Happy Days*, the semi-official newsletter of the CCC.

57. Salmond, *Civilian Conservation Corps*, 84.

58. Hill, *In the Shadow of the Mountain*, 37; Salmond, *Civilian Conservation Corps*, 86, 119.

59. Untitled document written by CCC Company 435, March 10, 1940, in State park project files, 1936–1945, box 3, folder "Highlands Hammock CCC," FSA.

60. Ibid.

61. The U.S. Forest Service oversaw projects dealing with forestry, and the Department of the Interior was in charge of Native American camps.

62. Untitled document written by CCC Company 435, March 10, 1940, in State park project files, 1936–1945, box 3, folder: "Highlands Hammock CCC," FSA.

63. Lacy, *Soil Soldiers*, 177.

64. Billy Hinson talks of the use of mess kits in the field in his article "The Civilian Conservation Corps in Mobile County, Alabama," *Alabama Review* (October 1992): 249. As Hinson explained, the truck driver would bring the food to the work site, along with large vats of hot water for washing hands and mess kits.

65. Hill, *In the Shadow of the Mountain*, 27.

66. Leonard Hendry, interview by Ranger Paul Benshoff, January 1985, Myakka River State Park files.

67. Ibid.

68. *C-bring C-amp C-ourier*, August 15, 1934.

69. US CCC, *Work Experience That Counts*.

70. Ibid.

71. For lists of the many jobs completed in Florida's state parks by the CCC, see Series 1270, State park project files, 1936–1945, FSA.

72. Narrative Report, December 1, 1935, FL SP-3, State park project files, 1936–1945, box 1, folder: "Highlands Hammock Misc. Mss. Files," FSA.

73. Richard Ives OH, SPOHP, 5.

74. Paul DeGirolamo OH, ROHP.

75. C. Codrington, interview by National Emergency Council state director Jack Guthrie, January 16, 1939, in National Emergency Council, *WJAX Radio Broadcast Transcripts*, Jacksonville, 1939, 4.

76. Malcolm Oliver, interview by Dave Nelson, November 2, 2002, ROHP.

77. Ibid.

78. Ansley Hall OH, ROHP.

79. Camp Inspection Report, January 13, 1935, SP-3, RG 35, entry 10, folder: "FL-SP-3, Sebring," NARA.

80. Terkel, *Hard Times*, 58.

81. Malcolm Oliver OH, ROHP.

82. For Florida's state park inspection reports, see RG 35, entry 10, box 1, NARA.

83. Camp Inspection Report, March 13, 1940, SP-5, RG 35, entry 10, box 1, folder: "FL SP-5, Starke", NARA.

84. Camp Inspection Reports, June 18, 1935 (SP-3), March 13, 1940, March 9, 1949 (SP-5), June 17, 1941 (SP-8), RG 35, entry 10, box 1, NARA.

85. "Inspection Report, State of Florida," by John H. Stone, August 16, 1937, 48, RG 95, entry 52A004, folder: "CCC Inspection—Florida FY1938 (2 of 2)," NARA.

86. Coney to McEntee, February 12, 1936, RG 35, entry 10, box 1, folder: "FL SP-3, Sebring," NARA.

87. Ibid.

88. Ibid.

89. Narrative Report, December 1, 1935, FL SP-3, State park project files, 1933–1942, box 1, folder: "Highland Hammock Mss. Files," FSA.

90. Ibid.

91. McEntee to Wirth, February 17, 1936, RG 35, entry 10, box 1, folder: "FL SP-3, Sebring," NARA.

92. Evison to McEntee, April 3, 1936, RG 35, entry 10, box 1, folder: "FL SP-3, Sebring," NARA.

93. Utley and Steely, *Guided With a Steady Hand*, 40.

94. Mrs. Dorothy Martin to Cone, November 22, 1937, RG 35, entry 29, box 1, folder: "Florida, 1937," NARA.

95. Persons to Horne, December 3, 1937, RG 35, entry 29, box 1, folder: "Florida, 1937," NARA.

96. Hillary Cowart OH, SPOHP, 12.

97. *Myakka Rattler* 2, no. 15 (January 1935).

98. Ibid.

99. Buck Heath OH, ROHP.

100. Lloyd Zorn to B. F. Harris, April 22, 1939; FPS director H. J. Malsberger to Colonel J. J. Fulman, July 11, 1939; Capt. George Buell to H. J. Malsberger, July 24, 1939, State park project files, box 4, folder: "Highlands Hammock Fire Control," FSA.

101. *C-bring C-amp C-ourier,* September 4, 1934.

102. "The Civilian Conservations Corps and Torreya State Park," undated manuscript in Torreya State park files, 5; H. J. Malsberger to Senator Charles Andrews, State park project files, 1933–1942, box 1, folder "Torreya state park," FSA; Lewis C. Horne to Ney Landrum, June 6, 1978, Florida state park survey, 1933–1942, 1988–1989, box 1, folder: "Torreya general files," FSA.

103. Myakka State Park, January 9, 1935, SP-4; Torreya State Park, February 1, 1936, SP-6; Fort Clinch State Park, June 17, 1941, SP-8, RG 35, entry 10, box 1, NARA.

104. As historian Jennifer Keene pointed out in her book *Doughboys, the Great War and the Remaking of America,* the U.S. Army used boxing to teach "aggressive ideals." During World War I the army hired professional boxers to train American soldiers for warfare. Boxing mimicked bayonet movements—it required athleticism, self-control, courage, and viril-

ity. It was the "masculine ideal." Keene, *Doughboys,* 41. See also Humberger, "The CCC in Nebraska," 294.

105. *Myakka Rattler,* January 1935.

106. Camp inspection reports, RG 35, entry 10, box 1, folder: "FL SP-5, Starke," NARA; *Pick and Spade,* November 11, 1936.

107. Thomas Hutcheson OH, ROHP.

108. Paul DeGirolamo OH, ROHP.

109. Malcolm Oliver OH, ROHP.

110. *Roger's Post,* October 16, 1935; October 30, 1935,

111. *Roger's Post,* November 6, 1935.

112. Ibid.

113. *Myakka Rattler,* January 1935.

114. Willie O'Neal, interview by Ben Houston, June 19, 2000, SPOHP, 25.

115. George LeCouris OH, ROHP.

116. Ansley Hall OH, ROHP. Malcolm Oliver and Paul DeGirolamo mentioned that they also often had to hitchhike to and from town.

117. Ansley Hall OH, ROHP.

118. Thomas Hutcheson OH, ROHP.

119. George LeCouris OH, ROHP.

120. *Myakka Rattler,* January 1935.

121. Best, *Nickel and Dime Decade,* 19; Kyrig, *Daily Life in the United States,* 72.

122. Best, *Nickel and Dime Decade,* 65–66.

123. Best, *Nickel and Dime Decade,* 70–75.

124. Wright, "Negro Youth," 398.

125. Persons, "Human Resources and the CCC," 323.

126. Oxley, "Growth and Accomplishments of CCC Education," 313; Fechner, "The Educational Contribution of the CCC," 305.

127. "Learn by doing" is from Fechner's "Educational Contribution of the CCC," 305.

128. Lacy, *Soil Soldiers,* 46.

129. Fechner, "Educational Contribution of the CCC," 305, Wright, "Negro Youth," 399; Untitled document written by CCC Company 435, March 10, 1940, in State park project files, 1936–1945, box 3, folder "Highlands Hammock CCC," FSA.

130. Wright, "Negro Youth," 400; US CCC, *Work Experience that Counts*; Clancy, "Conserving the Youth," 455. Historian Gorham referred to the educational program as an attempt to indoctrinate enrollees in modernization.

131. For example, US CCC, *Work Experience That Counts* and *The Civilian Conservation Corps Contributing to the Defense of the Nation.*

132. Salmond, *Civilian Conservation Corps,* 48; Gower, "Conservation, Censorship, and Controversy in the CCC, 1930s," 279.

133. Watkins, *Hungry Years,* 165–66.

134. Ibid.

135. Clancy, "Conserving the Youth," 440.

136. Cole, *African-American Experience in CCC,* 47; Wright, "Negro Youth," 399.

137. Camp Inspection reports: June 17, 1941 (SP-8), November 2, 1934 (SP-4), February 1, 1936 (SP-6), February 8, 1936 (SP-4), RG 35, entry 10, box 1, NARA; *C-bring C-amp C-ourier*, August 15, 1934.

138. Company 453, "Company 453, FL SP-10," State park project files, 1933–1942, box 1, folder: "Highlands Hammock Misc. Mss. Files," FSA.

139. State Librarian William T. Cash to R. B. Downs, January 1935, State librarian correspondence files, box 9, folder: "Correspondence, 1935," FSA.

140. The *Florida Advisor* can be found in the CCC Papers in the Major Manuscript Collection, P. K. Yonge Library, UF.

141. Reynolds to All Camp Commanders and Educational Advisors, June 9, 1934 (Circular Letter #2); June 27, 1934 (Circular Letter #4), CCC papers, box 1, folder: "CCC–University of Florida," Major Manuscript Collection, P. K. Yonge Library, UF.

142. Reynolds Circular Letters #2, #4.

143. *Florida Advisor*, February 22, 1935, June 29, 1935, CCC Papers, box 1, folder: "CCC–University of Florida," Major Manuscripts Collection, P. K. Yonge Library, UF.

144. Camp Inspection Report, February 23, 1939, folder: "FL SP-4, Sarasota"; Camp Inspection Report, March 13, 1940, folder: "FL SP-5, Starke," box 1, RG 35, entry 10, NARA.

145. Malcolm Oliver OH, ROHP.

146. Ansley Hall OH ROHP.

147. Buck Heath OH, ROHP.

148. Thomas Hutcheson OH, ROHP.

149. Buck Heath OH, ROHP.

150. Camp Inspection Report, March 13, 1940, SP-4, RG 35, entry 10, box 1, folder: "FL SP-4, Starke," NARA.

151. *Veterans Viewpoint*, September 1939.

152. *Veterans Viewpoint*, September 1939; *C-bring C-amp C-ourier*, September 4, 1934.

153. For information on the CCC camp newsletter, the best source is Alfred Emile Cornebise's "Heralds in New Deal America: Camp Newspapers of the Civilian Conservation Corps." Another good source is Gower's "Conservation, Censorship, and Controversy in the CCC, 1930s."

154. The *Roger's Post* was printed by the Sebring Chamber of Commerce and became a member of the Florida Press Association. Shofner, "Roosevelt's 'Tree Army,'" 451.

155. An enrollee term for someone who shirked work.

156. *Veterans Viewpoint* 3, no. 7 (July 1939), no. 9 (September 1939), no. 8 (August 1939).

157. Statement by Col. Hubert T. Andrews, September 27, 1939; Report of Investigation, October 3, 1939, RG 35, entry 10, box 45, folder: "FL SP-12, Marianna," NARA.

158. *Tent Town Topics*, December 7, 1934.

159. *Torreya Park Chronicle*, April 1936.

160. *Torreya Park Chronicle*, March 1, 1937; *The Barracks Bag*, December 1938; *Tent Town Topics*, December 7, 1934.

161. At the time, DePriest was the sole African American member of Congress.

162. Johnson, "The Army, the Negro, and the CCC," 82.

163. Ibid., 83.

164. Ibid.

165. Biles, *South and the New Deal*, 112; Friedel, "The South and the New Deal," 32.

166. Kennedy, *Freedom from Fear*, 18–19; Salmond, "The Civilian Conservation Corps and the Negro," 76.

167. Biles, *South and the New Deal*, 113.

168. Ibid.

169. By 1941 national enrollment for African Americans had reached 250,000. United States, Civilian Conservation Corps, *CCC and Colored Youth*.

170. For information on the KKK in Florida, see Newton, *Invisible Empire*.

171. Ibid., 75.

172. McGovern, *Anatomy of a Lynching*, 80–94.

173. George LeCouris OH, ROHP. LeCouris became very emotional while relating this story. He went into more detail only off the record.

174. A "side camp" was a branch off a main camp consisting of less than one hundred enrollees, working on a project less than an hour's drive away. The enrollees would stay onsite during the week, then would return to the main camp on weekends. To establish a side camp, the using service had to apply separately to the CCC Director's Office. They ran as smaller versions of the main camp, with their commander and project superintendent. Later a full camp of white veterans was established at the Florida Caverns.

175. *Myakka News* and *Torreya Park Chronicle*. Torreya's paper covered events at the Florida Caverns side camp.

176. See RG 35, entry 10, box 1, folders: "FL SP-4, Sarasota" and "SP-6, Bristol," NARA.

177. Willie O'Neal OH, SPOHP, 10.

178. Ibid., 10.

179. Ibid., 12.

180. Shofner, "Roosevelt's 'Tree Army,'" 448–49.

181. Randall to Sholtz, August 20, 1935, Sholtz papers, box 23, folder: "Conservation, CCC," FSA.

182. Trammel to Sholtz, August 20, 1935; Hardin to Sholtz, August 22, 1935; C. L. McKarig to Duncan Fletcher, August 20, 1935, Sholtz papers, box 23, folder: "Conservation, CCC," FSA.

183. Trammell to Sholtz, August 20, 1935, Sholtz papers, box 23, folder: Conservation, CCC," FSA.

184. B. Riley (editor of *Sarasota Herald*) to C. H. Schaeffer, August 27, 1935, Sholtz papers, box 23, folder: "Conservation, CCC," FSA.

185. Ibid.

186. H. Schaffer to Newell, n.d. (September 1935), Sholtz papers, box 23, folder: "Conservation, CCC," FSA; Sears to E. K. Burlow, August 23, 1935, RG 35, entry 2, box 607, folder: "300—FL (Negro Camps)," NARA.

187. Baker to Edwards, August 27, 1935, in FPS Public Relations and Historical Files, 1934–1964, box 1, folder: "Myakka River State Park—history (CCC files–1935)," FSA.

188. Schaeffer to Riley, August 25, 1935, in FPS Public Relations and Historical Files, 1934–1964, box 1, folder: "Myakka River State Park—history (CCC files–1935)," FSA.

189. Schaffer to J. H. Gadsby, September 4, 1935, Sholtz papers, box 23, folder: "Conservation, CCC," FSA.

190. Gadsby to Schaffer, September 7, 1935, Sholtz papers, box 23, folder: "Conservation, CCC," FSA.

191. Riley to Schaeffer, September 10, 1935, in FPS Public Relations and Historical Files, 1934–1964, box 1, folder: "Myakka River State Park—history (CCC files–1935)," FSA.

192. Ibid.

193. Dr. Charles Montague, Secretary, Kiwanis Club of Sarasota, to Schaeffer, September 24, 1935, in FPS Public Relations and Historical Files, 1934–1964, box 1, folder: "Myakka River State Park—history (CCC files–1935)," FSA.

194. Sholtz to Mosely, September 23, 1935; Mosely to Sholtz, September 23, 1935, Sholtz papers, box 23, folder: "Conservation, CCC," FSA.

195. Schaeffer to J. Hardin Peterson, September 24, 1935, in FPS Public Relations and Historical Files, 1934–1964, box 1, folder: "Myakka River State Park—history (CCC files–1935)," FSA.

196. See J. G. Tucker to Sholtz, August 10, 1935; American Legion to Millard Caldwell, August 9, 1935, Caldwell to Newell, August 9, 1935; and Newell to Caldwell, August 10, 1935, Sholtz papers, box 23, folder: "Conservation, CCC," FSA.

197. Vinten to Region One Director (NPS), September 10, 1940, State park project files, 1936–1945, box 2, folder: "Gold Head Camp Applications," FSA.

198. A search by the CCC's Director's Office for Florida success stories of former enrollees failed twice. Dean Snyder to Jack Horne, December 2, 1938, RG 35, entry 56, box 1, folder: "Florida," NARA; and there were no success stories in RG 35, entry 101, NARA.

199. Hillary Cowart OH, SPOHP, 20.

200. The figure comes from Shofner, "Roosevelt's 'Tree Army,'" 446.

Chapter 7. Improving Paradise: Nature as Commodity

1. Narrative Report, February 4, 1935, FL SP-4, Myakka State Park files.
2. *Pick and Spade*, March 1939.
3. Narrative Report, July 1934, Highlands Hammock State Park files.
4. Douglas, *Parks and Playgrounds of Florida*, 5.
5. Hale, "Florida's Scenic Highways," 31.
6. *Proceedings of the 46th Annual Meeting of the Florida State Horticultural Society*, 3.
7. *Proceedings of the 47th Annual Meeting of the Florida State Horticultural Society*, 2.
8. Ibid.
9. Florida State Planning Board, *Summary Report, March, 1934–December, 1936*, 17.
10. Jennings to Carlton, September 6, 1932, Carlton papers, box 9, folder: "Beautification Program," FSA.
11. Jennings to Sholtz, January 23, 1933, Sholtz papers, box 9, folder: "Beautification Program," FSA.
12. "City Beautification Called 'Investment' at Florida Meeting," *Christian Science Monitor*, May 25, 1933.

13. Florida Federation of Women's Clubs, *Year Book 1932–1933*, 105.

14. John Taylor, President's Annual Address, April 11, 1933, in *Proceedings of the 46th Annual Meeting of the Florida State Horticultural Society*, 3.

15. "Florida Bars Out 2,000 by 'Poverty Quarantine,'" *New York Times*, November 20, 1936.

16. "Florida Is Divided on Border Patrol," *New York Times,* December 20, 936.

17. "Florida Lifts Ban on Idle," *New York Times*, September 11, 1937.

18. Ibid.

19. State CCC Educational Adviser Porter G. Reynolds, "A Suggested Outline for a Course in Camp Beautification," Civilian Conservation Corps Records, 1934–1936, box 1, P. K. Yonge Library, University of Florida, Gainesville.

20. Ibid., viii.

21. Ibid.

22. For more on Phillips's park work, see Jackson, *Pioneer of Tropical Landscape Architecture*.

23. Ibid.

24. B. Taylor, NPS Regional Biologist, to M. Perkins, April 16, 1940, folder: "Florida-Fort Clinch," Records of the Wildlife Technician, RG 79, NARA.

25. Ibid.

26. Cutler, *Public Landscape*, 66.

27. Dr. Ludd Spivey address, April 11, 1933, in *Proceedings of the 46th Annual Meeting of the Florida State Horticultural Society*, 6–8.

28. *Proceedings of the 47th Annual Meeting of the Florida State Horticultural Society*, 2.

29. *Pictorial Review, Co 2444* (Starke, 1939), 25, found in State park project files, 1933–1942, 1988–1989, box 1, folder: "Gold Head Misc. Collection," FSA.

30. Narrative report by C. R. Vinten, November 19, 1934, SP-3, Highlands Hammock State Park files.

31. Narrative Report, November 26, 1934, FL SP-4, Myakka State Park files.

32. Buck Heath OH, ROHP.

33. Copies of these photos can be found in the Myakka State Park files.

34. Narrative report by A. D. Larson, June 1935, SP-4, Myakka State Park files.

35. Oscar Manigo oral history, 5, Myakka State Park files.

36. Ibid., 6.

37. Narrative report by A. D. Lawson, June 1935, Myakka State Park files.

38. For more information on the State of Florida's tick eradication program, see Record Group 293, Records of the State Sanitary Livestock Board, Tick Eradication files 1933–1951, FSA.

39. Interviews with longtime local residents by park staff in the 1980s mention the lack of deer in the 1930s and 1940s. A few attributed their absence to over-hunting. See Myakka River State Park files.

40. Ansley Hall OH, ROHP, 7.

41. Tracy Baker OH, FSA.

42. Mr. A. B. Weissinger was the camp superintendent. Tracy Baker OH, FSA.

43. *C-bring C-amp C-ourier*, August 15, 1934.

44. *Myakka Rattler*, February 1935.

45. Ibid.

46. *Tent Town Topics*, December 7, 1934.

47. Ibid.

48. *C-bring C-amp C-ourier*, August 15, 1934.

49. A copy of this report can be found in Chief Naturalist Jim Stevenson's Interpretation and Research Files, 1938–1977, box 1, folder 2: "Myakka—Animals," FSA. The report's full name is "Progress Report of Biological Reconnaissance, Myakka River State Park (Fla Sp-4) with Preliminary Check Lists of Vertebrate Fauna, December 31, 1941 by Gus Van Duyn, Wildlife Technician."

50. Ibid. A copy of McFarlin's floral report has apparently not survived.

51. Ibid.

52. Casual observations were made from November 16, 1939, to mid-April 1941; then full-time observations by Van Duyn were made from mid-April to December 1941, p. 3, Biological Reconnaissance Report, Chief Naturalist Jim Stevenson's Interpretation and Research Files, 1938–1977, box 1, folder 2: "Myakka—Animals," FSA.

53. Those numbers are comparable to the park's recent counts, after seventy years of observation, as found in the park's unit management plan: 23 amphibians, 33 mammals, 37 fish, and 52 reptiles. Only the bird counts are not close (254 species), unless one adds in the Payton Report's previously discredited 46 additional bird species. Florida Department of Environmental Protection, *Myakka River State Park Unit Management Plan*, Addendum 4.

54. Carol Beck, Chief Naturalist, to Guy Van Duyn, July 9, 1968, Chief Naturalist Jim Stevenson's Interpretation and Research Files, 1938–1977, box 1, folder 2: "Myakka—Animals," FSA. By this time Van Duyn was residing in Waldoboro, Maine.

55. Inspection Report, State of Florida, by S. M. Shanklin, February 17, 1937, General Correspondence, box 40, folder: "Supervision Policy—firebreaks and truck trails," RG 95, NARA.

56. F. Evans to Harry Lee Baker, March 8, 1934, General Correspondence, box 40, folder: "Supervision Policy—firebreaks and truck trails," RG 95, NARA.

57. Carl P. Russell to C. R. Vinten, March 11, 1938, Records of the Regional Wildlife Technician, 1936–1942, folder: "Florida–Fort Clinch," RG 79, NARA.

58. Fred White OH, SPOHP, 35.

59. Hoyt, *We Can Take It*, 66. This was a publication sanctioned by the federal government to promote the CCC. Hoyt was also the editor of the national CCC newspaper, *Happy Days*.

60. Baker to All Camp Superintendents, November 12, 1937, State park project files 1936–1945, box 3, folder: "Gold Head Protection—Fire Control," FSA.

61. "Fire Control Instructions to District Rangers and Project Superintendents," n.d. (1937), General Correspondence—ECW Inspections, AL-TX, box 30, folder: "ECW Inspections—Florida National Forests, 1937," RG 95, NARA.

62. "Firefighting Plan for 1938–9," by C. H. Vinten, 1938, State park projects files 1936–1945, box 3, folder: "Gold Head Protection—Fire Control," FSA.

63. George LeCouris OH, ROHP, 9.

64. *Tent Town Topics*, December 7, 1934.

65. For an examination of the evolution of federal policy on forest fires, see Pyne, *Fire in America*.

66. Florida State Chamber of Commerce Speech (1934), Jennings papers, box 19, folder: "Correspondence 1934—June-December," UF.

67. Florida State Board of Forestry, *Fifth Biennial Report of the Florida Forest and Park Service, July 1, 1936–June 30, 1938*, 11.

68. Vinten to NPS Regional Office, August 28, 1940, State park project files, 1936–1945, box 3, folder: "Gold Head reports," FSA.

69. Narrative Report by Earl Porter, November 26, 1934, Myakka State Park files.

70. Ibid.

71. In 1962 the Tall Timbers Research Station in north Leon County held the first annual Fire Ecology Conference, which presented the latest research on the benefits of fire to maintaining many of Florida's native ecosystems, such as dry prairies and longleaf pine forests. By the late 1960s, due in large part to Tall Timbers–sponsored research, many government agencies and private land managers were using controlled burns. Carle, *Burning Questions*, 117–19.

72. Florida State Chamber of Commerce Speech (1934), Jennings papers, box 19, folder: "Correspondence 1934—June-December," UF.

73. Florida State Planning Board, *Summary Report, March, 1934–December, 1936*, 20.

74. During research for this book while lodging at a CCC-built cabin in Gold Head Branch State Park, I witnessed the application of prescribed fire by park staff within yards of my accommodation. The fire's ferocity and intensity were matched only by the force of the sight of the huge swath of blackened land and trees. The negative reactions from tourists—and those hoping to attract tourists—to woodland fires and their aftermath seemed more than reasonable. But before I left the park five days later, fresh plant life could be seen dotting the burned-over area.

75. Myers, "Scrub and High Pine," 189.

76. Myers, "Scrub and High Pine," 189–90.

77. Highlands Hammock hosted one firefighting school in 1938. Every state park project superintendent attended, along with several foremen, FPS employees, and a few enrollees. "Report of the Fire Suppression and Prevention School, 18 November 1938," State park project files, 1936–1945, box 4, folder: "Highlands Hammock protection—fire control," FSA.

78. Altvater to Highlands Hammock foremen, December 6, 1938, State park project files, 1936–1945, box 4, folder: "Highlands Hammock protection—fire control," FSA.

79. Ibid.

80. Associate Civil Engineer J. H. Stone to Regional ECW Officers, December 8, 1938, General Correspondence—ECW Inspection, box 28, folder: "Inspection Reports—Florida, FY1937," RG 95, NARA.

81. George LeCouris OH, ROHP, 22.

82. Fire Control Instructions to Project Superintendents, 1937, pp. 3–4, General Corre-

spondence, ECW Inspections, folder: "ECW Inspections, Florida National Forests, 1937," RG 95, NARA.

83. Harry Bush OH, SPOHP, 22; George LeCouris OH, ROHP 11.

84. George LeCouris OH, ROHP, 11.

85. R. Brodie to Scoggin, June 21, 1941, State park project files, 1936–1945, box 3, folder: "Gold Head—fire control," FSA.

86. On March 6, 1941, Brodie wrote a three-page memo to Scoggin describing the fire. State park project files, 1936–1945, box 3, folder: "Gold Head—fire control," FSA.

87. Ibid.

88. "Notes of Fire Protection Conference, Florida State Parks," June 20, 1941, State park project files, 1936–1945, box 1, folder: "Florida Caverns—fire control," FSA.

89. Shofner, "Roosevelt's 'Tree Army,'" 434.

90. Mills, *Gifford Pinchot and the Making of the Modern Environment*, 134.

91. The Ocala and Choctawhatchee national forests were both created in 1908 by President Theodore Roosevelt. In 1940 the majority of the Choctawhatchee property was transferred to the War Department to form the nucleus of Eglin Air Force Base. The staff of the Apalachicola National Forest today administers the remaining property.

92. "Report of Inspection, Florida National Forests," October 18, 1937, RG 95, General Correspondence, box 12, folder: "CCC-Inspection—Florida," NARA.

93. H. Coulter to Schaffer, May 10, 1937, State park project files, 1936–1945, box 4, folder: "Plants and Plantings," FSA.

94. Fechner, "My Hopes for the CCC."

95. Oscar Manigo OH, 3, Myakka State Park files.

96. Florida Department of Environmental Protection, *Myakka River State Park Unit Management Plan*, 33; Myers and Ewel, *Ecosystems of Florida*, 117–18.

97. S. Wolfe to Assistant Forester C. H. Coulter, May 5, 1937, State park project files, 1936–1945, box 4, folder: "Plants and Plantings," FSA.

98. Coulter to FPS director C. H. Schaffer, May 10, 1937, State park project files, 1936–1945, box 4, folder: "Plants and Plantings," FSA.

99. FPS Ranger Paula Benshoff, personal communication, March 10, 2002.

100. Malsberger to SP-5 Landscape Architect, October 11, 1939, State park project files, 1936–1942, box 3, folder: "Gold Head reports—General," FSA.

101. Malsberger to SP-5 Landscape Architect, November 10, 1939, State park project files, 1936–1942, box 3, folder: "Gold Head reports—General," FSA.

102. Ibid.

103. Douglas, *Parks and Playgrounds of Florida*, 46.

104. Ibid.

105. Andrews, "McKee Gardens, an Outstanding Beauty Spot," in *Proceedings of the 48th Annual Meeting of the Florida Horticultural Society*, xvii–xviii.

106. Douglas, *Parks and Playgrounds of Florida*, 5, 11.

107. Notes from interview with Paul DeGirolamo, November 2, 2002, copy in author's possession. Interview stored with the New Deal Initiative, Florida State University.

108. Buck Heath OH, ROHP.

Chapter 8. The New Deal in Old Florida: Governor Fred Cone and Florida's Welfare System

1. For a sampling of such letters, see Green, *Looking for the New Deal*.
2. *Tampa Tribune*, July 18, 1937.
3. William A. Shands, interview by Dr. Samuel Proctor, March 1, 1971, SPOHP, 68.
4. Allen Morris, December 19, 1940, "Cracker Politics" files, vol. 1, Florida Collection, Florida State Library. All the Allen Morris "Cracker Politics" column clippings in this file were copied from the *Miami Herald*.
5. For the full story, see Shofner, "The White Springs Post Office Caper," 341–44.
6. Key, *Southern Politics*, 88; Green and Scher, *Florida's Gubernatorial Politics*, 71.
7. William A. Shands OH, SPOHP, 68.
8. Morris, "Cracker Politics," December 19, 1940.
9. Morris, "Cracker Politics," December 29, 1940.
10. Ibid.
11. In the November election Cone received over 80 percent of the vote. The Republican candidate was E. E. Callaway. Colburn and Scher, *Florida's Gubernatorial Politics*, 136.
12. William A. Shands OH, SPOHP, 66.
13. *Ocala Banner*, February 11, 1937; clipping found in box 1, Fred Cone Miscellaneous files, 1936–1948, FSA.
14. Howard, "Vigilante Justice," 234.
15. Howard, "Vigilante Justice," 234, fn. 6.
16. For a full transcription of Governor Cone's inauguration speech, see folder "Addresses, 1937," box 2, Governor Fred Cone Papers, FSA.
17. Folder "State Board of Social Welfare, 1935–1937," box 1, Florida Health and Welfare Council Records, 1921–1973, FSA.
18. Van Hyning's wife, Florella Van Hyning, died on January 13, 1937. *Florida Social Welfare Review* (February 1937), 2.
19. Biographical background on Van Hyning came from Cash, *A History of the Democratic Party in Florida*, 243–44; personal communication with Conrad's relative Amy Van Hyning, January 20, 2003, copy of e-mail in author's possession.
20. Jack Horne to Dean Snyder, Administrative Assistant, Office of the Secretary of Labor, June 17, 1937, folder: "Florida, 1937," entry 29, Correspondence with State Selection Officers, RG 35, NARA.
21. See untitled document in file: "Welfare, Social—Misc 1937," box 101, Fred Cone Papers, FSA. Several employees were paid between $250 and $300 a month. Van Hyning was paid $502.19. This figure was comparable to the pay of other state agency heads.
22. Ibid.
23. *Florida Newspaper News* (June 1936), n.p. Mapoles was first elected to the Florida House in 1912 and became a state senator in 1934. He introduced the 1915 bill that created Okaloosa County.
24. *Tallahassee Democrat*, May 7, 1937; *Tampa Tribune*, May 12, 1937.
25. *Tallahassee Democrat*, May 14, 1937; May 18, 1937.

26. *Tallahassee Democrat,* May 7, 1937.
27. *Tallahassee Democrat,* May 20, 1937.
28. *Tallahassee Democrat,* May 16, 1937.
29. *Tallahassee Democrat,* May 20, 1937.
30. *Florida Newspaper News* (June 1936), n.p.
31. *FTU,* May 1, 1937.
32. *Tallahassee Democrat,* May 16, 1937.
33. Stanley Sheip to Sholtz, September 7, 1935, Sholtz papers, box 105, "Forestry, 1934–1935," FSA.
34. Ibid.
35. Sam Ellis to Cone, February 7, 1938, Cone papers, box 34, folder: "Forestry Service, 1938," FSA.
36. Cone to Ellis, February 8, 1938, Cone papers, box 34, folder: "Forestry Service, 1938," FSA.
37. Ibid.
38. Ibid.
39. Baker to State Park Board, April 8, 1938, State park project files, 1936–1945, box 1, folder: "CCC camps," FSA.
40. See Sikes to Cone, July 27, 1937, folder: "Welfare, Social—Misc. 1937," box 101, Fred Cone Papers, FSA.
41. Drane, *Hank Drane's Historic Governors,* 108; "Cracker Politics," July 28, 1940. On Branch, Allen Morris wrote that Branch did not possess much in the way of politicking: "If he has such a grasp, Branch has yet to demonstrate it."
42. "Cracker Politics," July 28, 1940.
43. William A. Shands OH, SPOHP, 69.
44. Cone to J. E. Batts, March 19, 1937, folder: "Auditor, State 1937," box 5, Fred Cone Papers, FSA.
45. Vance, *May Mann Jennings,* 131.
46. Cone to L. P. Williams, June 17, 1937, folder: "Welfare, Social—Misc. 1937," box 101, Fred Cone Papers, FSA.
47. *FTU,* June 3, 1937.
48. See Cone to Clyde Taylor, George Shannon, T. T. Boozer, Ivy Futch, J. V. Roberts, W. H. Milton, and W. L. Cathorn, June 15, 1937, folder: "Welfare, Social—Misc. 1937," box 101, Fred Cone Papers, FSA.
49. Cone to James Farley, June 22, 1937; undated clipping from the *Okaloosa* found in folder: "Welfare, Social—Misc. 1937," box 101, Fred Cone Papers, FSA; *Florida Newspaper News* (Clermont, Fla.), June 1936; June 1937, n.p., a newsletter, available at Florida State Library, Tallahassee.
50. Gold, *History of Volusia County,* 394; Moyer, *Who's Who and What to See in Florida,* 71; State Welfare Board Minutes, July 1, 1937, folder: "Minutes, 1937," box 1, RG 897, FSA.
51. Paul DeGirolamo, interview by Dave Nelson, November 2, 2011, ROHP, 6.
52. George LeCouris OH, November 11, 2003, ROHP, 3.
53. James Keene, interview by Dr. Julian Pleasant, May 5, 1998, SPOHP, 5.
54. Hillary Cowart OH, SPOHP, 5.
55. Carol F. Burnette, interview by Dr. Julian Pleasants, February 8, 1999; Harry Bush,

interview by Ben Houston, July 3, 2000; Fred White, interview by Dr. Julian Pleasants, March 16, 1998, SPOHP.

56. Petition of Citizens of Alachua County [n.d., 1937] to State Rep. Fred Bryant, Fred Bryant papers, box 1, folder 1: "Correspondence," FSA.

57. State Welfare Board Minutes, June 28, 1937, folder: "Minutes, 1937," box 1, RG 897, FSA. They also praised Van Hyning's performance, adding that "probably no other man could in so short a time and under such handicaps have carried the program to the point that it reached under his administration."

58. Cone to J. B. Bragg, August 18, 1939, Cone papers, box 33, folder: "FL A&M," FSA.

59. *Fort Myers Press*, February 6, 1937.

60. Howard, "Vigilante Justice," 44.

61. Howard, "Vigilante Justice," 46, fn. 45.

62. Ibid. Letters referring to LaGuardia's snubbing can be found in Cone's paper at the State Archives of Florida.

63. Cone to Selwyn Jones, September 28, 1937, Cone Papers, box 34, folder: "Forest Service, 1937," FSA.

64. For details on his efforts, see files in box 34, Cone papers, FSA.

65. Although state-owned from the start, the memorial would not become a state park until 1979. Rep. Lex Green to Cone, October 14, 1940, box 34, folder: "Foster, Stephen Memorial Commission 1940"; Cone to H. T. Cole (PWA), October 21, 1938, box 34, folder: "Foster, Stephen Memorial Commission 1938," Cone papers, FSA.

66. "Florida, My Florida," was made state song by House Concurrent Resolution no. 24, *Laws of Florida* (1913), 517.

67. House Concurrent Resolution no. 22, *Laws of Florida* (1935) n.p. Cash to Kenneth Crouch, August 20, 1947. In later years, words such as "darkey" were removed from the official lyrics. State Librarian William T. Cash correspondence files, 1923–1955, box 12, folder: "Correspondence, A-Q 1947," FSA. Incidentally, Cash was convinced that Foster visited Florida. He maintained a box of "circumstantial evidence" proving Foster's visit. *St. Petersburg Times*, January 15, 1960.

Chapter 9. Florida Crackers and Yankee Tourists: Class, Conflict, and Rejection in Paradise

1. The recording of the original performance can be found on tape DAT D98-21, Recordings of the Florida Folklife Program, FSA.

2. On December 19, 2007, Hicks exited the stage for good when he passed away from complications of lung cancer.

3. Valerie Wisecracker (DC03-39), Frank Thomas, Lance Lazonby, and Cliff Buckosh (T83-106), Recordings of the Florida Folklife Program, FSA.

4. Quoted in Silverthorne, *Marjorie Kinnan Rawlings*, 86.

5. Lewis, "Cracker: Spanish Florida Style," 185; St. Clair, *Cracker Culture*, 29–36.

6. Lewis, "Cracker: Spanish Florida Style," 186.

7. Ibid., 187.

8. For years historians, folklorists, and anthropologists have attempted to define and describe a distinctive and unique cracker culture, arguing for a direct cultural lineage from Celtic Scots-Irish immigrants to present day South Georgia and North Florida culture. My stance is that the term *cracker* appears to be more like regional slang used to describe a somewhat homogeneous poor white southern culture. Having directed a Scotland Study Abroad Program for years, I see little "crackerness" in Scottish culture. But perhaps more work in the ethnology of Scotland and Ireland could further delineate and define the pre-commodified cracker culture. See McWhiney, *Cracker Culture*; Denham, *A Rogue's Paradise*; St. Clair, *Cracker Culture*; Bulger, *South Florida Folklife*; Kirby, *Mockingbird Song*.

9. "Illinois to Mississippi," *New York Times*, March 16, 1861; "The Florida Expedition," *New York Times*, March 30, 1864; "American Nicknames," *New York Times*, March 28, 1875.

10. For more examples, see *New York Times* articles: "Men of the Mountains," August 16, 1891; "With Cracker Hunters," July 13, 1891; "Orange Growers Troubles," February 26, 1894; "Mormons Roughly Handled," March 10, 1897; "With the 71st Regiment in Florida," May 29, 1898.

11. Harkins, *Hillbilly*, 4.

12. J. Rouse, "With the 71st Regiment in Florida," *New York Times*, May 29, 1898.

13. "Pepper v. Sholtz v. Wilcox," *Time*, May 2, 1938.

14. Ibid.

15. Bigelow, *Frontier Eden*, 10. This was the first serious and academic consideration of Rawlings's work.

16. Ibid., 11.

17. *Scribners*, February 1931, 127–34; April 1931, 351–66, May 1932, 283–90.

18. *Harper's*, June 1932, 21–33; July 1932, 225–34.

19. *Saturday Evening Post*, September 23, 1933.

20. For a version of this early 1930 manuscript, called "Florida Cracker," see Tarr and Kinser, *Uncollected Writings of Marjorie Kinnan Rawlings*.

21. Bigelow, *Frontier Eden*, 68.

22. Stetson Kennedy, *Palmetto Country*.

23. Ibid., 61.

24. Nina Oliver Dean, "Big Days in Florida," *New York Times*, February 18, 1940.

25. Cobb, *Away Down South*, 6.

26. The back flap of the novel *Suwannee Valley*, published in 1940, claimed it was "the natural successor to Marjorie Kinnan Rawlings." It was dedicated to Governor Fred Cone. Bernie Borchardt and Eugene Sears, *Suwannee Valley* (New York: Warringer House, 1940).

27. "Other Florida" was a phrase coined by journalist Gloria Jahoda in the 1960s, representing rural northern and northwest Florida, and later the title of her 1967 book.

28. Baker, *Forest Fires in Florida*, 26.

29. Stoddard, *Memoirs of a Naturalist*, 244.

30. Inman Eldredge OH, https://foresthistory.org/wp-content/uploads/2016/12/Eldredge.pdf.

31. Clinton H. Coulter, interview by Elwood Maunder, February 6, 1958, Forest History Society Papers, Duke University, 215.

32. Tucker, *Before the Timber was Cut*, 23.

33. Gerrell, *Illustrated History*, 45.
34. Ibid., 44.
35. Tucker, *Before the Timber Was Cut*, 23.
36. Ibid.
37. Florida State Board of Forestry, *13th Biennial Report, 1952–1954*, 12.
38. Florida Federation of Women's Clubs, *Year Book 1932–1934*, 169.
39. Arno and Allison-Burnell, *Flames in Our Forest*, 14.
40. Federal Writers' Project, *Agricultural Conservation*, 31.
41. Shea, "Our Pappies Burned the Woods."
42. Ibid.

43. The article was so influential that as late as 1995, historian Jack Temple Kirby repeated its basic arguments in his *Counter-Cultural South*, 48–56. He even argued that the Hank Williams song "Setting the Woods on Fire" was proof of the South's rampant arsonist tendencies. In 2006 Kirby revised his argument slightly with *Mockingbird's Song*, admitting that Shea's study was indeed biased and that Williams's song was probably allegorical. But he furthered a new but empirically deficient argument—that Florida's numerous fires were the product of poor laborers looking for relief work putting out "wild" fires. Kirby, *Mockingbird Song*, 137–43.

44. M82-8, box 23, folder: "Forest Farming," FSA. Incidentally, Coulter mentions in 1958 the use of "pine-tops" in firefighting before the advent of fire flaps. Coulter OH, 16.

45. M82-8, box 23, folder: "Forest Farming," FSA.
46. Ibid.
47. Ibid.
48. Ibid.
49. Coulter to Baker, May 4, 1936, S 278, box 46, folder: "Forestry, 1936," FSA.
50. Baker to Sholtz, June 22, 1935, S 278, box 45, folder: 14, FSA.
51. Stoddard, "Use of Fire in Pine Forests," 35.
52. Ibid., 32.
53. Ibid., 37.
54. Knapp to Davis, July 11, 1933, Tick eradication files, box 1, folder: "D misc (1933)," FSA.
55. Weaver to Sholtz, August 25, 1933, Sholtz papers, box 72, folder: "State Livestock Board (1933)," FSA.
56. Weaver to Fletcher, August 25, 1933, Tick eradication files, box 1, folder: "F misc (1933)," FSA.
57. Knapp to Fletcher, n.d. (August 1925), Tick eradication files, box 1, folder: "F misc (1933)," FSA.
58. The best source on tick eradication in the South is Strom's *Making Catfish Bait out of Government Boys*.
59. Although many scholars have written about Florida's ranching culture (e.g., John Otto, Joe Akerman, and Stetson Kennedy), the first and still authoritative source is Mealor and Prunty, "Open Range Ranching."
60. Harris Fussell, interview by folklorist Doris Dyen, May 7, 1983, Recordings of the Florida Folklife Program, 1936–2006, box 11, RG 158, FSA.

61. Ibid.

62. Note that like many who grew up in that period, she used the term *pioneer* instead of cracker. Inez Magill, *From Ticks to Politics* (n.d.), 1.

63. Ibid., 4.

64. Ibid., 17.

65. Mealor and Prunty, "Open Range Ranching," 364, 366.

66. Otto, "Traditional Cattle Herding," 319; Mealor and Prunty, "Open Range Ranching," 361.

67. Many maintain that the term *Florida cracker* derives from the cattle ranchers' use of the cow whip, the loud crack of which startled cattle into submission. See for instance Bulger, *South Florida Folklife*, 41. For more on Florida ranching folklife, see also Otto, "Traditional Cattle Herding," 219.

68. Florida passed its first branding law in 1828, while still a U.S. territory. Otto, "Traditional Cattle Herding," 303.

69. Trade with Cuba began in the 1850s. Otto, "Traditional Cattle Herding," 297–98.

70. Vance, *May Mann Jennings*, 123.

71. Dr. J. L. Kirby-Smith to Knapp, April 16, 1937, Governor Fred Cone papers, box 56, folder: "State Livestock Board (1937)," FSA.

72. Biographical information on Kay can be found in his *Miami Herald* obituary, October 6, 1977. He died at the age of eighty-five in Tampa. See also Kay's article in the *Florida Historical Quarterly*, "Tamiami Trail Blazers," January 1971, 279–88.

73. *Florida Newspaper News*, October 1934, n.p.

74. E. Williams, *Florida Cattleman*, October 1936, 5.

75. Williams, *Florida Cattleman*, November 1936 16.

76. Williams, *Florida Cattleman*, February 1937, 18.

77. Tucker, *Before the Timber Was Cut*, 43.

78. L. Perreault to Scoggin, January 4, 1942, State park project files, 1936–1945, box 3, folder: "Gold Head Supervision, 1941–1942," FSA.

79. Florida Research Bureau, *Florida and Its Money*, 98.

80. Ibid.

81. Ibid., 97.

82. Ibid.

83. In just one winter the FERA gave $2 million to tick eradication in 1933; T. W. Cole to Knapp, December 5, 1933, Tick eradication files, box 1, folder: Cole, TX (1933). The CWA also funded similar projects; Marcus Fagg to Knapp, December 21, 1933, box 1, folder: F misc (1933), FSA. Other agencies that contributed to the SLSSB were the WPA and the CCC; the WPA, CCC, and PWA all contributed to road building as well.

84. Knapp to Davis, August 29, 1933, Tick eradication files, box 1, folder: "D misc (1933)," FSA.

85. Ibid.

86. Ibid.

87. Knapp to Sholtz, September 11, 1933, Sholtz papers, box 72, folder: Livestock Board (1933), FSA.

88. Ibid.

89. Ibid.

90. Ibid.

91. See West, *Enduring Seminoles*, 90–91; Kersey, *Florida Seminoles*, 124–30; Tebeau, *History of Florida*, 382; and Derr, *Some Kind of Paradise*, 149–50.

92. Williams to Governor Fred Cone, November 6, 1937, Cone papers, box 56, folder: "Florida Livestock Board (1937)," FSA.

93. Cone to Williams, November 8, 1937, Cone papers, box 56, folder: "Florida Livestock Board (1937)," FSA.

94. Quoted in United States Senate, Committee on Indian Affairs, *Eradicating Cattle Tick*, 100–1.

95. Katherine Boyles to Cone, August 19, 1937, Cone papers, box 56, folder: "Florida Livestock Board (1937)," FSA.

96. Ibid.

97. Lillian Saunders to Cone, September 3, 1937, Cone papers, box 56, folder: "Florida Livestock Board (1937)," FSA.

98. References to starving and "scrawny" cattle results from a CCC program. As cattle in the West suffered from the ravages of drought, many were shipped to CCC camps in Florida, such as at Apalachicola National Forest, for fattening and then sold to local ranchers. These were sometimes referred to as "dust bowl cattle."

99. Elsie Beatty (Daytona Beach Humane Society) to Cone, August 20, 1937, Cone papers, box 36, folder: "Game and Fish Commission, Misc 1937," FSA.

100. Stokes to Cone, September 6, 1937, Cone papers, box 56, folder: "Live Stock Sanitary Board 1937," FSA.

101. At the time the novel's popularity was still on the rise. In 1938 Rawlings sold the film rights to MGM for $30,000.

102. Ackerman to Sholtz, Sholtz papers, box 48, folder: "Game and Fresh Water Fish, Dept. of 1933," FSA.

103. "Will Kill Deer to Save Cattle," *New York Times*, August 11, 1937.

104. Morris Ackerman to Sholtz, January 20, 1933, Sholtz papers, box 48, folder: "Game & Fresh Water Fish, Dept. of 1933," FSA.

105. Florida State Planning Board, *Summary Report, March 1934–December 1936*, 21–22, Cone papers, box 71, folder: "Planning Board, State 1937," FSA.

106. Reiger, *American Sportsmen and the Origins of Conservation*.

107. Kub, "Florida Black Bass," 4.

108. Davis (Conservation Commissioner), "Florida Wildlife Resources," 13.

109. Denmead, "Florida Bass," 5.

110. Merlin Mitchell to Cone, March 16, 1938, Cone papers, box 36, folder: "Game and Fish Commission—Misc," FSA.

111. John Rosch (White Plains, New York) to Sholtz, May 1, 1933, Sholtz papers, box 48, folder: "Game and Fresh Water Fish, Dept. of 1933," FSA.

112. Douglas, *Parks and Playgrounds of Florida*, 7.

113. Kub, "Florida Black Bass," 4.

114. J. Bodiford (City Fish Market) to Dowling, December 4, 1939, Cone papers, box 19, folder: "Conservation, State Board of 1939," FSA.

115. Y. Thompson (Gause Fish Company) to Cone, March 4, 1940, Cone papers, box 19, folder: "Conservation, State Board of 1940," FSA. Novelist Rawlings has the children of her neighbors playing fishers and game wardens instead cops and robbers or cowboys and Indians. Silverthorne, *Marjorie Kinnan Rawlings*, 69.

116. Fenton Jones to Cone, January 12, 1939, box 36, folder 14: "Game and Fish Commission 1939," FSA.

117. Ft. Pierce Chamber of Commerce to Cone, February 16, 1939, Cone papers, box 19, folder: "Conservation, State Board of 1939," FSA.

118. Jimmie Hughes et al. to Archie Clements, May 12, 1937, Fred Bryant papers, box 1, folder 1, FSA.

119. E. Knight to Cone, February 18, 1938, Cone papers, box 36, folder: "Game and Fish Commission—Misc," FSA.

120. Ibid.

121. E. Herring to Fresh Water Fish and Game Commission, February 23, 1938, Cone papers, box 36, folder: "Game and Fish Commission—Misc," FSA.

122. R. Mills (M.D., Tampa) to Rep. Fred Bryant, April 28, 1937, Bryant papers, box 1, folder 1, FSA.

123. Ibid.

124. O'Neal Cox to Bryant, Bryant papers, June 4, 1937, box 1, folder 1, FSA.

125. Longstreet, "Dollar Values of Florida Birds," 4.

126. Ibid.

127. Ibid.

128. Burghard, "Whaling in Florida Waters," 4–5.

129. Ibid., 5.

130. Ibid.

131. Ibid.

132. Hilton Crowe (NPS) to Robert Dowling (Chairman, State Board of Conservation), Cone papers, box 19, folder: "Conservation, State Board of 1940," FSA.

133. The first was reported in a telegram from Crow to Cone, October 10, 1940, Cone papers, box 19, folder: "Conservation, State Board of 1940," FSA.

134. Ibid.

135. Ibid.

136. Mrs. R. L. DeMuro in *Annual Report* (1938), in Florida Federation of Women's Clubs, *Year Book, 1936–1938*, 215.

137. FFWC *Annual Report* (1933), in Florida Federation of Women's Clubs, *Year Book, 1932–1934*, 223.

138. Carl Dickey to William J. Wood (State Conservation Board), March 15, 1938, Cone papers, box 19, folder: "Conservation, State Board of 1938," FSA.

139. Ibid.

140. Ibid.

141. Frances B. Newell (Chairman of Conservation, Bertha Hereford Hall Chapter, DAR, Leesburg) to Cone, February 12, 1938, Cone papers, box 19, folder: "Conservation, State Board of 1938," FSA.

142. Tebeau, *History of Florida*, 382.

143. That status would last less than a year. In the end the tick eradication program ran until 1961.

144. Maher, *Nature's New Deal*.

Chapter 10. The Sunshine State Emerges on the World Stage: Florida at the New York World's Fair

1. The study was published by the Florida State Planning Board in May 1939 as *Summaries of the Park, Parkway, and Recreation Areas Study and Forest Resources Survey*.

2. WPA, *The Florida Tourist*, 1.

3. Ibid., 4.

4. Ibid., 8.

5. Ibid., 9.

6. Ibid., 11–12.

7. Ibid.

8. Ibid., 13.

9. Ibid., 25.

10. Ibid., 18.

11. Ibid., 17.

12. Ibid., 20.

13. Taylor to Cone, July 25, 1939, box 46, folder: Hotel Commission—Misc 1939," FSA.

14. Ibid.

15. Florida Hotel Commission, *Biennial Report . . . January 1 1937 to December 31 1938*, 7.

16. Juliet Gorman points this out in her hypertext examination of the FWP's state guide to Florida, Jukin' It Out: Contested Visions of Florida in New Deal Narratives (May 2001), http://www.oberlin.edu/library/papers/honorshistory/2001-Gorman/FWP/contemporaryscene/contscene3.html.

17. For more on the FWP in Florida, see James A. Findley and Margaret Bing, "Touring Florida through the Federal Writer's Project," 289–305. Also see their web exhibit on the Federal Writer's Project, entitled An Exhibition of Works Progress Administration (WPA) Literature and Art from the Collections of the Bienes Center for the Literary Arts, http://www.co.broward.fl.us/library/bienes/lii10200.htm.

18. M. Taylor (hotel commissioner) to McCoy & Love (Lake Worth), March 29, 1938, Cone papers, box 46, folder: "Hotel Commission," FSA.

19. Henry Dew (Pres., Florida State Hotel Assn) to Taylor, December 10, 1938; J. A. Saeger to Cone, Cone papers, box 46, folder: "Hotel Commission," FSA.

20. *Miami Herald*, January 21, 1938.

21. Florida Department of Agriculture, *Agricultural Trends of the Day*, 30–31.

22. See for instance the published speech by State Marketing Director L. L. Rhodes, May 15, 1938, in Davenport, Cone papers, box 57, folder: "Marketing Bureau 1937," FSA; and *Agricultural Trends of the Day*, 30.

23. Walt Disney, who participated in the 1939 fair, was very influenced by its layout when

he designed both Disneyland in California and Disney World in Florida, with the fairy tale castles standing in for the New York Fair's unifying Theme Center. With Epcot, which opened in Orlando in 1983, Disney's plans for it from the 1950s, with its Geodome and World Showcase, modeled it even more closely upon both the New York and Century of Progress fairs in architecture, presentation, and content.

24. Hoffman, "From Augustine to Tangerine: Florida at the U.S. World's Fairs," 71. The original records of the 1939 New York World's Fair are housed at the New York Public Library.

25. FNE Press releases, October 14, 1939, and March 18, 1939, Cone papers, box 63, folder: "New York Fair," FSA.

26. Hoffman, "From Augustine to Tangerine," 75; FNE press release August 4, 1939, Cone papers, box 63, folder: "New York Fair," FSA; *Proceedings of the 52nd Meeting of the Florida State Horticultural Society*, 131.

27. FNE press release, August 4, 1939, Cone papers, box 63, folder: "New York Fair," FSA.

28. State of Florida, *Florida: Florida State Exhibit, New York World's Fair*, 5. This was a souvenir booklet sold at the fair.

29. Clipping can be found in Cone papers, box 63, folder: "New York Fair," FSA.

30. Ibid.

31. FNE press release, April 30, 1939, Cone papers, box 63, folder: "New York Fair," FSA.

32. Quoted in Hoffman, "From Augustine to Tangerine," 60.

33. FNE press release, April 1, 1939, Cone papers, box 63, folder: "New York Fair," FSA.

34. "Willie Saves Face of Surly Parrots," *New York Times*, July 12, 1939.

35. FNE press release, June 2, 1939, Cone papers, box 33, folder: "Florida National Exhibits," FSA.

36. FNE press release, August 4, 1939, Cone papers, box 63, folder: "New York Fair," FSA.

37. Cone to Chair of State County Commissioners Association, July 16, 1937, Cone papers, box 3, folder; "All-Florida Advertising Committee," FSA.

38. Cone to Harold Colee (President, State Chamber of Commerce) August 30, 1937, Cone papers, box 3, folder; "All-Florida Advertising Committee," FSA.

39. Branch Cone to E. J. L'Engle (Jacksonville), June 29, 1939, Cone papers, box 63, folder: "New York World's fair," FSA.

40. Ball to Cone, December 28, 1936, Cone papers, box 33, folder: "Florida National Exhibits," FSA. This would become Cone's official portrait, and today it hangs in the State Legislature.

41. Ibid.

42. Earl Brown to Cone, March 27, 1937, Cone papers, box 33, folder: "Florida National Exhibits," FSA.

43. Cone to Whalen, September 25, 1937, Cone papers, box 33, folder: "Florida National Exhibits," FSA.

44. Cone to Col. Cecil Harris (Live Oak), July 19, 1939, Cone papers, box 63, folder: "New York Fair," FSA.

45. The trains left Jacksonville at 5:10 p.m. on Sunday, August 27, and arrived at Penn Station in New York City at 8:00 p.m. the following day. Earl Brown to Cone, August 1, 1939, Seaboard Air Line Railway advertisement, Cone papers, box 63, folder: "New York Fair," FSA.

46. Ball to Cone, August 25, 1939, Cone papers, box 63, folder: "New York Fair," FSA.
47. Press release, August 17, 1939, Cone papers, box 63, folder: "New York Fair," FSA.
48. Brown to Cone, August 17, 1939, Cone papers, box 63, folder: New York Fair," FSA.
49. Brown to Cone, September 4, 1939, Cone to Brown, September 11, 1939, Cone papers, box 63, folder: "New York Fair," FSA.
50. Brown to Cone, September 4, 1939, Cone papers, box 63, folder: "New York Fair," FSA.
51. FNE, Press release, August 6, 1939, Cone papers, box 63, folder: "New York Fair," FSA; Seifert, "The World of Tomorrow: An Account of the 1939 New York World's Fair, 21.
52. See Cone papers, box 63, folder: "New York Fair," FSA.
53. See State of Florida, *Florida: Florida State Exhibit, New York World's Fair*.

Chapter 11. The End of the Beginning

1. Lewis Scoggin's notes on the conference, Holland papers, box 4, folder: "Forestry, 1942," FSA.
2. Ibid.
3. Ibid.
4. Ibid.
5. Robert Fechner died on New Year's Eve, 1939.
6. McEntee, "CCC and National Defense."
7. US, CCC, *Civilian Conservation Corps Contributing to the Defense of the Nation*.
8. Ibid.
9. Hoffman, "From Augustine to Tangerine," 75.
10. *New York Times* articles: "Florida Rounds Out Pioneering Epic," January 16, 1939; "Seven Floridas Welcome the Tourist," December 10, 1939; "It's More Than Miami," January 21, 1940; "Big Days in Florida," February 18, 1940; "Florida Lures Summer Host," June 30, 1940; "Florida Awaits Tourist Host," November 10, 1940.
11. Minutes of the Meeting of the Southeastern Regional Planning Commission, October 8, 1940, 7, Cone papers, box 71, folder: "Planning Board, State 1940," FSA.
12. Mormino, "World War II," 323.
13. Tebeau, *History of Florida*, 406.
14. Wirth, *Civilian Conservation Corps Camps*.
15. Sixteenth period directory: Florida, RG 35, entry 13, folder: "Florida," NARA; Vinten to Malsberger, March 2, 1940, State park project files, 1936–1945, box 2, folder: "Gold Head Camp Applications," FSA.
16. Eighteenth period directory: Florida, RG 35, entry 13, folder: "Florida," NARA.
17. S. Billings to James McEntee, January 23, 1942, RG 35, entry 10, folder: "FL SP-8, Fernandina," NARA.
18. Ibid.
19. Emmett Hill to Malsberger, January 16, 1942, State park project files, 1936–1945, box 1, folder: "Fort Clinch CCC," FSA.

20. Billings to Charles Kesler, Asst. to Director, RG 35, entry 10, folder: "FL SPP-12, Marianna," NARA.

21. *Jackson County Floridian*, February 27, 1942.

22. Scoggin to Region 1, NPS, March 18, 1942, State park project files, 1936–1945, box 1, folder: "CCC Camps," FSA.

23. Scoggin to John B. McFarlin, March 20, 1942, State park project files, 1936–1945, box 1, folder: "CCC Camps," FSA.

24. *Jackson County Floridian*, February 29, 1942.

25. Camp Inspection report, February 2, 1942, SP-4, RG 35, entry 10, folder: "FL SP-4, Sarasota," NARA.

26. Florida State Board of Forestry, *Seventh Biennial Report of the Florida Forestry and Park Service, 1 July 1940–30 June 1942*, 13.

27. One of these was Ranger M. L. Sibley, who left Gold Head Branch State Park for Camp Blanding because it offered "better pay." B. H. Griffin to Scoggin, April 2, 1943, State park project files 1936–1945, box 3, folder: "Gold Head Supervision, 1942–1943," FSA.

28. Green to Malsberger, December 8, 1942, State park project files 1936–1945, box 2, folder: "Fort Clinch Supervision, 1942–1943," FSA.

29. Clayton Perreault to Scoggin, May 2, 1942, State park project files 1936–1945, box 3, folder: "Gold Head Supervision, 1942–1943," FSA.

30. Griffin to Scoggin, April 2, 1943, State park project files 1936–1945, box 3, folder: "Gold Head Supervision, 1942–1943," FSA.

31. B. Taylor to Vinten, December 10, 1941, RG 79, entry 92, folder: "Florida—general," NARA.

32. Ferreira to Scoggin, June 19, 1942, State park project files, 1936–1945, box 2, folder: "Fort Clinch—park use," FSA.

33. Hollis, *Dixie Before Disney*, 46.

34. Scoggin to Simpson, April 30, 1943, State park project files, 1936–1945, box 1, folder: "Florida Caverns Supervision, 1941–1943," FSA.

35. Simpson to Scoggin, May 23, 1943, State park project files 1936–1945, box 1, folder: "Florida Caverns Supervision, 1941–1943," FSA.

36. Griffin to Park branch, May 17, 1943, State park project files, 1936–1945, box 2, folder: "Gold Head Supervision, 1941–1943," FSA.

37. Scoggin to Griffin, June 3, 1943, State park project files, 1936–1945, box 2, folder: "Gold Head Supervision, 1941–1943," FSA; Scoggin to Simpson, June 3, 1943, State park project files, 1936–1945, box 1, folder: "Florida Caverns Supervision, 1941–1943," FSA.

38. Simpson to Scoggin, May 25, 1943, State park project files, 1936–1945, box 1, folder: "Florida Caverns Supervision, 1941–1943," FSA.

39. Ibid.

40. Ibid.

41. Ibid.

42. Ibid.

43. Captain W. Z. Bancroft to Scoggin, July 18, 1942, State park project files, 1936–1945, box 2, folder: "Gold Head State Park—Misc. Correspondence, 1942–1943," FSA.

44. Green to Scoggin, February 19, 1942, State park project files, 1936–1945, box 2, folder: "Fort Clinch Supervision, 1942–1943," FSA; Simpson to Scoggin, January 7, 1943, State park project files, 1936–1945, box 1, folder: "Florida Caverns supervision, 1942–1943," FSA.

45. Alvater OH, 8, Sebring Historical Society.

46. C. Altvater, "Chronology of Events of Highlands Hammock," n.d. (unpublished manuscript), Sebring Historical Society.

47. Malsberger to F.N.K. Bailey, November 2, 1942, Holland papers, box 4, folder: "Florida Forestry and park Service, 1942–1943," FSA.

48. Green to Scoggin, August 2, 1942, State park project files, 1936–1945, box 2, folder: "Gold Head misc. correspondence, 1942–1943," FSA.

49. Florida State Board of Forestry, *Seventh Biennial Report of the Florida Forestry and Park Service*, 13.

50. Mormino, "World War II," 323.

51. Simpson to Scoggin, January 7, 1943, State park project files, 1936–1945, box 1, folder: "Florida Caverns supervision, 1942–1943," FSA.

52. Scoggin to Simpson, January 20, 1943, State park project files, 1936–1945, box 1, folder: "Florida Caverns supervision, 1942–1943," FSA.

53. Annual Report of the Park Director, July 1, 1945 to June 30, 1946, 3, Chief of Education and Information Charles H. Schaeffer's administrative and reference files, 1936–1959, box 2, folder: "Misc.," FSA.

54. Scoggin, "History of Florida State Parks," 16.

55. United Daughters of the Confederacy, *Minutes of the 36th Annual Convention*, 56.

56. Ibid., 23.

57. Ibid., 56.

58. *Minutes of the 38th Annual Convention, Florida Division, United Daughters of the Confederacy*, 46.

59. *Minutes of the 40th Annual Convention, Florida Division, United Daughters of the Confederacy*, 57.

60. Ibid., 58.

61. *Minutes of the 43rd Annual Convention, Florida Division, United Daughters of the Confederacy*, 70.

62. *Minutes of the 44th Annual Convention, Florida Division, United Daughters of the Confederacy*, 20, 69.

63. *Minutes of the 45th Annual Convention, Florida Division, United Daughters of the Confederacy*, 54.

64. Ibid., 25.

65. Ibid., 24.

66. Mattson, *Small Town*, 40.

67. *Tallahassee Democrat*, June 17, 1940.

68. Ibid.

69. *FTU*, June 17, 1940.

Bibliography

Archival Sources, Interviews, and Unpublished Sources

Anderson, Sherry. "Pre-1955 Tourist Attractions in Florida: A Developmental History and Analysis of Significance." M.A. Thesis, University of Georgia, 1995.

Altvater, A. C. Papers. Sebring Historical Society, Sebring, Fla.

———. Interview by Herbert Evison. Spring 1971. Sebring Historical Society, Sebring, Fla.

Baker, Tracy. Interview by Capt. Alogna and Ranger Worthington. November 26, 1977. State park project files, 1933–1942, 1988–1989, box 1, folder: "Gold Head Misc. Collections," Florida State Archives, Tallahassee.

Bethea, John. Biographical file. Florida Collection, Florida State Library, Tallahassee.

Bryant, Fred. Papers. RG 900000. Florida State Archives, Tallahassee.

Burnette, Carroll F. Interview by Dr. Julian Pleasants. February 8, 1999. Samuel Proctor Oral History Project. University of Florida, Gainesville.

Bush, Harry. Interview by Ben Houston. July 3, 2000. Samuel Proctor Oral History Project. University of Florida, Gainesville.

Campbell, State Veterinarian Clarence. Correspondence. RG 293. Florida State Archives, Tallahassee.

Carlton, Governor Doyle. Correspondence. RG 102. Florida State Archives, Tallahassee.

Cash, State Librarian William. Correspondence. RG 198. Florida State Archives, Tallahassee.

———. Administration files, 1927–1954. RG 198. Florida State Archives, Tallahassee.

Cone, Governor Frederick. Correspondence. RG 102. Florida State Archives, Tallahassee.

Coulter, Clinton. Biographical file. Florida Collection. Florida State Library, Tallahassee.

———. Interview by Elwood Maunder. February 6, 1958. Forest History Society Papers. Duke University, Durham, N.C. https://foresthistory.org/wp-content/uploads/2016/12/CoulterOHI.pdf

———. Interview. Reichelt Oral History Program. Florida State University, Tallahassee.

Cowart, Hillary. Interview by Dr. Julian Pleasants. April 30, 1998. Samuel Proctor Oral History Project. University of Florida, Gainesville. https://foresthistory.org.

DeGirolamo, Paul. Interview by Dave Nelson. November 2, 2011. Reichelt Oral History Program. Florida State University, Tallahassee.

Drew Family. Papers, 1856–1999. RG 900000. Florida State Archives, Tallahassee.

Dunn, James William. "The New Deal and Florida Politics." Ph.D. dissertation, Florida State University, 1971.
Eldredge, Inman. Interview by Elwood Maunder. February 3, 1959. Forest Society History Papers. Duke University, Durham, N.C. https://foresthistory.org/wp-content/uploads/2016/12/Eldredge.pdf.
Evans, Jon S. "Florida Politics in the Shade of War: The 1940 Governor's Race." Master's thesis, Florida State University, 2000.
Florida Caverns State Park. Park Files. Marianna, Fla.
Florida Department of Agriculture. *24th Biennial Report of the Dept. of Agriculture from July 1, 1934 to June 30, 1936.* Tallahassee: Florida Department of Agriculture, 1937.
Florida Division of Historical Resources. Florida State Park Project Files, 1933–1942, 1988–1989. RG 155. Florida State Archives, Tallahassee.
Florida Division of Recreation and Parks. Chief of Education and Information Charles H. Schaeffer's administrative and reference files, 1936–1959. RG 510. Florida State Archives, Tallahassee.
———. Florida Caverns State Park and other state park plans, 1935–1939. RG 510. Florida State Archives, Tallahassee.
———. Fort Clinch exhibit materials, 1820–1940. RG 510. Florida State Archives, Tallahassee.
———. Public relations and historical files, 1934–1964. RG 510. Florida State Archives, Tallahassee.
———. State park project files, 1936–1945. RG 510. Florida State Archives, Tallahassee.
———. State park surveys, 1934–1935. RG 510. Florida State Archives, Tallahassee.
Florida Folklife Program. Recordings of the Florida Folklife Program, 1936–2006. RG 158. Florida State Archives, Tallahassee.
———. Maritime Heritage Files, 1986–1987. RG 158. Florida State Archives, Tallahassee.
Florida Forestry Service. Minutes. Office of the Director. Tallahassee, Fla.
Florida Health and Welfare Council. Records, 1921–1973. RG 900000. Florida State Archives, Tallahassee.
Florida Park Service. Central Office Historical Files. Tallahassee.
Florida State Livestock Sanitary Board. Tick eradication files, 1933–1951. RG 293. Florida State Archives, Tallahassee.
Florida Office of the Governor. *Message of Fred P. Cone, Governor of Florida, to the Florida Legislature, Session of 1937.* Tallahassee, 1937.
Florida State Board of Conservation. Minutes, 1933–1970. RG 592. Florida State Archives, Tallahassee.
Florida State Board of Forestry. *Biennial Reports* and *Annual Reports*, 1927–1970. Florida State Archives, Tallahassee.
Florida Merit System Council. Minutes, 1936–1967. RG 196. Florida State Archives, Tallahassee.
Florida State Defense Council. *First Biennial Report of the State Defense Council, 1941–1942.* March 25, 1943. Florida State Library, Tallahassee.
Florida State Planning Board. Clippings. RG 192. Florida State Archives, Tallahassee.

———. *Directory of State Officers, Boards, Departments and Commissions of Florida.* Tallahassee, 1936.

———. Florida recreation facilities surveys, 1938. Florida State Archives, Tallahassee.

———. Minutes. Florida State Archives, Tallahassee.

———. *Summaries of the Park, Parkway, and Recreational Areas Study and Florida Resources Survey.* Tallahassee, 1939.

———. *Summary Report, March 1934–December 1936.* Tallahassee, 1937.

Florida Statewide Library Project. *WJAX Radio Broadcast: U.S. Government Reports.* Jacksonville, 1939.

Florida State Welfare Board. Minutes, 1927–1969. RG 897. Florida State Archives, Tallahassee.

Florida, Trustees of the Internal Improvement Fund. Minutes, 1855–1973. RG 194. Florida State Archives, Tallahassee.

Fort Clinch State Park. Park Files. Fernandina, Fla.

Fussell, Harris. Interview by folklorist Doris Dyen. May 7, 1983. Recordings of the Florida Folklife Program, 1936–2006, box 11, RG 158. Florida State Archives, Tallahassee.

Gold Head Branch State Park. Park Files. Keystone Heights, Fla.

Gufford, Albert. Interview by folklorist David Taylor. August 8, 1986. Maritime Heritage Survey files, 1986–1987, box 7, RG 158. Florida State Archives. Tallahassee, Fla.

Hall, Ansley. Interview by Dave Nelson. November 2, 2002. Reichelt Oral History Program, Florida State University, Tallahassee.

Hamburger, Susan. "And They're Off! The Development of the Horse Racing Industry in Florida." Ph.D. dissertation, Florida State University, 1994.

Heath, Buck. Interview by Dave Nelson. July 12, 2003. Reichelt Oral History Program, Florida State University, Tallahassee.

Hendry, Leonard. Interview by park ranger Paula Benshoff. January 1985. Myakka River State Park. Files. Sarasota, Fla.

Highlands Hammock State Park. Files. Sebring Historical Society. Sebring, Fla.

———. Park files. Highlands Hammock State Park, Sebring, Fla.

Hillsborough River State Park. Park Files. Thonotosassa, Fla.

Holland, Governor Spessard. Correspondence. RG 102. Florida State Archives. Tallahassee, Fla.

Holmes, Talmadge. Interview by Dr. Julian Pleasants. May 5, 1998. Samuel Proctor Oral History Project. University of Florida. Gainesville, Fla.

Howard, Walter. "Vigilante Justice: Extra Legal Executions in Florida, 1930–1940," Ph.D. dissertation, Florida State University, 1987.

Hutcheson, Thomas. Interview by Dave Nelson. November 2, 2002. Reichelt Oral History Program, Florida State University, Tallahassee, Fla.

Ives, Richard. Interview by Ben Houston. June 19, 2000. Samuel Proctor Oral History Project. University of Florida. Gainesville, Fla.

Jennings, May Mann. Papers. P. K. Yonge Library. University of Florida, Gainesville, Fla.

Keene, James. Interview by Ben Houston. May 5, 1998. Samuel Proctor Oral History Project. University of Florida. Gainesville.

Knapp, State Veterinarian Jean. Correspondence. RG 293. Florida State Archives. Tallahassee, Fla.
———. Biographical files. Florida Collection. Florida State Library, Tallahassee.
LeCouris, George. Interview by Dave Nelson. November 2, 2002; November 11, 2003. Reichelt Oral History Program, Florida State University, Tallahassee, Fla.
Leslie, Vernon. "The Great Depression in Miami Beach," M.A. Thesis, Florida Atlantic University, 1980.
Mackle, Elliot, Jr. "The Eden of the South: Florida's Image in American Travel Literature and Painting, 1965–1900," Ph.D. dissertation, Emory University, 1977.
Morris, Allen. *Cracker Politics* files. Florida Collection. Florida State Library, Tallahassee.
Myakka River State Park. Park files. Sarasota, Fla.
Oleno State Park. Park Files. High Springs, Fla.
Oliver, Malcolm. Interview by Dave Nelson. November 2, 2002. Reichelt Oral History Program. Florida State University, Tallahassee.
O'Neal, Willie. Interview by Ben Houston. June 19, 2000. Samuel Proctor Oral History Project. University of Florida. Gainesville, Fla.
Pleasants, Julian. "The Forgotten Men: The Civilian Conservation Corps, 1933–1942." Manuscript, n.d., copy in possession of the author.
Rawick, George. "The New Deal and Youth: the Civilian Conservation Corps, the National Youth Administration, and the American Youth Congress." Ph.D. dissertation, University of Wisconsin, 1957.
Seifert, Harry. "The World of Tomorrow: An Account of the 1939 New York World's Fair," M.A. Thesis, Florida State University, 1974.
Shands, Senator William A. Interview by Dr. Samuel Proctor. March 1, 1971. Samuel Proctor Oral History Project. University of Florida. Gainesville, Fla.
Sholtz, Governor Dave. Correspondence. RG 102. Florida State Archives. Tallahassee, Fla.
Stevenson, Jim. Chief Naturalist Research Files, 1938–1977. RG 510. Florida State Archives. Tallahassee, Fla.
———. Interview by Robin Sellers. September 24, 1999. Reichelt Oral History Program. Florida State University, Tallahassee, Fla.
Thompson, Fred. Interview by Park Ranger Paula Benshoff. n.d. Myakka River State Park. Files. Sarasota, Fla.
Thompson, Sam. Interview by Ben Houston. June 19, 2000. Samuel Proctor Oral History Project. University of Florida. Gainesville, Fla.
Torreya State Park. Park Files. Bristol, Florida.
Trescott, Dan. Interview with the author. 2003. Reichelt Oral History Program. Florida State University, Tallahassee.
United States, Bureau of the Census. *Thirteenth Census of the United States: 1910*.
———. *Fourteenth Census of the United States: 1920*.
———. *Fifteenth Census of the United States: 1930*.
United States. Civilian Conservation Corps. Camp directories, 1933–1942. RG 35. National Archives. College Park, MD.

———. Camp inspection records, 1933–1942. RG 35. National Archives. College Park, MD.
———. Correspondence with governors, 1933–1937. RG 35. National Archives. College Park, MD.
———. Correspondence with state selection agencies, 1933–1942. RG 35. National Archives. College Park, MD.
———. General correspondence, 1933–1942. RG 35. National Archives. College Park, MD.
———. Letters of instruction and local selection agencies, 1938–1942. RG 35. National Archives. College Park, MD.
———. Records, 1933–1936. P. K. Yonge Library. University of Florida. Gainesville, Fla.
———. Reports of field trips, 1935–1941. RG 35. National Archives. College Park, MD.
———. Success stories. RG 35. National Archives. College Park, MD.
United States. Forestry Service. ECW Inspection correspondence. RG 95. National Archives. Atlanta, GA.
United States. National Park Service. Regional Biologist, Reports. RG 79 National Archives. Atlanta, GA.
———. Regional Geologist. Reports. RG 79 National Archives. Atlanta, GA
Walston, Kathleen Anne. "A Case for the Revival of the CCC in Florida," M.A. thesis, University of Florida, 1986.
White, Fred. Interview by Dr. Julian Pleasants. March 16, 1998. Samuel Proctor Oral History Project. University of Florida, Gainesville.
Williams, Fred. Interview by folklorist Doris Dyen. April 16, 1983. Florida Folklife Program Recordings. RG 158. Florida State Archives, Tallahassee.
Zangara, Joseph. Case Files, 1933. RG L47. Florida State Archives, Tallahassee.

Articles, Books, and Miscellaneous Sources

Akerman, Joe. *Florida Cowman: A History of Florida Cattle Raising*. Kissimmee: Florida Cattlemen's Association, 1976.
Allen, Frederick Lewis. *Since Yesterday: The Nineteen Thirties in America*. New York: Harpers and Brothers, 1939.
Ammidown, Margot. "Edens, Underworlds, and Shrines: Florida's Small Tourist Attractions." *Journal of Decorative and Propaganda Arts* 23 (1998).
Andrews, A. H. "McKee Gardens, an Outstanding Beauty Spot." In *Proceedings of the 48th Annual Meeting of the Florida Horticultural Society*. Deland, Fla.: Florida State Horticultural Society, 1935.
Antonelli, Paola. "Of Imagination and Concrete Fantasies." In *Exit to Tomorrow: World's Fairs Architecture, Design, Fashion, 1933–2006*, ed. Andrew Garn. New York: Universe Publishing, 2007.
Arsenault, Raymond. *St. Petersburg and the Florida Dream: 1888–1950*. Gainesville: University Press of Florida, 1996.
Arno, Steven, and Steve Allison-Burnell. *Flames in Our Forest: Disaster or Renewal?* Washington: Island Press, 2002.

Attevy, John A. *Hurricanes and Florida Agriculture*. Lake Alfred: Florida Science, 1999.
Baker, Harry Lee. *Forest Fires in Florida*. Tallahassee: Florida Forestry Association, 1927.
Balbridge, Kenneth. "Reclamation Work of the Civilian Conservation Corps, 1933–1942." *Utah Historical Quarterly* (Summer 1971).
Barnes, Jay. *Florida's Hurricane History*. Chapel Hill: University of North Carolina Press, 1998.
Barron, Stephanie, Sheri Bernstein, and Ilene Susan Fort, eds. *Reading California: Art, Image, and Identity, 1900–2000*. Berkeley: University of California Press, 2000.
Bauer, Ruthmary. "Sarasota: Hardship and Tourism in the 1930s." *Florida Historical Quarterly* (Fall 1997).
Beach, Rex. *Paradise in Florida*. Sebring, Fla.: Highland Hammock, Inc., 1930.
Beck, Carol. *Nature on Parade*. Tallahassee: Florida Department of Natural Resources, 1970.
Best, Gary Dean. *Nickel and Dime Decade: American Popular Culture in the 1930s*. Westport: Praeger, 1993.
Bicentennial Commission of Florida. *Florida Bicentennial Trail: A Heritage Revisited*. Tallahassee: Bicentennial Commission of Florida, 1976.
Bigelow, Gordon E. *Frontier Eden: The Literary Career of Marjorie Kinnan Rawlings*. Gainesville: University Press of Florida, 1966.
Biles, Roger. *The South and the New Deal*. Lexington: University Press of Kentucky, 1994.
Black, Allida M., ed. *Courage in a Dangerous World: The Political Writings of Eleanor Roosevelt*. New York: Columbia University Press, 1999.
Blevins, Brooks. *Hill Folks: A History of Arkansas Ozarkers and Their Image*. Chapel Hill: University of North Carolina Press, 2002.
Breslauer, Ken. *Roadside Paradise: The Golden Age of Florida's Tourist Attractions, 1929–1971*. Sebring: Retro Florida, 2000.
Brinkley, Alan. *The End of Reform*. New York: Vintage Books, 1995.
———. *Voices of Protest*. New York: Vintage Books, 1982.
Brundage, W. Fitzhugh. *The Southern Past: A Clash of Race and Memory*. Cambridge: Harvard University Press, 2005.
Bulger, Peggy, et al. *South Florida Folklife*. Jackson: University Press of Mississippi, 1994.
Burghard, August. "Whaling in Florida Waters." *Florida Conservator* (April–May 1935).
Buhite, Russell D., and David W. Levy, eds. *FDR's Fireside Chats*. Norman: University of Oklahoma Press, 1992.
Butler, Ovid. *American Conservation in Picture and Story*. Washington, D.C.: American Forestry Association, 1935.
Carle, David. *Burning Questions: America's Fight With Nature's Fire*. Westport, Conn.: Praeger, 2002.
Carr, Archie, III. "A Century of Sea Turtles." In *Proceedings of the 20th Annual Symposium on Sea Turtle Biology and Conservation*. Orlando: National Oceanic and Atmospheric Administration, 2000.
Cash, William T. *A History of the Democratic Party in Florida*. Tallahassee, 1936.
Chalmers, David. "The Ku Klux Klan in the Sunshine State: The 1920s." *Florida Historical Quarterly* (January 1964).

Chandler, David Leon. *Henry Flagler: The Astonishing Life and Times of the Visionary Robber Baron Who Founded Florida*. New York: Macmillan, 1986.
Chicago: A Century of Progress, 1833–1933. Chicago: Marquette Publishing Company, 1933.
Clancy, Patrick. "Conserving the Youth: The Civilian Conservation Corps Experience in the Shenandoah National Park." *Virginia Magazine of History and Biography* (Autumn 1997).
Clarke, Jeanne Nienaber. *Roosevelt's Warrior: Harold L. Ickes and the New Deal*. Baltimore: Johns Hopkins University Press, 1996.
Cobb, James C. *Away Down South: A History of Southern Identity*. Oxford: Oxford University Press, 2005.
Cobb, James C., and Michael Namorato, eds. *The New Deal and the South*. Jackson: University of Mississippi Press, 1984.
Cohen, Stan. *The Tree Army: The History of the Civilian Conservation Corps, 1933–1942*. Missoula: Pictorial Histories Publishing Company, 1980.
Colburn, David R. "Florida Politics in the Twentieth Century." In *The New History of Florida*, ed. Michael Gannon. Gainesville: University Press of Florida, 1996.
———. *From Yellow Dog Democrats to Red State Republicans: Florida and Its Politics since 1940*. Gainesville: University Press of Florida, 2007.
Colburn, David, and Lance DeHaven-Smith. *Government in the Sunshine State*. Gainesville: University Press of Florida, 1999.
Colburn, David, and Richard Scher. *Florida's Gubernatorial Politics in the Twentieth Century*. Tallahassee: University of Florida Press, 1980.
Cole, Alison, et al. *The Forest Service and Civilian Conservation Corps: 1933–1942*. Washington, D.C: Government Printing Office, 1986.
Cole, Olen. *The African-American Experience in the Civilian Conservation Corps*. Gainesville: University Press of Florida, 1999.
Conkin, Paul. *The New Deal*, 2nd edition. Arlington Heights: Harlan Davidson, 1975.
Conrad, David Eugene. *The Forgotten Farmers: The Story of Sharecroppers in the New Deal*. Urbana: University of Illinois Press, 1965.
Cornebise, Alfred Emile. "Heralds in New Deal America: Camp Newspapers of the Civilian Conservation Corps." *Media History Monographs* 2, no. 1 (1998).
Cox, Merlin. "David Sholtz: New Deal Governor of Florida." *Florida Historical Quarterly* 43 (Fall 1964).
Cresap, Ida Keeling. *The History of Florida Agriculture: The Early Era*. Gainesville: Florida Agricultural Experiment Station, 1982.
Cutler, Phoebe. *The Public Landscape of the New Deal*. New Haven: Yale University Press, 1985.
Dacy, George. *Four Centuries of Florida Ranching*. St. Louis, Mo.: Britt Printing, 1940.
Danese, Tracy. *Claude Pepper and Ed Ball: Politics, Purpose, and Power*. Gainesville: University Press of Florida, 2000.
Daniel, Pete. "The New Deal, Southern Agriculture and Economic Change." In *The New Deal and the South*, ed. James C. Cobb and Michael Namorato. Jackson: University of Mississippi Press, 1984.

———, ed. *Official Images: New Deal Photography.* Washington, D.C.: Smithsonian Institution Press, 1987.
Davis, George. "Florida Wildlife Resources." *Florida Conservator* (February 1935).
Davis, Jack. "Alligators and Plume Birds: The Despoliation of Florida's Living Aesthetic." In *Paradise Lost? The Environmental History of Florida*, ed. Jack Davis. Gainesville: University Press of Florida, 2005.
———, ed. *Paradise Lost?: The Environmental History of Florida.* Gainesville: University Press of Florida, 2005.
Davis, Kenneth. *FDR: The New York Years, 1928–1933.* New York: Random House, 1994.
Davis, Kingsley. *Youth in the Depression.* Chicago: University of Chicago Press, 1935.
Dearborn, Ned H. "Educational Opportunities for Enrollees." *Phi Delta Kappan* 19 (May 1937).
Denham, James. *A Rogue's Paradise: Crime and Punishment in Antebellum Florida, 1821–1861.* Tuscaloosa: University of Alabama Press, 2005.
Denmead, Talbott. "Florida Bass." *Florida Conservator* (January 1935).
Derr, Mark. *Some Kind of Paradise: A Chronicle of Man and the Land in Florida.* Gainesville: University Press of Florida, 1998.
Douglas, Marjory Stoneman. *The Parks and Playgrounds of Florida.* Tallahassee: Florida Department of Agriculture, 1935.
———. *The Parks and Playgrounds of Florida* (revised). Tallahassee: Florida Department of Agriculture, 1937.
Douglas, Marjory Stoneman (with John Rothchild). *Voice of the River: An Autobiography.* Sarasota, Fla.: Pineapple Press, 1987.
Dovell, J. E. "The Florida State Parks." *University of Florida Economic Leaflets* 13 (February 1954).
Doyle, Wilson, et al. *The Government and Administration of Florida.* New York: Thomas Crowell Company, 1954.
Drane, Hank. *Hank Drane's Historic Governors: Their Impact on the Sunshine State.* Ocala, Fla.: Ferguson Printing, 1994.
Dreary, George. *Four Centuries of Florida Cattle Ranching.* St. Louis: Britt Printing Company, 1940.
Educational Policies Commission. *The Civilian Conservation Corps, the National Youth Administration and the Public Schools.* Washington, D.C.: Educational Policies Commission, National Education Association of the United States, and American Association of School Administrators, 1941.
Everhart, William C. *The National Park Service.* Boulder, Colo.: Westview Press, 1983.
Fairbanks, Charles H., and Jerald T. Milanich. *Florida Archaeology.* New York: Academic Press, 1980.
Fausold, Martin. *Gifford Pinchot: Bull Moose Progressive.* Syracuse: Syracuse University Press, 1961.
Fechner, Robert. "The Educational Contribution of the Civilian Conservation Corps." *Phi Delta Kappan* 19 (May 1937).
———. "My Hopes for the CCC." *American Forests,* January 1937.

Federal Writers' Project, comp. *Agricultural Conservation*. Tallahassee: Florida Department of Agriculture, 1939.

———. *Florida: A Guide to the Southernmost State*. New York: Oxford University Press, 1939.

Florida Board of Parks and Historic Memorials. *Biennial Report of the Florida Board of Parks and Historic Memorials, July 1, 1955–June 30, 1957*. Tallahassee, 1959.

Florida Department of Agriculture. *Agricultural Trends of the Day: Addresses on Pertinent Problems Pertaining to Florida Agriculture and Economy*. Tallahassee: Florida Department of Agriculture, 1938.

———. *Florida Facts and General Statistics*. Tallahassee: Florida Department of Agriculture, 1932.

Florida Department of Environmental Protection, Division of Recreation and Parks. *Florida Caverns State Park Unit Management Plan*. Tallahassee, 2018.

———. *Fort Clinch State Park Unit Management Plan*. Tallahassee, 1998.

———. *Hillsborough River State Park Unit Management Plan*. Tallahassee, 1999.

———. *Myakka River State Park Unit Management Plan*. Tallahassee, 2004.

———. *Tomoka State Park Unit Management Plan*. Tallahassee, 2012.

———. *Torreya State Park Unit Management Plan*. Tallahassee, 1999.

Florida Federation of Women's Clubs. *Year Book, 1932–1934*. Tampa: Florida Federation of Women's Clubs, 1934.

———. *Year Book, 1936–1938*. Tampa: Florida Federation of Women's Clubs, 1938.

Florida Forestry Service. *Florida Commercial Forestry Conference* (Bulletin #5). Tallahassee, June 1931.

Florida Hotel Commission. *Biennial Report of the Hotel Commission of the State of Florida from January 1 1937 to December 31 1938*. Tallahassee: Florida Hotel Commission, 1938.

Florida House of Representatives, Clerk of the House. *The People of Lawmaking in Florida, 1822–2001*. Tallahassee: Florida House of Representatives, 2002.

Florida Research Bureau. *Florida and Its Money*. St. Augustine: Record Company, 1938.

Flynn, Stephen J. *Florida: Land of Fortune*. New York: Van Rees Press, 1962.

Flynt, Wayne. *Duncan Upshaw Fletcher: Dixie's Reluctant Progressive*. Tallahassee: Florida State University Press, 1971.

Foster, Mark S. *Castles in the Sand: The Life and Times of Carl Graham Fisher*. Gainesville: University Press of Florida, 2000.

Friedel, Frank. *FDR and the South*. Baton Rouge: Louisiana State University Press, 1965.

———. *Franklin D. Roosevelt: A Rendezvous With Destiny*. Boston: Little Brown and Company, 1990.

———. *Franklin D. Roosevelt: Launching the New Deal*. Boston: Little Brown and Company 1973.

———. "The South and the New Deal." In *The New Deal and the South*, ed. James C. Cobb and Michael V. Namorato. Jackson: University of Mississippi Press, 1984.

Gallagher, Hugh G. *FDR's Splendid Deception: The Moving Story of Roosevelt's Massive Disability—and the Intense Efforts to Conceal It from the Public*. New York: Dodd Mead, 1985.

Gannon, Michael, ed. *New History of Florida*. Gainesville: University Press of Florida, 1996.

Garn, Andrew. *Exit to Tomorrow: World's Fairs Architecture, Design, Fashion, 1933–2006.* New York: Universe Publishing, 2007.

Garrett, Gary. "Blasting through Paradise: The Cost and Consequence of the Tamiami Trail." In *Paradise Lost?: The Environmental History Florida*, ed. Jack Davis. Gainesville: University Press of Florida, 2005.

George, Paul S. "Passage to the New Eden: Tourism in Miami from Flagler through Everest G. Sewell." *Florida Historical Quarterly* (April 1981).

Gerrell, Pete. *Illustrated History of the Naval Stores (Turpentine) Industry.* Kearney: Morris Publishing. 1997.

Gittner, Cory H. *Miami's Parrot Jungle and Gardens.* Gainesville: University Press of Florida, 2000.

Gold, Pleasant Daniel. *History of Volusia County.* Deland, Fla., 1927.

Gorham, Eric. "The Ambiguous Practices of the Civilian Conservation Corps." *Social History* 17 (May 1992).

Gower, Calvin W. "Conservation, Censorship, and Controversy in the CCC, 1930s." *Journalism Quarterly* 1 (Summer 1975).

Gray, R. A. *The Government of Florida.* Philadelphia: John C. Winston Company, 1941.

———. *The Power and the Glory.* Tallahassee: Rose Printing, 1965.

Green, Elna C., ed. *Looking for the New Deal: Florida Women's Letters during the Great Depression.* Columbia: University of South Carolina Press, 2007.

Hale, Arthur. "Florida's Scenic Highways," in *Florida's Government for 1939* (St. Augustine: Record Company, 1939), 31.

Harkins, Anthony. *Hillbilly: A Cultural History of an American Icon.* Oxford: Oxford University Press, 2005.

Heinemann, Ronald L. *Depression and New Deal in Virginia: The Enduring Dominion.* Charlottesville: University Press of Virginia, 1983.

Highlands Hammock State Park brochure. Tallahassee: Florida Forest and Park Service, 1940.

Hill, Edwin G. *In the Shadow of the Mountain: The Spirit of the CCC.* Pullman: Washington State University Press, 1990.

Hinson, Billy G. "The Civilian Conservation Corps in Mobile County, Alabama." *Alabama Review* 45 (October 1992).

Hoffman, Joel M. "From Augustine to Tangerine: Florida at the U.S. World Fairs." *Journal of Decorative and Propaganda Arts* 23 (1998).

Hollis, Tim. *Dixie Before Disney: 100 Years of Roadside Fun.* Jackson: University Press of Mississippi, 1999.

———. *Florida's Miracle Strip: From Redneck Riviera to Emerald Coast.* Jackson: University Press of Mississippi, 2004.

Howard, Walter T. "Vigilante Justice and National Reaction: The 1937 Tallahassee Double Lynching." *Florida Historical Quarterly* (July 1988).

Hoyt, Roy. *We Can Take It: A Short Story of the CCC.* New York: American Book Company, 1935.

Humberger, Charles E. "The CCC in Nebraska: Memoirs of Company 762." *Nebraska History* 75 (Winter 1994).
Humphrey, Hubert. "In a Sense Experimental: The Civilian Conservation Corps in Louisiana, Pt. II." *Louisiana History* 6 (Winter 1965).
Ickes, Harold. *The Secret Diaries of Harold Ickes: The First Thousand Days*. New York: Simon and Schuster, 1953.
Ingalls, Robert P. *Urban Vigilantes in the New South: Tampa, 1882–1936*. Gainesville: University of Florida Press, 1998.
Ingram, Tammy. *Dixie Highway: Road Building and the Making of the Modern South, 1900–1930*. Chapel Hill: University of North Carolina Press, 2014.
Jackson, Faith Reyher. *Pioneer of Tropical Landscape Architecture: William Lyman Phillips in Florida*. Gainesville: University Press of Florida, 1997.
Jacobs, William F. "Wild Fire and Game." *Florida Conservator* (December 1934).
James, Marquis. *Alfred Dupont: Family Rebel*. Indianapolis: Bobbs-Merrill Company, 1969.
Johnson, Charles. "The Army, the Negro and the CCC." *Military Affairs* 36 (October 1972).
Keene, Jennifer D. *Doughboys, the Great War, and the Remaking of America*. Baltimore: Johns Hopkins University Press, 2001.
Kennedy, David. *Freedom from Fear*. Oxford: Oxford University Press, 1999.
Kennedy, Stetson. *Palmetto Country*. New York: Duell, Sloane and Pearce, 1942.
Kersey, Harry. *The Florida Seminoles and the New Deal, 1933–1942*. Gainesville: University Press of Florida, 1989.
Key, V. O. *Southern Politics in State and Nation*. New York: Alfred Knopf, 1949.
Kirby, Jack Temple. *Counter-Cultural South*. Athens: University of Georgia Press, 1995.
———. *Mockingbird Song: Ecological Landscapes of the South*. Chapel Hill, N.C.: University of North Carolina Press, 2006.
Kiwanis Club of Tallahassee. *Who's Who*. Tallahassee: Kiwanis Club of Tallahassee, 1933.
Kub, C. D. "Florida Black Bass: Dollars or Cents?" *Florida Conservator* (March 1935).
Kulterman, Udo. "Anticipating the Future: The Origins and History of World's Fairs." In *Exit to Tomorrow: World's Fairs Architecture, Design, Fashion, 1933–2006*, ed. Andrew Garn. New York: Universe Publishing, 2007.
Kyrig, David E. *Daily Life in the United States, 1920–1939: Decades of Promise and Pain*. Westport, Conn.: Greenwood Press, 2002.
Lacy, Leslie Alexander. *The Soil Soldiers: The Civilian Conservation Corps in the Great Depression*. Radnor, Pa.: Chilton Book Company, 1976.
Lancek, Lena, and Gideon Bosker. *The Beach: The History of Paradise on Earth*. New York: Viking Press, 1998.
Landrum, Ney, ed. *Histories of the Southeastern State Park Systems*. Tallahassee, Fla.: Association of Southeastern State Parks, 1992.
Lay, Fred. "Two Decades of State Forests in Arkansas." *Arkansas Historical Quarterly*, 24 (Autumn 1965).
Leuchtenburg, William. *Franklin D. Roosevelt and the New Deal*. New York: Harper and Row, 1963.

———. *Perils of Prosperity*. Chicago: University of Chicago Press, 1958.
Lewis, James A. "Cracker: Spanish Florida Style," *Florida Historical Quarterly* 63 (October 1984).
Lindenmeyer, Kriste. *The Greatest Generation Grows Up: American Childhood in the 1930s*. Chicago: Ivan R. Dee, 2005.
Lindley, Betty, and Ernest Lindley. *A New Deal for Youth: The Story of the National Youth Administration*. New York: Viking Press, 1938.
Linley, Tom. "History of the Florida Park System." Tallahassee: Florida Park Service, n.d., www.myflorida.com/communities/learn/stateparks/information/history.
Lippman, Theo. *The Squire of Warm Springs: FDR in Georgia, 1924–1945*. Chicago: Playboy Press, 1977.
Little, Charles. "Smokey's Revenge." *American Forests* 99 (May–June 1993). http://www.majbill.vt.edu/history/barrow/hist3144/readings/little.html.
Lombard, Joanna. "The Memorable Landscapes of William Lyman Phillips." *Journal of Decorative and Propaganda Arts* 23 (1998).
Longstreet, R. J. "The Dollar Values of Florida Birds." *Florida Conservator* (February 1935).
Lowitt, Richard, and Marine Beasley, eds. *One Third of a Nation: Lorena Hickok Reports on the Great Depression*. Urbana: University of Illinois Press, 1981.
Lutts, Ralph. "The Trouble with Bambi: Walt Disney's Bambi and the American Vision of Nature." *Conservation History* 36 (October 1992).
Magill, Inez. *From Ticks to Politics*. N.d. Copy in Florida Room, Florida State Library, Tallahassee.
Maher, Neil M. *Nature's New Deal: The Civilian Conservation Corps and the Roots of the American Environmental Movement*. Oxford: Oxford University Press, 2008.
Maney, Patrick. *The Roosevelt Presence*. Berkeley: University of California Press, 1992.
Matthews, Janet Snyder. *Venice, Journey from Horse and Chaise: A History of Venice, Florida*. Sarasota: Pine Level Press, 1989.
Mattson, Gary Armes. *Small Town, Sprawl and the Politics of Policy Choices: The Florida Experience*. New York: University Press of America, 2002.
May, Kirse Granat. *Golden State, Golden Youth: The California Image in Popular Culture, 1955–1966*. Chapel Hill: University of North Carolina Press, 2002.
McCally, David. *Everglades: An Environmental History*. Gainesville: University Press of Florida, 1999.
McClelland, Linda. *Building the National Parks: Historic Landscape Design and Construction*. Baltimore: Johns Hopkins University Press, 1998.
McElvaine, Robert S. *The Great Depression: America, 1929–1941*. New York: Random House, 1984.
McEntee, James. "CCC and National Defense." *American Forests* (July 1940).
McGovern, James. *Anatomy of a Lynching: The Killing of Claude Neal*. Baton Rouge: Louisiana State University Press, 1982.
McWhiney, Grady. *Cracker Culture: Celtic Ways in the Old South*. Tuscaloosa: University of Alabama Press, 1988.

Mealor, Theodore, and Merle C. Prunty. "Open Range Ranching in Southern Florida." *Annals of the Association of American Geographers* 66, no. 3 (September 1976).
Merrian, Dr. Charles. "The Spirit of Planning." *Conservation* 3 (April–May 1937).
Mertz, Paul. *New Deal Policy and Southern Rural Poverty.* Baton Rouge: Louisiana State University Press, 1978.
Meyer, Jessie Hamm. *Leading the Way: A Century of Service, Florida Federation of Women's Clubs, 1895–1995.* Lakeland: CFWF Federation of Florida Women's Clubs, 1994.
Mills, Char. *Gifford Pinchot and the Making of the Modern Environment.* Washington, D.C.: Island Press, 2004.
Mormino, Gary. "World War II." In *The New History of Florida*, ed. Michael Gannon. Gainesville: University Press of Florida, 1996.
Moyer, Homer, ed. *Who's Who and What to See in Florida.* St. Petersburg: Current Historical Company of Florida, 1935.
Mueller, Edward. *Along the St. Johns and Ocklawaha Rivers.* Charleston, S.C.: Arcadia Press, 1999.
Myers, Ronald L. "Scrub and High Pines." In *Ecosystems of Florida*, ed. Ronald L. Myers and John J. Ewel. Gainesville: University of Florida Press, 1990.
Myers, Ronald L., and John J. Ewel, eds. *Ecosystems of Florida.* Gainesville: University of Florida Press, 1990.
Nash, Gerald D. *The Crucial Era: The Great Depression and World War II.* New York: St. Martin's Press, 1992.
National Emergency Council. *WJAX Radio Broadcast Transcripts.* Jacksonville, Fla.: National Emergency Council, 1939.
National Resources Committee. "The States and Planning." *Conservation* 4 (November–December 1938).
Nelson, David J. "Camp Roosevelt: A Case Study of the NYA in Florida." *Florida Historical Quarterly* 86 (Fall 2007).
———. "The Great Suppression: State Fire Policy in Florida, 1920–1970." *Gulf South Historical Review* 21 (Spring 2006).
———. "'Improving Paradise': The Civilian Conservation Corps and Environmental Change in Florida." In *Paradise Lost? The Environmental History of Florida*, ed. Jack Davis. Gainesville: University Press of Florida, 2005.
———. "A New Deal for Welfare: Governor Fred Cone and the Florida State Welfare Board." *Florida Historical Quarterly* 84 (Fall 2005).
———. "Rejecting Paradise: Tourism, Conservation, and the Birth of the Modern Florida Cracker in the 1930s." *Florida Historical Quarterly* 97 (Summer 2018).
———. "When Modern Tourism Was Born: Florida at the World Fairs and on the World Stage in the 1930s." *Florida Historical Quarterly* 89 (Spring 2010).
Newton, Michael. *The Invisible Empire: The Ku Klux Klan in Florida.* Gainesville: University Press of Florida, 2001.
Nolan, David. *Fifty Feet in Paradise: The Booming of Florida.* New York: Harcourt Brace Jovanovich, 1984.

Otis, Alison, et al. *The Forest Service and the Civilian Conservation Corps: 1933–42*. Washington, D.C.: Government Printing Office, 1986.
Otto, John Solomon. "Traditional Cattle Herding Practices in Florida." *Journal of American Folklore* 97 (July–September 1984).
Owens, A. L. Reisch. *Conservation Under FDR*. New York: Praeger, 1983.
Oxley, Howard W. "Growth and Accomplishments of CCC Education." *Phi Delta Kappan* 19 (May 1937).
Paige, John C. *The Civilian Conservation Corps and the National Park Service: 1933–1942*. Washington, D.C.: Government Printing Office, 1985.
Patterson, James T. *America's Struggle Against Poverty, 1900–1994*. Cambridge: Harvard University Press, 1994.
———. *The New Deal and the State: Federalism in Transition*. Princeton: Princeton University Press, 1969.
Perkins, Frances. *The Roosevelt I Knew*. New York: Viking Press, 1946.
Persons, W. Frank. "Human Resources in the Civilian Conservation Corps." *Phi Delta Kappan* 19 (May 1937).
Philip, Kenneth R. "Turmoil at Big Cypress: Seminole Deer and the Florida Cattle Tick Controversy." *Florida Historical Quarterly* 56 (July 1977).
Pictorial Review, District I, Company 2444, SP-5 Starke, Florida (Starke, 1939).
"Planning from the Ground Up." *Conservation* 3 (November–December 1937).
Preston, Howard Lawrence. *Dirt Roads to Dixie: Accessibility and Modernization in the South, 1885–1935*. Knoxville: University of Tennessee Press, 1991.
Proceedings of the 46th Annual Meeting of the Florida State Horticultural Society. Deland: Florida State Horticultural Society. Available at Florida State Library, Tallahassee.
Proceedings of the 47th Annual Meeting. Deland: Florida State Horticultural Society.
Proceedings of the 48th Annual Meeting. Deland: Florida State Horticultural Society.
Proceedings of the 52nd Annual Meeting. Deland: Florida State Horticultural Society.
Putnam, Lt. Col. Carl M. "The CCC Experience." *Military Review* 53 (September 1973).
Putz, Francis E. "Are Rednecks the Unsung Heroes of Ecosystem Management?" *Wild Earth* (Summer 2003).
Pyne, Stephen. *Fire in America: A Cultural History of Wildfire and Rural Fire*. Princeton: Princeton University Press, 1982.
Reagan, Patrick D. *Designing a New America: The Origins of New Deal Planning, 1890–1943*. Lawrence: University of Kansas Press, 1999.
"Recreational Industry in Florida." *Conservation* 7 (September–October 1941).
Reiger, John F. *American Sportsmen and the Origins of Conservation*. New York: Winchester Press, 1975; rev. ed., Corvallis: Oregon State University Press, 2001.
Reiman, Richard. *The New Deal and American Youth: Ideas and Ideals in a Depression Decade*. Athens: University of Georgia Press, 1992.
Revels, Tracy J. *Sunshine Paradise: A History of Florida Tourism*. Gainesville: University Press of Florida, 2011.
———. *Watery Eden: A History of Wakulla Springs*. Tallahassee, Fla: Sentry Press, 2002.

Reynolds, Charles B. *The Story of Ask Mr. Foster.* St. Augustine: Ask Mr. Foster, 1937.
Rogers, Ben F. "Florida in World War II: Tourists and Citrus." *Florida Historical Quarterly* 39 (July 1960).
Rogers, William. "The Great Depression." In *New History of Florida*, ed. Michael Gannon. Gainesville: University Press of Florida, 1996.
———. "The Paradoxical Twenties. In *New History of Florida*, ed. Michael Gannon. Gainesville: University Press of Florida, 1996.
Rowe, Anne. *The Idea of Florida in the American Literary Imagination.* Gainesville: University Press of Florida, 1992.
Rydell, Robert W. *World of Fairs: The Century of Progress Experience.* Chicago: University of Chicago Press, 1993.
Salmond, John A. *The Civilian Conservation Corps, 1933–1942.* Durham, N.C.: Duke University Press, 1967.
———. "The Civilian Conservation Corps and the Negro." *Journal of American History* 52 (June 1965).
Schlesinger, Arthur. *Age of Roosevelt*, vol. 2: *Coming of the New Deal.* Boston: Houghton Mifflin, 1958.
Scoggin, Lewis. "History of Florida State Parks." *Florida Park Service News* 5 (June 1947).
Scott, John M. *Livestock in Florida.* Bulletin 12. Tallahassee: State of Florida, Department of Agriculture, 1929.
Sebring Historical Society. *Highlands Hammock.* 1966; repr. Sebring, Fla.: Sebring Historical Society, 1979.
Shea, John. "Our Pappies Burned the Woods." *American Forests* (April 1940), 159–70.
Shofner, Jerrell. *Jackson County, Florida: A History.* Marianna: Jackson County Heritage Association, 1985.
———. "Roosevelt's 'Tree Army': The Civilian Conservation Corps in Florida." *Florida Historical Quarterly* 65 (Spring 1987).
———. "The White Springs Post Office Caper." *Florida Historical Quarterly* 56 (January 1978).
Silverthorne, Elizabeth. *Marjorie Kinnan Rawlings: Sojourner at Cross Creek.* Woodstock, N.Y.: Overlook Press, 1988.
Simmons, Glen, and Laura Ogden. *Gladesmen: Gator Hunters, Moonshiners and Skiffers.* Gainesville: University Press of Florida, 1998.
Skaggs, Jimmy M. *Prime Cut: Livestock Raising and Meatpacking in the United States, 1607–1983.* College Station: Texas A&M University Press, 1986.
Solo-Gabriele, Helena, et al. *Quantities of Arsenic Within the State of Florida.* Gainesville: Florida Center for Solid Waste and Hazardous Waste Management, State University System of Florida, 2003.
Standiford, Les. *Last Train to Paradise: Henry Flagler and the Spectacular Rise and Fall of the Railroad that Crossed an Ocean.* New York: Broadway Books, 1998.
Starge, Maren. "Publicity, Husbandry and Technocracy: Fact and Symbol in Civilian Con-

servation Corps Photography." In *Official Images: New Deal Photography*, ed. Pete Daniel. Washington, D.C.: Smithsonian Institute Press, 1987.

St. Clair, Dana. *The Cracker Culture in Florida History*. Daytona, Fla.: Museum of Arts and Science, 1998; repr., Gainesville: University Press of Florida, 2007.

Steen, Harold. *The U.S. Forest Service: A History*. Seattle: University of Washington Press, 1976.

Stoddard, Herbert L. *Memoirs of a Naturalist*. Norman: University of Oklahoma Press, 1969.

———. "Use of Fire in Pine Forests and Game Lands of the Deep Southeast." In *Tall Timbers Fire Ecology Conference Proceedings, Volume 1*. Tallahassee, 1962.

Strom, Claire. *Making Catfish Bait out of Government Boys: The Fight Against Cattle Ticks and the Transformation of the Yeoman South*. Athens: University of Georgia Press, 2009.

———. "Texas Fever and the Dispossession of the Southern Yeoman Farmer." *Journal of Southern History* 66 (2000).

Sullivan, John J. "The Civilian Conservation Corps and the Creation of Myakka River State Park." *Tampa Bay History* 9 (Winter 1987).

Sweet, John F. "The Civilian Conservation Corps in Florida." *Apalachee* 6 (1967).

Tarr, Rodger L., and Brent E. Kinser, eds. *The Uncollected Writings of Marjorie Kinnan Rawlings*. Gainesville: University Press of Florida, 2007.

Taylor, Bob Pepperman. *Our Limits Transgressed: Environmental Political Thought in America*. Lawrence: University of Kansas Press, 1992.

Tebeau, Charlton. *History of Florida*. Coral Gables: University of Miami Press, 1971.

Terkel, Studs. *Hard Times: An Oral History of the Great Depression*. New York: Random House, 1970.

Tilden, Freeman. *The State Parks: Their Meaning in American Life*. New York: Alfred A. Knopf, 1962.

Tucker, Gilbert A. *Before the Timber Was Cut*. Self-published, 1999.

United Daughters of the Confederacy, Florida Division. *Minutes of the 36th Annual Convention, Florida Division, United Daughters of the Confederacy*. Opelika, Ala: Post Publishing Company 1933.

———. *Minutes of the 38th Annual Convention*. Opelika, Ala: Post Publishing Company 1935.

———. *Minutes of the 40th Annual Convention*. Opelika, Ala: Post Publishing Company 1937.

———. *Minutes of the 43rd Annual Convention*. Opelika, Ala: Post Publishing Company 1940.

———. *Minutes of the 45th Annual Convention*. Opelika, Ala: Post Publishing Company 1942.

United States, Civilian Conservation Corps. *Memories of District "I" Fourth Corps Area, CCC 1940*. Washington, D.C: Government Printing Office, 1940.

———. *The CCC and Colored Youth*. Washington, D.C.: Government Printing Office, 1941.

———. *The CCC and Public Recreation*. Washington, D.C.: Government Printing Office, 1941.

———. *The Civilian Conservation Corps Contributing to the Defense of the Nation.* Washington, D.C.: Government Printing Office, 1941.
———. *CCC Standards of Eligibility for Enrollment.* Washington, D.C.: Government Printing Office, 1941.
———. *Work Experience That Counts.* Washington, D.C.: Government Printing Office, 1941.
United States Senate, Committee on Indian Affairs. *Eradicating Cattle Tick, Seminole Indian Reservation, Florida.* Washington, D.C.: Government Printing Office, 1941.
Utley, Dan K., and James W. Steely. *Guided With a Steady Hand: The Cultural Landscape of a Rural Texas Park.* Waco: Baylor University Press, 1998.
Vance, Linda. "May Mann Jennings and Royal Palm State Park." *Florida Historical Quarterly* 55 (Summer 1977).
———. *May Mann Jennings: Florida's Genteel Activist.* Gainesville: University Press of Florida, 1985.
Vickers, Raymond. *Panic in Paradise: The Florida Banking Crisis of 1926.* Tuscaloosa: University of Alabama Press, 1994.
Vinten, C. R. "The Conservation of Historic Sites in Florida." *Florida Historical Quarterly* 23 (Fall 1944).
Wandall, Luther C. "A Negro in the CCC." *Crisis* 42 (August 1935).
Ware, Susan. *Holding Their Own: American Women in the 1930s.* Boston: Twayne Publishing, 1982.
Warner, Joe G. *Biscuits and Taters: A History of Cattle Ranching in Manatee County.* Bradenton, Fla.: Warner, 1980.
Watkins, T. H. *Great Depression: America in the Great Depression.* New York: Little Brown and Company, 1993.
———. *The Hungry Years: A Narrative History of the Great Depression in America.* New York: Henry Holt and Company, 1999.
———. *Righteous Pilgrim: The Life and Times of Harold L. Ickes, 1874–1952.* New York: Henry Holt and Company, 1990.
Weigall, T. H. *Boom in Paradise.* New York: Alfred H. King, 1932.
West, Patsy. *The Enduring Seminoles: From Alligator Wrestling to Ecotourism.* Gainesville: University of Florida Press, 1998.
Whitfield, Stephen J. "Florida's Fudged Identity." *Florida Historical Quarterly* 74 (Summer, 1995).
Wilson, Lorenzo. "Florida at the Century of Progress Exposition," *Proceedings of the 47th Annual Meeting of the Florida Horticultural Society.* Deland: Florida Horticultural Society, 1934.
Wirth, Conrad L., Department of the Interior. *Civilian Conservation Corps Camps of the U.S. Department of the Interior, March 1933–June 20 1933.* Washington, D.C.: Government Printing Office, 1944.
———. *Parks, Politics and the People.* Norman: University of Oklahoma Press, 1980.
"With the Civilian Conservation Corps." *American Forests* 39 (July 1933).

Woodruff, Nan. *As Rare as Rain: Federal Relief in the Great Southern Drought of 1930–1*. Urbana: University of Illinois Press, 1985.

Woodward, Hugh M. "Recreation: A Philosophy of Joyful Living." *Conservation* 4 (January–February 1941).

Works Progress Administration (WPA). *The Florida Tourist: A Preliminary Report of the Florida Tourism Survey Project*. Florida State Chamber of Commerce, September 1939.

Wright, Marian Thompson. "Negro Youth and the Federal Emergency Programs: CCC and NYA." *Journal of Negro Education* 9 (July 1940).

Wynne, Nick. *The Tin Can Tourists in Florida*. Charleston, S.C.: Arcadia Press, 1999.

Index

Ackerman, Morris, 182
African Americans, 169; CCC and, 129, 132; CCC Company #5480 and, 129; Gov. Cone and, 161; economic conditions of in Florida, 27; Florida Caverns State Park and, 203; Little Talbot Island State Park and, 96, 203; Myakka River State Park and, 134–35; New York World's Fair (1939) and, 195; state parks and, 96, 134–36, 203; Torreya State Park and, 135–36; tourism and, 203. *See also* Lynchings; Segregation
Agricultural Adjustment Administration (AAA), 20, 26
Agriculture: citrus, 7, 11, 26, 35; cotton, 10, 11, 12; livestock, 174–81; Mediterranean fruit fly, 26; strawberries, 11. *See also* Cattle ranching; Ranching; Sharecroppers and sharecropping; Turpentine industry; Turpentiners
Air conditioning, 72
Alachua County, 160, 166
Albright, Horace, 60
Allapattah Flats Swamp, 180
All-Florida Advertising Campaign, 70–75; abolished by Gov. Cone, 195; European campaign of, 73–74; Florida Forestry Service and, 75; funding of, 71; Grassfield as secretary, 70; national media, 71–72; Overman as vice chair, 70; success of, 72–73; Gov. Sholtz as chair, 70; William Wilson and, 73; WPA and, 73
Alligators, 46, 177
Alsberg, Henry, 192
Altvater, A. C., 81, 89, 120, 122–23, 146

Amelia Island, 95, 203
American Beach, 203
American Federation of Labor (AFL), 24
American Folkways series, 169
American Forest Association (AFA), 52
American Forests, 200
American Tree Association, 31
Amos, Ernest, 207
Andrews, A. H., 150
Apalachicola National Forest, 142, 144, 148, 152; CCC and, 85
Apalachicola River, 58, 117, 124
Appleyard, Thomas J., 7, 209
Archaeology, 77, 85–86, 95
Association of County Commissioners of Florida, 70
Atlanta, 201
Audubon Society, 80
Avon Park, 33, 34

Babson, Roger, 40
Bacon, E. J., 135
Baker, Harry Lee, 31, 32, 35, 39, 50, 51, 57, 65, 66, 206; anger over African Americans at Myakka River State Park, 135; author of *Forest Fires in Florida*, 50; creation of FPS and, 53, 58; criticisms of, 75; FAIR and, 53; fire and, 144, 170–74; fire prevention and, 170–74; on Florida Caverns, 76; Santa Rosa Island and, 158; on state forests as tourist attractions, 52, 61; state parks, 60–61, 90; on state parks as tourist attractions, 76; C. R. Vinten and, 158. *See also* Florida Forestry Service; Florida Park Service

Ball, Edward, 40, 47, 196; Century of Progress, 61; chair, park and playgrounds subcommittee, 62; purchase of Wakulla Springs, 62. *See also* Century of Progress International Exposition; Wakulla Springs
Barbour, George, 45
Barnes, Foster, 193
Barracks Bag (CCC newsletter), 131
Baynard, Oscar: author, *Birds of Hillsborough River,* 80; biography of, 78, 80; bird lists of, 78; Everglades and, 80; Hillsborough River State Park and, 78, 79, 203; as ornithologist, 80; park interpretation and, 80; publicity, 80. *See also* Park interpretation
Beach, Rex, 34, 35
Beall, Philip, 157
Beautification, 138–40
Beck, Carol: park interpretation and, 92; as park naturalist, 92. *See also* Park interpretation
Bennett, Charles E, 95–96
Bentley, E. R., 32
Benton, Felix, 62, 79
Benton (Florida), 154
Billings, J. S., 201
"Binder boys," 14, 192
Birch, Hugh Taylor, 94
Bishopp, Dr. F. C., 180
"Black Thursday," 9
"Black Tuesday," 9
Blair, Alexander, 35
Board of Workman's Compensation, 64
Boca Raton, 13
Bohleber, Carl, 117
Bok, Edward, 33
Bok Tower, 33–34, 41, 48, 140
Boll weevil, 170
Bonita Springs, 15, 150
Bonus Marches, 24
Brodie, L. R., 147
Brooksville, 55, 93, 150
Broward County, 94, 180
Brown, Earl W., 40, 41, 185, 195. *See also* Florida National Exhibits

Bryan, William Jennings, 14
Bullock, Orin, 35
Bureau of Immigration, 37–38, 43; advertising fund of, 37

Caldwell, Erskine, 169
California, 21, 43, 70, 197; forest fires and, 50; rivalry with Florida, 39–40, 43, 70; state parks and, 60; tourism and, 70
Caloosahatchee Valley, 175
Camp Benning, 115
Camp Blanding, 201
Camping, 199
Cape Florida State Park, 199
Carlton, Gov. Doyle, 7, 28, 38–39, 138
Castillo de San Marcos National Monument, 186–87
Cattle, 174–80
Cattle dipping, 26, 175, 176
Cattle fencing, 165
Cattle ranching, 26, 172–74; cattle on highways, 47; reactions to Baker, 172–74. *See also* Agriculture; Cattle dipping; Ranching
Cattle tick fever, 175, 180
C-bring C-amp C-ourier (CCC newsletter), 142
CCC Company #AF-5, 201
CCC Company #2444, 83, 122, 129, 130, 141, 201
CCC Company #262, 124
CCC Company #453, 118
CCC Company #5480, 129
Century of Progress International Exposition, 36, 37, 61; Court of States, 41, 42; FDR on Florida exhibit, 70; Florida exhibit, 39–42, 43, 44, 49, 69, 70, 71, 177, 208; Florida Hall, 43; number of visitors, 43; origin of, 38. *See also* Florida National Exhibits; World Fairs
Cermak, Anton, 18
Chicago, 18, 36, 38–39, 41, 44, 49, 70, 193, 194, 199, 207
Chicago Tribune, 72
Chipley, William D., 45

Chipola River, 84
Choctawhatchee National Forest, 148
Christmas (Florida), 12
Civilian Conservation Corps (CCC): abolished, 201; accidents in, 124; African Americans and, 131, 136; archaeology and, 77; beautification and, 138–41; boxing in, 125, 240n104; building state parks, 69, 76–87; camp educational advisers, 128–29, 130, 133, 140; camp newsletters, 126, 130, 131, 132; camps, 25, 30, 36, 58, 59, 60, 62, 64, 67, 117, 117–30, 142, 144, 201; communities reject African American CCC camps, 131, 134–35, 224n26, 243n174; conditioning camps, 114–15; creation of, 20–21; criticisms of, 24, 25; death of two CCC enrollees at Torreya State Park, 124; deer and, 182, 142, 143; drainage of wetlands, 144; economic benefits of, 30; education and, 22–23, 115, 127, 131; enrollees and local romances, 126; enrollees' attitudes about CCC education, 129–30; enrollees, 24, 30–31, 69, 91, 113, 115, 116, 118, 119–34; exotics and, 148, 149; fire and, 143, 149; fire prevention and, 53, 145, 146, 147, 172; first camp, 25; Florida and, 30–31, 158, 160; Florida State Planning Board and, 63; food and, 121–22; FPS and, 69, 89–90, 116; general cleanup projects, 141–42, 144; hazing and, 123–24; inspection of CCC camps, 122; job training and, 22, 120–21; labor and, 23–24; LEMs, 119, 120; mosquitoes and, 144; Native Americans and, 31; nature and, 118, 137–41, 144–49; NPS and, 24, 115; Office of the Director, 122; origins of, 21, 22; palmettos and, 142; pay for enrollees, 126–27; popularity of, 25–26, 30, 53; project designations, 224n26; publicity, 113; racism and, 133–34; recreation and, 59, 124–27, 133; recruitment, 113–14; salaries, 24; segregation and, 131–34; snakes and, 143; sports and, 124–25; staffing Florida state parks, 69, 78, 80–82, 115, 116–17, 206; state parks and, 58–59, 115, 116, 118–19, 137, 201; tree planting and, 25, 141, 147–49; typical day in, 119–20, 124; U.S. Army and, 24, 114–15, 119, 124, 127; U.S. Congress and, 201; U.S. Forest Service and, 116; venereal diseases and, 122; vocational training and, 129–30; weekend trips to local communities, 126–27; weight gain in, 121; woods improvement, and, 141–42; WWII and, 200–201; youth and, 21, 22. See also Fechner, Robert; Florida Forestry Service, Florida Park Service, National Park Service; U.S. Forestry Service
Civil Works Administration (CWA), 20, 30, 32, 61
Clarke-McNary Act (1924), 51, 52
Cleveland, 70, 159, 182, 193, 201, 207, 208
Clyde Line Steamers, 73
Coachman, Walter, 62
Cobb, James, 169
Codrington, Clayton C., 121; campaign manager for Cone, 159; Florida State Welfare Commissioner, 21, 159
Coldwell, Walter, 62, 79
Coldwell, William, 66
Collier, Baron, 48
Collier County, 48
Columbia County, 154
Columbia Forests and Farms, Inc., 83
Committee on the Century of Progress Exposition, 36, 37, 39–40
Cone, Branch, 159
Cone, Charles, 155
Cone, Gov. Fred, 123, 153, 187, 191, 192, 196; African Americans and, 161; ambitions for U.S. Senate, 160–61, 208; anger of, 155; attempted murder of Morrison, 155; background of, 153–55; Harry Lee Baker and, 158; cronyism of, 160; Democratic Party and, 154; election of, 159; FDR and, 154; governing style of, 155–56, 161; his political base and, 159, 160; lynchings and, 161; New Deal and, 153–54, 159; New York World's Fair and, 195–97; non-Floridians ("foreigners") and, 153–54, 156, 157; NPS and, 158; NYC and, 155,

Cone, Gov. Fred—*continued*
  161, 195–97, 258n45; politics of, 153–54; Santa Rosa Island and, 158; segregation and, 161–61; Joseph Shoemaker and, 161; Gov. Sholtz and, 155, 158, 160; State Board of Public Welfare and, 153; State Board of Social Welfare and, 157, 158, 160; State Welfare Board and, 158, 159; tick eradication and, 181, 182; tourism and, 140, 154, 161, 162; U.S. 19 and, 207; white supremacy and, 161
Coney, Neill, 122–23
Conkin, Paul, 21
Conner, Doyle, 37
Conservation, 182–87; laws and, 184, 185; tourism and, 184–85
Conservation magazine, 59
Coral Gables, 13
Coulter, C. H., 75, 170, 174
Cowart, Hillary, 115–16; on FDR, 160; on hazing in CCC, 123
Crackers, 153, 154, 159, 163–70, 182; fire and, 253n43; historical debates over, 252n8; as marker of class, 165, 167; *New York Times* and, 166–67; origins and evolution of term, 166–70, 252n8; as racial term, 167; Marjorie Kinnan Rawlings and, 166, 168–69, 172, 173; as a reaction to tourism, 169–70; tourism and, 165; as tourist attraction, 199; wildlife and, 185, 186
Cracker song tradition, 165
Crestview, 157
Cross Creek, 168, 169
Crowley, Allen, 80
Crystal River, 54
Cuba, 167, 176
Cunard White Star Lines, 73, 74
Cutler, Phoebe, 141
Cypress Gardens, 150, 198

Dade County, 16, 55, 63, 140, 160
Davis, George, 174, 180
Davis, Jack, 41
Dawes, Rufus, 38, 39
Daytona, 75, 194
Daytona Humane Society, 181
DDT, 45, 72
Decker, William, park superintendent, Fort Clinch State Park, 202
Deer, tick eradication and, 175, 179–83, 187–88; tourism and, 182
DeGirolamo, Paul, CCC enrollee at Hillsborough River State Park, 116, 118; on CCC, 116; on Depression, 116; on FDR, 160
Deland, 40, 41
Denham, Thomas, 189
DePriest, Oscar, 132
Dick Tracy, Florida tourism and, 72
Disney, Walt: world fairs and, 257n23
Dixie County, 65, 166
Donaldson, C. S., 34
Douglas, Marjory Stoneman, 56–57, 138, 182; author, *Parks and Playgrounds of Florida*, 77, 91, 138, 182; on fishing, 183–84; house owned by the FPS, 199; May Mann Jennings and, 57; state parks and, 77; on tourism, 150, 151, 183–84
Dowling, George, 184, 187
Dunedin, 150
DuPont, Alfred, 47, 61
Duval County, 36, 58, 63, 66, 95, 96
Dye, Dewey, 76

Eagle's Nest Gardens, 150
Eastman, Scott, and Company, 71
Edwards, A. B., 76, 117; donated land for Myakka River State Park, 83; Little Talbot Island and, 95; park board member, 95
Edwards, W. T., 67
Ellaville, 93
Everglades, 14, 42, 48, 55, 56, 64, 80; at Century of Progress, 42
Everglades National Park, 56, 67–68, 76, 94, 208; and Pan-American State Park, 94. *See also* Jennings, May Mann; National Park Service; Pan-American State Park
Everglades Park Commission, 64, 67
Evison, Herbert, 123

Fairbanks, Charles, 86
Famous Trees Botanical Gardens, 150
Fanning Springs State Park, 78
Farmers, 70
Fechner, Robert, 58–59, 63, 117; chosen as CCC director, 24; education in CCC and, 127, 128; on state parks, 59; on tree planting, 148
Federal Emergency Relief Administration (FERA), 11, 20, 32, 62, 66, 129; state park surveys, 62, 95, 158
Federal Parks, Parkways and Recreation Study Act, 189–90
Federal Roads Act, 47
Federal Writers' Project, 59, 169, 191–92; fire and, 172; *Florida: A Guide to the Southernmost State*, 169, 191–92; tourism and, 191–92
Federated Garden Clubs of Florida, 36
Fenn, T. J., 157
Fernandina, 134, 203
Finlayson, D. A., 79, 84
Fire, prescribed burns, 171–72, 253n43; Gold Head Branch State Park and, 247n71
Fire prevention, 165
Fisher, Carl, 13
Fishing, 42, 53, 182–83, 189, 190; black bass banned for commercial fishing, 182; tourism and, 183
Flagler, Henry, 13, 45, 46
Fletcher, Duncan Upshaw, 29, 134, 175, 180
Florida: advertising and, 69, 71–73, 161; African Americans and, 27, 161; agriculture and, 7, 10, 11, 15, 16, 20, 174–81; banks and banking, 16, 28; beautification and, 15, 138–41; birds and, 185–86; citrus and, 16, 177; climate and weather and, 13, 15, 45; conservation and, 182–87; convict labor and, 138–39; Depression in, 9, 26, 153, 165; economic conditions, 26–27; exotics and, 198; fire and, 144, 149, 165, 170–74, 177; forestry and, 170; gardens and, 149, 150; image of in Europe, 74; lynchings and, 161; nature and, 137–49; nature as tourism and, 149–52; New Deal and, 63, 154–55, 159, 191, 192; number of visitors to, 43–44, 45, 76; politics and, 28; popular image of, 9, 33, 41, 44–45, 72, 74, 162–64, 169–70, 182–83; population, 15; poverty and, 11–12, 13; real estate and, 13, 14; relief and welfare, 17, 26, 27; roadside attractions, 149–52; songs about, 162–63, 164–65; southern image of, 7, 162–64, 206–7, 208; springs and, 149–50; state song, 162–63; taxes and, 13–14, 27; timber and, 16, 50, 170; tourism and, 17, 38, 39–40, 42, 45–49, 69, 90, 93, 115, 161, 165, 170, 179, 184–85, 189; tourists and, 15, 190, 192–93; unemployment and, 17; wildlife and, 177, 181–87, 190
Florida Agricultural College, 162
Florida Agriculture and Industrial Relief Commission (FAIR), 53
Florida Agriculture and Mechanical University (FAMU), 161, 195
Florida Asylum for Indigent Insane, 27
Florida Banking Act, 28
Florida Board of Forestry, 56, 75, 158; creation of, 57; Highlands Hammock State Park and, 81, 82
Florida Board of Forestry and Parks, 94
Florida Board of Parks and Historic Memorials, 79
Florida Cabinet, 37, 161
Florida Cattleman, 178
Florida Cattlemen's Association, 178, 181
Florida Caverns State Park, 130, 133, 152, 201, 203, 205; African Americans and, 203; archaeology and, 85–86; beautification and, 138–40; caves and, 84, 85–86; CCC company #1445 and, 85; CCC involvement ends, 202; CCC park supt. A. D. Lawson and, 81; construction of by the CCC, 84–86, 88–89, 90, 117; diorama exhibit of, 79; discovery of new caves, 85–86; discovery of whale fossil (Zeuglodon), 86, 87; hazing at CCC camp, 123; location of, 75; Native Americans and, 85, 180; park naturalist Leonard Giovanoli, 80; park supt. Clarence Simpson, 79, 80,

286 · Index

Florida Caverns State Park—*continued*
85–86; plans for, 78; publicity, 79; PWA and, 85; "Sholtz Park," 78; staffing, 80; tourism and, 75–76, 198–99; visitation, 91; WWI veterans and, 84; WWII and, 204. *See also* Civilian Conservation Corps; Florida Park Service; Marianna; National Park Service

Florida Citrus Commission, 64

Florida Clipping Service, 177

Florida Conservator, 186

Florida Dept. of Agriculture, 35, 37, 43, 71, 77

Florida Dept. of Conservation, 186

Florida Dept. of Environmental Protection, 198

Florida East Coast Railway, 17, 45, 62

Florida Emergency Relief Administration, 156, 157

Florida Federal Writers' Project, 59, 169

Florida Federation of Women's Clubs (FFWC), 55, 56, 139, 171, 187; conservation and, 177; wildlife and, 177. *See also* Jennings, May Mann; Royal Palm State Park

Florida Folk Festival, 164–65

Florida Forestry and Parks Board, 189, 202

Florida Forestry Association, 50

Florida Forestry Board, 31, 79; creation of, 52; Florida Park service and, 64

Florida Forestry Service (FFS): All-Florida Advertising Campaign and, 75; creation of in 1927, 49, 51, 52; fire prevention and, 171; NPS and, 158; tourism and, 75; tree planting and, 148, 149. *See also* Baker, Harry Lee; Jennings, May Mann

Florida Garden and Arboretum, 36, 65, 82, 118; closed, 204

Florida Geological Society, 80, 85

Florida governor, office of the, 27

Florida Grower, 194

Florida Health and Welfare Council, 156

Florida Highway Patrol, 192

Florida Highways, 194

Florida Horticultural Society, 138, 141, 150; beautification and, 141

Florida Hotel Commission, 190–91

Florida Land Boom, 8, 16, 37, 48, 73, 192

Florida Land Crash, 16

Florida Legislature, 30, 56, 66, 196; created FPS, 64; legalized pari-mutuel betting, 71

"Florida, My Florida" (state song), 162

Florida National Exhibits (FNE), 40–41, 42, 193–95, 208; creation of, 40

Florida Panhandle Hotel Corporation, 17

Florida Park Service (FPS), 32, 36, 142, 153, 164, 192, 196, 207; administration of, 79–80, 115; admission fees, 82, 90; African Americans and, 161, 203–4; beer parties in parks, 203; budget, 64, 91, 204; cabins and, 83; camping and, 91; CCC and, 69, 80–81, 89–90; CCC enrollees staffing parks, 69, 80–81, 91, 202, 204–5; CCC involvement ends, 201–2; closed parks because of WWII, 204–5; conflicts with NPS, 69, 76, 87–90; creation of, 53, 58, 64; dynamite and, 91; employees, 79–80, 92–93, 202, 231n81; exotics and, 150; expansion of, 93, 96; fires and, 144–49; first employee hired, 69; first female field employee (Carol Beck), 92; first state park, 223n15; gas rationing and, 202–3; Highlands Hammock and, 36; locations of parks, 75; NPS and, 69, 80, 83, 87, 158; NPS staffing parks, 80–81; park caretakers, 91–92; park interpretation, 78–79, 92, 148; park maintenance, 80–81; park rules, 91; parks as tourist attractions, 53, 75–76, 87–88, 90, 205, 206; plans for state parks, 77–78; post-WWII, 205–6; publicity, 76–77, 78–79, 81, 148, 182; radio program (WTAL), 78; Santa Rosa Island and, 158; segregation and, 96, 160, 161, 162, 203–4; U.S. Army and, 203; visitation, 90, 206; war workers and, 203; wildlife and, 187; WWII and, 96, 198–200, 202. *See also* Civilian Conservation Corps; Florida Forestry Service; Jennings, May Mann; Malsberger, Henry J.; National Park Service; Schaeffer, Charles H.; Scoggin, Lewis; *individual parks*

Florida Park Service News (newsletter), 206

Florida Research Bureau, 179
Florida Senate, 157
Florida Southern College, 141
Florida State Chamber of Commerce, 29, 70, 145, 182, 189
Florida State Liquor Board, 64
Florida State Planning Board, 53, 61–62, 94, 138, 146, 182, 189, 201; CCC and, 63–64; tourism and, 75
Florida State Road, 61
Florida State University, 174
Florida State Welfare Board, 63
Florida Times Union, 29
Florida Tourist: A Preliminary Report of the Florida Tourism Survey Program, 189–90
Flushing Meadows, NY, 193
Foley, Harold, 75
Forest Capital State Park, 199
Forest Fire Prevention Week, 31
Forest fires: changes in attitudes toward, 49–50; "Dixie Crusaders," 52; prescribed fires and controlled burns, 50; prevention of, 31, 51–53; state policy on, 49. *See also* Civilian Conservation Corps; Florida Forestry Service
Forest Fires in Florida, 170
Fort Barracas, 115
Fort Caroline, 95–96
Fort Caroline National Monument, 96
Fort Clinch (Fernandina, Florida): history of, 84; restoration of, 87. *See also* Fort Clinch State Park
Fort Clinch State Park, 134, 140, 201, 202, 203; admission fees and, 90; CCC project SP-8, 83, 115–16; CCC projects ends, 202; closed because of WWII, 204; condition of CCC camp, 122; construction of by CCC, 84, 87, 117, 140; erosion control and, 83; hazing at CCC camp, 123; location of, 75; mosquitoes and, 144; publicity, 79; as tourist attraction, 75, 76; visitation and, 90–91
Fort Lauderdale, 73
Fort Matanzas, 76
Fort Myers, 150, 177

Fort Pierce, 184–85
Foster, Stephen, 42, 90, 162, 194
Foster, Ward G., 46
Fox Movietone News, 186
Fussell, Harris, 175

Gainesville, 159
Galbraith, John Kenneth, 15
Gamble Plantation State Park, 198, 206–7
Game and Fresh Water Fish, 184
Ganiere, George E., 42, 193
Gas rationing, 199–200, 202–3
Gas tax, 27, 178
General Inspection Fund, 37
General Revenue Fund, 37
Germany, 73–74
Giovanoli, Leonard, 80, 231n85
Glisson, Vera, 79, 231n81
Goggin, John, 85–86
Gold Head Branch State Park, 115–16, 125, 128, 130, 137, 141, 150, 178–79; acquired by FPS, 83; admission fees and, 90; African Americans and, 135–36; bobcats and, 142; cabins and, 83; CCC Company #AF-5, 201; CCC Company #2444, 83, 122; CCC involvement ends, 201; construction of by the CCC, 87–88, 117, 119; deer and, 142–43; fires and, 145, 147; "improving" natural features, 149; Lake Johnson, 83; land donated by Mike Roess, 83; location of, 75; opened for public, 90; plans for, 78; publicity and, 79; ravine and, 77, 149; sawmill and, 78, 119; as tourist attraction, 75; traveling exhibit and, 79; U.S. Army and, 203; visitation and, 90; WWII and, 204
Good, Albert, 81
Goodwood Plantation, 39, 208
Gore, Robert Hayes, 94
Gormes, Gen. Samuel, 203
Granberry, Julian, 85
Grassfield, Robert, 70
Gray, R. A., 29
Great Britain: Florida tourism and, 73–74; image of Florida, 74
Great Bull Market, 8

Great Depression, 8–9, 19, 165, 174; causes of, 8–9; tourism and, 48–49; unemployment and, 19, 22
Great Lakes Exposition, 70
Green, Ray, 34
Green, William, 24, 25
Green Cove Springs, 55
Greene, M. B., 80, 81, 202
Greynolds Park, 65, 140
Griffin, B. H., 80, 202, 203
Gross, George, 201, 225n61
Gufford, Albert, 47
Gunter, Herman, 86–87

Hale, Arthur, 138
Hall, Ansley, 11, 121, 126, 130: CCC enrollee at Highlands Hammock State Park, 121; on vocational training in CCC, 130
Hall, Stanley, 22
Hardee, Gov. Cary, 37
Hawkins, Joe, 35
Heath, Buck, 12, 86, 151–52; on removing palmettos from Florida Caverns, 142; on vocational training in CCC, 130
Hickok, Lorena, 11, 32; on citrus industry, 212n27; on Florida tourism, 49; on Sholtz, 32
Hicks, Bobby, 164, 165
Highlands County, 35, 182
Highlands Hammock: became a state park, 35–36, 82; CCC and, 36; funding of, 82; as Hooker's Hammock, 34; publicity and, 82; purchased by Roebling family, 33–35; and Tropical Parks Association and, 34–35
Highlands Hammock, Inc., 34, 36, 82
Highlands Hammock State Park, 65, 69, 89, 91, 121, 137, 150, 151; admission fees and, 82, 90; budget of, 118–19; cabins, 83; CCC Company #262 and, 124; CCC Company #453 and, 118; CCC involvement ends, 201; CCC reunion and, 151; condition of CCC camp, 122–23; construction of by CCC, 34–35, 81–83, 119, 140; dances at, 125, 126; deer and, 142–43; designed by William Lyman Phillips, 140; fires and, 148, 247n77;

Florida Garden and Arboretum and, 36, 65, 82, 119; funding of, 82; location of, 75; opened to public as state park, 35; publicity and, 78, 79, 82; snakes and, 143; staffing and, 69, 80; as tourist attraction, 75; tree planting in, 148; visitation and, 90; WWI veterans and, 116; WWII and, 204
Highways, 178, 179, 190; A1A, 95; cattle on, 47; complaints about, 47; Federal Roads Act, 47; Heckscher Drive (A1A), 95; Highway Survey, 190; Tamiami Trail, 177; U.S. 1 (Dixie Highway), 47; U.S. 17 (St. Johns River Trail), 48; U.S. 19 (Stonewall Jackson Memorial Highway), 207; U.S. 27 (Orange Blossom Trail), 33, 47; U.S. 41, 34, 48; U.S. 441 (Uncle Remus Route), 48; U.S. 90 (Old Spanish Trail), 47, 78
Hill, Emmett, 231n81
Hillbilly, as a label, 166, 167
Hillsborough County, 47, 63, 115
Hillsborough Lighthouse, 186
Hillsborough River, 77, 83
Hillsborough River State Park, 77, 116, 129, 140, 203; CCC involvement ends, 201; closed because of WWII, 204; park construction by CCC, 83, 117, 118, 120; park superintendent Oscar Baynard, 78, 79–80; publicity, 78, 80; swing bridge, 83; as tourist attraction, 75, 76; and U.S. Army, 204
Hinely, Minnie and S. A., 94
Hodges, William C., 39, 40, 58, 66, 96, 208–9
Holland, Gov. Spessard, 90, 95, 96, 208
Hollywood (Florida), 13
Holmes, Talmadge, 115, 116
Homestead, 55, 56
Homosassa Springs, 62, 93, 150, 182, 198
Hooker's Hammock, 34; renamed Highland's Hammock, 35
Hookworm, 12, 26
Hoover, Herbert, 8, 19, 28
Hopkins, Harry, 20, 22, 24, 32, 49, 63; Florida and, 156
Horne, Jack, 114, 123, 156–57

Hotels, 190–91, 192
Hoyt, Ray, 119, 144
Hugh Taylor Birch State Park: acquisition by FPS, 94; opened to the public, 96
Huguenot City Park, 96
Hunting, 42, 53, 182–87, 189, 190
Hurricanes, 15, 16
Hutchison, Thomas, 126; on vocational training in CCC, 130

Ickes, Harold, 61, 128, 215n48
Inman, Eldredge, 51, 170
Inter-Island Association for Conservation, 187

Jackson County, 12
Jacksonville, 29, 32, 47, 48, 55, 70, 73, 75, 90, 93, 150, 165, 167, 203
James, William, 21
Jane Green Swamp, 180
J. C. Deagan Company of Chicago, 194
Jeffreys, Mrs. Linwood, 62, 87
Jenkins, Valworth, 161
Jennings, May Mann: background of, 54–57; campaign to be FPS director, 65, 67–68; Gov. Cone and, 159; convict labor and, 138–39; creation of the Florida Forestry Board and, 57, 64; Marjory Stoneman Douglas and, 57; the Everglades and, 55, 56, 67–68; fire and, 145, 146; the Florida Federation of Women's Clubs and, 54, 56; the Florida Forestry Association and, 51; the Florida Park Service and, 54, 65–68, 206; the Internal Improvement Fund and, 58; William S. Jennings and, 54, 55; National Conference on State Parks and, 65; political influence of, 56; Royal Palm State Park and, 56–57, 118; state parks and, 58, 62; Suwanee River State Park and, 78; Tropical Everglades National Park Association and, 57. *See also* Florida Federation of Women's Clubs; Florida Forestry Service; Florida Park Service; Royal Palm State Park
Jennings, S. Bryan, 56, 57; creation of the FPS and, 64, 66; Everglades Park Commission and, 67; Florida Forestry Board and, 56; the Internal Improvement Fund and, 58
Jennings, Gov. William S., 54–55
Johnston's Island Game Preserve, 180
Judah P. Benjamin Historic Memorial, 206–7
Junior State Chamber of Commerce, 184

Kary, William, 85
Kay, Russell, 177
Keene, James, 115; on FDR, 160
Kennedy, Stetson, 13, 169, 192; on crackers, 169; *Palmetto Country* and, 169
Keystone Heights, 83, 136
Key West, 46
Kingsley Plantation: as national park, 96; as state park, 96
Kirby, Jack Temple, 253n43
Knapp, Jean: deer reduction program and, 180; as state veterinarian, 174–75; ticks and, 174–75, 180
Knight, J. E., 185
Ku Klux Klan, 132

LaGuardia, Fiorello, 161, 193
Lake City, 48, 78, 91, 117, 159, 161, 201
Lake City Reporter, 159
Lake Kissimmee State Park, 199
Lakeland, 32, 73
Lake Okeechobee, 15, 76
Lake Placid, 33, 34
Lake Wales, 33
Lane, Frederick, 60
Lawson, A. D.: CCC project superintendent, Florida Caverns State Park, 81, 89–90, 91; CCC project superintendent, Torreya State Park, 81, 91; conflicts with FPS directors, 89–90; at Myakka River State Park, 89–90, 137
LeCouris, George, 11; on CCC conditioning camps, 115; on FDR, 160; on fighting fires, 145, 147; on pay in the CCC, 127; on witnessing a lynching in Quincy, 133
Lee County, 16

Leesburg, 187
Leon County, 62
Liberty County, 124, 133
Little Talbot Island, 94–95; owned by Florida State Road Department, 95
Little Talbot Island State Park, 95; segregated, 96, 203
Live Oak, 47, 93
Livestock: cattle dipping and, 26; fencing and, 177; ticks and, 26, 174–80
Local Experienced Men (LEMs), 119, 120
Longstreet, R. L., 185–86
Lowrie, John, 85
Lynchings, 132–33, 161

MacArthur, Gen. Douglas, 128
Mackinnon, A. E., 193
Maclenny, 159
Macon (Georgia), 85
Madison, 78, 93
Magill, Inez, 175–76
Malaria, 12, 26, 45
Malsberger, Henry J., 149; conflicts with CCC, 89–90; conflicts with NPS, 88; Fort Clinch and, 87; as FPS director, 79, 87–88, 91
Mann, Austin, 54
Mapoles, William H., 157
Marianna, 16, 118, 202; Florida Caverns and, 84, 90; tourism and, 75–76
Marianna Air Base, 203
Marietta, 134
Marineland, 189, 198, 203
Marion County, 37, 47–48
Martin, Gov. John, 14, 52, 57
Mason, Dorothea, 174
Mather, Stephen, 60, 199
Matheson Hammock Park, 58
Maxwell, Carlos: hired as park supt., Oleno State Park, 91
Mayo, Nathan, 36, 37, 38, 40, 61, 71
McCrory Ranch, 180
McEntee, James, 24; as assistant CCC director, 122–23; as CCC director, 200
McKee Jungle Gardens, 65, 150, 182

McRae, W. A., 37
Mediterranean fruit fly, 26
Meineche, E. P., 81
Merrick, George, 13, 14
Miami, 13–16, 46, 48, 49, 73, 93, 150, 177; Greynolds Park and, 65; hurricane and, 15
Miami Herald, 15, 181, 192
Milton, 32
Mizner, Addison, 13
Monkey Jungle, 93
Monticello, 207
Moore Haven, 15
Moral Equivalence of War, The, 21
Morgenthau, Henry, 24
Mormino, Gary, 205
Morris, Allen, 155
Morrison, C. L., 155
Mosely, Gen. George Van Horn, 119, 135
Munro, Kirk, 56
Myakka Rattler (CCC newsletter), 131, 141
Myakka River, 117
Myakka River State Park, 117–18, 129, 133, 137, 141, 142, 150–51; African Americans and, 134–35, 143, 161–62; cabins and, 83; CCC involvement ends, 202; CCC Project SP-4, 83; construction by CCC, 83, 118, 143; deer and, 141, 182; fires and, 145; fish and, 141; hazing at CCC camp, 123; land donated by A. B. Edwards (Phoenix Insurance Company), 83; location of, 75; natural features and, 144; opening of, 76; prairie, 148; rattlesnakes in, 118; segregation and, 161–62; tensions over African American CCC camp, 134, 135; as tourist attraction, 75, 76; tree planting in, 148; WWII and, 204

Nassau County, 58, 66
National Conference on State Parks, 65, 199–200
National Park Service (NPS), 24, 25, 34, 62, 64, 76, 135, 149, 186–87, 201–7; archaeology and, 85; beautification and, 141; caverns and, 77; CCC and, 24, 60, 115, 116, 119, 142; conflicts with FFS, 137; conflicts with

FPS, 76, 80–81, 87, 88, 89–90; creation of, 59–60; fire, 144–49; Florida and, 80–81, 158; Florida Caverns and, 84–85; Florida Forestry Service and, 158; Fort Clinch and, 87–88; FPS and, 69, 76, 80–81, 119, 158; FPS director and, 67, 87–88; Highlands Hammock and, 25; hiring FPS staff, 81; master plans for state parks, 141; no-fire policy, 145–46; park design, 81; park planning, 88–89; Regional Office (Richmond VA), 80; "rustic style" of, 81; Santa Rosa Island and, 158; Southeastern Archaeological Center (SEAC), 85; staffing of FPS parks, 78, 80–82; state parks and, 62, 69
National Relief Administration (NRA), 20
National Youth Administration (NYA), 20, 23
Natural Bridge State Park, 206
NBC (radio), 195, 196
Neale, Claude: lynching of, 132–33
New Deal, 19, 154–55, 191, 205; recreation and, 189–90; South and, 19, 20; state parks and, 59, 207; tourism and, 59, 207; WWII and, 200; youth relief, 21–23
Newell, James (Jim), 31, 134
New Jersey, 72, 190, 197
New River, 94
New York City, 17, 70, 156, 159, 161, 193; Florida tourism and, 73, 74; world's fair and, 177, 193–97. *See also* Sholtz, Gov. Dave; World fairs
New York state, 19, 72, 131, 156, 190; state parks and, 59
New York State Fish and Game Commission, 20
New York Times, 70, 72, 140, 195, 197; Florida crackers and, 166–67, 169; Florida promoter Harry Sims and, 72; Gov. Dave Sholtz and, 72
New York World's Fair (1939), 177, 193–98, 208, 209; Gov. Cone and, 195–97; Florida Exhibit, 193, 195; Florida Week, 196–97; Fred Cone Day, 196–97; visitation, 193
New York World's Fair (1940), 201
No-Fence League, 177

Ocala, 55, 150, 199
Ocala National Forest, 148
Ocmulgee National Monument, 85, 86
Ohio, 156, 159, 190
Okaloosa County, 158–59
"Old Folks at Home" (song), 42; becomes Florida's state song, 162–63
Oleno State Park: CCC involvement ends, 201; construction by CCC, 91; construction by WPA, 91; as forestry training camp, 78, 91, 227n119; opened to public, 91; park supt. Carlos Maxwell and, 91; publicity of, 78; transferred to a state park, 91; visitation and, 91; WWI veterans and, 116
Oleto River, 140
Oliva, Albert, 124
Oliver, Malcolm, 121; boxing in CCC, 125; CCC enrollee at Highlands Hammock State Park, 121; on food and weight gain in CCC, 121
Olmsted, Frederick Law, 34, 60
Olustee, 91, 117, 134, 149
Olustee Battlefield State Park, 206, 223n15
Olustee National Forest, 30
O'Neal, Willie, 126, 133–34
Orange County, 180, 182
Orange Lake, 168
Oriental Gardens, 93, 150
Orlando, 26, 34, 73, 132
Ormond Beach, 94, 182
Osceola County, 182
Osceola National Forest, 148
Overman, Charles, 70
Oxley, Harold, 128

Palatka, 150
Palmetto Country, 169
Panama City (Florida), 184, 203
Pan-American State Park, 94
Paradise Key, 55–56
Paradise Park, 203
Pari-mutuel betting: legalized by Florida legislature, 71
Park interpretation, 78–79, 92

292 · Index

Park, Parkways, and Recreational Study, 59, 60
Parrot Jungle, 93, 150, 189
Pellagra, 12
Pennsylvania, 131
Pensacola, 15, 47, 76, 157, 158, 207
Pepper, Sen. Claude, 162
Perkins, Frances, 23, 24
Perreault, Clayton: CCC employee, 80; park superintendent, Gold Head Branch State Park, 80, 202
Perry, 199
Persons, Frank W.: CCC director of selection, 123; idea for education in CCC, 128
Phillips, William Lyman, 65, 140
Pick and Spade (CCC newsletter), 131, 145
Pinchot, Gifford, 54
Pine Island, 187
Plank, Donald K., 80
Plant, Henry, 13, 45, 46
Plant City, 185
Plastow, Charles, 41
Polk County, 180
Pompano Beach, 186
Porpoises, 186–87
Port Everglades, 73, 74, 186
Prescribed burning, 145, 171–72
Public Works Administration (PWA), 20, 61; construction of Stephen Foster Memorial and, 162; excavations at Florida Caverns and, 85
Putnam Lumber Company, 65

Queen Mary (HMS), 73
Quincy: lynching in, 133

Radio, 78
Ragan, Claude, 81, 83
Rainbow Springs, 62, 93, 198
Ranchers, 70, 175, 176, 177, 180–81
Ranching, 170–71, 70, 180–81, 182; fencing and, 175–77. *See also* Cattle ranching; Livestock; Ticks
Randall, George, 134
Rankin, W. H., 73, 74

Rattlesnakes: CCC and, 118
Ravine Gardens, 93, 150, 198
Rawlings, Marjorie Kinnan, 165–66, 168–70, 185; background of, 166; Cross Creek and, 168, 169, 198; Florida crackers and, 166, 168, 169; home owned by the FPS, 198; *South Moon Under* and, 165–66, 168; *The Yearling and*, 168, 169, 182
Reconstruction Finance Corporation (RFC), 28–29
Reinsmith, Winton, 58
Rex Beach Lake, 118, 124
Reynolds, P. G., 129
Richmond (Virginia): NPS regional office, 80
Riley, J. B., 135
Riley, Virgil, 157
Rockefeller Center, 70
Roebling, John, 33–35, 36, 65; created Highlands Hammock, Inc., 82; donation of land for Highlands Hammock State Park, 119
Roebling, Margaret, 33, 35
Roebling, Ronald, 33
Roess, Mike, 83
Rogers, Will, 43
Rogers Post (CCC newsletter), 131
Rollins College, 41
Roosevelt, Eleanor, 22
Roosevelt, Pres. Franklin Delano, 7, 11, 18, 31, 128, 156; assassination attempt, 18, 30, 213n4; conservation and, 20–21; creation of CCC, 21, 22, 25; fire and, 172; Fireside Chats, 25; Florida and, 72, 160; on Florida exhibit, Century of Progress, 70; Florida Gov. Cone and, 154; Florida Gov. Sholtz and, 18, 29, 31; forestry and, 20; Hyde Park (New York) and, 20; "Hundred Days," 19; as New York governor, 19, 20; polio and, 19; recreation and, 59; reputation in Florida, 160; state parks and, 63; Warm Springs and, 19; youth and, 22
Ross Allen Reptile Institute (Silver Springs), 150
Royal Palm State Park, 56, 58, 65, 118; CCC

and, 56, 206; CCC Company #453 and, 118; CCC Project SP-1, 56, 58. *See also* Everglades National Park; Jennings, May Mann

Salmond, John, 116, 132
Santa Rosa Island, 158; FPS and, 158; as a national park, 159; as a possible state park, 158
Santa Rosa Island National Monument, 76
Sarasota, 14, 48, 76, 125, 161–62; tensions over African American CCC camp, 134–35
Sarasota American Legion Arena, 125
Sarasota Chamber of Commerce, 135
Sarasota Herald, 135
Sarasota Kiwanis Club, 135
Schaeffer, Charles H.: and anger over African Americans at Myakka River State Park, 135; becoming FPS director in 1935, 67, 79
Scoggin, Lewis, 147, 179, 202, 203, 204; on Oscar Baynard, 78; CCC and, 69, 202, 206; criticisms of CCC supt. Lawson, 89–90; criticisms of NPS, 69, 76; conflicts with NPS, 69, 87–88, 202; conflicts with Vinten, 87, 88; as FPS director (1940–1952), 79, 69, 76, 91, 96; fired as FPS director, 79; segregation and, 203–4
Scott, R. H., 72
Scrub cattle, 176
Seaboard Air Line Railway, 196
Sebring, 33, 34
Segregation, 134–35, 161, 203; effects on tourism, 161; WWII, 200
Seminoles, 31, 169, 180
Shands, William, 155, 159, 162; on Gov. Cone, 155
Sharecroppers and sharecropping, 10–12, 19, 26, 115
Shea, John, 172, 253n43
Sheeler Lake, 147
Shoemaker, Joseph: lynching of, 161
Sholtz, Gov. Dave, 29–32, 36–37, 38, 57, 64, 138, 175, 180, 182, 217n121; anger over African Americans at Myakka River State Park and, 135; CCC and, 31, 36; Century of Progress and, 36; charges of corruption and, 32, 154; Gov. Cone and, 160; FDR and, 30, 32; FPS director and, 66, 67; Highlands Hammock and, 35; May Mann Jennings and, 67; New Deal and, 31, 32, 36, 62–63; New York City and, 156; public image of, 31, 32; Sarasota rejecting African American CCC camp and, 134–35; "Sholtz Park" (Florida Caverns), 78; state song and, 162; tourism and, 70, 140, 155; Conrad Van Hyning and, 156; welfare and, 63; Joseph Zangara and, 18
Shuffleboard, 190
Sikes, Bob, 157; Santa Rosa Island and, 159
Silver River State Park, 150, 199
Silver Springs, 42, 93, 150, 182, 189, 203
Simpson, Clarence, 79–80, 203, 205
Sims, Harris, 72
Smith, Al, 18
Snakes, 143
Sneads, 11
Society of American Foresters, 21
Southeastern Archaeological Center (SEAC), 85
Southeastern Regional Planning Commission, 201
Southern Forest Association, 52
South Moon Under, 165–66, 168. *See also* Rawlings, Marjorie Kinnan
Spivey, Ludd, 141
Springs, 62, 149–50
St. Andrews State Park, 203
Starke, 90
State Audit Board, 157, 159
State Board of Public Welfare, 30–31, 156; abolished, 153; budget of, 28; CCC and, 31; creation of, 28. *See also* State Board of Social Welfare; State Welfare Board
State Board of Social Welfare: abolished, 157–58, 159; audit of, 157; budget of, 156; Gov. Cone and, 160; creation of, 156. *See also* State Board of Public Welfare; State Welfare Board

State forests, 189
State Livestock Board, 142, 174; cattle dipping and, 175, 176; deer reduction program, 175, 179, 183; tick eradication program, 174, 188
State parks, 58, 62, 81, 115, 189; FERA state park survey and, 62; gas rationing and, 202–3; history of, 60; "Meineche plan," 81; park design and, 81; tourism and, 162, 198–99; WWII and, 201, 204. *See also* Florida Park Service; National Park Service; *individual state parks*
State Racing Commission, 71
State Road Department, 138, 139, 179, 190; created in 1915, 47; Highway Survey and, 190. *See also* Highways
State Tuberculosis Board, 64
State Welfare Board, 90, 153; CCC and, 114; creation of, 157–58, 159. *See also* State Board of Public Welfare
St. Augustine, 27, 39, 42, 54, 75, 87, 93, 186–87, 203, 207
Steinbeck, John, 169
Stephen Foster Memorial State Park, 194, 198; CCC and, 162; creation of, 162–63; Florida Folk Festival and, 164; PWA and, 162
Stetson University, 72
Stevenson, Jim, 92–93, 236n193; on Carol Beck, 92; on park interpretation, 92
St. Johns River, 45, 178
St. Lucie County, 180
Stock market, 8–9, 13, 48
Stoddard, Herbert, 174
Stokes, Betty, 182
St. Petersburg, 46, 47, 48, 207
St. Simons Island, 87
Stuckey, William, 49
Sulphur Springs, 122
Sun City, 17
Sunken Gardens, 93, 150
Suwanee River, 39, 42, 65, 162, 167, 195
Suwanee River State Park, 66, 78; FPS acquisition of, 78, 93–94; opened to the public, 96; plans for, 78

Suwanee River State Park Association, 93

Tallahassee, 32, 51, 70, 73, 90, 134, 208; lynching in, 161
Tall Timbers Research Station, 247n71
Tamiami Trail, 177
Tamiami Trail Blazers, 177
Tampa, 17, 28, 46, 73, 76, 83, 167, 194
Tarpon Springs, 160, 194
Taussig, Charles, 22
Taylor, John, 138, 139, 141
Tebeau, Charlton, 64
Tenant farmers, 10, 26. *See also* Agriculture; Sharecroppers and sharecropping
Tennessee Valley Administration (TVA), 20
"Tent cities," 47
Tent Town Topics (CCC newsletter), 145
Thomasville, 7
Ticks, 118, 142, 170, 174–83; *Babesia bovis*, 175; *Boophilus annulates*, 175, 180; cattle tick fever, 175, 180; cattle ticks, 26, 175, 187–88; deer reduction program and, 142, 179–83, 187–88; deer ticks, 13, 180; eradication of, 142, 174–83, 187–88. *See also* Cattle ranching; Ranching; State Livestock Board
Time magazine, 71, 196; and "crackers," 167
Timucuan Ecological and Historic Preserve, 96
"Tin can tourists," 46–47, 49
Tomoka State Park, 94; acquisition by state, 94; as Volusia State Park, 94
Torreya Park Chronicle (CCC newsletter), 131
Torreya State Park, 133, 141; admission fees, 90; African Americans and, 135–36; bluffs, 77; CCC and, 83; CCC involvement ends, 202; CCC park supt. A. D. Lawson, 81; CCC Project SP-6, 83, 117; death of two CCC enrollees, 124; description of, 76–77; "Indian relics" and, 77; Gregory House, 77, 83–84, 124; location of, 75; plans for, 76, 77–78; state acquisition of, 58; topography of, 76–77; as tourist attraction, 75; visitation, 91; WWII and, 204. *See also* Florida Park Service

Torreya tree, 58, 77
Tosahatchee Game Preserve, 180
Tourist attractions, 93; becoming state parks, 198–99
Townsend, Francis, 20
Trammell, Gov. Park, 56, 134
Treadway, C. B., 61
Trescott, Dan: on park ranger training, 236n193
Tropical Everglades National Park Association, 57
Tropical Hollywood, 93
Tropical Parks Association, 34–35
Tropical Sportsmen Club, 175
Truman, Harry, 68
Trustees of the Internal Improvement Fund, 57–58, 64
Tucker, Gilbert, 12, 171
Turpentine industry, 12
Turpentiners, 12–13, 17, 70, 159, 170–71
Tyler, Glen, 32

United Daughters of the Confederacy (UDC), 206–7
University of Florida, 148, 149; CCC education and, 129
U.S. Army, 24, 60, 167, 200, 205, 125–26; CCC and, 24, 114–15, 119, 124–27, 140, 240n104; education and, 127–28; Fourth Army Corps, 135; hazing and, 123
U.S. Army Corps of Engineers, 95
U.S. Congress, 19, 20, 23, 24; abolishes CCC, 201
U.S. Dept. of Agriculture (USDA), 23, 175; tick eradication and, 175, 180, 188
U.S. Dept. of Labor, 23
U.S. Dept. of the Interior, 23, 31, 60
U.S. Dept. of War, 23
U.S. Forest Service (USFS), 50–51, 75, 144; CCC and, 116; fire and, 146, 170; no-fire policy of, 145, 146. *See also* Florida Forestry Service; Florida Park Service; Shea, John

Van Duyn, Gus, 143
Van Hyning, Conrad, 63, 156–57, 158; background of, 156; charges of corruption, 157; as Florida Commissioner of Welfare, 156; salary of, 157, 159. *See also* State Board of Public Welfare
Veterans Viewpoint (newsletter), 131
Vickers, Raymond, 16
Vilas, 142
Villard, Oswald, 48–49
Vinten, C. R., 202, 123, 136; Harry Lee Baker and, 158; conflicts with FPS and, 87, 88; conflicts with FPS director Malsberger, 88; conflicts with FPS director Scoggin, 87, 88; fires and, 145; Florida state parks and, 80–81, 87–88; Myakka River State Park opening and, 75; as NPS administrator in Florida, 80; Santa Rosa Island and, 158; state inspector, NPS, 80–81. *See also* Malsberger, Henry J.; National Park Service; Scoggin, Lewis
Virginia, 21
Volusia County, 180, 185

Wainwright, William, 157
Wakulla Springs, 62, 149–50, 194, 198; Ed Ball and, 62; Henry the Pole-Vaulting Fish, 194
Wallace, Henry, 25
Wall Street, 16
Walsh, David, 22
Wand, Ben, 36, 37, 38; editor, *Southern Lumber Journal*, 51; Florida Forestry Association and, 51
Ward-Banks Bill, 63
Warm Springs, 19, 30
Washington, D.C., 18, 134, 166
Waugh, C. V., 162
Weaver, Scott, 175
Weeki Wachee, 93, 149–50, 198
Weeks Act (1911), 51
Weissinger, Arthur B: CCC project superintendent, Gold Head Branch State Park, 81, 90
West Florida Industrial School, 117
West Palm Beach, 46, 184
Wewahitchka, 12

Whalen, Grover, 193, 196
Whales, 186
White, Fred: CCC enrollee at Fort Clinch State Park, 115; sharecropping, 115
White Springs, 155, 164–65, 194
Wilcox, James, 167
Williams, Aubrey, 22, 23, 24
Williams, Fred, 12
Williams, Hayden: as park superintendent, Highlands Hammock, 80
Williams, Whistling Willie, 195
Willis, Bryan, 36
Wilson, Lorenzo, 61
Wilson, William L., 63; All-Florida Advertising Campaign and, 73
Wilson, Woodrow, 59, 60
Winter Haven, 150
Winter Park, 174
Wirth, Conrad, 60, 123
WJAX (radio), 115
Works Progress Administration (WPA), 13, 20, 25, 30, 32, 59, 142, 160, 169, 172
World fairs, 39–39, 41, 70, 177, 193–97; Century of Progress International Exposition, 36, 37, 38–44, 49, 61, 69, 70, 71, 177; Florida and, 49, 70; Great Lakes Exposition, 70, 177; New York World's Fair (1939), 177, 193–97; Walt Disney and, 257n23
World War I, 9, 11, 125
World War I veterans, 12, 24; Bonus marches of, 24; CCC and, 83, 116; Gold Head Branch State Park, and, 83; Hillsborough River State Park and, 116; Oleno State Park and, 116
World War II, 115, 128, 198–206; CCC and, 201–2, 205, 206; FPS and, 201, 202, 204–6; New Deal and, 200; as replacement for tourism dollars, 205; segregation and, 200; the South and, 200; tourism and, 202–6
Wright, Marian, 127
WTAL (radio), 75, 78

Ybor City, 42
Young, Joseph, 13
Youth unemployment, 22
Yulee, 95

Zangara, Joseph (Giuseppe), 18, 30, 213n4
Zook, George, 128

DAVE NELSON is professor of history at Abraham Baldwin Agriculture College–Bainbridge. Originally from Jacksonville, Florida, he received his B.A. in history from the University of North Florida and his M.A. and Ph.D. in history from Florida State University. David also served four years as a park ranger with the Florida Park Service and worked six years as an archivist at the Florida State Archives in Tallahassee. He lives with his wife and son in Quincy, Florida.

MICHAEL V. GANNON FUND

In honor of Michael Gannon's lasting legacy and his dedication to the scholarship of our state's history, the University Press of Florida has established the Michael V. Gannon Fund to provide continued support for first publications in Florida history. Royalties and gifts donated to this fund underwrite the costs of these monographs, helping to keep the price as affordable as possible.

Special thanks to Dr. Gary R. Mormino for his very generous contribution to further publications about the Sunshine State's long and fascinating history.

History of Florida, edited by Michael Gannon (2018)